German Women
as Letter Writers:
1750–1850

# German Women
# as Letter Writers:
# 1750–1850

Lorely French

Madison • Teaneck
Fairleigh Dickinson University Press
London: Associated University Presses

Associated University Presses
440 Forsgate Drive
Cranbury, NJ 08512

Associated University Presses
16 Barter Street
London WC1A 2AH, England

Associated University Presses
P.O. Box 338, Port Credit
Mississauga, Ontario
Canada L5G 4L8

The paper used in this publication meets the requirements
of the American National Standard for Permanence of Paper
for Printed Library Materials Z39.48-1984.

**Library of Congress Cataloging-in-Publication Data**

French, Lorely, 1957–
    German women as letter writers, 1750–1850 / Lorely French.
        p.   cm.
    Includes bibliographical references.
    ISBN 0-8386-3664-0 (alk. paper)
    1. German letters—Women authors—History and criticism.
    2. German prose literature—19th century—History and criticism.
    3. German prose literature—18th century—History and criticism.
    4. Women and literature—Germany—History—19th century.   5. Women
    and literature—Germany—History—18th century.   6. Women authors,
    German—Correspondence.   7. Women—Germany—Correspondence.
    I. Title.
    PT811.F74   1996
    836.009'9287—dc20                                                    95-53145
                                                                          CIP

*Dedicated to Elsa French,*
*one of the best letter writers of them all*

# Contents

Acknowledgments 9

Introduction 13

1. Reclamation of the Sources and Genre 29
2. Letters, History, and Gender 48
3. "Let us rather exchange letters of friendship": Women's Friendship in Letters 75
4. "Thousand Lives, Thousand Forms": Letter Writing and Publication 112
5. An Aesthetics of Letter Writing: Caroline Schlegel-Schelling and Rahel Varnhagen 162
6. Storytelling and Poetry in Letters: Bettine von Arnim's *Goethes Briefwechsel mit einem Kinde* and *Die Günderode* 203
7. Corresponding with the World: Letters and Women around the 1848 Revolution 238

Notes 254
Works Cited 293
Index 317

# Acknowledgments

MOST acknowledgments usually thank personal friends and relatives last. I wish to reverse that order, if only to stress the importance of the connection between one's personal and professional lives. This book is dedicated to my mother, Elsa French, who writes some of the best letters I have ever read. I thank her and the rest of my large family on all sides for their continued moral support. James Draznin deserves special thanks for his patience and undaunted help in all aspects of my life. I really can say that I could not have completed this book without him. I sincerely thank Leif Draznin-French for his love, humor, energy, and stories. His preschool antics have taught me a lot about friendship, gender relations, creativity, and human nature, and I thank him especially for those insights, however unwittingly he may have shared them. Matyáš Bečvárov has helped me during all stages of writing this book, from initial research, to transcribing letters, to editing various versions of the manuscript; I remain very grateful to him for that assistance. Diane Young, whose name comes up at various times throughout this book, has remained a close friend whose intelligence and wit I greatly admire. I am indebted to Doris Merkl for carefully reading over my translations and offering her thoughtful suggestions for changes. As Pacific University's 1994–95 Foreign Language Assistant from Austria, she has acquired a very special place in many people's hearts, mine included. I thank Helga Heckmeier for her lasting friendship over these many years and for generously welcoming me into her apartment in Berlin during my several research trips there. Thank you, too, Max Heckmeier, for keeping me in touch with American culture during my stays in Berlin. My Polish family, the Wójcikiewicz family, receives my most heartful thanks for their hospitality and generosity during my research trips to Krakow, Poland. Many thanks to Linda, Laura, Christina, and Matthew Carmichael for providing a second home for my son while I researched and worked.

The research for this book has been long in the process, and the final product would not be possible without the financial support of several organizations and people. A grant in 1983–84 from the Deutscher Akademischer Austauschdienst (German Academic Exchange Service, DAAD) for research in Berlin on my dissertation on Bettine von Arnim provided me initially with funds to begin gathering materials from libraries and archives. Postgraduate grants from the DAAD in summer 1987 and from the American Council of Learned Societies in Summer 1989 aided me in finding materials on women's letter writing in general and on those women participating in the 1848 Revolution in specific. For writing the book, I am sincerely grateful to John Meyer and Pacific University, whose endowed faculty research and teaching award allowed me to make final research visits to Berlin and Krakow in 1992–93 and to complete the first draft of the manuscript.

For archival materials, I thank the Jagiellonian University Library in Krakow for allowing me access to the enormous wealth of the Varnhagen Collection. I extend special thanks to Elżbieta Burda, who administered the Varnhagen Collection during my five visits there, for her expertise and continued interest in my project. I also wish to thank the Berlin-Brandenburgische Akademie der Wissenschaften, Akademie-Archiv, and especially Dr. Klaus Klauß, for assuring that I received copies of documents I needed from them. I am also grateful to the Staatsbibliothek Preußischer Kulturbesitz in Berlin and the Freie Universitätsbibliothek in Berlin for their help in locating rare books and in making microfilms, photos, and copies of materials I needed.

Several people at Pacific University deserve many thanks. Michelle Campbell Christensen helped me immensely as a research assistant, tracking down obscure books and formatting the manuscript. I cannot thank her enough for her patience, accuracy, intelligence, and good-heartedness. I am also grateful to Ramona Matzke, who served as a research assistant during the final stages of formulating the bibliography and footnotes. I thank Hannah Pratt for her help with the index. Charles O'Connor, Associate Professor of Business Administration at Pacific University, generously lent his services and computer for transferring disks from one system to another. The librarians at Pacific University deserve special thanks, especially considering the extenuating circumstances under which they are working in a small library with limited funds. I recognize their trials in tracking down the many older books I needed, and I especially thank Lucinda Huffine and Elaine Bortles for their persistence and good humor.

Last, but not least, I am grateful to members of the Women in German organization for the much-needed encouragement and networking that all women academics need. I extend my heartfelt thanks to Sara Friedrichsmeyer for reading an earlier version of my manuscript and offering insightful criticism. I also thank Lisa Cornick, Elke

Frederiksen, Katherine Goodman, and Irina Hundt for their words of encouragement.

\* \* \*

I gratefully acknowledge permission to reprint quotations and to translate from the following works:

Bettine von Arnim, *Werke und Briefe*, edited by Gustav Konrad, 4 vols., Frechen: Bartmann Verlag, 1958–63, and *Briefe*, edited by Johannes Müller, vol. 5., Frechen: Bartmann Verlag, 1961, with permission from Buchhandlung/Antiquariat Thomas and Curt Brauns.

Clemens Brentano and Sophie Mereau, *Lebe der Liebe und liebe das Leben: Der Briefwechsel von Clemens Brentano und Sophie Mereau*, edited by Dagmar von Gersdorff, Frankfurt a. M.: Insel, 1981, with permission from Insel Verlag.

Karoline von Günderrode, *Der Schatten eines Traumes: Gedichte, Prosa, Briefe, Zeugnisse von Zeitgenossen*, edited with an essay by Christa Wolf, Darmstadt und Neuwied: Luchterhand, 1979, with permission from Morgenbuch Verlag.

Anna Louisa Karsch, *Die Karschin: Friedrichs des Grossen Volksdichterin. Ein Leben in Briefen*, edited by Elisabeth Hausmann, Frankfurt a. M.: Societäts-Verlag, 1933, with permission from Societäts-Verlag.

Caroline Schlegel-Schelling, *Caroline. Briefe aus der Frühromantik*, edited by Erich Schmidt, revised and enlarged by Georg Waitz, 2 vols., Leipzig: Insel, 1913, with permission from Insel Verlag.

Rahel Varnhagen, *Briefe an eine Freundin: Rahel Varnhagen an Rebecca Friedländer*, edited by Deborah Hertz, Köln: Kiepenheuer und Witsch, 1988, with permission from Verlag Kiepenheuer and Witsch.

Rahel Varnhagen, *Gesammelte Werke*, edited by Konrad Feilchenfeldt, Uwe Schweikert und Rahel E. Steiner, Munich: Matthes und Seitz, 1983, with permission from Matthes and Seitz Verlag.

An earlier version of parts of chapter 4 originally appeared as an essay entitled "'. . . ich wandte mich höflich an den Mann und schrieb in seinem Beysein schnell ein Versbriefchen': Poetry in Letters of German Women in the Late-Eighteenth and Early Nineteenth-Century" in *Pacific Coast Philology 29.1* (September 1994), used with permission of the Philological Association of the Pacific Coast.

Parts of chapter 7 appeared in an essay entitled "Strategies of Female Persuasion: The Political Letters of Bettina Brentano-von Arnim" in *Bettina Brentano-von Arnim: Gender and Politics*, edited by Elke P. Frederiksen and Katherine R. Goodman, Detroit: Wayne State University Press, 1995, used with permission of Wayne State University Press.

# Introduction

In fall 1990 the University of Nebraska Press published the anthology *Bitter Healing: German Women Writers 1700–1830*, edited by Jeannine Blackwell and Susanne Zantop and containing English translations of German women's writings.[1] The positive reception of this anthology in the United States, and especially among publications with wide circulation, suggests that eighteenth- and nineteenth-century German women writers are receiving attention internationally.[2] The accessibility of works in English translation assures a more diverse audience for critical discourse, a trend that a growing group of "German-American Germanist Feminists" has continued by concurrently publishing collections of relevant critical essays.[3]

In the field of *Germanistik*, however, *Bitter Healing* is just one of several anthologies and reprinted editions of eighteenth- and nineteenth-century German women's works that have appeared in the past two decades, including texts by Meta Klopstock, Anna Louisa Karsch, Sophie von LaRoche, Sophie Mereau, Dorothea Mendelssohn-Veit-Schlegel, Caroline Schlegel-Schelling, Bettine von Arnim, and Rahel Varnhagen.[4] In such publications, the importance of letter writing for the development of women's literary talents becomes especially clear—seven of the fifteen entries in *Bitter Healing*, for example, include letters.

Fascination with women's letters is not only a German phenomenon. This interest, heightened during the past decade, is due largely to the direction that feminist scholarship in general has taken. Elaine Showalter's proposal to study women as writers, a process she termed "gynocritics," as opposed to critiquing how women appear in male writers' works, which she called androcentric criticism, has contributed to analysis of genres outside the canon, such as the letter and diary, in which women had historically found outlets for their creativity.[5] In conjunction with the work started in the 1970s by many literary historians eager to rediscover women hidden from history, the profusion of published letters by women points to a continuous desire to study women's voices in their own texts.

From another angle, an interest in the letter as a basis for philosophical, psychological, and linguistic analysis of the feminine, in

13

contrast to its historical role in the lives of women, has led to recent investigations of women's relationship to the "letter."[6] "Letter" here is placed in quotations to signify what various English-speaking post-structuralists have connoted as the alphabetic character, the epistle, the distinguishing mark of a "man of letters," and the literal, as in "living by the letter."[7] The dialogue that began with Lacan and Derrida on the role the letter plays in Poe's short story *The Purloined Letter* has sparked a fascination with the letter as signifier engaged in a complex relationship with the signified. Within this context, the letter also functions as a means for psychoanalytical interpretations of the feminine and Woman. Whereas Lacan sees the letter in the story as representing a "lack," in which the Woman becomes the feminine Other, for Derrida, the feminine become one term in a series of binary oppositions. These two interpretations have led to such deconstructive feminist readings as that of Barbara Johnson, who sees the letter as a "knot . . . where words, things, and organs can neither be definably separated nor compatibly combined."[8] Woman, in her relation to the letter and the signifier, in Johnson's interpretation, remains a nonhierarchical figure of the knot. Breaking down the binary oppositions that weave the knot has become one task of the so-called French deconstructive feminists.[9]

In all their complexities then, these two directions in criticism, in which the letter acts as either a historical or psychological phenomenon, risk confrontation with each other in the same way that the diverse methodological approaches of feminist literary criticism have in the past two decades. These approaches have assumed many dimensions, definitions, and labels, the most prominent being a break between the so-called "Anglo-American" and "French" feminist literary theory. Scholars have often equated the former with espousing a pragmatic view of gender roles as being socially and culturally constructed; in contrast, the latter seeks to undermine dualistic thought modes and cultural systems, resituate the female Other within those systems, and rely on a woman-centered language to deconstruct existing modes of linguistic communication.[10] This break has found reference in numerous other attempts to trace a history of feminist criticism. In the study of letters, for example, an "Anglo-American" approach sees epistolary writings, for the most part, as a historical means by which women have been able to enter the male-dominated literary canon.[11] The "French" methodology attempts to deconstruct the way Woman as a signifier in her relation to the "letter" as alphabetic character, literature, or learning, has been marginalized from the phallocentric symbolic order.[12] Despite both sides' efforts to eliminate binary modes that marginalize women socially and linguistically, there still remains a significant demarcation be-tween the Anglo-American and the French, at least in the continued reflections on the state of feminist criticism. Unfortunately, the result of the break has been to adopt terminology reflective of the binary thinking that feminisms have attempted to dispel. The most heated opposition centers on the debate between essentialism and construc-tionism, or, at the risk of oversimplification, the question whether woman is born or made.[13]

On the one hand, one could claim that apparent tensions between methodological approaches leave feminists at an impasse that threat-ens any cohesive bond between various approaches to women's writ-ings. In fact, discussions until the mid 1980s on how to define "a feminist literary criticism" attempt to establish one set of criteria that could prevent disunity. Efforts to draw all analytical methods under one rubric now seem more like answers to demands for struc-tures imposed from outside than important challenges to those struc-tures from within feminism.[14] On the other hand, one could state that feminists stand on the threshold of encompassing more diversity and of formulating the basis for a truly radical literary criticism that embraces different theoretical models in a nonhierarchical, non-threatening manner. Emphasis on diversity in the late 1980s could bring about an engagement of productive dialogue, as would an un-derstanding of the commonalities that differing methodologies share in their goals.

Instead of perceiving such a tension as a battle between the poles, it now seems better to call attention to the healthiness of debate and to listen to those who have convincingly shown the viability and feasibility of combining the strengths of many positions. Reaching a balance between what appear to be opposing views has been the task in articles by Anne Hermann, Ruth-Ellen Joeres, and Siegfried Weigel.[15] Diana Fuss, in her book *Essentially Speaking*, takes on the essentialist/constructionist debate, arguing how each side can be turned around and manipulated, depending on how terms are de-fined and used. She concludes that the antagonism between essential-ists and constructionists is "largely artificial" and sees elements of both theories in both sides' arguments. The crux of her thesis, how-ever, questions equating "Anglo-American" and "French" Feminisms with essentialists and constructionists respectively. The debate be-tween the two sides will probably continue, she concludes, but more importantly and positively, she warns against being unnecessarily paralyzed by what she calls the "overvalued binarism."[16]

Avoidance of a "paralyzing binarism" is important. Philosophical interpretations need not be divorced from social and historical considerations and vice versa. Recent discussions arising around the value of incorporating the work of anthropologists, historians, and cultural critics into literary analysis, referred to as new historicism, present a viable option for a critical recognition of necessary shared associations and add yet another dimension to the value of studying women's letters.[17] Through self-reflective, textual archeological work, new historicists have been engaged in discovering their own roots in various methodological approaches. Implicit in the process of reevaluating the relationship of literature and history is the recognition of the author's/historian's/critic's highly subjective job of choosing, interpreting, and elaborating on the associations connecting what might appear to be a highly eclectic, even arbitrary selection of texts. In this way, many scholars claiming new historicism as their method hark back to a synthesis, or rather a combination, as Hohendahl suggests,[18] of a variety of critical methods. References to Marxism appear as new historicists try to account for literature's relation to "developing material conditions" or "shifting ideologies."[19] Poststructuralism surfaces in the attempt to amalgamate literary and nonliterary texts, high and low culture, past and present.[20] Hence, new historicists draw on writings from a variety of sources. British cultural studies figure prominently, especially those on the anthropology and experimental ethnography of Clifford Geertz, who, in works such as *The Interpretation of Cultures*, questions the possibility of "objective" observation and calls for anthropologists to recognize the influence of their often imperialist, colonialist roots in compiling ethnographies.[21] The writings of Michel Foucault also receive much attention, particularly his investigation into how a culture's discourse on subjects such as sexuality, knowledge, madness, punishment, and power, as seen in nonliterary documents from a specific historical period, affect our interpretation of a literary work addressing that same topic. Scholars also cite Walter Benjamin with his belief that the relationship between the past and present is a dynamic, fluctuating one.

Feminists, too, rightly see how much their methodologies have influenced what others have labeled new historicism, although that influence, according to Judith Newton and, most recently, to Jeanette Clausen and Sara Friedrichsmeyer, has not always been duly recognized, nor have new historians accounted for the important role that gender relationships play in the interactions between text, history, and society.[22] As Newton outlines, numerous "new historicist" assumptions should look familiar to participants in the women's movement. In general, the feminist critic of the hegemonic patriarchal structure shares the position that there is no transhistorical or human essence, that human subjectivity is constructed by cultural codes, that various forms of representation ought to be read in relation to each other and in relation to events, and that "history," as contradictory and fragmented, represents a series of power relations and struggles. In connection with new historicism, feminists have called for more historical focus, with a critical eye toward all-out consumption of male-centered views of history that tends to view "History" as a monolithic construct upon which to measure literary accomplishments.[23] Many have also advocated an identification of one's "positionality" in literary analysis, situating oneself in one's social, political, personal background and locating one's questions and purpose within the framework of one's expected audience.[24] Like Newton's criticism before, Lennox has asked that gender be taken into account in every literary analysis, while recognizing that gender may not always be the single nor the most important category of literary analysis.[25]

While researchers still have much to iron out, apply, and understand about new historicism, the processes of self-definition and of drawing associations from a variety of texts and methodologies are ones that feminist criticism has in its own background and upon which it can rely. Implicit in the way in which some critics have traced a history of feminist literary criticism is the assumption that each new stage is better and more progressive than the last. Instead, feminism stands to gain more from a continual reevaluation of the strengths and weaknesses of its diverse methods and a reassessment of methods in association with each other. Moi criticizes Showalter's gynocritics for espousing a patriarchal humanist tradition of women's history, but that criticism should not throw out the baby with the bathwater. Maybe at this time of what journalist Susan Faludi has identified as a backlash against feminism,[26] the designs to "discover women lost from history," the work begun by feminists in the 1960s, or of exploring the notion of a tradition of writing by women, as Showalter advocates, are not all wrong. Maybe what Ruth-Ellen Joeres calls a pessimistic criticism, or the analysis of how the patriarchal canon has suppressed women's writing, has to accompany an optimistic one, or investigation into how women have broken away from that suppression through subversive forms, images, and metaphors, in order to reevaluate continually the cultural codes that inform our readings of women's works.[27] Maybe an androcentric stance has to join with a gynocritical one to understand the ideology that has informed women's and men's choices; maybe a discovery of the "not-so-greats" has to combine with a new look at the "greats" in order to respect the diversity we promote.

The desire that Joan Kelly expresses when she states that feminist historians do not want only "to restore women to history," but also "to restore our history to women" offers another way to look at amalgamating the diverse sides of the previously outlined debate surrounding feminist literary criticism.[28] The process of working within a system that is just beginning to define its own limitations and of working outside the system to create a new kind of dialogue requires a dual outlook. Kelly clearly places both of her goals side-by-side. Whether we want to label the new way of perceiving intersections of literature and history as "new historicism," or look at it as an extension of amalgamating dialogues on history, psychology, anthropology, literature, and other disciplines, the combination seems welcome. The developments in new historicism as they relate to feminism necessitate looking back at the documents available to us, assessing the gender ideology they present, and working toward seeing the influence of that ideology on women's writing. In addition, the call for more interaction between text and history requires that we continually examine each for intersections and fissures, for cooperation and disruptions, for conformity and subversion.

How, then, will the ideas espoused by the new historicists, as heavily influenced by feminist methodologies, lead us to a better understanding of women's letters? And how well does a study of letters lend itself to such ideas? Certainly, letters, traditionally considered neither literary nor historical, form a major part of what Newton refers to as the "cross-cultural montage" that historians and literary critics have been compiling in attempts to show an interactive relationship between writing and events.[29] In fact, contrary to the widespread belief that letters represent largely personal writings penned within the confines of the home, letters also appear frequently in a number of public contexts, including newspapers, etiquette manuals, collections, political treatises, essays, and novels. In these instances, the letter exhibits its particular qualities of mediator between writing and the material world. In the case of personal correspondence, the letter as a form promotes communication between two or more people while at the same time allowing a semi-fictive, semi-autobiographical text to emerge. Such a form seems ideal to reveal interactive dialogue between literature, history, and society. Thus, an analysis of the intersection between private and public as represented by the letter will reveal the ways in which various texts and events contributed to the development of women's writing, and vice versa, the ways in which letter-writing practices challenged or confirmed the image the public held of women. Interpretation of the various sources in which letters appear, including letter-writing manuals, novels, autobiographies, private correspondences, and political treatises, will help illuminate those developments.

Yet proponents of new historical methods should not allow history to stand as a monolithic privileged entity by which to validate literature's worth. Scholars should also not have the illusion of reaching any "one" understanding of "History" through the study of letters. For letters, not only is historical interpretation important for the material presented, but that material is important for our formulation of history and how that history has been presented. Louis Montrose expresses the relationship between text and history when he coins the terms "historicity of texts" and the "textuality of history."[30] The former he defines as the cultural and social climate out of which all texts, primary and secondary, arise. The latter refers to the reasoning that it is impossible to have access to an "authentic" past, unmediated by the texts we use to interpret that past and by the process by which those texts have been compiled, preserved, and effaced. Likewise, the "history" that comes out of those texts remains mediated through social constructions.[31] In using texts such as letters, which often were not compiled by the original writer, we must also evaluate the ways in which the compilations have been "historicized," that is, mediated to us through editing processes. In turn, we can recognize how edited correspondences have created a certain "history" of letter writing that speaks from a certain ideological position. In the first chapter of my study here, a survey of existing anthologies and editions in which letters by women appear provides apt examples of how the historicization of women's texts has ultimately obscured major parts of their lives and letters and thereby conditioned analysis in secondary literature.

Another main criticism leveled against new historicist methodology is that it creates aesthetic relativity, relegating all forms of writing to the level of discourse involved in the interplay of other kinds of social, political, or legal documents. How can a letter stand up aesthetically to the dramas of Goethe? critics might ask. In addition, new historicists, so opponents maintain, have an overwhelming desire to emphasize the new and the unique, so much so that they ignore the obvious evidence of interpretations that the literary text itself and other texts within a writer's own *oeuvre* might signal. The concentration on texts traditionally not considered aesthetic or literary threatens to undermine the privileged position that literature has assumed within categories of aesthetic beauty.[32]

A rereading and reinterpretation of women's letters holds no covert or overt intention to make various kinds of literature aesthetically relative. Adding forgotten texts to the lists of those that have carried through the years does not entail the elimination of other texts. Further, a reevaluation of women's letters as aesthetic writings is not new. The second chapter examines the cultural and historical milieu out of which a prolific tradition of women's epistolary practices rose and fell so as to confirm the central position those practices held in the creation of a cultural life during the eighteenth and nineteenth centuries. Problems of categorization and periodization that affect the study of women's letters, as discussed in chapter one, though not caused solely by gender, are gender-related. As chapter two will demonstrate, the gender norms manifest in documents from the time and in editions of women's letters have influenced greatly the attitude that literary critics assume toward creativity. Women's continued use of private, personal narrative forms also results from gender socialization. Told that by "nature" their instincts were largely maternal and domestic, women were excluded from the public sphere and from the intense exposure that men had to studying and writing in the formal, "good," classical literary forms. Many women therefore established their own kind of "traditional" literature, mostly in letters and diaries. While a historical explanation of women's creativity should not rule out the importance individual choice has assumed in selecting a mode of expression, it does demonstrate the continual intertwining of social norms and literary production.

If we take as a premise the idea that texts are not produced in isolation from their cultural, social, political, personal, and historical contexts, then the letter lends itself particularly well to such a new-historicist reading, for its levels of interaction are varied. The immediate surroundings include not only the particular audience to whom the letter is addressed, but, as in the case of the eighteenth and nineteenth centuries, also any readers who formed the audience of various salons that often included letter reading. For many women, the circles of correspondence were often enormous, a fact that does not surface immediately due to the nature of collections that present only the one-sided correspondence of singular women. In the third chapter, I look at some examples of women's friendship to emphasize the very public nature that women's private letters could assume through expansive circles of correspondents. In many cases, especially that of Helmina von Chézy, such an evaluation necessitates going back to the archives to find original documents. And indeed, as one proponent of new historicism exclaims, the archives are again becoming places of discovery and wonderment.[33] In the case of the Karl Varnhagen von Ense Collection, now located in the Jagiellonian University Library in Krakow, the selection of what Varnhagen and subsequent scholars deemed worthy to publish from the collection exemplifies the process of exclusion and the establishment of criteria that justify that exclusion. The diverse correspondence that women held with each other becomes particularly visible when one digs deeply into the folders of writers such as Chézy, whose documents were once considered great enough to warrant collecting, but who have since become relegated to near invisibility.

If, then, the process of compiling and interpreting history is a conscious one that involves positioning oneself within one's own social milieu, the process by which the letter writers positioned themselves vis-à-vis their correspondents, letter writing, geographical location, social milieu, personal lives, and particular historical situations becomes especially important. Self-reflection and self-consciousness of the writer as both observer and mediator play large roles in showing the process of a never-ending production of meaning and identities. Changing attitudes towards writing within the authors' own personal lives as well as the cultural life of the times become reflected in the construction of changing selves. Rather than searching for one authentic self in the way that a traditional historian would search for objective history or the literary critic for one interpretation of a text, the writers of letters display a recognition of the existence of multiple selves that evolve in relationship to others and to their cultural and social milieu. This varying perspective surfaces in the letters of Anna Louisa Karsch, Sophie Mereau, and Karoline von Günderrode, all publishing writers who continually repositioned themselves according to the diverse roles they assumed in life. Rather than view the construction of multiple selves as negative or somehow dishonest, however, analysis in the fourth chapter sees it as a positive way to pose options in their otherwise restrictive social milieu.

Clifford Geertz, in his *Interpretations of Cultures*, remarks: "Cultural forms can be treated as texts, as imaginative works built out of social materials."[34] Both the art work and the cultural form out of which it arises "are not merely reflections of a pre-existing sensibility analogically represented; they are positive agents in the creation and maintenance of such a sensibility."[35] These comments inspire a new look at the letters of women who, in the eyes of many scholars, "wrote merely letters and never published anything." Women's letters have long served to access biographical and cultural information. Rarely, though, have scholars seen them concurrently possessing aesthetic merit, a hesitation due mostly to standards that view letters as too trivial, subjective, and lacking in literary intent. Male writers of the early nineteenth century began to regard the letter as a questionable literary form and established a standard for women's letters, questioning their artistic value. The fifth chapter of my study turns to select passages from letters by Rahel Varnhagen and Caroline Schlegel-Schelling, two women known specifically for their letter writing, to show them expressly reacting to men's devaluation of the artistic worth of the letter form. Varnhagen's and Schlegel-Schelling's responses grant importance to the trivial and aestheticize the everyday through skillful narration. In letters, the stories the two women tell, the impressions they have, the critiques they exert, all have a meaning whose value is heightened by the narrative process. What might have become a mere fact recorded in a literary history earns the status of an elaborate and artistically crafted explanation. In the context of men's skepticism toward the letter form, women's epistolary aesthetics appear even more poignant.

A final major tenet of new historicist methodology is a recognition of the roles that power can play on many levels of literary and historical writing, analysis, interpretation, and compilation. The efforts of new historicists to study the experience of those literary figures who remained on the margins of culture and society join with an investigation into the powers that can exist between the writer and the text, the text and the reader, the text and the interpreter, and the interpreter and his or her position or situation.[36] In many cases, the new historicist tries to unveil the power that ideologies exert on the compilation and interpretation of texts. For feminists, the negative implications that the forces of power exert in deconstructive thought processes have presented a paradox. If feminism has as its major function the empowerment of women, how can women relinquish that power without denying its value? How can women deconstruct that power if they have never been within the systems of power themselves? The call for more contextual background to ground the motives for the power serves as the best way to address that paradox. Marilyn French, for example, differentiates between *having power over* and *giving power to* something or someone.[37] The need for feminists to recognize this distinction and to opt in favor of the latter will empower them in a way that does not fall into the dangerous trap of being co-opted by destructive patriarchal power structures.

Because of the exclusion of women writers from the realm of literary power, the potential for power held by the relationship between author and text, and between text and audience, can represent access to empowerment. The power to change in order to attain one's own goals becomes especially evident in the process of compilation that Bettine von Arnim carried out when she edited and then published her correspondence with famous writers of her day, including Goethe, Karoline von Günderrode, and Clemens Brentano. An analysis of selected changes in Arnim's publications will reveal how many of her alterations suggest a move toward reaching a more communicative, dialogic relationship in which literature, history, and art coalesce into a highly personal expressive form. The letter form builds her confidence as a writer.

Recognition of the power of knowledge and rhetoric also surfaces in the various ways that women engaged in the democratic struggle around 1848 employed the letter as a means to address political concerns. In overstepping the boundaries of a prescribed feminine nature that excluded women's participation from the political realm, women relied on what was still considered a feminine literary device to exhibit their concerns. The use of letters in writings by Louise Aston, Fanny Lewald, Emma Herwegh, and Mathilda Franziska Anneke shows fissures with the canonical definition of literature and the historical essay and thus is conducive to interpretation from a new-historicist perspective that promotes a radical expansion of textual material for study.

In connection with many of the questions posed by new historical methods, the issues that recent feminist inquiry has raised about diversity among women, about ruptures, fissures, and fragmentation in their "history," and about ambiguities in each woman's individual life challenge any reference to a "tradition" of women's letter writing.[38] Considering Fox-Genovese's observations on the differences that even a few decades can make in women's history, the century between 1750 and 1850 seems too vast for narrowing down specifics of a women's epistolary tradition.[39] My idea here is not to trace a teleological development in women's letter-writing production, with a specific beginning and end point. Nor do I intend to complete a comprehensive comparative study that would show that women wrote more or better letters than men. Within the context of women's writings, however, and in proportion to other genres, letters were crucial in encouraging women in the writing process, in helping to establish a literary and cultural solidarity amongst themselves, and in bridging the gap between their personal and public lives. Given the state of resources and research on the topic and women's repeated reliance on the epistolary form in the face of social and literary restrictions, it would be wrong to dismiss automatically the existence of a continuity.

My reconstruction is thus not what Schlaffer calls the formation of idols, which suffers from a chronic lack of material and obscurity.[40] On the contrary, my research builds on voluminous, multifaceted texts with a wide reception and an underestimated history. The first purpose of my study is to demonstrate the multitudinous dimensions of selected German women's letters so as to challenge interpretations that have pejoratively categorized women's concerns in their writing. At the same time that my investigation poses options for evaluating women's letters, it also challenges criteria that have questioned the aesthetic merit of personal correspondence. My discussion of individual letters and letter writers encompasses a wide array of themes, including friendship and professional literary contacts among women, psychological identities, aesthetics and the literary process, and politics. Close readings of texts disclose that vehicle to be not only convenient, but also consciously selected. I hope that emphasis on this diversity will incite further discussions on the relation between gender and genre, on a "tradition" of women's writing, on canon formation, on the determination of aesthetic values, and on intersections between the text's creation and reception.

Second, analysis of these multifaceted texts brings attention to the rich cultural, aesthetic, and literary resources that German women have to offer scholars in other parts of the world and in other disciplines. Research in Germany on women's letter writing has begun to pose questions within a cross-cultural arena. Essays in the collections *Die Frau im Dialog*, edited by Runge and Steinbrügge, and *Frauen Literatur Geschichte*, edited by Gnüg and Möhrmann, examine letters by English-speaking women.[41] In contrast, few English-speaking feminists incorporate studies of German women writers into their discussions of literary theory or texts. Language definitely poses a barrier, as does accessibility of materials. Thus, although my own study is not a cross-cultural comparison, the continued appearance of studies in English on German women writers in conjunction with translations of primary sources will foster further appreciation of the accomplishments of German women.

Third, analysis of German women's letters offers a viable means to address the larger theoretical debate surrounding feminism and the incorporation of history, culture, and psychology into the study of women's writing. Sara Lennox, in an article showing Germanists how gender can be used as a historically specific category of literary analysis, defines culture as an "arena where the contradictions of a society both express themselves and contend with each other." Accordingly, ". . . All forms of cultural production, including literature, are thus sites for the expression of historical contradictions as well as active interventions into history—in terms shaped, if not dictated, by history—and both writers and readers are actors in their society's history of signification."[42] Letters by women in my study continually reflect a struggle, manifested by contradiction and contention, between adhering to outside norms and following inner ambitions. But letters also serve as forums for the kind of healthy debate that the diversity among feminist positions continues to incite today. In several passages from women's letters, scholars have consistently detected signs of general resignation to the expectation that the writers remain passively voiceless and reticence to challenge social norms in public.[43] Assertions against literary or publicly educated women, abnegation of one's own writing, expressed lack of self-confidence in one's own work, and efforts to combine femininity with a literary profession reveal acquiescence to restrictive gender norms. In contrast, there is much evidence of strong, independent women who took hold of their own destiny by creating new ways of life that contradicted social norms. Letters by Louise Gottsched, Meta Klopstock, Anna Karsch, Caroline Schlegel-Schelling, Helmina von Chézy, Rahel Varnhagen, Sophie Mereau, Karoline von Günderrode, Bettine von Arnim, Louise Aston, Fanny Lewald, Mathilde Franziska Anneke, and others show how they dealt with such biographical aberrations as being single, having childless marriages, forming strong female friendships, working on communal literary projects, divorcing, remarrying, having extramarital love relationships, engaging in political movements, and writing literature. Through the letters they write, the friendships they form, the different personae they adopt, the liberty of expression they take, and the publications they undertake, these women represent historical contradiction and active intervention into history. An examination of the text and context of the letters in which ambiguities reveal strength and weakness will help us understand better the intricate web intertwining gender, history, literature, and culture.

✳ ✳ ✳

All translations in the manuscript are mine, unless otherwise noted.

German Women
as Letter Writers:
1750–1850

# 1

# Reclamation of the Sources and Genre

Ärgerlicher Weise fehlen auch hier, wie in allen solchen Briefwech-
seln, die Briefe der Dame, ich weiß nicht, woher das kommt, aber
es ist fast immer so und ist ein Mißbrauch, daß die eine Hälfte
solcher Korrespondenz immer auf die Seite gebracht wird. Man
fährt immer im Nebel herum, da man nicht weiß, was die andere
Partei wert ist.

[In an aggravating way, even here the letters of the lady, as in all
such correspondence, are missing, I do not know where that
comes from, but it is almost always so and is a misuse that the
one half of such correspondence is always brushed aside. One
always drives around in the fog in that one does not know how
valuable the other party is.]
    —*Gottfried Keller to Ludmilla Assing, 24 October 1872*[1]

GOTTFRIED Keller's response to Ludmilla Assing's publication of
Pückler-Muskau's letters in the *Frankfurter Zeitung* conveys a frustration still valid today. Several anthologies and editions in which
women's letters appear provide apt examples of how historicization
can ultimately obscure major parts of lives and texts. Editing of letters, omitting them from relevant collections, restricting their content
and themes to stereotypical categories of love and other emotions,
publishing them only in association with famous men—such are the
ways in which editions of women's letters become less than adequate
research tools. Without accurate primary sources and reassessment
of the editing process, scholars will continue to perpetuate the stereotypes that prevent a more thorough understanding of the relationship
between women, letter writing, and history.

One of the most disturbing drawbacks of many anthologies of letters has been the editorial license taken to omit entire letters and
passages considered unimportant. One can argue that correspondence often needs editing to strengthen its coherence and vitality.
More often than not, however, editors have omitted passages by

women or about women's lives, mostly because those passages have appeared too private, domestic, and mundane, and are thus judged to be irrelevant to readers' interests. The editor might describe the cuts, but without explaining exact reasons for them or recognizing fully their effect. Kletke, for example, in the introduction to his *Auserwählte Briefe deutscher Männer und Frauen* [*Selected Letters of German Men and Women*], claims merely that the content of the letters will not be affected by omitting what he calls meaningless and incomprehensible passages.[2] Gundolf prefaces his collection of letters from the Romantics by admitting that he deleted everything that he considered too private, biographical, literary, or fabricated, or that did not capture the spirit of Romanticism.[3]

In selecting which letters to include and which to exclude, Gundolf focuses on letters as a vehicle to present overarching concepts about an entire age. Gundolf, of course, working as a proponent of *Geistesgeschichte*, in which a nebulous "History" stood in the foreground of the literary text, represents an extreme in arbitrariness, but other editors of letters also prioritize more "public" subjects, such as historical events or important personalities. The correspondence between Friedrich and Dorothea Schlegel includes Finke's explanation of his editorial criteria: publishing Friedrich's reports on apartment hunting and travel preparation and Dorothea's about her sickness would create a "Wüste des Kleinlichen" [desert of triviality],[4] a repetitive, uninteresting collection for readers who might wish to see more variance of themes and topics. For him, the private concerns are too trivial to engage the reader.

There are two problems with excluding what one deems unimportant: the first concerns content; the second, the process of letter writing. Regarding content, Finke ignores the fact that in relating their trials and tribulations, letter writers can also weave fascinating stories that captivate readers. For the scholar exploring women's perspectives, the passages in which females describe domestic or personal problems can provide important insights into the relation between a woman's creativity and her life. Women's letters become historicized according to criteria the editor finds universally worthy and interesting, but which, as different interests and methodologies influence reading habits, can change over time. Concerning the process of writing letters, if everyday ordeals recur in letters, as they do in those of Dorothea and Friedrich, omitting them from a correspondence risks losing a unity throughout the epistolary dialogue and excluding a powerful emotional interaction. Barbara Hahn, in her extensive research on Rahel Varnhagen's correspondence, discusses the important aspect of dialogic exchange in letters.[5] To take the term

"Briefwechsel" seriously, one needs to include both sides of the letter exchange as much as possible. Especially for women, who have been either silenced or censored through drastic cuts, mutual interaction between two letter partners is significant.

Of course, Finke's decision to leave the everyday concerns out of his edition of Friedrich and Dorothea Schlegel's letters also affected men's letters: Finke also cleansed Friedrich Schlegel's letters of private concerns. Vortriede, the editor of the 1981 edition of letters between Achim and Bettine von Arnim, included a number of ellipses in both partners' letters. In the epilogue, Vortriede explains but does not really justify his omissions. He states that he has excluded everything that does not relate to the marriage and that has little cultural or historical interest, such as domestic stories, accounting records, or servant affairs.[6] In fact, there appear to be as many ellipses in Achim's letters from Wiepersdorf as in those by Bettine from Berlin.

Brockmeyer, in his dissertation on the history of the letter in the mid-eighteenth century, gives certain criteria that women's letters in the eighteenth and nineteenth centuries had to meet to be published: the women had to be respected personalities, have something culturally interesting to report, be members of a renowned circle of people, and have written letters that contributed to a general social history of the time.[7] One could of course argue that such criteria affect the publication of men's letters as well. In other words, the decision as to whose personal documents will be published and whose will not has hinged upon the question of famous and not famous, not solely on the question of the sex of the letter writer. But upon close examination of anthologies that do include women's letters, one can narrow Brockmeyer's criteria down to state that women's letters have most often been published because they allow the scholar to disseminate views of the predominant male figures of the day. Emil Burger prefaces his collection of *Deutsche Frauenbriefe aus zwei Jahrhunderten* [*German Women's Letters of Two Centuries*] by stating: "Manche von den Frauen dieser Epoche [Goethe's] sind allerdings nicht um ihrer selbst willen hier aufgenommen worden, sondern weil sie Beiträge liefern zur Erkenntnis des Wesens und Wirkens unserer großen Geistesheroen" [Many of the women of this epoch are included here not because of themselves, but rather because they contribute to knowledge about the personalities and deeds of our great intellectual heroes.][8] Women's letters have been published in various collections that define their role by a relationship, either explicitly to a specific man, or implicitly to certain prescribed gender roles of lover, wife, or mother. Wasserzieher, whose *Briefe deutscher Frauen* [*Letters of German Women*] underwent four editions between 1907 and 1925, sees the women whose letters he includes as having no literary impact. Rather, the women, as mothers, brides, wives, sisters, or daughters, exerted only a personal influence on the men in their lives.[9] Titles of anthologies that include women's letters preserve stereotypical roles: Gotsmann's *Deutsche Briefe der Liebe und Freundschaft* [*German Letters of Love and Friendship*] (1937), Zeitler's *Deutsche Liebesbriefe* [*German Loveletters*] (1907), Westermann's *Briefe der Liebe aus drei Jahrhunderten deutscher Vergangenheit*, [*Letters of Love From Three Centuries of German Past*], Schmidt-Fischer's "*... und immer weiter schlägt das Herz:*" *Briefe deutscher Frauen*, ["*... the heart continues to beat*": *Letters of German Women*] (1938), and Elbogen's two collections—*Geliebter Sohn: Elternbriefe an Berühmte Dichter* [*Dear Son: Parents' Letters to Famous Poets*] (1930), and *Liebste Mutter: Briefe berühmter Deutscher an ihre Mütter* [*Dearest Mother: Letters of Famous Germans to Their Mothers*] (1930).[10] This context reveals little about women's creativity or artistic ambitions and presents incomplete ideas and stories. Even in anthologies that claim to publish men's and women's letters, the quantity of women's letters falls short, and the same personalities—mostly those connected with Goethe and Schiller, such as Bettine von Arnim, Elisabeth Goethe, Charlotte von Lengefeld, Caroline Flachsland, and Karoline von Humboldt—appear over and over.[11] The role of Goethe as great man looms in the foreground of many major anthologies of women's letters between 1790 and 1830, as exemplified in the titles of the often-cited edition *Frauen der Goethezeit in Briefen, Dokumenten und Bildern* [*Women in the Goethe-Era in Letters, Documents, and Portraits*] (1960), edited by Haberland and Pehnt. Clearly, women's letters are often published because of their contacts with renowned men.[12] Rare, however, is the edition of a man's letters published because of his relationship to a famous woman.

Further, editions of letters between famous men and women have often been published as one-sided correspondences, presenting only the man's letters. Sometimes the woman's letters remain absent because she destroyed her own correspondence for reasons of discretion, such as in the case of Charlotte von Stein's correspondence with Goethe. Several other women of the period did not want to have their letters published due to the risk of losing status in a culture that frowned upon them publishing their own writings. Gottsched, for example, tried to publish Louise Kulmus Gottsched's letters to him in 1734, but apparently her consent did not seem enthusiastic enough for him to follow through with his intent. Not until a decade after her death did her friend Dorothea Runckel publish Louise Gottsched's letters.[13] Whereas the first volume contains the husband Gottsched's responses, Runckel does not include her own responses to Louise Gottsched's letters that appear in the subsequent two volumes. Likewise, Meta Klopstock's sister, Elisabeth Moller Schmidt, wanted to publish Meta's letters, but, as with Gottschedin, Meta showed hesitation about such publication, saying that her letters were too personal and intimate. Such hesitation makes Hahn's call for publishing both sides of the epistolary exchange difficult to fulfill. Consequently, one must assess the context in which opposition to publication occurs as well as reevaluate women's supposed nonconsent. My study attempts to address this dilemma in subsequent chapters by investigating historical situations that might predicate decisions, such as the increasing split between private and public realms and the norms that confined women to their so-called natural place in the domestic sphere, and by closely analyzing passages in which women talk about publication of their letters.

In instances in which only the man's letters have appeared in a collection of a correspondence with a woman, however, the omission of the woman's half of the correspondence often signals a devaluation of the cultural and aesthetic worth of her letters. Many letters exchanged between men and women—including the correspondence between Gellert and Fräulein von Schönfeld, and between Friedrich Schiller and Sophie Mereau—were first published without the woman's letters.[14] The letters of Dorothea Schlegel appear in the section of correspondence in the critical edition of Friedrich Schlegel's writings, of which only three volumes have been published to date.[15] One-sided correspondence not only omits the recipient's reaction, an important part of a correspondence; it also continues to make women passive recipients with no regard for their active voices. In many cases, there is no evidence that the woman would not have consented to having her letters published. Instead, someone else made the decision for her. In 1823, Goethe proudly published Solger's correspondence and then, in 1828/29, the correspondence between him and Schiller, extolling the letters as evidence of productive, unifying friendship.[16] Before his departure to Switzerland in 1779 and to Italy in 1797, however, he burned—apparently without regret—letters from his mother, his sister Cornelia, Friederike Brion, Charlotte Buff, and Lili Schönemann, as he writes in his diary on 9 June 1797.[17] After Karoline von Günderrode committed suicide, her friend, Susanne von Heyden, sent the letters of Karoline's lover, Friedrich Creuzer, back to him, upon his request, and in turn received Karoline's letters from him, which she then apparently burned.[18] The issue of ownership is one that comes up over and over again within the discussion of letter publication, and the particulars of each case justify individual attention in any critical study. Charlotte von Stein meticulously saved Goethe's letters. She requested her own letters back from Goethe, however, and burned them shortly before her death. Lack of Stein's letters has not prevented analysis of the "correspondence" and relationship between her and Goethe. Susman, in her study of the relationship through Goethe's letters, concludes that Stein's portrait comes across clear enough in Goethe's letters so there need be no worry about Stein's absent viewpoint. Instead, the difficulties of interpretation lie not in Stein's silence, but in Goethe's own secrecy and concealment.[19] Recent scholarship on Stein's own texts, however, suggests that Goethe and Stein may have had very different images of themselves and their relationship.[20] Whether women destroyed their own letters, whether other people destroyed their letters, or whether their letters exist to be published, editors should justify any omission and recognize the impact that any exclusion may have on the study of correspondence.

When women's letters were published during their lifetime, it was usually done anonymously and under the pretense of shedding light on their contemporary culture, but with little or no emphasis on the authors or their writing. Some of Rahel Varnhagen's letters first appeared anonymously in the widely read literary newsletter *Morgenblatt für gebildete Stände* in 1812.[21] Rahel's letters were included in this series for the purpose of relating interesting perspectives on Goethe. Thus, her letters were not published out of interest for Rahel the person, or out of admiration for the aesthetic beauty of the letters themselves; instead, they were considered important merely because they illuminated the life of a great person. Only in 1834, after Rahel's death, did Karl August reveal the identity of their author.[22] The letters of other female intellectuals were also published anonymously for the insights they could lend into the nineteenth-century milieu. J. F. Unger anonymously published some letters of his wife, the writer Helene Unger, in the *Jahrbücher der preussischen Monarchie* for the glimpses they gave into cultural life in Berlin. These letters were subsequently reprinted in book form entitled *Briefe über Berlin*. Not until the reprinted version appeared in 1930, however, was Helene Unger revealed as their author.[23] Fanny Lewald's first publications were her letters, appearing anonymously and without her consent in 1839 in her cousin's newspaper *Europa*. Although Lewald, as she relates in her autobiography *Meine Lebensgeschichte*, was astonished and overjoyed at discovering that "meine sorg-und absichtslos geschriebenen Briefe" [my careless and purposeless letters] were worthy enough to be published, their publication still did not instill in her any self-confidence in her talents, for she read them as if another person had written them.[24]

"Anonym, verschollen, trivial" [anonymous, lost, trivial]—so reads the title of Jeannine Blackwell's article on methodological hindrances in researching German women's literature.[25] Working with women's personal letters involves confronting the same hindrances to researching women's published fictional works. The irony of disguised publications of private letters is that behind the mask of non-identity, women could often formulate a new style or assert radical ideas without fearing the harsh admonishments or possible ostracism from a society that frowned upon women who expressed themselves publicly. Rahel's anonymous publication in 1812, entitled "Über Goethe. Bruchstücke aus Briefen" ["On Goethe. Excerpts From Letters"], does not, as Hahn observes, treat Goethe as much as it does the author Jean Paul. In contrast to giving a literary or cultural portrait of Jean Paul the author, Rahel presents him as Jean Paul her friend, who advises her never to get married. As Hahn describes, the letter belongs to the kind of dialogic writing that exists outside of the conventional relationships of author as husband and reader as wife.[26] From such ruptures of expectations and interweavings of personal and cultural experiences arises the demand to reevaluate and analyze entire texts and contexts of women's letters.

Still, the publication of women's letters creates a conundrum. To create separate anthologies of women's letters is to risk delineating the same dichotomies of "masculine" and "feminine" in writing that can create gender tension. Given ingrained biases and lack of properly edited sources, however, fair integration of women's texts with men's seems at present unattainable. In those anthologies that have tried to integrate more women's texts in with men's, that integration often does not include enough women's letters, either proportionately to the number they wrote or to the number men wrote. The recent anthology *Deutsche Briefe 1750–1950* [*German Letters 1750–1950*], edited by Mattenklott, Schlaffer, and Schlaffer, shows an inadequate attempt at integration.[27] Although the editors devote a large part of their introduction to the talents of women as letter writers, only one in every sixth letter writer included is a woman. With due respect for a feminist literary criticism that calls for more integration of women's works into the standard canon, it seems as if we still need separate anthologies on women's writings as compensation for all that has been lost, ignored, or excised. At this point, specialized studies are still the best way to begin working through the maze. While separate anthologies provide a highly convenient research tool when such tools are extremely rare, one does hope that the time will come in which women's letters become integrated into general anthologies, collections of research essays, conference sessions, and university lectures. Presenting the woman's voice alongside the man's will lead to what Kolodny terms a more "humane" literary criticism.[28]

Standard categorization will have to change, too, if scholars insist on justifying the publication of women's letters. A recent worthy project for anyone interested in examining private letters has been the reproduction on microfiche of letter collections of what the editors have called German philosophers living between 1750 and 1850.[29] The foci of the collection are older, less accessible editions of letters by lesser-known writers. Given the desire to reprint and catalogue such important, out-of-print works, one might welcome and expect inclusion of women's collections. For women's studies, however, this project is interesting because of its omissions—rarely were women considered philosophers, and thus less accessible correspondences by Louise Gottsched, Dorothea Runckel, Anna L. Karsch, Sophie Mereau, and Fanny Lewald, among others, are missing from the series. In fact, the contents of the more than seven-hundred-volume reprint collection, as well as the extensive list of senders and recipients of letters, contain very few women as senders. Without undermining the importance of those who are included, one must question the arbitrariness of the selection. Why reprint the letters of Malwida von Meysenbug and not Fanny Lewald? Why Elisa von der Recke and not Sophie Mereau, whose original correspondence with Schiller would have fit within the scope of the project? Even more puzzling is the inclusion of writings by certain men—for example, A. W. Schlegel and Schelling—without those by their female counterpart, Caroline Schlegel-Schelling. Justification for women's inclusion seems to lie in connections with famous male philosophers as well as in the criteria that constitute men as main members of the category "philosophers."

The editorial omissions found in first editions of women's letters have led to inevitable deficiencies in subsequent editions. Of the many recent editions of women's letters reprinted or newly collected, very few have been based on consultation of original sources, and thus research has had to contend with incomplete collections.[30] With the loss of archival materials and primary sources, we may never know the complete extent of the damage or ever be able to recreate the originals. Likewise, deficits in source material create inadequacies in secondary literature. Even recent anthologies are problematic in their continued tendency to place women's letters next to famous men and standard literary periods, a placement that the secondary literature treating the history and form of the letter substantiates. One of the main reasons for inadequate treatment of women's letters in tradi-

tional scholarship is a gender-biased perspective that resorts to transhistorical biological factors as explanations for the difference between
the two sexes and how they have opted to express themselves. Such
a separation has placed women's creative works and deeds on the
periphery of literary scholarship, for the man's world becomes that of
culture.[31] Closer scrutiny of what have come to be standard secondary
works on the history and form of the letter will confirm the need for
a more detailed look at the role that gender plays in literary and
historical interpretation.

Georg Steinhausen's antiquated, yet richly documented and therefore still valuable work, *Die Geschichte des deutschen Briefes* [*The
History of the German Letter*], focuses mainly on the development of
the epistolary form in Germany from its beginnings in the fourteenth
century to what he views as its acme in the eighteenth century.[32]
As Hahn observes, the subtitle "Zur Kulturgeschichte des deutschen
Volkes" [*On the Cultural History of the German People*] implies that
the letter has one primary purpose: to purvey messages that reveal
cultural and historical information.[33] Steinhausen is very clear about
keeping a disciplinary agenda. He stresses that he is not writing a
literary historical account of the letter form;[34] instead, he chooses to
concentrate on social and cultural transformations that instigated
changes in letter-writing practices, such as shifts in social classes
and structures, continuous modernization of the postal system, and
alterations in writing materials. In the sense of conveying a monolithic history that changed letter writing, he is relying on diachronic,
categorical historiography. Despite the well-demarcated line he draws
between a historical and a literary study, he cannot escape the close
connection between the two when he treats the use of the letter
during certain periods: he continues to employ a well-established
classification of literary periods as they apply to various epistolary
styles. His periodization of the different epistolary styles during the
eighteenth century, for example, coincides with that of traditional
literary history, proceeding through the periods of Enlightenment,
Storm and Stress, and Sentimentalism. The figures he chooses to concentrate on remain largely well-known authors or those in their immediate circles.

In Steinhausen's estimation, the eighteenth century was the century
of the letter, not only because people were such productive correspondents, but also because they consciously strove for a naturalness of
style and form that opposed the preceding era's rigid norms for letter-
writing. Steinhausen maintains that the value of the letter diminished
in the early nineteenth century. New technology facilitated travel and
advanced communication, the laconic postcard replaced the eloquent

letter, and people had less time to write letters. He stresses how materialistic and somber attitudes supplanted the previous eighteenth-century emotional expressiveness. In connection with the "downfall" of the letter, he alludes to one gender-related development that had a large impact, namely, the eventual defining of letter writing and of the expression of the very personal emotions that letter writing represented as being "feminine," and thus inappropriate for men. He cites a passage from a letter from Friederike Krickeberg to Tieck in 1841, in which Krickeberg replies to Tieck's request that she let him read letters that Friedrich Gentz had written to her in 1794 and 1795. She replies:

> Sie wünschen Briefe von Gentz an mich, um sie der heutigen krittlichen Welt zu übergeben? Fordern Sie das nicht von mir! Ihnen durfte ich Sie damals vertrauen, Sie würden sie noch heute fühlen—aber wer sonst? Auch diese Zeit ist vorüber; die Liebe hat ein anderes Gewand umgehängt; die zarten Stoffe sind verweht, und ich glaube, ein junger Mann, der jetzt solche Briefe schrieb, würde sich nicht mehr männlich erhaben vorkommen.

> [You wish to have letters from Gentz to me in order to give them over to today's critical world? Don't demand that of me! I could trust you to them then, you would feel them today, but who else? Even this era is over; love has another disguise; the tender subject matter has blown away, and, I believe, a young man who would write these letters today would not consider himself very masculinely exalted.][35]

In the 1840s, Krickeberg was referring to a major shift in gender expectations that had occurred in the past century. Men had become too "masculine" to write the emotions contained in Gentz's love letters from the late eighteenth century. The implicit equation of letter-writing with feminine traits also betrays attitudes undermining the worth of private letters. Steinhausen does not delve any further into this attitudinal change and the eventual categorization and evaluation of the "masculine" and "feminine" in writing. Thus, his analysis supports an unexplained polarization of gender roles in social interactions and editions of letters.

Throughout his extensive study of the letter, Steinhausen does not hesitate to extol the quality of women's letters and the influence that women have had on letter-writing style and content.[36] There is a certain contradiction between his praise of women's letter-writing talents, which he claims were evident past the middle of the nineteenth century, and his statements regarding the general degeneration of letter writing at the end of the eighteenth century. The fact that he finds women still excelling at letter writing long after male literary figures have abandoned writing epistles causes one to question the traditional classifications of mainstream literary activity and to devise alternative methods of studying women's personal writings. In defining the decline in the epistolary tradition, Steinhausen refers to both a diminishing quality and quantity in letters, factors that no longer allow the letter to be classified as literature as it had been in the eighteenth century. After observing that the epistolary productivity of only men and not women decreases at the beginning of the nineteenth century, Steinhausen does not probe further for possible definitions of literature, for the expectations certain men and women placed on the poet, and for the gender norms that would cause categorization of a "masculine" and "feminine" letter-writing style.

Thus, although Steinhausen makes sex a determinant in the success of letter-writing culture, his desire to focus on social and cultural developments reflected in the letter omits gender as a category of historical interpretation. Other critics have shared his views on the downfall of the letter after the eighteenth century, skimming over the early nineteenth century and Romanticism when discussing the letter.[37] In such cases, the classification of the letter as literature is based primarily on its increased public function.[38] These critics see a turn away from public-oriented statements in letters towards expressions of extremely private emotions, and thus they locate the beginnings of the decline in letter writing in Romanticism.[39] They imply one main reason why scholars rarely include letters in discussions of works defined as "high art": the letter, written in private and usually without the thought of publication, is not a self-consciously created work designated to reach a public audience through commercial distribution. Without proper definitions of what constitutes "good" art and without the recognition that criteria of art, like those of history and literature, are based on the historical context out of which they arise, these scholars do not emphasize that correspondence cannot, and should not, be read like a novel, a drama, or a poem. Instead, a study of letters, as scholars of personal narratives have recognized, calls for an approach to literary examination that views artistic creation as a process, not as a cumulative set of products.[40] In other words, such a study would emphasize the circumstances of production, including the social, historical, and psychological conditions of both the letter writer and the letter reader. The scrupulous reader should give particular attention to the individual imagination that produces and reads the text in order to see, as Culley points out, the interaction between letter writing and other forms of literary self-expression.[41] Where scholars have not addressed questions of social context, reader reception, and intentionality in the individual texts, their articles represent a scholarship that still remains negligent of the function of the letter in its historical context, and especially of women's contributions in continuing and developing the epistolary tradition.

With the interest in structuralism and phenomenology in the 1960s and 70s came studies on the form and structure of the letter and the significance of the letter as a literary entity. Albert Wellek's article on the phenomenology of the letter and Honnefelder's informative structural study on the use of letters in German fictional literature represent perspectives of literary philosophy on the epistolary form.[42] Discussion of the letter in these cases revolves around what constitutes literature. Wellek differentiates between documentary letters and literary letters, which he terms "offene Briefe," and the private, or intimate, letter. Unlike many researchers before and after him, however, Wellek considers all these forms literature, whether produced for the public or in private. In contrast, Bürgel presents a heuristic model that sees the private letter as an autobiographical, historical document or as a sociological communication form.[43] But because the letter possesses mostly functional, one-dimensional, nonsymbolic, nonfictional qualities, any instances detected as aesthetic occur purely as accidents. Wellek, drawing upon the theories of Roman Ingarden, classifies letters as literature based on the belief that the consciousness of the letter writer pervades his or her letter, and that the letter writer has produced a text intentionally directed at an object.[44]

In identifying the letter as literature, however, Wellek distinguishes between the quality of different forms of literature and implies the existence of a "high art," which rarely includes letters written within the past two centuries. Like the previous scholars, Wellek, too, identifies a downfall in the art of both letter writing and letter reading since the early nineteenth century, a development that he attributes to the" de-domestication" of modern life, to the "Entpersönlichung" [depersonalization] and "Versachlichung" [objectification] of humans, and to the modern attitude that one "has no time" to write letters.[45] In his discussion of how gender and letter writing relate to one another, Wellek, again like his predecessors, turns to biological sex differences to classify women's letters. He distinguishes between naive and sentimental, extroverted and introverted, feminine and masculine letter writers, whereby the woman is extroverted, reaching out more readily for response and giving more warm and open response. Although the correlation between women and extroversion seems to represent a new one, given that "femininity" has been stereotyped as passive and introverted, there is no role reversal here. Instead, Wellek sees the reason for women's warmth and openness in their personality, which biologically distinguishes them from men.[46] Furthermore, instead of causing women to develop their own style, this so-called extroverted feminine compassion, Wellek postulates, has caused women letter writers to adopt the epistolary styles of their male letter partners. As examples of this adoption, he mentions the Romantic women, and Bettine von Arnim in particular, who took the chance of adapting their letters to the circumstances. He concurs with other scholars before him in saying that Arnim falsified three letters she received from Beethoven. Attributing Arnim's attempts to emulate another person's epistolary style to "einer hysteroid-übereinfühlsamen und wandelbaren, 'proteischen', typisch romantischen Briefschreiberin" [a hysteric-over-empathetic and inconstant 'proteic,' typically romantic letter writer],[47] Wellek stereotypes Arnim's letters with clichés that are not further supported or defined in his article.[48]

Wellek's assertions on the difference between men's and women's letters have carried through in scholarship into the present. In 1970, this essay reappeared in a collection of his writings. As late as 1985, Wolfgang Müller, in an essay on the letter published in a volume of essays devoted to nonfictional artistic prose, cites Wellek's differentiation in the context of pointing out how much the letter is oriented toward the receiver.[49] Müller's essay looks at the changing views towards the function of the letter by examining transformations in the constellation formed by the writer, the reader, and the subject of the letter. Like Wellek, and unlike Bürgel, he also recognizes the possibility that letters have artistic and literary merit. In describing those changes, however, he draws only on the example of one woman, Bettine von Arnim in the context of publishing her works. As with Wellek and others, he neglects to support universal statements about women's letter-writing techniques with specific examples, thus leaving them out of the larger critical debate on the aesthetic value of letters.

While copious studies of the personalities of Bettine von Arnim, Dorothea Veit-Schlegel, Caroline Schlegel-Schelling, and Rahel Varnhagen exist, their letters, which constitute their main texts, receive little attention within the context of a larger literary tradition. Unfortunately, even informative and important studies on the letter in German history appearing during the past two decades still neglect women's contribution to the long epistolary tradition. This critical absence suggests that sexual bias still prejudices scholarship. The published proceedings of the 1975 conference on the problems of letter editing, conducted by the Deutsche Forschungsgemeinschaft and edited by Wolfgang Frühwald, present a study that contributes

much information to the history of letter editions.[50] The collection
claims an interdisciplinary approach that combines scholars from
history, theology, musicology, philosophy, and literature. The study
incites the interested scholar to pursue publication of personal letters
because the contributors all assume a very positive attitude towards
the published letter and view it as a valuable research tool for the
serious scholar.[51] Conspicuously absent in this collection of essays,
however, is any study on the many editions of women's letters that
have appeared within the past two centuries.

Likewise, and more recently, the 1989 volume of essays *Brief und
Briefwechsel in Mittel-Osteuropa im 18. und 19. Jahrhundert*, the first
volume in the series, *Brief und Briefwechsel im 18. und 19. Jahrhundert als Quellen der Kulturbeziehungsforschung* [*Letter and Correspondence in Central-Easteurope in the 18th and 19th Century; Letter and
Correspondence as Sources of Research on Cultural Relations*], contains no in-depth study on women's letters.[52] Oellers, in his article on
the letter as a form of private and public communication in Germany
during the eighteenth century, mentions Louise Gottsched, Meta Klopstock, and Anna Karsch as well-known letter writers, but for the most
part in negative contexts. For the age of Sentimentality, he lumps all
women together as contributing to an eventual overemotionality.[53]
While he admits in his analysis of men's letters that literary sentimentality could not have gained popularity without the participation of
men, he differentiates among their forms and styles without resorting
to universal characteristics, as he does with the women. Both these
important collections of essays would have been appropriate forums
for discussing women's letters within the context of general problems
of editing and publication of private letters, a subject that Frühwald's
collection addresses, and issues of cultural and literary development,
which the volume *Brief und Briefwechsel in Mittel-Osteuropa* treats.
Furthermore, the unique questions raised by publications of women's
letters deserve their own analysis within such studies, for at the root
of this continuous stereotyping and neglect lie primary resources in-
adequately developed by a scholarly community that devalues
women's texts.

The reasons for this devaluation form a complex mixture of sexual
discrimination, literary periodization, and genre categorization. Difficulties with categorization surface in two often-quoted studies on
women in Romanticism, Irmgard Tanneberger's *Die Frauen der Romantik und das soziale Problem* [*The Women of Romanticism and
the Social Problem*] and Margarete Susman's *Frauen der Romantik*
[*Women of Romanicism*].[54] Both these scholars express their hesitation
about using Romantic women's letters as either historical testimony

or literature. As historical testimony, Tanneberger finds letters too subjective and too bound to their times to be reliable as objective evaluations of the social climate. Instead, she opts for what she sees as more "objective" sources—facts about historical events in the early nineteenth century, the impressions others had of the women she discusses, and the women's biographies—against which she weighs what the women say about themselves and the times in their own letters.[55] Susman, whose study is oriented towards the women's individual personalities within their literary context, doubts the literariness of letters because of their subjectivity. Even though Susman finds what she calls a totally great system of thought in many women's letters, she still does not view women's thought processes as profound as those of the "great people."[56]

Restrictive genre categorization that neglects women's contributions to literary culture appears in several essay collections on Romanticism. The papers presented at the interdisciplinary symposium on Romanticism in Germany published by Brinkmann in 1978, Lützeler's two anthologies, *Romane und Erzählungen der deutschen Romantik* [*Novels and Stories of German Romanticism*] and *Romane und Erzählungen zwischen Romantik und Realismus* [*Novels and Stories Between Romanticism and Realism*], and Klaus Peter's essay collection, *Romantikforschung seit 1945* [*Research on Romanticism Since 1945*] do not contain studies on women writers.[57] The marginality of women letter writers in these three literary discussions seems due in large part to the letter's own tenuous position within the traditional literary canon, and not solely to sexual discrimination. Discussions of women's letters do not comfortably fit into Lützeler's collection of studies on novels and stories in the early nineteenth century. If one is interested in studying the woman writer, one must often look outside of those forms legitimized in the literary canon toward those personal forms that many women have used continuously, such as the letter. Often, the traditional definition of "literature" as public-oriented, self-consciously produced writing displaying a unity of form and content excludes the private letter. In addition, the historical continuity of women's letter writing does not corroborate the traditional notion of an ebb in epistolary communication at the beginning of the nineteenth century.

Another stumbling block that scholarship will have to overcome is the cult of personality usually focused on publicly recognized men. Schlawe's two-volume reference work on editions of nineteenth-century Germans offers an example of how this kind of selectivity excludes women.[58] He includes the editions of letters of those who were at least ten years old by 1830 and who were born before 1880, with part A listing the collections alphabetically by the main name, part B the individual receivers of letters, and part C, individuals who wrote the letters. The selection of women included in part A seems arbitrary, for although the list includes letter collections of Bettine von Arnim, Fanny Stahr-Lewald, and Helmina von Chézy, it cites no edition of Rahel Varnhagen's or Dorothea Schlegel's letters. Part C identifies many women as avid letter writers, but their published letters are scattered in publications of men's letters.

Continual stress on the heroic male artist precludes women from consideration as agents of larger cultural transformations. Oellers attributes the downfall of letter writing in the nineteenth-century to "Destruktion von persönlicher Größe" [the destruction of personal greatness] without recognizing the continuity of women's letter-writing. The anthologies *Briefe deutscher Philosophen* [*Letters to German Philosophers*], *Briefe an den Vater* [*Letters to the Father*], and *Briefwechsel mit Autoren* include few, if any, letters by women.[59] Inclusion depends mostly on connection with "great men," seldom on intrinsic literary merit. In a commentary essay at the end of the volume *Brief und Briefwechsel im Mittel-Osteuropa im 18. und 19. Jahrhundert*, Wolfgang Kessler continues this ideology of the "greats" by proposing it as a model for a slavistic research series entitled "Briefwechsel deutschsprachiger Philosophen," a collection, which I mentioned earlier, whose very categorization largely excludes women.[60]

The inability that scholars show to combine both literary and historical understanding of the letter, that is, to show how the letter can intersect both the aesthetic and the cultural realm, manifests itself in the dichotomization that studies of the letter exhibit. On the one hand, in the past two decades, various scholars have used the letters of early nineteenth-century women as a source of important social and historical information. By employing letters to cull historical information, scholars are reading letters in what is called an "efferent" manner in Louise Rosenblatt's *The Reader, the Text, the Poem*, and subsequently, in Susan Kissel's article on colonial women's letters: an approach to letters with the intention of "carrying away" facts, figures, and data about the women's lives and times.[61] As efferent readers, scholars search letters for current events of the recipient or writer, and for information on traditions, economic conditions, gender roles, and psychological states.[62]

In contrast to efferent letter readers, Rosenblatt and Kissel describe those who read a letter "aesthetically"—they approach writing in terms of the emotions that the words, style, structure, and subjects of the letter evoke for both readers and writers. While efferent readings of letters help discern women's views of their times and situation, the aesthetic value of the letters should not be underestimated nor separated. In other words, the scholar should not ignore the emotions that the beauty of letters aroused in the letter writer and her contemporary letter readers, a beauty that can still affect readers today.

As literary creations, letters present many complex and interesting formal and thematic elements. The tradition and structure of the genre, the interaction of a narrative self with an authentic or implied reader, and the images of the self that the letter writer creates in relation to time and experience provoke questions relevant to literary criticism. Studies of German women's letter writing within the past decade have concentrated on the texts of the so-called Romantic women in an attempt to explore the issue of aesthetic sensibilities.[63] These studies demonstrate that extensive and comparative research on the poetics and aesthetics of Romantic women's letters is necessary for an understanding of the woman's perspective of her creativity and the opportunities she has had to express it. In calling for an evaluation of the aesthetic worth of letters, scholars do not necessarily state that all letters have an aesthetic worth or that efferent readings of letters cannot be rewarding. Rather, they show that the letter represents a mode of literary production in which language and text give shape and meaning to a life. That mode also need not force separations between the writing process and its cultural context, between the inner and outer world. By narrating to an actual or implied audience, the letter writer creates a direct form of self-expression that asks for a response to her experiences. Letters by women underrepresented in the traditional literary canon may disclose strong desires to enter the literary realm and the social or psychological inhibitions that block their way. Women's letters may suggest enforced silences, socially inflicted modesty about writing for the public, and physical barriers. But concurrently, and just as importantly, women may exhibit a self-conscious effort to create an alternative aesthetic mode of self-expression.

The most exciting and thorough work on women's letters is coming from scholars who go back to the archives in order to represent and reinterpret the original texts. On the forefront of such scholarship are several Germanists working with original documents of Rahel Varnhagen, located in the Karl Varnhagen von Ense Collection in the Jagiellonian Libary in Krakow. Barbara Hahn's books and essays on women's letter writing prove especially noteworthy.[64] Along with discoveries of Rahel's intentions to publish her own letters, Hahn is undertaking a new edition of Rahel Varnhagen's correspondence, which will try to adhere to the true sense of the word *Briefwechsel*.

Thus, Hahn has addressed the larger question of the process of compiling and editing letters. Through carefully rereading Rahel Varnhagen's published and unpublished correspondence together with Rahel's brief notes and comments to Karl Varnhagen von Ense regarding the collection and publication of her letters, Hahn has shown that Rahel did indeed want to see her letters published and did express ideas on inclusions and exclusions in the edition. Such discoveries certainly justify reexamination of the archives and attention to nonliterary documents in the interpretation of literary and cultural discourses. Without actually defining her work as new historicism, Hahn substantiates the most innovative work that new historical tenets uphold: she reevaluates the historicity of texts, scrupulously examines the archives for diverse texts that allow history and literature to unfold simultaneously, and reissues a new collection that encompasses a dialogic interaction between people and their histories.

The impact of over twenty years of feminist research is beginning to show. In addition to the previously mentioned primary and secondary literature, a recent edition of Karoline von Günderrode's letters signifies an important progressive step toward making women's correspondence more accessible.[65] Gert Mattenklott's work on connections between Jews and German letters, in which he includes analysis of correspondence between Henriette Herz and Rahel Varnhagen, recognizes women's contributions within their social milieu.[66] The collection of excerpts from primary literature in Brieftheorie des 18. Jahrhunderts [Theory of the Letter in the 18th Century], edited by Angelika Ebrecht, Regina Nörtemann, and Herta Schwarz, makes primary texts more accessible.[67] The insightful, interdisciplinary, cross-cultural studies in the collection Die Frau im Dialog: Studien zur Theorie und Geschichte des Briefes [Woman in Dialogue: Studies on the Theory and History of the Letter], edited by Anita Runge and Lieselotte Steinbrügge, stress the significance of letter writing for women's participation in the cultural life of their time.[68] In addition to increasing the quantity of publications and reprints, however, we should continue to improve the quality of research. As Becker-Cantarino has pointed out, it is now inexcusable that Michael Maurer's 1985 edition of Sophie von LaRoche's correspondence does not list the archival sources for the letters.[69] Scholars should be critical of inconsistencies and incompleteness of documentation, such as that exhibited by Dagmar von Gersdorff in her biography of Sophie Mereau, which does not include a complete listing of the documents' locations.[70] Particularly in editing and publication, precision remains vital, especially when documenting the sources and explaining what has been omitted and why. As I hope to demonstrate in subsequent chapters, the private and domestic concerns expressed in letters are often significant public issues. As the next chapter will show, we should also become skeptical of any ideology that devalues the personal realm and recognize the role that gender plays in that devaluation, as women often become associated with the private sphere.

# 2

# Letters, History, and Gender

My decision to use the century between 1750 and 1850 as a framework in which to study German women's letter writing challenges the belief that letter writing as a personal and literary act diminished after 1800. When considering gender as a category of historical and literary interpretation, traditional periodization comes into question. The mid-eighteenth century ushered in a new image of women, which promoted their "natural," biological roles as mothers and hearthkeepers. That change conflicted with the perception of women as social individuals capable of participating in an enlightened, intellectual community, even if in a limited way, through reading, writing, and informal education. This conflict exerted an increasing influence on women's writing until well into the nineteenth century. The mid-eighteenth century also brought increased separation of the private and public spheres as the developing free market economy encouraged a workplace divorced from the home. While the ensuing duality legitimized the public life of the middle class, it concurrently devalued the private sphere by attributing to it less cultural and social impact. Hence, praise of women for their "natural talents" became ambiguous when those talents went public.

The history of letter writing intersects with these social changes. The year 1751 marks the date when Gellert published his *Briefe, nebst einer praktischen Abhandlung von dem guten Geschmacke in Briefen* [*Letters, in Conjunction with a Practical Guide to Good Taste in Letters*]. In short, because this handbook contained what Gellert considered model letters by women, it gave them an unprecedented legitimacy to write and offered an influential model for their writing and the presentation of that writing to the public. From the 1750s—when Louise Adelgunde Victorie Gottsched's letters to Dorothea Runckel reached heightened intimacy, and Meta Moller Klopstock engaged in her lively correspondence with friends and fiancé—to 1850, the publication date of Fanny Lewald's *Erinnerungen aus dem Jahr 1848* in the form of letters to a friend, women took confidence in the epistolary form as a primary means of literary and political self-expression. The period's large number of unpublished and published epistolary writings also contributed immensely to women's growing public image as writers.

Just as the intellectual role of women was changing from one socially cultivated to one viewed as biologically innate, however, so the history of men's encouragement of women as writers became fraught with contradictions. From 1750 on, women were discouraged from publishing, while at the same time, men extolled their talents in the private genre of the letter. In fact, the fame and fecundity of women's letter writing seemed to grow proportionately to the increase in limitations placed on their social and creative freedom. By the 1848 Revolution, women had entered the literary field in such numbers, largely through the practice and legitimacy that letter writing had afforded them, that men issued public warnings against a phenomenon they saw as standing in radical defiance of prescribed feminine roles.[1] The culmination of the discouragement against women's writing occurred in 1850, when conservative forces enacted the *Preußisches Vereinsgesetz*, outlawing women from participation in any political organizations, meetings, and publications.

Using 1750 as a starting date for a study of women letter writers does not imply they did not write letters earlier. On the contrary, letter writing has always represented a means to communicate personal experiences in the most accessible style and language. As Steinhausen points outs, women wrote some of the first letters in German prose, medieval love letters during the early fourteenth century, mostly because they lacked the education to correspond in Latin or in poetry, the language and form that men had traditionally used in epistles.[2] Walter Ong describes the European Latin educational system from the Middle Ages onwards as a male initiation rite.[3] When the split between colloquial and learned Latin occurred between the sixth and the eighth centuries, a corresponding hiatus between the sphere of the formal, public language and the vernacular developed. Because women had limited access to the public sphere, formal Latin, as Ong observes, became a "sex-linked language, a kind of badge of masculine identity. . . . The Latin world was a man's world."[4] Writing from outside this formal, rhetorical tradition, women found the letter form highly suited to their capabilities and needs. In Barbara Becker-Cantarino's studies of women and literature from 1500 to 1800, the prominence of letters as personal correspondence and as public treatises on religious matters during the sixteenth century is especially noteworthy. The letter form as rhetorical device created a personal relationship between writer and audience, thus making the pleas of women who wrote in the vernacular, for instance, of Katharina Zell and Argula von Grumbach, more effective.[5]

Although the letters of sixteenth-century German women were not always published, as Becker-Cantarino observes, much of their private correspondence with such people as Luther and those in the court circles displays public characteristics.[6] Letter writing helped these women fulfill expectations of social norms that existed to limit their public participation. In her essay on Dorothy Osborne's letters to William Temple during the seventeenth century, Virginia Woolf points out that a woman writing in private genres did not demonstrate a desire to become a public literary figure, an ambition that could endanger her social reputation.[7] Thus, letter writing proved an important step in the tradition of women's public literary development. Woolf explains: "Had she been born in 1827, Dorothy Osborne would have written novels; had she been born in 1527, she would never have written at all. But she was born in 1627, and at that date though writing books was ridiculous for a woman there was nothing unseemly in writing a letter. And so by degrees the silence is broken; . . . ."[8] Woolf also discusses how convenient letter writing was for women because it could be accomplished at any time or place without disturbing her "feminine" domestic duties: "It was an art that could be carried on at odd moments, by a father's sickbed, among a thousand interruptions, without exciting comment, anonymously as it were, and often with the pretence that it served some useful purpose."[9]

By the mid-eighteenth century, many women continued to find the letter accessible and convenient. What made the latter half of the eighteenth century markedly different from earlier times, however, was that many influential men of the time, and especially Gellert, held selected women's letters up as models for other writers to follow and openly encouraged women to display their letter-writing talents in public, either in letter-writing manuals, epistolary novels, or essays. The recognition that many women gained as talented letter writers helped formulate a culture in which the letter assumed an important role in both the private and public lives of literate, middle-, upper-middle-, and upper-class people. In general, many letters did not remain private during the period between 1750 and 1850, despite the growing fear of publication at the end of the century, to be discussed later in this chapter. Salon frequenters and participants in reading circles often discussed letters aloud, or a recipient would recopy and send a letter along to a mutual friend. Letters became a public means to convey political news, literary notes, or travel descriptions. The reader had access to a variety of published letters in the form of travelogues, satire, etiquette manuals, narrative accounts, and declarations of love and friendship. As Jürgen Habermas observes in *Strukturwandel der Öffentlichkeit*, many of the letters that correspondents such as Gellert, Gleim, and Goethe wrote were originally composed to be published.[10] One of the highest compliments that one could have paid a letter writer was to say that his or her letter was "zum Druck schön,"[beautiful enough for printing] as Gellert once praised the letters of his correspondent, Fräulein Erdmuth von Schönfeld.[11] Moreover, the epistolary novel, the genre that has its roots in the second half of the eighteenth century, grew out of the public-oriented subjectivity as represented by the private letter in the eighteenth century. Richardson's *Pamela* offers a classic example of how fictional epistolary works arose from the private letter. *Pamela* originally evolved from model letters Richardson had composed for a letter-writing manual entitled *Letters Written To and For Particular Friends* (1741).[12] As one of the first epistolary novels in Europe, *Pamela* became a model for novels in other European countries.

Women's participation in the public epistolary exchange grew out of and heightened the attention paid to women's education, which began at the beginning of the century. Although this education did not imply providing opportunities for formal public schooling for women, as Engelsing aptly points out, it did help to improve women's literacy and to encourage more women to write.[13] At the exhortation of men that they develop their reading and writing skills, several women turned to letter writing as the most appropriate form to "practice" these skills. But the men's agenda included little that promoted learning for the sake of women's own betterment. On the contrary, according to theorists, education would not only make them better wives, but also produce a more distinctive national culture and language.[14] To that end, Gottsched's and Gellert's programs both insisted that women learn to write in German. For many middle- and upper-class women, that meant further study. As mentioned before, many women of earlier centuries relied on the German language for corresponding. Since the beginning of the eighteenth century, however, the value that the aristocracy placed on French as the courtly language had influenced the education of women, encouraging them to write and read in languages other than the vernacular. In 1731, Louise Gottsched lauded her own successful efforts to correspond in German, a task that Gottsched had inspired her to undertake: "Sie stellen mir die Mannigfaltigkeit des Ausdrucks und die männliche Schönheit meiner Muttersprache so lebhaft vor, daß ich sogleich den Entschluß faßte, mich mehr darinne zu üben, und ich fieng schon an gerne deutsch zu denken und zu schreiben" [You portray the multifarious nature of expression and the masculine beauty of my mother tongue so vivaciously that I immediately decided to practice it more, and I gladly began to think and write German].[15] Gottsched's reference to the masculine beauty of her mother language establishes a telling paradox indicative of ambiguous gender norms.[16] Despite Gellert's and Gottsched's attempts to convince German-speaking people to write in their mother tongue, several women still wrote in the literary language they knew best. Among the women who continued to write their letters in French were Sophie von LaRoche (to Wieland), Cornelia Goethe (to her friend Katharina Fabricius), and Caroline Michaelis (to Julie von Studnitz). Among those who peppered their letters with French phrases Rahel Varnhagen figures prominently. That continuity attests both to the vestiges of their previous education and, as we shall see through textual analysis, to their spirit of originality that resisted conformity.

Besides entailing learning to write in a language that had previously been used mostly in spoken form, Gellert's "natürliche Schreibart" [natural writing style], as R. M. G. Nickisch has pointed out, required study and an extensive knowledge of ancient Greek, Latin, and classical French literature.[17] Gellert demanded that the letter writer continually work on his or her own style through translation exercises, especially from French to German, and learn the elements of a certain stylistic grace.[18] Although Gellert insisted upon dismissing the affected, formulaic, and highly stylized letter form that had characterized letters in preceding centuries, he still called for an educated naturalness that the letter writer could accomplish only through studying examples and reading famous letters in other languages. According to Nickisch, the "Natürlichkeit" [naturalness] that Gellert sought was not one that any layman could immediately acquire and master, but rather one that could be practiced mostly by someone in correspondence with an educated person with a cosmopolitan, humanistic, and literary background.[19] When discussing the vitality and originality in women's letters, Gellert stresses that model letters come from women who are not, by any means, uneducated: "Wir reden nicht von Frauenzimmern, die unter Leuten von verderbtem Geschmacke aufgewachsen sind; die ihren Verstand und ihre Sprache noch durch keinen vernünftigen Umgang, durch kein gutes Buch ausgebessert haben; nein" [We are not talking about women who have grown up among people with vulgar tastes; who have not improved their reasoning and their language through any intelligent company, through any good book; no].[20] The so-called "naturalness" of writing also comes into question when one remembers that the best letters were those considered worthy of publication. Subsequent scholars have continued to follow that criterion when they consider that the best letters are those that have been published. In order to insure that women, too, acquired the proper style, manuals of epistolary style written expressly for the female sex appeared.[21] Many women demonstrated their education in their letters, for instance, Demoiselle Lucius, Gellert's long-time correspondent, who states her opinion on literary works by Wieland and Uz and continually asks Gellert for reading suggestions.[22]

A second transformation grew concurrently with women's partici-pation in the eighteenth-century epistolary cult and linked letter writ-ing and education: the emphasis on friendship that the century heralded. Friendships provided an outlet for women to expand their own contacts and to develop epistolary communication. For the de-veloping middle-class in general, the warmth of personal friendship became an ideology that set out to oppose the sterile and artificial atmosphere found in aristocratic court circles.[23] Public proclamation of friendship, such as the forming of groups like the "Göttinger Hain," was carried out further in the publication of letters. That proclama-tion expressed the wish to build an intellectual community on the foundation of personal emotions, and thus combined the push for education with the growth of sentimental literature. The 1750s wit-nessed the first published collections of private letters, an act inspired by the desire to demonstrate open and genuine friendship in public.[24] Although most of these first collections included letters between groups of male friends, both men and women engaged in friendships.

Whereas in previous centuries the letters that members of both sexes had written to each other had been mostly love letters, those that passed between eighteenth-century men and women were fre-quently based more on friendship than romantic relationships. In his *Gedanken von einem guten deutschen Briefe* [*Thoughts on a Good German Letter*], Gellert opines that the letters women write out of friendship are so genuine and natural that they should be displayed as models for others to emulate. Referring specifically to women's correspondence with "vernünftigen Mannspersonen" [intelligent man], Gellert writes: "Es wäre zu wünschen, daß solche Briefe zu Beförderungen des guten Geschmacks unter dem Frauenzimmer an das Licht käme" [It would be desirable that such letters would come to light as promotion of good taste among women].[25] Letters of friendship between men and women, however, must be kept in hid-den, ". . . so lange man das Vorurteil voraussetzt, daß die Freundschaft unter unverehlichten Personen stets mit einer tadelhaf-ten Liebe vergesellschaftet sei . . ." [as long as one presupposes the prejudice that friendship amongst unmarried people is always associated with a scornful love].[26] In his own life, Gellert strove to break down prejudices against friendship between the two sexes: his two most famous correspondences were with Fräulein Erdmuth von Schönfeld and Demoiselle Lucius, neither of whom were romantically involved with him. In fact, Gellert and Lucius had not met each other before she wrote to him requesting that he become her correspondent; for many years, they knew each other only through letters. The correspondence between Goethe and Auguste Stolberg is another such platonic friendship in which neither ever met the other. The exchange of letters between C. M. Wieland and Sophie von LaRoche continued long after their romance was over and she was married. Even the letters between Meta Moller and Klopstock, which in hindsight read as love letters leading to their eventual marriage, began in friendship, and even after marriage, Meta Klopstock stresses the importance of initial friendship between the two.[27] The mid-eighteenth century also marks a period in which women formed close bonds with one another through letters as well, considering the affectionate correspondence that passed between Dorothea Runckel and Louise Gottsched, Charlotte von Lengefeld Schiller and Caroline von Dacheröden von Humboldt, Caroline Michaelis and Luise Gotter, and Bettine von Arnim and Karoline von Günderrode. The next chapter will discuss the significance of these correspondences between female friends for building confidantes and confidence within their own intellectual community, phenomena that scholars have generally ignored.

The activity of women letter writers after 1750 was also due to a third factor, the philosophical turn towards empirical theory and the subsequent emphasis on the feelings of the individual within an empirical reality. Mary Poovey, in her analysis of the effect that norms of "femininity" exerted on the works of late eighteenth and early nineteenth-century English women writers, observes how interest in philosophical empiricism at the time aided in the development of the novel, a genre whose subject matter frequently centered on domestic and emotional affairs, and that thus coincided with women's personal experiences.[28] By mid-century, although criteria for a good letter presumed a humanistic literary background, the display of book learning was considered best when tempered with exposés on individual feelings. Previously excluded from mainstream intellectual activities because they were not educated in the necessary Greek and Latin language and texts, women could now write about their individual feelings and be praised for their very natural mode of expression, rather than be condemned for their unfamiliarity with rhetoric and "intellectual" subjects. For letter writers, this emphasis on the individual emotions brought further recognition to their epistolary talents and, in fact, stimulated many women to publish their letters in many of the popular letter-writing manuals of the time, or to branch out into related public genres, such as the epistolary novel. Gellert frequently extolled the letter-writing talents of women for what he saw as their beauty and naturalness, qualities that he did not always find in letters by men.[29]

Indeed, many readers have been struck by what they have called the natural and comfortable attitude that women showed towards the letter-writing process. The gender-based ideology that underlies that label, however, leads them to ignore individual inflection of style and theme. In discussing the connection between education, empiricism, friendship, and letter writing, one has to recognize the early eighteenth-century belief in the abilities of women to be educated, and to use that education to contribute to the intellectual community. That belief stands opposed to the mid-century perception of women's biological nature as the source of gentleness and passivity, which makes women mere vessels for receiving male culture. Several scholars have studied the relation between views on the biological nature of women and their creativity. In the German realm, Sally Winkle convincingly argues that the latter half of the eighteenth century demonstrates a shift toward attributing nature to women's biological facilities for educating themselves, whereas the early eighteenth century promoted education for women and believed in women's abilities to improve intellectually.[30] Bovenschen expresses the major difference between the early and mid-eighteenth century in stating that Rousseau and others at mid-century promoted a gender ideology that saw women and men as opposites, whereas Gottsched, a major proponent of women's education in the early part of the century, had wanted women to be like men, or at least to conform to men's norms.[31] Eva Walter traces that shift in personal documents. Walter contends that the transformation to theory that centered on women's biological needs became manifested in attitudinal changes creating a "neue Mutterliebe" [new motherly love], whereby the woman's role as nurturer and educator of her children at home gained heightened significance.[32]

At this point, the controversial work of French theorist Elisabeth Badinter raises some relevant issues.[33] Badinter follows the premise that maternal instinct is an ideological construct derived from eighteenth-century philosophies, mostly those put forward by Rousseau, that reinforce changes in women's roles to aid national security and the rise of the bourgeoisie. She argues against the concept of maternal instinct, drawing on the then-common practice of giving a newborn over to a wet nurse, the result of which was high infant abuse and mortality. If philosophers spent so much time and energy promoting the "natural instinct of women to bear and raise children," Badinter queries, how then could women have shown that "instinct" so naturally?

Within the context of the transformation to a biologically centered calling, women's active participation in the mid-eighteenth-century epistolary cult could possibly be viewed as evidence in support of the idea that women were by nature more subjective, sentimental, intuitive, and domestic than men. That image began surfacing in the latter decades of the eighteenth century, promoted particularly by the writings of Rousseau, Goethe, Schiller, and Wilhelm von Humboldt.[34] The importance of women's letter writing was unquestionably very great, but some scholars have also pointed out its limitations. Silvia Bovenschen, in her extensive work on the representation of the feminine ideal in eighteenth-century fiction by men and women, identifies the epistolary form as a "Trojan Horse" given to women as a kind of trick to defeat any literary ambitions they may have harbored.[35] By excelling in their letter writing, and by striving to meet the ideals of spontaneity and naturalness that men placed on their talents, women risked adopting a form that could eventually segregate their written productivity from more publicly accepted forms of literary expression. According to Bovenschen, in limiting themselves to a very subjective form such as the letter, women acquiesced to the established norms of "feminine" creativity.

When one reads men's praise about women's letters, one certainly recognizes the predicament in which Bovenschen sees women. Gellert, for example, lauded women's letters for their sentimentality, naïveté, and simplicity, qualities that had little value in public life. He writes in his *Praktische Abhandlung von dem guten Geschmacke in Briefen:*

> Die Empfindungen der Frauenzimmer sind zarter und lebhafter, als die unsrigen. Sie werden von tausend kleinen Umständen gerührt, die bei uns keinen Eindruck machen. Sie werden nicht allein öfter, sondern auch leichter gerührt, als wir. Eine Vorstellung macht bei ihnen geschwind der andern Platz, daher halten sie sich selten bei einem guten Gedanken zu lange auf: wir fühlen ihn stärker, und darum gehen wir oft zu lange mit ihm um. Ihre Gedanken selbst sind, wie ihre Eindrücke, leicht; sie sind ein scharfes, aber kein tiefes Gepräge. Die Frauenzimmer sorgen weniger für die Ordnung eines Briefes, und weil sie nicht durch die Regeln der Kunst ihrem Verstande eine ungewöhnliche Richtung gegeben haben: so wird ihr Brief desto freier und weniger ängstlich.

[The sentiments of women are more tender and lively than ours. They are moved by thousands of small conditions that make no impression on us. They are not only more often, but also more easily moved that we. With them, an image makes room for another one quickly, thus a good thought seldom stays with them a long time: we feel it more strongly, and therefore we often ponder it for a long time. Even their thoughts, like their impressions, are light; they are a sharp, but no profound impression. Women worry less about the order of a letter, and because they have not provided their minds with an unusual direction through artistic rules: the letter thus becomes for them more free and less anxious].[36]

Gellert's description of women's nature is meant to explain why women write better letters than men, and is thus intended as a compliment. He places the facility, gentleness, and lightness with which women write letters above the heaviness and order found in men's letters. Because of women's unfamiliarity with the rules of language and art, they are able to write with the freedom and ease that men lack, due to their exposure to rigorous training.

Gellert's praise, however, presents a paradox that affected the status of women's writing particularly from 1750 to 1850, and one that still persists today. Continually flattered for remaining within the boundaries established for "feminine" writing, women risked confinement within the marginal realms of literary production, being expected to write without disturbance to their "feminine" role. There existed little encouragement for independence or self-assertion outside of the private sphere. Gellert writes in a letter to a female correspondent in 1756:

Gelehrte Frauenzimmer braucht die Welt, denke ich, nicht sehr; aber ein Frauenzimmer, das gleich Ihnen, sich durch das Lesen guter Bücher, den Verstand, das Herz und den Geschmack bildet, ist ihrem Hause, ihren Freunden, einem künftigen Manne, Vergnügen, Glück und Ruhe. Sie wird schreiben, ohne ihre andere Pflichten zu vergessen, und dadurch, daß sie gut zu denken weis, wird sie ihren übrigen Verrichtungen, auch den geringern, noch einen gewissen Reiz, und ihren Tugenden eine größre Anmuth geben.

[I think the world does not need educated women very much; but a woman like yourself who educates herself through the reading of good books, intelligence, heart, and taste brings pleasure, happiness, and peace to her household, her friends, her future husband. She will write without forgetting her other duties and thereby, because she knows how to think well, will give to her other tasks, even the slighter ones, a certain charm, and to her virtues a greater grace.] (*Briefe* 115)

Women are expected to develop talents and taste not for themselves, but for the sake of homes, friends, and future husbands. Their writing is not to disturb their domestic duties, which Gellert, among other eighteenth-century philosophers, writers, and pedagogues, considered to be more important. Similarly, one looks in vain in the popular moral weeklies of the eighteenth century for passages that condone women's entrance into the public literary domain through their private letters.[37] When men encouraged women to write letters, it was not to incite them to pursue literary ambitions. Letter writing, education in the arts, and the reading of suggested moral weeklies and books should not stimulate a woman to take up the pen professionally, but rather should make her a socially virtuous woman and a partner of greater intellect and charm for her husband.

Consequently, Gellert's compliments are very restricting, for in assessing women's talents he continues to place them in the private, domestic sphere and leaves women little space for public positions of power. Nickisch, in his article "Die Frau als Briefschreiberin im Zeitalter der deutschen Aufklärung," recognizes the great contributions that women's letters made to eighteenth-century cultural and literary life (59), but he also points out limitations that men imposed upon women to dampen any literary ambitions.[38] Nickisch claims that when Gellert and other pedagogically engaged men encouraged women to write letters, it was not with any eventual literary goal in mind for the woman, but rather so that the men could improve their own epistolary skills and reputation through practice with women.[39] Suppressing women's public voices by restricting them to "feminine" duties in the domestic realm and discouraging them from any literary ambitions consequently excluded women's letters from any competition with men's writing. Women were not supposed to pose a threat to men, and as letter writers they did not.

Without examination of individual women's letters over a long period of time, it is difficult to generalize about how women conformed to norms of writing. The letter as a form certainly offered a convenient vehicle through which to conform. Paradoxically, the one form in which women were encouraged to write constituted one of the limitations that the domestic sphere imposed on them. There was another paradox, however: the epistolary form could also act as a disguise for resistance to restrictions. Textual analysis discloses ambiguities that show not only submission but also defiance in letter writers' texts. Required as well is close attention to the continual interplay between historical and epistolary transformations as reception of the letter and the relation between gender and genre altered.

Beginning in the mid-eighteenth century, writers praised sentimentality and openness of emotions in every person, and the domestic enterprises of the burgeoning middle class became major topics in literature by men and women alike. Nontraditional genres and styles provided one means by which the developing middle class could break away from the classical models used in court-commissioned literary works. From the very beginning of this new emphasis on the individual's feelings and imagination, women became associated with sentimental literature, both as writers and as readers. In general, readers welcomed women's epistolary novels and letters that dealt with affairs of the heart in order to teach moral virtues. The positive reception of Sophie von LaRoche's novel *Das Fräulein von Sternheim* offers a good case in point.[40]

By the end of the century, however, the very private, subjective nature of the letter eventually evoked mistrust of the epistolary form, especially for male writers, whose remarks determined the nature of the literary canon. That mistrust accompanied doubt of the value that private letters can hold for the general public. What had turned from a subjective, private medium to a subjective, literary one in the 1750s, after Gellert published his famous letter-writing manual, retreated back into the private realm in the following decades.[41] The fact that "over-sentimentality" became synonomous with "feminine nature" surfaces in a variety of sources, including a letter from Wieland to La Roche in 1793 in which he writes: "Unsere heutigen Mädchen sind, Gott sey's geklage, fast durchgängig auf Schwermuth und Empfindsamkeit gestellt" [Our girls today are, to complain to God, almost universally oriented toward melancholia and sentimentality.].[42] Because of the growing skepticism towards overt or excessive emotionality in public, readers and scholars have, since the end of the eighteenth century, frequently disregarded letters as too personal and spontaneous and thus not public-oriented enough to be considered literature. This opinion surfaces in the various anthologies and scholarly treatments of women's letters examined in the previous chapter.

The devaluation of women's subjective emotions has a direct correlation to the changing relationship between the public and private realms in Germany in the late eighteenth century. In centuries preceding the eighteenth century, both men and women in the agrarian and trade sectors of society frequently shared administration of the household. When much of the industry remained in the home, the demarcation between the public and private functions of men and women was often vague. In many households, both sexes managed food production, oversaw workers, helped educate the children, and contributed to the household industry that supplied the family's livelihood. Although equality between the sexes did not exist and there were definite limitations on women's participation in such organizations as the guilds, at least women's work in the domestic sphere was not considered economically unproductive.[43] With the rise of the middle classes in the eighteenth century, women's and men's roles were largely redefined. Many men began to work away from the home in industry, small businesses, and managerial jobs that slowly began to replace the work previously done at home. Women often became managers of the private, household sphere, performing the domestic duties considered their only legitimate occupation.

Slowly, the realm of public work became distinct from the private sphere, both physically and psychologically. Without the materially productive function it once served, the household became a locus of sentiment. Friedhelm Neidhardt speaks of a *"Privatisierung"* [privatization] and an *"Emotionalisierung"* [emotionalization] of the family that, as the private and the public sphere grew further apart, stand opposed to a "Versachlichung" [objectification] and "Durchrationalisierung" [rationalization] of the spheres outside the family.[44] To the man, the house became an emotional and personal refuge to which he returned after a day of work in the public sphere, which was narrow, one-sided, factual, and impersonal. The qualities of human warmth and safety attributed to the domestic sphere may seem positive, but as a social entity, the household lost its value as a unit of economic productivity. Consequently, women's duties within the house were devalued because they provided no monetary income for the family, whereas the man's work outside the house did. In addition, the home was the main sphere in a woman's life, the place where she received her education, worked, and relaxed, whereas it was only one of many realms in a man's life. Being sequestered, the woman remained distant from those activities reserved for men, such as formal education, independent travel, and work opportunities, activities that brought about a greater sense of worth in a society driven by the work ethos and *Bildung*. In the eyes of society, such isolation can lead, as the sociologist Dahrendorf points out, to underdevelopment of civic engagement and political interest, as well as to a one-sided emphasis on privatized values, such as "Innerlichkeit" [inwardness], "Direktheit" [directness], and "Gemeinschaftlichkeit" [communalism] (284–85).[45]

Granted, an ideology of separate spheres existed in medieval and early modern periods in Europe, too, as recent historical work has shown.[46] But as historian Elizabeth Fox-Genovese points out, the extent to which the dominant culture used that ideology to enforce separate and unequal education for women and to justify the exclusion of women from professional and public life increases as the economy advances. The separation of the domestic and political realms resulted in descriptions of masculine and feminine traits as innate qualities, and not social roles, a polarization that would affect gender roles in work. Sociologist Karin Hausen explains how sex characteristcs are introduced as a combination of biology and natural determinacy and thus become attributed to innate human characteristics (369–70).[47] According to the chart that Hausen compiles based on material gleaned from late eighteenth-century encyclopedias and philosophical treatises dealing with women, stereotypes emerging in the latter part of the century show characteristics such as activity, rationality, strength, and independence being attributed biologically to masculinity, whereas passivity, emotionality, weakness, and dependence become pejorative traits of femininity. In relation to the previous discussion on women's equation with nature, Richard Sennett's observations in his book *The Fall of Public Man* prove useful. In the eighteenth century, he states, citizens "attempted to define both what public life was and what it was not. The line drawn between public and private was essentially one on which the claims of civility— epitomized by cosmopolitan, public behavior—were balanced against the claims of nature—epitomized by the family."[48]

Scholars have studied the effect of this polarization of subjectivity and rationality, of private and public, of culture and nature, on the portrayal of men and women in literature and on the two sexes' literary production.[49] Recently, Ulrike Prokop, in her examination of the generation of women born around 1750, explains the silences these women show as a form of depression brought on largely by social transition to a market economy.[50] Women such as Cornelia Goethe, Caroline Flachsland, and Maximiliane Brentano were unable to overcome the profound paradox between encouragement to educate themselves and discouragement against using that education in a publicly productive manner; through teachings in the early eighteenth century, they had been led to believe in the value of intellectual curiosity, or *Wißbegierde*, and yet, as the century progressed, the ideology of the private sphere relegated them to a position of economic dependency on their fathers or husbands. This silent generation had as its models only literary images of weak, passive girls submitting to aggressive males, a paradigm that promotes opposing binary gender roles. Their foremothers were women who for the most part idealized the roles and works of famous men in their lives, such as Susanne von Klettenberg in the role of the bride of Christ, Elisabeth Goethe as Goethe's mother, and Meta Klopstock as Klopstock's lover.

The power that sexual dichotomization has held over readers' evaluation and categorization of literature is most relevant to a discussion of the history of the letter, and particularly women's letters. The devaluation of the private realm, and of the emotionality and subjectivity that came to be associated with this realm in the late eighteenth and early nineteenth centuries also caused a general contempt of literature written either about domestic concerns or with emotional and subjective tones, leading eventually to the derogatory classification of such works as *Trivialliteratur,* or *Frauenliteratur.*[51] The letter, being the most accessible form in which women especially could express their very private concerns poignantly, was soon questioned for its public worth and its literary value.

The end of the eighteenth century saw a growing hostility towards publishing private documents. The greatest controversy over the publication of private letters occurred in reaction to Wilhelm Körte's posthumous collection of letters between his great uncle, the writer Johann Wilhelm Ludwig Gleim, and two of his correspondents, Wilhelm Heinse, and Johannes von Müller. As administrator of Gleim's manuscripts, Körte published, as volumes two and three of his *Briefe deutscher Gelehrten* [*Letters of German Scholars*] his *Briefe zwischen Gleim, Wilhelm Heinse und Johannes von Müller* [*Letters Between Gleim, Wilhelm Heinse and Johannes von Müller*] in 1806. Dedicating the volume to "den theuren Jünglingen meines deutschen Vaterlandes" [the dear youths of my German fatherland], Körte wished to honor the affectionate and virtuous friendship between the three men. A heated debate ensued, led by Johann Heinrich Voß and Friedrich Heinrich Jacobi, manifesting itself in a series of attacks against Körte's right to publish very personal letters and a call for more discretion when evaluating which letters may have been intentionally written for a large readership.[52] Körte's foreword to the edition and his printed rebuttals to Voß and Jacobi suggest that he had anticipated no scandal through his publication, intending only to honor the affectionate and virtuous friendship between the three men. But, as Heinrich Mohr observes in his detailed account of the controversy, the opinions of Jacobi and Voß towards confidential letters coincided with a change in attitudes towards friendship cults and the manifestation of these in public.[53] For Gleim and Körte, whose values were embedded in eighteenth-century culture, expression of friendship in public through exposure of intimate letters was the most positive thing that could happen to a relationship. In contrast, the beliefs of Jacobi and Voß represent a retreat of friendship and private emotions into more intimate circles from which private letters should not be removed by publication.

Each of the major debates over the publication of private letters in the latter half of the eighteenth century, however, shows a growing concern over publishing rights versus personal rights. The apprehension that private letters could one day be published, and thus reveal an important part of one's personal self, incited many letter writers to destroy their correspondence, as I discussed in the previous chapter. Other factors also contributed to the skepticism against the public worth of personal documents, including the flourishing and burgeoning book trade, which increased people's beliefs that the literary market would be glutted by numerous unimportant books.[54] Dorothea Schlegel, in 1833, expresses Friedrich's and her fear of increased publication of letters when she explains that she has burned many of Rahel Varnhagen's letters:

> . . . auch war der zu unsrer Zeit immer mehr überhandnehmende Mißbrauch der gedruckten Briefe kürzlich verstorbner Personen ihm [Friedrich] sehr zuwider—(eine Empfindung die ich ganz mit ihm teilte) und so entschlossen wir uns, lieber alle Briefe, besonders von geliebten Personen, nicht der Gefahr auszusetzen, von fremden Personen, für deren Augen sie nicht bestimmt waren, gelesen zu werden; und so war ich Zeuge vom Verbrennen eines Pakets sämtlicher Briefe der seligen Rahel.

> [. . . Friedrich was also very much against the increasing misuse of the published letters of recently deceased people in our time—(a sentiment that I totally shared with him), and thus we decided not to subject all the letters, especially those from dear people, to the danger of being read by strangers for whose eyes they were not intended; and thus I was witness to the burning of a package of collected letters of our blessed Rahel.][55]

Changes were taking place at the end of the eighteenth century, changes in the value bestowed on private letters, the choice of letters that were published, and the content of letters. Caroline von Humboldt's exclamation to Wilhelm von Humboldt in 1789 about the worth of their own correspondence would soon become an anomaly: "Wilhelm! wir sollten ein Archiv unsrer Papiere anlegen, damit sie sich in der Folge durch keinen unvorhergesehenen Zufall etwa zerstreuten. Ich versichere Dich, einer, der einmal darüber käme, könnte etwas gar Schönes daraus machen" [Wilhelm! we should establish an archive of our papers so that they do not become scattered all over because of any unpredictable accident. I assure you that anyone who came across them could make something very beautiful out of them].[56]

Because of the differing social conditions under which men and women were encouraged and allowed to develop and to display their creativity, private letters assumed a function that was different for the two sexes. By the late eighteenth century, the ambiguity between praise from men about women's talents and natural calling as letter writers and the limited options such praise allowed had escalated. On the negative side, social and economic norms increasingly discouraged female writers from playing an active public role as writers. Although the early part of the century had not been one of total emancipation for women, at least men's concurrent focus on women's education had provided a legitimacy to women's writing that did not need constant justification. That legitimacy lost ground as middle-class women become more economically dependent and legally confined. Helga Brandes points to the challenges faced by the editors Sophie von LaRoche, whose publication *Pomona* appeared from 1783 to 1784, and Marianne Ehrmann, who published *Amaliens Erholungsstunden* from 1790 to 1794 and *Die Einsiedlerin aus den Alpen* from 1793 to 1794. La Roche, publishing within a culture that still valued women's education, if only to provide stimulating housewives and educated mothers, did not need to justify her role as an editor. In contrast, Marianne Ehrmann had constantly to legitimate her role as publisher by stressing her ability to publish without neglecting her household duties. Likewise, as Brandes points out, criticism by men such as Wieland of women's *Lesewut* contributed to the harsh discouragement against women's writing and reading.[57]

In addition to psychological discouragement and economic limitations, specific laws during the late eighteenth and early nineteenth centuries had a direct influence on women's chances of choosing a public career such as writing. The "Allgemeines Landrecht der Preußischen Staaten" [General Federal Rights of the Prussian States] of 1794 and the Napoleonic Code, adopted by many of the German states in the early nineteenth century, forbade women from taking part in business transactions and legal proceedings.[58] Women were, by law, under the father's authority or, if he died, under the guardian of another male. There was never any age of majority for women. In the first decade of the century, women's participation in certain political and social groups became more limited because most societies and clubs did not allow membership to women, the "Christlich-Deutsche Tischgesellschaft" [Christian-German Social Group], founded by Achim von Arnim in 1810, representing the most prominent of these groups. In 1850, the *Preußisches Vereinsgesetz* outlawed women from participation in any political organizations, meetings, and publications.[59] Although this law was not enacted until later in the century, its harbinger was already evident in the mounting hostility toward women's public activities during the early half of the century. In regards to education, women who tried to attend university or to learn outside of their private tutelages, when allowed, risked scorn and ridicule.[60] Only in 1906 did the Prussian government officially allow women to attend universities.

Laws comprise the institutionalized social forces that established the boundaries of a woman's expectations and goals. The ideological stereotypes that literature and philosophy propagated psychologically affected women's creativity by offering the aspiring female writer few role models outside of the muse, priestess, mother, or wife. As Virginia Woolf postulates in *A Room of One's Own*, the effect such discouragement has upon the mind of the female artist has still not been totally measured.[61] Being told that they were by nature not destined to be writers, women received little encouragement from those men who were in the position to promote and publish their works. In fact, certain prolific nineteenth-century female letter writers, such as Rahel Varnhagen, were praised by contemporary scholars and readers for *not* publishing their works because publication for women meant stepping out of their proscribed domestic sphere and relinquishing their "femininity."[62]

The letter still offered the early-nineteenth-century woman a convenient and accessible form; she did not risk her reputation as a virtuous mother and wife by demonstrating a desire to become a public literary figure, and consequently neglecting the domestic duties relegated to her in popular journals, novels, and etiquette handbooks. But this by no means signaled total acquiescence. The growth of a bourgeois private sector and the loosening of moral standards at the beginning of the century facilitated women's participation in acceptable alternative social groups, such as salon culture. Social transformations found parallels in literary developments that emphasized fragmentariness, subjectivity, and formlessness, qualities found in the letter form. Through letter writing, women could perpetuate an artistic form that took direct root in their everyday lives. Close readings of letters reveal in many cases a choice of form based on aesthetic preference.

In recent years a number of informative articles have appeared that treat the silencing of women in the literature and philosophy of the period designated as German Romanticism.[63] It would be counterproductive to reiterate in detail the many statements, treatises, and laws that oppressed women in this period. Of particular relevance to my study is the ambiguity that characterizes the contrast between encouragement and restriction of women's creativity, which seemed to grow in proportion to women's success as writers. By the end of the eighteenth century, this ambiguity becomes most apparent in Friedrich Schlegel's inconsistent attitude towards women and their position in society. In two early essays, "Über die weiblichen Charaktere in den griechischen Dichtern" (1794) [On the Feminine Characters in the Greek Poets], and "Über die Diotima" (1795) [On Diotima], Schlegel criticizes the sexual behavioral norms of society and calls for freedom of categorization of the two sexes. In "Über die Diotima" Schlegel states: ". . . die Weiblichkeit soll wie die Männlichkeit zur höhern Menschlichkeit gereinigt werden" [femininity should, as masculinity, be purified toward greater humanity].[64] He then queries: "Was ist häßlicher als die überladne Weiblichkeit, was ist ekelhafter als die übertriebne Männlichkeit, die in unsern Sitten, in unsern Meinungen, ja auch in unsrer bessern Kunst, herrscht?" [What is uglier than overdone femininity, what is more disgusting than exaggerated masculinity, which dominates in our customs, in our opinions, yes even in our best art?] (KFSA 1:92) Refuting Rousseau's contention that women should not be educated, Schlegel holds up examples from Greek drama and culture in which numerous women received the same education and attained the same power as their male counterparts. According to Schlegel, women do not neccessarily have to be docile, and men do not have to be sovereign; he even calls for a reversal of such roles: "Nur selbständige Weiblichkeit, nur sanfte Männlichkeit ist gut und schön" [Only independent femininity, only gentle masculinity is good and beautiful] (KFSA 1: 93).

Although these early essays by Schlegel were also riddled with contradictions and misinterpret the role that women actually did play in Greek society, as Becker-Cantarino and Friedrichsmeyer have observed, many of Schlegel's early ideas do seem progressive in comparison to those of Schiller and Rousseau, who see no place for the woman in the public world.[65] Both the late-eighteenth-century reader and the modern reader of these two early essays by Schlegel would find evidence that he calls for a revamping of the stereotypical sex roles accepted by other eighteenth-century philosophers.

Schlegel did not maintain his liberal stance for very long, though. In the later essay "Über die Philosophie. An Dorothea" (1799) [On Philosophy. To Dorothea], in the Athenäum Fragments, and in the novel Lucinde, he turns to defining the sexes in dichotomous categories whose ideal amalgamation will be a harmonizing principle for a world of chaos and will combine the variety of life into one unit. Although the love between Julius and Lucinde represents a new form of free and open emotional expression, however, that kind of free love is not emancipatory for the woman. Schlegel's categories of male and female, no matter how equal he intended them to be, still served to reinforce the traditional belief that women are passive, subservient, irrational, and subjective as opposed to men, who are active, independent, rational, and objective. His separation of women as domestic beings and men as public figures further reinforces the division of sexual roles according to the private and public spheres. "Das Weib ist ein häusliches Wesen" [Woman is a domestic being] (*Werke* 2: 105) he states in "Über die Philosophie,"[66] and thus he reasons: ". . . daß die weibliche Organisation ganz auf den einen schönen Zweck der Mütterlichkeit gerichtet ist" [that the feminine organization is totally oriented toward the beautiful purpose of motherliness] (*Werke* 2: 109). And, as other scholars have pointed out, in drawing up his ostensibly symmetrical pattern of the sexes, Schlegel was mostly concerned with the development of the male and considered the female's importance only in relation to her role in aiding that development.[67] In *Lucinde*, Julius acquires greater hopes for becoming an artist through his uniting with Lucinde, whereas Lucinde, in realizing her love of Julius, turns away from her artistic endeavors to tranquil domesticity.

The "naturalism" of women's letters, so lauded by Gellert and others, finds a parallel to the dualism between nature and culture that Schlegel uses most frequently to contrast woman and man respectively. Women are referred to as plants, the earth, "das Vegetabilische," whereas men are animals, the air, "das Animalische."[68] Romantic male writers other than Schlegel also perceived women's role as aligned with that of nature.[69] Sara Friedrichsmeyer, who examines the androgynous model in texts by German and English Romantics, points out that the "marriage" Romantics believe will amalgamate the two sexes into one harmonious being is usually described as one between man and nature.[70] Friedrichsmeyer draws her German example from Hölderlin's Hyperion, who, in longing for Diotima, his feminine complement, conjures up a vision of universal harmony in which man and nature unite "in Eine allumfassende Gottheit" [in an all-encompassing divinity].[71]

Even before Romanticism, in the philosophies of Rousseau, Schiller, and Humboldt, women had been responsible for bringing nature to society.[72] Some half a century later, male writers, by equating women directly with nature, further warrant the exclusion of women from society. Women also become ostracized from the more influential and cultural civilization, not by their own choice, but by the view that they are instinctively and biologically closer to nature. Novalis maintains: "Die Frauen wissen nichts von Verhältnissen der Gemeinschaft. Nur durch ihren Mann hängen sie mit Staat, Kirche, Publikum etc. zusammen. Sie leben im eigentlichen Naturzustande." [Women know nothing about the relationships of the community. They are connected to the state, church, public, etc. only through their husband. They live in a truly natural state.][73] Friedrich Schlegel also supports the idea of an innate quality in women that causes them to withdraw from public activity: "Die Lebensart der Frauen hat die Neigung, sie immer enger und enger zu beschränken, und ihren Geist noch vor seinem seeligen Ende in den mütterlichen Schoß der Erde zu begraben" [The way of life of women has the tendency to limit them more narrowly and narrowly, and to bury their spirit before its blessed end in the maternal lap of the earth] (*Werke* 2: 106–7). In the fragment that the physicist Johann Wilhelm Ritter wrote on femininity, women are again analogized to plants and relegated to passive indifference: "Das Menschenweib ist die concentrierteste Pflanzenindifferenz" [the human female is the most concentrated indifference of the plants] (*Werke* 2: 176). This concept of women's "indifference" was then expanded to contrast with men's "difference": "Das Weib wird immer Indifferenz seyn, der Mann dagegen Differenz, Pol" [Woman will always be the indifference, man, in contrast, difference, pole] (*Werke* 2: 176).

Each of these statements shows the woman as abstractly idealized in her connection to nature; her "natural" goodness and simplicity stand juxtaposed to a mechanical and impersonal world. However intentionally damaging this apposition was meant to be in its original theory, in practice it could only dissuade women from involvement in mainstream public events. Placing women on par with nature led to a widespread belief that they were incapable of participating in the activities of certain public institutions, such as universities and lawmaking bodies, which are intrinsic to a progressive society. Through discouraging them from, and even denying them institutional education, the freedom to appear publicly, and an independent choice of livelihood, society also hindered women from developing a sense of belonging to a social whole and hence made them marginalized in society.

Many men certainly saw the creativity of the women around them, and they also recognized the limitations on that creativity. Instead of fighting restrictions, however, they opted to encourage the women in their writing, but protectively. In writing to Sophie Mereau on 10 January 1803, Clemens Brentano outlines limitations that middle- and upper-class women faced in their everyday activities. On the literary front, he instructs her, it is dangerous for a woman to write, even more dangerous for her to edit a journal; on the social front, women should not enter cafés; professionally, women should not be academics; for pleasure, women should avoid the "unfeminine" activities of coach driving and horseback riding (Brentano/Mereau 104).[74] Brentano then jokingly sketches the research he has completed for a work on the attitudes of other authors towards literary women. He derides many of the roles to which men relegated women, such as cooking, mothering, and midwifery, all stemming from a loathing, such as that of Tieck, of the educated woman. In the works by men, the domestic chores are patronizingly idealized by making them into an art; there is "Kochkunst" [culinary art], and "die Kunst Kinder zu bekommen" [the art of having children], and "Hebammenkunst" [the art of midwivery]. Clemens plans to collect these studies and present them all under the guise of a pocketbook for unhappy lovers. As examples, Clemens ironically mentions the two renowned (or infamous) "unfeminine" bluestockings of the day, Madame de Staël and Frau von Krüdener.

It may be reassuring that Clemens Brentano was aware of women's limited career choices as well as their restricted public freedom. Still, he is not completely free of these stereotypical ideas about women himself, and thus he jokingly threatens with them. He later pokes fun at the numerous famous authoresses he sees journeying incognito, and at the reactions from other travelers when they recognize these famous women. He forgets his banter, however, when he talks about his own response to Mereau's publications:

> Als Sie mich noch liebten, da erschrak ich immer, wenn ich etwas Gedruktes von Ihnen sah, und nichts war mir quälender, als etwas von Ihnen zu lesen, nicht als wenn es mir zu schlecht sei, oder gut genug, nein es kam mir so unnatürlich vor, daß Etwas, was Sie sagten, schlecht genug, und gut genug sein könne, so mit dem bleiernen Buchstaben fest genagelt zu werden, jedes Format schien mir ein Gedicht von Ihnen komisch oder pitoiabel zu machen, ja das Gedicht selbst mache sich komisch oder bedaurenswert, . . . .

> [When you still loved me, I was always shocked whenever I saw something published by you, and nothing was more painful to me than to read something by you, not as if it was bad to me or good enough, no it appeared so unnatural, that something that you said could be bad enough or good enough so that it became nailed with leaden letters, this format seemed to make a poem by you strange or pitiable to me, yes the poem made itself strange or regrettable.] (Brentano/Mereau 106)

For Brentano, it is allowable when other women write; he can even ridicule other men's criticism of publicly active females. When the woman who is so close to him publishes her writings, however, he cannot accept the fact that she has opened up her thoughts and her interests to the public, and that she stands to be judged by others. Her words stare at him, reified, alienated, and intimidating in print. The main impetus for Brentano's letter was that Sophie Mereau had decided not to publish some of his poems in her *Göttinger Musen-Almanach*. Brentano found it easy to discuss women's creativity from a distance, but concerning his own lover, wife, or sister, he had difficulties accepting the idea that a woman could display public ambition. One way to enforce his own kind of limitations was to hark back to the same backhanded flattery of women's talents as letter writers that Gellert had introduced. In a letter loaded with diminutives, Brentano, to his sister Gunda, declares that women will always excel in these "smaller" tasks because it accords with their nature:

> Ich beneide euch zierliche Mädchen wahrlich um euer Talent, Briefchen zu schreiben, ihr seid ein wunderliches Geschlecht, alles wird in euren Händen bedeutend . . . und ich glaube, etwas Kleines ist heiliger und verzauberter, wenn es ein Weib tut, als etwas Großes, denn im Weibe ist nicht die Handlung das Große, sondern die ewig hervorspringende erste menschliche Bestimmung. Alles was ihr tut, muß Liebreiz werden oder Pflege und hängt einzig mit eurer einzigen Bestimmung zusammen, uns zu locken und aus dem Staat in jedem Augenblick zum bloßen Leben zurückzuführen, und dann Mutter zu werden.

> [I envy you dainty girls really for your talent at writing little letters, you are a strange sex, everything becomes meaningful in your hands . . . and I believe something small is more holy and magical when a woman does it than something great, for in the woman it is not the deed that is great but rather the first destiny that springs forth eternally. Everything that you do must become charm or nurturing and goes along with your true destiny to seduce us and in every moment to return us from the public state to pure life, and then to become mother.][75]

The paradox persists. On the one hand, Clemens acknowledges in women an admirable talent for writing letters. On the other hand, this talent confirms, in his mind, the "feminine" propensity they have for small endeavors, which can only lead them to fulfill what he views as their goal and mission in life—to captivate a man, to assume domestic duties, and to become mothers. Sexual bias and a traditional view of letter writing as an insignificant creative act prohibit him from imagining that women's epistolary talent might result in the creation of anything artistically great. Brentano's undermining of letter writing belongs to a larger skepticism of many early-nineteenth-century male writers towards the epistolary form.

A subtle example of ideological subversion occurs in a letter from Friedrich Schlegel to Caroline Schlegel in 1797. Here he extols her ease at letter writing but precludes her capacity to compose adequately outside the epistolary form:

Man erschwert sichs gewiß sehr, wenn man, besonders bey wenig Uebung, eine Form wählt, die Einem nicht natürlich und also nur durch große Kunst und Anstrengung erreichbar ist.—Sollten Sie jemahls einen Roman schreiben: so müßte vielleicht ein andrer den Plan machen, und wenn nicht das Ganze aus Briefen bestehen sollte, auch alles darin schreiben, was nicht in Briefen wäre.

[One certainly struggles when one choses, especially without much practice, a form, that does not come naturally and thus is attainable only through great art and effort. If you should ever write a novel: then another person would perhaps have to draw up the plan, and, if the whole thing should not be comprised of letters, then also write everything in it that is not in letters.] (*Caroline* 1: 439)[76]

Friedrich's admiration for Caroline's "natural" letter-writing talent has served to support subsequent estimations of the high aesthetic value of her letters.[77] When read closely, however, the praise reveals much about Friedrich Schlegel's underestimation of the letter as a literary genre. He implies that Caroline lacks artistic organizational skills that would help her plan a novel. Considering his view that women are destined mainly for domestic tasks, and not for public professions, his low estimation of Caroline's capabilities reflects his own gender bias. But his inability to see her writing in other genres stems also from his belief that letter writers are ultimately dilettantes. Her talent is entirely "natural," that is, unconscious, so she is held to be incapable of possessing a self-conscious will as a creative writer.

Friedrich subsequently questions how Caroline's letters fit in with the goals of the intellectual group formed at Jena:

Sie können wohl Fragmente sprechen und auch in Briefen schreiben: aber sie sind immer grade nur in dem, was ganz individuell und also für unsern Zweck nicht brauchbar ist.—Ihre Philosophie und Ihre Fragmentheit gehn jede ihren eignen Gang.—Seyn Sie also ja vorsichtig bei der Wahl der Form, und bedenken Sie, daß Briefe und Recensionen Formen sind, die Sie ganz in der Gewalt haben.

[You can certainly speak fragments and also write letters: but they belong to that which is totally individual and thus for our purpose not useful. Your philosophy and your fragmentation go each their own way.—Therefore, be careful in choosing the form, and remember that letters and reviews are forms in which you have power.] (*Caroline* 1: 439–40)

The individuality and fragmentariness of Caroline's letters do not adhere to Friedrich's required objectivity and completeness in a published work, criteria advocated in his theoretical and literary works as well. The benefits of his encouragement seem few: if Caroline continues to write letters, a genre in which she excels, but that does not comply with an aesthetic program seeking more objectivity in art, she cannot expect her writings to be published. Friedrich does have a suggestion for a publishable form for her letters: if he were to edit them and compose his own "große philosophische Rhapsodie:"

> Was sich aus Ihren Briefen drucken ließe, ist viel zu rein, schön und weich, als daß ich es in Fragmente gleichsam zerbrochen, und durch die bloße Aushebung kokett gemacht sehn möchte. Dagegen denke ich, es würde mir nicht unmöglich seyn, aus Ihren Briefen Eine große philosophische Rhapsodie zu—diaskeuasiren. Was meynen Sie dazu?—Das wäre etwas für den Sommer, wenn ich wieder bey Ihnen bin.

> [What can be published from your letters is much too pure, beautiful, and gentle for me to want to see it broken, as it were, into fragments and be made coquettish through merely raiding. On the contrary, I think it would be impossible for me to—diaskeuasize—a great philosophical rhapsody out of your letters. What do you think about that?—That would be something for the summer, when I am with you again.] (*Caroline* 1: 440)

Friedrich's offer to compose a "philosophical rhapsody" from Caroline's letters demonstrates the back-seat position that women and their personal writings were expected to assume in literary production. Encouraged to donate raw material in a "pre-aesthetic" form, such as letters, so that their male colleagues could shape it into a finished product, many women contributed to published works signed by men. Caroline's own production offers an apt case in point, for most of her writing, often penned in the letter form or originating from material in a personal letter, appeared under her male colleagues' names. A. W. Schlegel's foreword to his 1828 published *Kritische Schriften* admits that some essays are "nicht ganz" [not entirely] by him, "sondern zum Teil von der Hand einer geistreichen Frau,welche alle Talente besaß, um als Schriftstellerin zu glänzen, deren Ehrgeiz aber nicht darauf gerichtet war" [but rather in part by the hand of a clever woman who possessed all the talents to shine as a writer, whose ambition, however, was not oriented for that].[78] The letters about Shakespeare's *Romeo und Julia*, which Schlegel includes word-for-word in the collection, are by Caroline, as perhaps is, scholars suspect, work on the essays about the Dresden Art Gallery. A statement she wrote—"Fast alles, was bei Cotta jetzt unter der Presse ist, ist von meiner Hand . . ." [Nearly everything that is in press at Cotta now is by my hand]—is ambiguous enough to provoke speculation on whether she acted not only as Schelling's secretary, but also as a major contributor to reviews he wrote between 1805 and 1807. Private letters reveal that Caroline also did not receive sufficient credit for her editorial work on the *Atheneum*, on Friedrich Schlegel's *Lucinde*, on A. W. Schlegel's drama *Ion*, and on Gottfried August Bürger's poetry and translations. Every text that we know did come from her—the satirical poem about Fichte's *Wissenschaftslehre*, her parody about Fr. Schlegel's dissertation, the review of *Ion* for the *Zeitung für die elegante Welt*, her draft of a novel, and her more than four hundred extant letters—remained published anonymously or not at all.

The "feminine" duties that came with being a woman, that is childbearing, housekeeping, and care of the husband, followed a woman throughout her life. Only when these tasks were done could she even think about putting pen to paper. Even in the circles at Jena, where women such as Caroline Schlegel-Schelling and Dorothea Schlegel held organizing positions, women were still relegated to the performance of domestic chores.[79] Thus Friedrich Schlegel writes to Schleiermacher in 1798 about Caroline Schlegel, who was then thirty-five, and, he concluded, approaching the end of her childbearing years: "Nun, sage ich, kann sie tun, was wir alle wollen—einen Roman schreiben. Mit der Weiblichkeit ist es nun doch vorbei . . ." [Now, I say, she can do what we all want—write a novel. But it's all over now with femininity].[80] For Schlegel, writing and "femininity" cannot exist side by side. One must, however, credit Schlegel for his recognition of women's talent to write at all. For others, like Novalis, who sees women as subordinate creatures (*Werke* 2: 161) who in marriage and in relation to men remain "der sogenannte ungebildete Theil" [the so-called uneducated part] (*Werke* 2: 164), the existence of any kind of creativity in women stays hidden. Later, Eichendorff, in his essay "Die deutsche Salon-Poesie der Frauen" [The German Salon-Poetry of Women][81] and Karl Gutzkow entirely denied women the creative power to write; so contends Gutzkow: "Da der Geist der Frauen nie schöpferisch wird, so kann ihre höchste Bildung immer nur eine unglaubliche Steigerung der Empfänglichkeit sein" [Because the intellect of women will never be creative, thus her highest education can always be only an unbelievable increase in receptability].[82]

In discussing letter writing, gender becomes one obviously important historical determinant. Faced with other options, men did not need a personal form such as the letter for entrance into the literary realm: they could chose from a gamut of genres, occupations, and styles and could play a large part in determining their conditions, while women's options remained limited. Any creativity a woman might show publicly or privately risked relegation to what men labeled the less-significant, trivial realms of life. The talented salonières, such as Rahel Varnhagen, who masterfully conducted intellectual circles standing outside conventional society and coupled the love of conversation with dialogic forms such as the letter, had by the 1830s lost their reputation as organizers of tolerant and avant-garde gathering places. Instead, women's function within salon culture came to be viewed as an extension of their roles as nurturers and inspirators of men.[83]

Individually, women certainly lauded the letters of their male correspondents, but they did not universalize their statements to read that men wrote better letters than women. This is, of course, not to say that women themselves did not make statements that generalized gender experiences. On the contrary, there are many assertions in which they acquiesce to gender roles, and their concern about submission applies almost always to their own sex. Worrying about overstepping the boundaries of the "feminine," criticizing other women for challenging norms, resigning themselves to remaining anonymous, wishing to be men, such are the signs of acquiescence that continue to trouble scholars who might wish for more assertiveness.

Ambiguities do not make research easier. Surges of creativity were not always rewarded; indeed, they were often undermined. But neither did restrictions prove totally effective, as reading between the lines often reveals. Against the backdrop of writing in a "natural" form, women were engaging in some quite subversive activities—forming bonds of friendship amongst themselves; empowering and aiding each other in the publishing process; creating aesthetic metaphors of their selves to deal with ambiguities that both limited and encouraged them; and writing about taboo subjects such as politics and literature. Such are the cases to which we turn now.

# 3

# "Let us rather exchange letters of friendship":[1]
# Women's Friendship in Letters

THE absence of notable friendships among women, as a theme both in biography and fiction, is no new discovery to feminist inquiry. From Virginia Woolf, in *A Room of One's Own*, to Carolyn Heilbrun, in *Writing A Woman's Life*, readers in the English-speaking realm have criticized writers for this void, which suggests women lead a monotonous, simple life that no one would wish upon either gender.[2] For German studies, Sylvia Bovenschen's article "Vom Tanz der Gedanken und Gefühle" ["On the Dance of Thoughts and Feelings"] in the *Frankfurter Allgemeine Zeitung* and the collection of essays entitled *Frauenfreundschaft—Männerfreundschaft: Literarische Diskurse im 18. Jahrhundert* [*Women's Friendship—Men's Friendship: Literary Discourse in the 18th Century*] address the lack of treatment of friendships among women in contrast to the abundant attention paid to those between Goethe and Schiller, Lessing and Mendelssohn, and Clemens Brentano and Achim von Arnim.[3]

An overview of previous scholarship on women's friendships validates the criticism. Research has often recognized the importance of salon circles for encouraging women to interact more with famous men than with other women.[4] For the most part, literary history stresses rivalry and not solidarity among women.[5] For obvious reasons, the most widely known friendships between women are those depicted in published works, such as between Bettine von Arnim and Karoline von Günderrode. One might argue, too, that the absence is justifiable. Within the literary canon there are few models for women to follow, for they appear mostly as possessed objects in love relationships with men. Traditional theories and definitions emphasize the importance of autonomy, equality, choice, and self-sufficiency for survival of a friendship; a patriarchal society that restricted a woman's legitimate activities to the home made it difficult for her to develop any of these qualities.[6] Lack of opportunity for personal contacts due to restrictions on travel could inhibit a relationship. Moreover, as

Bovenschen observes, the equation of women's friendships amongst themselves with lesbianism has made the subject threatening, even taboo, for many researchers.[7]

Two tracts on friendship in the eighteenth century represent very different views that men and women had of women's friendship: the chapter on friendship in Dorothea Henriette von Runckel's *Moral für Frauenzimmer nach Anleitung der moralischen Vorlesungen des sel. Prof. Gellerts und anderer Sittenlehrer* [*Morality for Women Under the Guidance of the Moral Lectures of the Honorable Professor Gellert and Other Moralists*] and that in the second volume of Carl Friedrich Pockels's *Versuch einer Charakteristik des weiblichen Geschlechts* [*Attempt at a Characterization of the Female Sex*].[8] Runckel, the widow of a Saxon lieutenant colonel, was a writer, translator, and governess to several aristocratic girls in Dresden. She was involved in Gottsched's attempts to educate women on issues of morality and virtue, and her works reflect that allegiance as well as her indebtedness to Gellert's guidelines for letter writing. *Moral für Frauenzimmer* appeared first in 1774 and then in revised form in 1784 and 1796.[9] Although Runckel's target audience for the book was obviously women, her opening remarks in the chapter on friendship do not define different expectations for the two sexes. All successful friendships need a "gegenseitige Hochachtung und Neigung tugendhafter Gemüther" [mutual respect and inclination of virtuous minds] (*Moral*, 326). Using the first person, she draws on her own experiences as she gives advice. She cites only positive examples, the prominent one being that of a woman called Caroline, who enhances friendship by being willing to forgive, slow to anger, and cheerful. Runckel showed practical application of her theories on letter writing in her *Sammlung freundschaftlicher Originalbriefe, zur Bildung des Geschmacks für Frauenzimmer* [*Collection of Original Letters On the Formation of Taste for Women*], a three-part collection of letters published from 1777 to 1783, and then revised in 1790. It contains a preface promoting letter writing for women and model letters by such people as Madame Lucius, Gellert, and Gleim.[10] Another tribute to the link between letter writing and women's friendship occurs in her publication of Louise Gottsched's letters, which I will examine later.

Pockels published his treatise in 1798, two decades later than Runckel's exposé on women's friendship. In contrast to Runckel's picture, which does not deny women the ability to form close bonds with one another, Pockels sees friendship among women as neither possible nor desirable for society at large. Envy, jealousy, and vanity, in connection with both their beauty and their abilities, prevent women from ever forming close bonds. The result can only be the neglect of duties related to their "natural" status as wives and mothers anyway, he argues, and thus, not desirable. He draws a negative correlation between writing, reading, gender, and the formation of friendships. Even when women show friendship, he claims, it is artificial. Books in which women's friendships often occur have a "schwärmerische Art" [passionate style] and "haben ihre [die Frauen] Gefühle zu sehr verfeinert, ihren Egoismus zu sehr erhöht, ihre Nerven geschwächt, und ihre Launen unzählbar gemacht" [have refined their (the women's) feelings too much, escalated their egotism too much, weakened their nerves, and made their moods innumerable] (*Versuch* II: 216). In this connection, letter writing figures prominently: "Alle ihre—selbst häuslichen Geschäfte, ihre Erziehungsmethoden, ihre Briefwechsel, ihre Besuche sind sentimental" [All their—even domestic affairs, their methods of raising children, their correspondence, their visits are sentimental] (*Versuch*, II: 217). The word "sentimental," which twenty years previously would have had a positive connotation, now has a negative effect on prescribed gender roles: "Übrigens habe ich öfters gefunden, dass eben diese sentimentalen Weiber, die mit andern gleichgestimmten oder gleich verstimmten Frauen so leicht gewisse schwärmerische Herzensverbindungen errichten konnte, und ihnen ihr ganzes Leben widmeten, selten die bessern und glücklichern Mütter und Gattinnen waren" [Moreover, I have often found that exactly these sentimental women, who could establish such passionate connections of the heart with equally minded and equally ill-humored women, and who devoted their entire life to them, were rarely the better and happier mothers and wives.] (*Versuch*, II: 217–18).

Letters prove that friendships did exist and formed an essential part of women's personal and professional lives. In fact, there seems to be a strong correlation between the low value that traditional scholarship has placed on women's private writings, as discussed in chapter one of my study, and the equally low estimation of women's contacts with one another. That underestimation has resulted in the inaccessibility of relevant documents, which has in turn contributed to the paucity of scholarship. In addition, the ambiguous ways in which the letter form could serve either as a way to affirm norms of the feminine or to break out of them through writing find echoes in the contradictions that arise in women's friendships. On the one hand, close ties with other women could reaffirm affinity to the private realm, centered around what some scholars have identified as the ongoing female rituals of courtship, marriage, pregnancy, birth, and weaning.[11] On the other hand, letters reveal that close relationships could, and often did, react against, rather than result from, specific socially prescribed female relations and values. Writers formed supportive bonds with each other not because they were carrying on traditions, but because they remained outside the realms of female rituals. Letter writing became itself a ritual to address and, in many cases, to combat actively norms of femininity, including passivity and noncreativity.

Close readings suggest that we must recognize the complexities of women's friendships. An attempt to define the term necessitates a closer look at historical context. Mobility and technology have multiplied the amount of support friends can give each other today. Two centuries ago restricted travel and resources limited communication. Barriers blocking women's contact with one another were especially strong. It was a woman's duty to follow her husband to his place of residence after marriage, often uprooting her from her childhood confidantes. In a society that frowned upon the woman who traveled alone, letters became the main means to cultivate friendship. Letters often disclose that the bonds between women were obviously quantitatively and qualitatively more than what traditional scholarship has portrayed. But letters also prove the ties that bind to be more diverse and varying. Many friendships had their trying times as women attempted to sort out their opinions on restrictions that affected their lives and writings. Some ended in quarrels and misunderstandings; some overcame differences to become even stronger. The contradictions letters hold should make us think twice when we talk about any all-encompassing characteristics of women. Instead, the picture letters paint is nonstatic, multifaceted, and human. Widesweeping condemnation or idealization would be unrealistic.

My exploration concentrates on three writers' friendships as manifested in letters, namely Louise Adelgunde Kulmus Gottsched, Margaretha (Meta) Moller Klopstock, and Helmina von Chézy. I must stress that each of the women came from a middle-class or upper-middle class background, which allowed them the time, skills, and legitimacy for such engagement. Also of note is that the theme of friendship is not restricted to this chapter and runs throughout the correspondence of Karoline von Günderrode with Gunda Brentano and Bettine von Arnim, Caroline Schlegel-Schelling with Louise Gotter, Rahel Varnhagen with Pauline Wiesel, and Bettine von Arnim with Elisabeth Goethe.

Louise Adelgunde Kulmus Gottsched and her works have been enjoying new critical interpretations.[12] Because she showed very little desire to break away from gender norms categorizing her chiefly as wife and helpmate to her husband, many scholars on eighteenth-century women writers have hesitated to place her with women such as Ziegler and Zäunemann, who showed a strong awareness of restrictive gender norms.[13] Despite the fact that Louise Gottsched displayed few signs of consciously espousing women's rights, studies cannot ignore her work and her role in early enlightenment philosophy, especially her promotion of education for girls and women. By the sheer number of plays and translations she produced, she was surely one of the most prolific writers of her time. Scholarly inquiry has also led to unprecedented analysis of her correspondence, and rightly so.[14] The letters reveal, as Becker-Cantarino states, "her intelligence, erudition, her keen understanding and sensitive relationship to others and her time."[15] Furthermore, the edition of letters is unusual because it was published by a woman, Dorothea Runckel, the same woman to whom the letters were written, and represents one of the first, but certainly not the last, collection of publicized letters exchanged between two female friends.

Louise Kulmus was born in 1713, the daughter of a physician in Danzig.[16] When Gottsched was traveling though Danzig in 1729, he asked her parents for permission to correspond with their daughter, a request showing the parameters of a male-dominated society. The two corresponded six years before they married, when he received a professorship at the University of Leipzig. The marriage remained childless. Louise became the main helpmate and secretary for her husband, researching, translating, and writing scholarly articles and literary works for his reform program. Through her own comedies, translations, and letters, she acquired a reputation as a writer and learned woman.

The three-volume edition of letters contains Louise Gottsched's letters to her husband, to her friend Dorothea Runckel, and to others who asked her advice on a variety of topics, including educational methods, translating, and letter-writing techniques. But the edition includes not only letters. The second volume has Louise Gottsched's travelogue to Frau Thomasius, in which Gottschedin describes her trip that carries her to Karlsbad, Bayreuth, Erlangen, Nürnberg, and Regensburg (II: 4–16).[17] Runckel notes that these reports have already been published. The third volume includes a mixture of texts: an essay from Runckel on education, written upon Louise Gottsched's request; a letter from a friend to Louise Gottsched lauding the latter's translations (III: 155–62); Gottschedin's letters in French (III: 172–76), to stand, as Runckel states, as proof of Gottschedin's ability to write in French (III: 172); the tragedy *Panthea* (III: 177–270); an essay-letter to Dorothea von Runckel entitled "bey Absterben Ihres Mannes" [upon the death of her husband] (III: 299–303); and a request for a correction of orthography and grammar, which

Gottschedin honors, but with a modest excuse and surprise that he is asking a woman to correct him. Runckel notes the importance of that request and reply, for they were written in 1748, before Gottsched's reforms about language were published.

Hence, under the auspices of an edition of letters, Runckel presents texts exemplifying Louise Gottsched's multifarious talents and literary interests. Readers approaching the edition to find "just letters" have to reformulate their expectations. In fact, Runckel must have realized the edition's unconventionality, for in the forewords to the three volumes she prepares readers for the content while anticipating negative reactions from those who might perceive the independence and diversity in the texts as too progressive for a woman. To that end, she fits Gottschedin in with the ideal woman writer who was able to accomplish her literary feats without neglecting her domestic duties. In the prologue to the second volume, she states her intent has been to present a multi-sided perspective of her friend and colleague, with an emphasis not only on Gottschedin's public roles as "die originelle Schriftstellerin, die scharfsinnige Kunstrichterin, die erhabenste Dichterin" [the original writer, the astute judge of art, the most dignified poet], but perhaps more importantly on her capacities as "die zärtliche Tochter, die tugendhafte Ehegattin, die treuste Freundin, die Christin, die Philosophin" [the tender daughter, the virtuous wife, the most loyal friend, the Christian, the philosopher] (II: 3). If the letters are not of literary worth, Runckel states, they should at least serve as useful contributions to compliment her sex (II: 4). The prologue to the third volume relies on feminine traits to offset any masculine ones. Louise Gottsched had "[e]ine glückliche Mischung von dem Ernste, der Standhaftigkeit und Entschlossenheit des männlichen Geschlechts mit der Sanftmuth, Zurückhaltung und Bescheidenheit, die die größte Zierde des unsrigen ausmachen" [a happy mixture of seriousness, steadfastness, and decisiveness of the male sex with the gentleness, reserve, and modesty that comprise the greatest ornament of our sex] (III: [9]). According to Runckel, Gottschedin was proud to possess knowledge that other women did not have, yet she preferred to remain modest. Her intellectual curiosity and industriousness were inexhausible, yet she still kept an orderly house.

The letters reflect the continual tension Gottschedin felt between her desire to express her personal will and her fear of overstepping boundaries defined by public norms. Her correspondence with Gottsched reveals how she worked toward combining enlightened ideas and intellect under Gottsched's direction. In one of her first letters to him she admires his guidance toward making her virtuous while admitting that many women never fully attain that virtue. The condemnation of her own sex spurs her to rise above the common inadequacies and to hope "auf dem Wege der Tugend nicht zurücke zu bleiben, sondern darauf immer weiter zu kommen" [not to stand behind on the path to virtue, but rather always to come further along on it] (I: 4). She follows Gottsched's recommendations for reading and comments on them (I: 5–6; 9–10). When Gottsched mildly reprimands her for her criticisms, she thanks him subserviently: "Sie haben mir gezeiget, wie leicht unser Geschlecht seine Schwäche vergißt, und wie oft es sich unterfängt, seinen Meister zu tadeln . . . Ich erschrack über meine Kühnheit und verspreche Ihnen mich niemals wieder so sehr zu vergessen [You have shown me how easily our sex forgets its weakness and how often it ventures to scold its master . . . My boldness astonished me, and I promise you that I will never again forget myself so much] (I: 26). To him, she expressed a position against formal public education for women and especially against bestowing doctorates on them (I: 22–23).

As time goes on, however, she begins to reveal her own independence of thought and goals. She eventually branches out to comment on books she has found on her own (I: 32). She questions openly the worth of the education she has received, for example, when she wonders why Gottsched will not allow her to write in French "Zu welchem Ende erlernen wir diese Sprache, wenn wir uns nicht üben und unsere Fertigkeit darinnen zeigen sollen?" [To what end do we learn this language if we should not practice and show our skills with it?] (I: 6) She criticizes works freely—a letter-writing manual whose model letters follow the rules outlined for a good letter nevertheless lacks wit ("Witz") and expression (I: 21–22). The examples provided in a manual of style on the German language do not follow the criteria in their overuse of foreign words (I: 29–30). She recognizes her work as an anomaly for her sex (I: 259). She wants him to be genuine and does not want him to idealize her: "Eins bitte ich nur von Ihnen, machen Sie Ihren Freunden kein gar zu reitzendes Bild von mir" [I ask only one thing of you, do not paint such a glowing image of me to your friends] (I: 133). She does not want to undertake the translations Gottsched sends her and requests that she be allowed to choose the works she translates (I: 162–63). In general, the wit in her letters displays her defying her own concessions.

Letters to other correspondents in the volumes show the pendulum could swing from adherence to gender norms to defiance of those norms, such as her response to a letter from a certain Mademoiselle Schulz. Along with the letter to Schulz, Gottschedin sends *Gottscheds deutsche Sprachkunst* [*Gottsched's German Art of Language*]. She praises Schulz for pursuing her education: "Sie besitzen viele Vorzüge vor vielen Ihres Geschlechts, die mit der ekelhaften Entschuldigung, ein Frauenzimmer dürfe nicht viel lernen, ihre Unwissenheit noch unerträglicher machen" [You possess many advantages over many of your sex, who make their lack of knowledge even more unbearable with the disgusting excuse that a woman should not learn much] (II: 28). But she warns her not to neglect her household chores, and, in her pursuit of knowledge, not to read dangerous books, but to let herself be advised on good books to read. She advises Schulz to become a teacher or governess. Accompanying her advice, almost as if in a slash of the pen, however, comes the wish that the German bourgeoisie would make sure their daughters receive a good education so that when the fathers died, the daughters could at least make a respectable living. Her promotion of planned economic independence seems radical for a time in which arranged marriages that would secure women's financial dependence on the man were still commonplace.

Thus, Gottschedin's promotion of the image of woman as wife and mother occurs side-by-side with statements on financial and intellectual independence for women. Whereas her correspondence with Gottsched shows wit and humor in confronting him with criticism, her comments to Runckel become more somber. Louise Gottsched obviously placed a high value on her friendship with Runckel, as Runckel herself emphasizes in the forword to the third volume, when she lauds their powerful friendship, but admits that Gottschedin did not extend her openness to everyone (III: [11]). Foremost, we should value Runckel's edition as one of the first publicly recorded documents of friendship between women, and one that until recently received no scholarly attention in studies on eighteenth-century friendships. It is also significant, especially for future discussions of the relationship between letters, women's friendships, and literature, that their friendship began in a literary context. On 12 February 1736, Gottschedin sent Runckel a translation of Cato and asked her opinion, considering that she knew English and admired Addison (I: 231). Although the focus on literary endeavors never falls by the wayside, the relationship consciously becomes one of deep friendship. On 24 March 1754, Louise Gottsched decides not to send a promised translation of Socrates and Plato, but opts instead that their correspondence be more intimate: "Lassen Sie uns lieber freundschaftliche Briefe wechseln. Dieses sey und bleibe unsere reitzenste Beschäftigung; so lange wir getrennt leben müssen" [Let us rather exchange letters of friendship. This is and remains our most stimulating occupation; as long as we must live separately] (II: 216).

Letters to Runckel after 1750 become very expressive. In inviting

Runckel to correspond with her, Gottschedin makes clear her expectations of openness and consistency: "Erlauben Sie mir Ihnen oft zu schreiben, und oft meinen Kummer, davon Sie die unschuldige Ursache sind, zu klagen" [Allow me to write to you often, and often to complain about my sadness for which you are an innocent reason] (II: 45). The metaphors expressing her friendship are rich: "Mein Gewissen sagt mir, daß ich mit Ihnen im Briefwechsel einen eben so eigenützigen Handel treibe, als die Holländer nach der neuen Welt, welche Gold für Tändeleyen einholen" [My conscience tells me that I am carrying on such a selfish trade with you as the Dutch to the New World obtain gold for trifles] (II: 69). Her self-interest, she honestly admits, presides over any other pressing needs Runckel might have (69). Frequent remarks on friendship show a woman realizing, most likely for the first time, her need for friendship with another woman; she writes: "Mein Herz ist zur Freundschaft mehr, als zu irgend einer andern Leidenschaft geschaffen" [My heart is made for friendship more than any other passion] (II: 66); and again later: "Ihre Freundschaft, meine Theuerste, rechne ich unter die wesentlichsten Glücksgüter, die ich gegenwärtig in der Welt besitze . . . [Your friendship, my dearest, I count as one of the most essential happinesses that I own presently in the world] (II: 108). The friendship she wants to build with Runckel will be unique, she asserts: "Unser Herz ist immer voller Wünsche; wir sagen uns täglich dasjenige, was andre kaum des Jahres einmal denken, und was sie ganz vergessen würden, wenn der Neujahrstag sie nicht daran erinnerte" [Our heart is always full of wishes; we tell each other daily what others can hardly think of in a year, and what they would totally forget if New Year's Day did not remind them of it] (II: 263–64). At one point, she stresses that she lives only for her friend (II: 267). Luise Gottsched's longing for death leads her to contemplate a mutual suicide with Runckel (II: 276–77). She lets on that she would prefer a visit to her friend, "der Freundin" [the female friend], implying Runckel, over an excursion with "dem Freund" [the male friend] Gottsched (III: 18–19).

Correspondence is the lifeline of their friendship. On a trip, Gottschedin emphasizes the three things that have occupied her: "Die Begierde mich mit Ihnen schriftlich zu unterreden, die Sehnsucht nach Ihren Briefen, und das Verlangen näher bei Ihnen zu seyn" [The desire to talk with you in writing, the longing for your letters, and the need to be closer to you] (II: 144). Runckel's letters are her "schriftliche Besuche" [written visits] (II: 248) and "schrifliche Unterredung mit meiner besten Freundin" [written conversations with my best friend] (II: 211). The letters are replete with statements linking their correspondence and their lives. She claims she cannot live without her letters (II: 218). Runckel's letters become her mainstay: "Erheitern Sie durch Ihre Briefe die trüben Tage eines Lebens, das ich noch überdieses fern von Ihnen zubringen muß. Kein Geschäft ist mir so wichtig, keine Zeit so besetzt, die hier nicht weichen müßte" [Brighten up with your letters the gloomy days of a life that I must spend away from you. No occupation is so important to me, no time so occupied that I must not yield here] (II: 248). A letter from 29 January 1755 is remarkable for its emotional pleas:

> Kurz, ich lebe nur für Sie, um Sie zu lieben, und mein ganzes künftiges Leben aller Freude und allem Schmerze, aller Zufriedenheit und aller tödlichen Unruhe, kurz allen Empfindungen zu überlassen, die die Begleiterinnen dieser göttlichen Leidenschaft sind.
>
> Leben Sie wohl, einzige Freundin; Schreiben Sie mir öfter als ich, und längere Briefe als ich, weil Sie mehr Muße haben als ich. Jedes Wort ist mir theuer, was mir Ihre Feder sagt. Ungedultig bey jedem Anfang Ihrer Briefe, eile ich das Ende zu wissen; und fange sie wieder an zu lesen, weil ich zu bald fertig damit werde.

> [In short, I live only for you, in order to love you, and to leave my future life to all the joys and all the pains, all the contentment and all the fatal restlessness, in short all the sentiments that are the accomplices of this divine passion.
>
> I fare you good-bye, my only friend; write to me more often than I, and longer letters than I because you have more leisure time. Every word that your quill says is precious to me. Impatient at every beginning of your letters, I rush to know the end, and begin to read again because I have finished too quickly.] (II: 269–70)

It would be, of course, easy to attribute the strong emotional statements in this letter to the rhetoric of friendship visible in many eighteenth-century correspondences. With Louise Gottsched's letters to her husband at hand, however, the genuineness of sentiments in the correspondence with Runckel becomes comparatively more visible. The openness Gottschedin hopes to cultivate emerges in statements about the everyday reality of her life as a helpmate of her husband and restrictive gender roles. Interjected with talk about her work with her husband, her life at home, her travels, or her commentary on what she has been reading come complaints about her isolation, exhaustion, and loneliness. She refers to her tiredness (II: 111; 118; III: 39; 149–51; 165–68), and "das Schreibejoch, welches mir täglich aufliegt" [the writing yoke that lies upon me daily] (II: 82). Conscious of the more tedious duties that she as a woman must perform, she laments the difference:

Hier muß ich meinen Kopf täglich mit wahren Kleinigkeiten, mit Haus-
und Wirthschaftssorgen füllen, die ich von Kindheit an, für die elendesten
Beschäftigungen eines denkenden Wesens gehalten habe; und deren ich
gern entübriget seyn möchte. Allein ein wesentliches Theil der vorzüg-
lichen Glückseligkeit des männlichen Geschlechts, sollte in der Ueberheb-
ung dieser nichtsbedeutenden Dinge bestehen; und wir dürfen nicht wider
das Schicksal murren, daß uns diese beschwerlichen Kleinigkeiten vorbehalten hat. Sie verlieren nichts, liebste Freundin, daß wir in einer gewissen
Entfernung leben, die Ihnen meine Schwäche nur von weiten erblicken
läßt. Ich bin jetzt zuweilen so verdrüßlich, und so niedergeschlagen, daß
ich alsdenn zu dem Umgange mit einer Person, der ich niemals mißfallen
möchte, gar nicht fähig wäre.

[Here I have to fill my head daily with real trivialities, with household
and financial worries, which, since childhood, I have considered the most
terrible preoccupation of a thinking being, and which I would like to be
relieved of. Thus, an essential part of the fine mental happiness of the
male sex should consist of the strain of these meaningless things; and
we are not allowed to grumble against the fate that has reserved these
burdensome trivialities for us. You do not lose anything, dearest friend,
by having us live at a certain distance, which lets you view my weakness
only from far away. I am sometimes now so ill-tempered and depressed
that I would certainly not be able to associate with a person whom I
never would want to displease.] (II: 151–152)

In another letter we can detect a resignation to norms, but one that
ultimately questions submission: "da die Männer, so wie ihr Herz
gegenwärtig beschaffen ist, unsre ganze Neigung an sich zu ziehen
wissen; was bliebe uns übrig, Ihnen aufzuopfern, wenn sie uns an
Redlichkeit und Treue überträfen? Sie sind darzu geschaffen, unser
lebhaftes Vergnügen, und unsern bittersten Gram zu veranlassen;
darzu mußten sie recht so seyn, wie sie sind" [because the men, as
their heart is presently so constituted, know how to attract our entire
affection to themselves; what remains for us but to sacrifice ourselves
to them if they surpass us in their integrity and fidelity? They are
made to cause our most ardent pleasures and our most bitter grief;
thus they really have to be as they are] (II: 61). Her final sickness,
which results in her death on 26 June 1762, is, she relates to Runckel
on 4 March 1762, "Acht und zwanzig Jahre ununterbrochene Arbeit,
Gram im Verborgenen und sechs Jahre lang unzählige Thränen sonder
Zeugen, die Gott allein hat fließen sehen; [Twenty-eight years of uninterrupted work, concealed grief, and six years long of countless tears
without witnesses, which only God has seen flow] (III: 167).

Defiant or questioning statements about her duties accompany almost always a submission to limitations. Just when Gottschedin

seems bold enough to complain about the everyday tiring tasks she must accomplish, she retreats into the mold of the submissive woman who cannot follow "den Empfindungen seines Herzens" [the sentiments of the heart], but rather must accept "die Pflichten der bürgerlichen Gesellschaft und die Umstände der Zeit" [the duties of the bourgeois society and the conditions of the time] (II: 310). Her remarks about the uniqueness of their friendship remain obscure or are rescinded, as if she senses something unusual about the two women's relationship, which society might condemn. In a letter from 24 May 1754, she analyzes why she is bothered so much over Runckel's long silence. She reasons that it is because she had imagined herself as Runckel's lover and that Runckel had not approved. She writes a message in French declaring her friendship, and not love (II: 218–19).

As in her correspondence with her husband, Gottschedin oscillates between viewing her intellectual pursuits as unusual and wanting to continue anyway; between believing society's warnings against the harm she could be causing to herself and still following her desires. She recognizes that she performs work "die vielen meines Geschlechts ganz fremd sind" [that is entirely foreign to many of my sex] and believes the advice of her doctor, who states that her health would be better without so much activity (III: 259). Still, she cannot deny her own drive to work and its possible positive impact on her health: "Mein eigner Trieb hingegen sagt mir, daß die Beschäftigung mit allem, was meine Neigung befriediget, und meinen Geist zufrieden stellt, meiner Gesundheit nicht schädlich seyn kann. Diesem Trieb will ich folgen, so lange meine Maschine nicht ganz baufällig wird" [My own drive, in contrast, tells me that the preoccupation with everything that satisfies my desires and makes my intellect content cannot harm my health. I want to follow this drive as long as my machine does not become dilapidated] (III: 259–60). Publicly, however, she has a difficult time acknowledging that she herself is a poet (I: 75). Instead, she sees herself as "Gehülfin" [helpmeet], "unwürdigen Secretair" [unworthy secretary], "Hausmuse" [house muse] of her husband and thus as an educated woman and poet second (I: 282; II: 287; III: 154). She definitiely supports the idea of a good education for girls and women, but she still sees women's destiny in marriage and believes that their talents and ambitions should play a secondary role to marriage duties (III: 21). Representative of her adherence to the idealization of motherhood developing in the middle of the century is her letter on 4 January 1752 to Frau S., praising her for nursing her child herself (II: 41–42) and her advice to a new mother to give her child his own mother's milk (II: 209). Her frequent mention of her own childlessness emphasizes she has not chosen her lot, but that divine will has intervened. Unable to break the traditional image of women's role as childbearers, she wonders whether her lack is a sign that she is incapable of educating children anyway (I: 233). Ultimately, her question turns into a statement of her belief that God sees it as best not to give her children (II: 73–74; II: 208–209). Although she believes that destiny to have limited her experiences in some fields, she still suggests, and certainly not remorsefully so, that her life of continual learning would have been hampered with a child as well (I: 233–34).

Intertwined with hesitation against becoming too public a figure and a projected image of adherence to her husband's wishes come ambiguous statements about the publication of the letters. In the introduction to the first volume, Runckel asserts that Gottschedin desired not to have her letters published. A closer look at the two places where Gottschedin talks about publication evidences that her wishes were not asserted solely out of modesty or lack of ambition, which would have fit in with desired feminine traits. In response to Gottsched's request, Gottschedin writes:

> Welchen Anschlag haben Sie auf meine Briefe gemacht? Es ist am besten, daß diese ganz im Verborgenen bleiben. Ich habe keinen Roman schreiben wollen. Tugend und Aufrichtigkeit sind die Richtschnur meiner Handlungen und meiner Gesinnungen von je her gewesen; diese sollen auch immer meine Führerinn bleiben. Von ihnen geleitet, will ich die Bahn meines Lebens muthig durchwandeln. Aus der Fülle meines Herzens habe ich geschrieben, und wem die Art unserer Freundschaft nicht gefällt, der wird an diesen Briefen viel zu tadeln finden. Nur wenig Leser würden ihnen Beyfall geben. Ein falscher Anstrich, ausgesuchte, nichtsbedeutende Worte sind der Mode Styl; diesen werde ich niemals nachahmen, und wenn Sie nur mit meinen Briefen zufrieden sind, so mögen solche der ganzen Welt unbekannt bleiben.

> [What kind of a scheme have you made for my letters? It is best that the whole thing remain entirely secret. I did not want to write a novel. Virtue and sincerity have always been the directional lines of my actions and my convictions; these should also stay my leaders. Led by them, I want to wander courageously through the course of my life. I have written from the depths of my heart, and whoever does not like our friendship will find a lot to scorn in these letters. Only a few readers will applaud them. A false air, exquisite, meaningless words are the fashionable style; I will never imitate these and if you alone are content with my letters, then they should stay unknown to the rest of the world.] (I: 101–2)

Louise Gottsched does not undermine her talents nor feign modesty in the face of publication. Rather, she anticipates misunderstanding from a public readership. She surmises that readers would object to the style of her letters, composed from the depth of her heart. The context in which those emotions would appear to outsiders could cause scorn. In historical perspective, her fears are real: a society that frowned upon women's public expression in general would only condemn such emotional exchange between the sexes. Louise Gottsched's later answer to the same request is more ambiguous, suggesting that she was not totally against publication:

> Für die Gewährung meiner Bitte in Absicht auf meine Briefe, danke ich Ihnen recht sehr. Die guten Zeilen haben das ihrige gethan; Sie haben Ihnen mein ganzes Herz gezeiget, lassen Sie solche nunmehro vergessen seyn. Wenn sie ganz Deutschland lesen möchte, so würde ich diese Ehre nicht mehr empfinden, als daß sie von Ihnen gelesen worden. Alles, was ich Sie bitte, ist dieses: Verhindern Sie den Druck dieser Briefe, oder verschieben ihn, bis nach meinem Tode.

> [I truly thank you for respecting my request regarding my letters. The good lines have done their work; They have shown you my entire heart, from now on just let them be forgotten. If all of Germany would like to read them, then I would not feel as honored as if they had been read by you. Everything that I ask you is this: Prevent the publication of these letters, or delay it until after my death.] (I: 126)

Runckel as editor uses this subtle consent to publish the letters posthumously as justification for her edition. Her edition includes footnotes that try to mediate Gottschedin's attempts to deny herself public recognition. A footnote from Runckel at this point in the edition speculates on the pleasure Gottschedin would have taken in knowing that readers did enjoy the letters: "Diese Besorgung war mir vorbehalten. Wie glücklich, wenn ich meiner Freundin den Beyfall der Leser erworben hätte" [This provision was reserved for me. How lucky, if I would have procured for my friend the acclaim of the readers] (I: 126). Runckel thus also indiscreetly acknowledges her precarious role as editor and facilitator of Gottschedin's ideas. At one point, Gottschedin writes about not wanting to accept the invitation into the society of poets, for the minute women overstep their boundaries: "so gerathen wir in ein Labyrinth, und verliehren den Leitfaden unserer schwachen Vernunft, die uns doch glücklich ans Ende bringen sollte" [thus we become entangled in a labyrinth and lose the guidance of our weak mind that should really bring us happily to our end] (I: 27). Runckel clarifies this position in a less harsh tone, emphasizing the fine difference between earning a place in an honorable society and accepting recognition for the reward: "Ein Vorsatz den unsre Kulmus genau erfüllet hat. Sie fand mehr Ehre, einen Platz in dieser Gesellschaft zu verdienen, als sich darum zu bewerben, oder ihn anzunehmen" [A resolution that our Kulmus fulfilled exactly. She found more honor in earning a place in this society than to strive for one or to accept one] (I: 27).

Runckel is aware of the uniqueness of Louise Gottsched's correspondence and admits it in her foreword. Runckel also believes herself to have been respectful of Gottschedin's wishes in publishing the correspondence. Except for the few instances in which she clarifies the context of certain statements, she lets the letters speak for themselves. Gottschedin's letters to Runckel add elements of frustration and weariness to the ostensibly contented relationship between a famous man and woman. They also prove Runckel's belief that women are capable of friendship with one another, a friendship in which sorrow and happiness, discouragement and hope can have an audience. The next generation of women letter writers would seize that opportunity.

Two years before Louise Kulmus began her correspondence with Gottsched, Meta Moller was born, on 16 March 1728, the daughter of a rich Hamburg merchant.[18] When Meta's father died, her mother remarried. Meta was left independent and had access to her own inheritance left by her father. In remarrying, her mother had no power over her daughter, and their relationship shows a resulting tenseness, especially concerning Meta's future. Her mother wanted her to marry rich and was against her marriage to Klopstock, a not-so-wealthy poet. But Meta convinced her mother, who eventually could not deny the marriage. Meta and Klopstock, who had met on 4 April 1751, were married on 10 June 1754. Meta continued her witty correspondence after her marriage, writing letters to her sisters, Elisabeth and Catharina, and to Klopstock, when he was away. Her life ended abuptly, though, during the birth of her first son on 28 November 1758.

Meta's short life leaves us with her correspondence and other works that her husband published after her death. Her works were subsequently included in his collected works until the 1859 edition, when they were omitted. Consequently, access to her works has been limited. It was also believed that Klopstock had burned their correspondence, which turned out to be untrue. Nearly two hundred years after her death, in 1956, Hermann Tiemann published a three-volume edition of her correspondence.[19] That edition, now out of print, appeared in abridged form in 1988 in the series *Bibliothek des 18. Jahrhunderts*, published by Beck.[20] Inclusions in this new, accessible edition focus on the letters as biographical indices, especially for the relationship between Meta and Klopstock. The edition starts with a series of letters that Meta writes between September 1753 and March 1754, in which she relates to her friends Dieterich and Eleonore Giseke the story of Meta's and Klopstock's first meeting. Chronologically, the content of Meta's whimsical report belongs at the beginning of her relationship, and not her correspondence, with Klopstock. The focus of the edition thus becomes the relationship between Meta and Klopstock. Stylistically, however, the narration demonstrates a wit and an emotional openness that Meta develops with time and in correspondence with friends and relatives other than Klopstock. These other relationships, however, assume second priority: whereas the editors have included the correspondence between Meta and Klopstock in its entirety, they have edited out letters and passages in letters from friends and family members, which, the editors claim, do not take anything essential away from the total picture.[21] Once again, subtle editing criteria restrict a woman's contacts and influence.

Meta's correspondence with Klopstock shows her using letters to turn friendship into love. She views her correspondence with Klopstock as rooted in a mutual friendship. When it began, Klopstock was still in love with his cousin, Maria Sophia Schmidt, the "Fanny" in his early love poems. Fanny's parents and brother were against the relationship developing into anything serious, for Klopstock had no financial security. In 1751, Klopstock went to Copenhagen in order to present himself to the Danish King, Friedrich V. The King had offered to sponsor Klopstock while he finished the rest of the *Messias*, whose first three parts had appeared in 1748. Klopstock left his cousin in Langensalza, Switzerland. When he and Meta began writing in April, it had been a half a year since he had heard from Schmidt.

On 13 April 1751, Meta begins one of her earliest letters to him, declaring, "Ihr Brief, den ich lange noch nicht erwarten konnte, hat meine Freundschaft zu Ihnen gewiß viele Jahre älter gemacht" [Your letter, which I could not have expected so soon, made my friendship with you certainly many years older] (24). She continually stresses her intentions to build a strong friendship with him (36–37; 52; 60; 152). Klopstock, too, stresses his need for friendship and makes no secret of his continued love for Fanny. He laments to Meta the fact that he receives no letters from his cousin, even though he has written her several. When a letter from Fanny finally comes, he sends it to Meta to ask her opinion (47–48). He talks openly about his unrequited love and asks Meta for her advice. She readily sympathizes with him without making any demands, only trying to explain Fanny's reactions. Their language is very affectionate and intimate, and thus the modern reader finds it difficult to discern where friendship stops and love begins. Meta, too, later talks about her sentiments in these early letters. To the English writer Samuel Richardson, with whom she had a brief correspondence in 1757 and 1758, she mentions how her friends had tried to convince her that she really was engaged in a correspondence of love, but that she had denied their observations.

No denying, the friendship that Meta and Klopstock developed was genuine. But there was a definite element of role-playing, which manifested itself also later in Meta's ironic, witty style. The most apparent indication of such performance is in Meta's assuming the persona Klopstock assigns to her. Klopstock calls her his "Babet," (40; 44). He compares her talents as a letter writer to those of Madame de Sevigny (221). Meta repeats this praise proudly. Influenced by Klopstock's reading of Richardson's *Clarissa* and his exclamations of feminine virtue, he asks if he can call her "Klärchen," (142) and Meta soon begins signing her letters as "Clärchen," or "Klärchen," or "K." In fact, Klopstock borrows often from Richardson's works to formulate his image of Meta, sending her appropriate writings such as the ode "Die todte Clarissa" (132). As their relationship proceeds through many stages, she adopts her respective roles as lover, fiancée, and then wife. His letter on 3 July 1752 lists the names and parts he has assigned to her throughout their relationship: "'Mein Mädchen . . . Babet . . . Clärchen' (u dann eine Menge Beywörter zu Clärchen) 'meine Clarissa' 'meine Geliebte' (hier kömmt [es] besonders auf den Ton an) u zulezt, was alles wieder zusammen nimmt, 'Meine Moller'" ['My girl . . . Babet . . . Clärchen (and then a number of epithets for Clärchen) 'my Clarissa' 'my beloved' (here the tone is especially important) and lastly, what brings everything together again, 'my Moller'] (159).

Letters offer a venue for both confirming traditional roles and playing out new ones. Klopstock notices differences between their letters (105; 117). To Gleim, he remarks that men's friendship with women is different than that with other men. To Klopstock, Meta, too, observes differences between the sexes and their epistolary styles: "wir Mädchens lassen unsere Herzen niemals so weit fliegen, daß sie aus unserer Macht kommen" [we girls never let our hearts fly so far that they come out of our power] (67). Assumption of certain traditional roles, however, also occasionally leads to imagined role reversal. They both recognize that their friendship would be different if they were of the same sex. They frequently discuss the different gender roles they each play and how those roles affect their relationship. She calls herself the "female Klopstock," seeing in him a "Mädchenherz" (143). She states that she and Klopstock are the masculine and feminine sides of one person (204; 223) and uses the name "Friedrikchen Moller" to express this unity (202). At one point, she wishes that

Klopstock were a girl (132). He, too, imagines reversal: "Wenn Du ein Junge wärst, so würdest Du ich seyn; u wenn ich ein Mädchen wäre, so würde ich Du seyn" [If you were a boy, then you would be I, and if I were a girl, then I would be you] (181; 219).

Toying with other roles does not eliminate social pressures to conform though. In general, Meta's letters to Klopstock convey her adapting to the idealization of a perfect woman as projected by the image emerging in the mid-eighteenth century. Although she knows French, Italian, English, and Latin, is well read, and well known in her circle of friends as an actress in little dramas performed on social occasions, she denies that she is a "gelehrtes Frauenzimmer" [learned woman]. After she marries, she mentions her desire to have a child, but then interprets her childlessness as perhaps a sign from the divine powers of her own deficiencies, an attitude that haunted Louise Gottsched, too.

In contrast to this often playful acquiescence, however, Meta expresses to her female friends and sister sentiments that she rarely shows in letters to Klopstock. A letter to Eleonore Cruse after she has married Diederich Giseke unveils a wider emotional spectrum than what she had demonstrated with Klopstock. First, in a letter addressed to the couple, she congratulates them on their marriage and describes how she and her friends had celebrated the marriage in the couple's absence. She then specifies that the latter part of the letter is for Eleonore. Here she first queries: "Aber sagen Sie mir doch, ob es denn wirklich so süß ist, eine Frau zu seyn. Ich weis nicht" [But tell me truly, if it is really so sweet to be a wife. I do not know.] She then concedes that after hearing anecdotes from other newly married friends, "ich halte es mit dem heiligen, verehrungswürdigen, u in aller Welt so hochgeachteten Jungfernstande" [I am staying with the sacred, most honorable, and in the whole world highly esteemed maidenhood]. The advantages of remaining a virgin are numerous:

Sie wissen, welche Schönheit eine gute Taille ist. Und das ist nun unstreitig der Vorzug des Jungfernstandes. Zweitens wissen Sie, wie süß blühende Wangen sind. (Sehen Sie geschwinde in den Spiegel, *vielleicht* können Sie das noch itzt sehen) Aber mein liebes Hannchen, ach, [mir ist angst um Ihre Wan]gen, diese rothe Wang[e könnte in kurzer Zeit] in eine blasse verwandelt w[erden. Vielleicht wird] sie verblühen, noch eher, als die [Blume] ihre [Schön]heit verlieren wird!

[You know what a beauty a good waist is. And that is now unarguably the advantage of maidenhood. Second you know how sweet rosy cheeks are. (Look quickly in the mirror, *maybe* you can still see that). But my dear Hannchen, ah, I am worried about your cheeks, this red cheek could transform into a pale one in a short time. Maybe it will pass, still sooner than the flower will lose its beauty.] (251)

As Prokop has observed, despite the ironic form of the letter, there is still an unmistakable undertone of fear in Meta's letter. For Meta, that fear assumed real causes. Here was a woman who tried to live up to the ideals of a man who had expressed on more than one occasion his admiration of her slim waist, among other characteristics he deemed beautiful in a woman; who was enjoying full vigor and health after being a sickly child; and who, along with her husband, would become very sick right after her marriage, fall into a fever that would last fourteen days, and then have to nurse her husband back to wellness for the next several months.

After marriage she turns to her sisters and wives of childhood friends through letters that continue to have undertones of fear and profound emotions different than love. Whereas the letters between Klopstock and Meta center on each other's fondness and care for each other, those that Meta writes to her female friends, including her sister, show more personal fears and concerns, as well as interaction with her own social world, in general a more diverse gamut of human emotions. Especially the dreams she describes to her sister show prevalent images of death and sorrow. The letter she writes to Klopstock before the childbirth that will bring her own death seems eerily cogent of the reality of her fears. Given the high rate of infant mortality and death of the mother in childbirth, eighteenth-century women had much to fear before giving birth. Meta herself had witnessed her sister's difficult labor and her loss of her infant daughter, the subject of a sympathtic letter to her (457–58).

Most important, it is to her sisters that Meta talks about her writing. The topic of the writing process comes about through an interactive exhange of praise, encouragement, and suggestions. Within the exchange comes even the demand from Meta's sister Elisabeth Schmidt that Meta write a book in her usual engaging, descriptive style (402). As if responding to this suggestion, Meta reveals to her sisters the fact that she has been keeping a secret journal in which, unbeknownst to Klopstock, she has been recording what he has been doing (408). She thus hints that she has been preparing a biography of Klopstock. She also talks about the process of writing her *Briefe von Verstorbenen an Lebendige* [*Letters of the Dead to the Living*], talking about her modesty at even beginning such a work and then at reading what she had written (410–11). Her lengthy description of the process of writing the letters betrays that modesty though, as do her promises to send the poetry she has written (413) and her talk about how she came to write her tragedy called *Abel* (426–27).

Discussions about writing between the sisters usually center on Meta's marvelous letters and their value. Her sisters encourage her to write out her travel descriptions. They praise her for her letters and their value; Elisabeth Schmidt even stresses that Meta must have her letters published, suggesting her own son as a possible editor (386). Through her sisters' praise of her letters, Meta admits her talents: "Es sind wunderliche Dinger, meine Briefe, u ich mache sie manchmal aus einer närrischen Ursache noch wunderlicher" [They are odd things, my letters, and sometimes I make them even odder for some crazy reason] (366). The subject then turns to the familiar one of publication. She imagines a grandson eventually wanting to publish them because she had been Klopstock's wife. She surmises, however, that the naturalness of her style will prevent such a publication. In reading Madame de Sevigny's letters, she concludes that Sevigny had written such beautiful letters because she did not face the threat of publication.

Like Louise Gottsched, in fearing publication, Meta does not underestimate the quality or beauty of her letters. More frightful is the possibility of misinterpretation, especially considering publication within a context totally different from that in which the letters were written. Meta implies that she writes out of love and friendship, not out of fame in conjunction with a well-known author. The loss of control she has over her correspondence with a famous person seems to disturb her most, not the content of the letters or her own inadequacies. In her letters to Klopstock, Meta also continually recognizes the worth of her letters, although she more than once expresses her unwillingness to publish them. One particularly involved exchange shows her reservations about opening her letters up to the public. Spurred by a request by her friend Giseke that she acquire his letters back from the family of his dead friend, she is fearful about the possible fate of her own letters. Meta, like Giseke, is afraid her letters, meant for a private reader, will fall into the hands of another person. When Meta asks the friend's brother for the letters, he consents, but only after he has read them and bragged about them. This attitude, with which not only the correspondent's privacy is invaded, but also misinterpreted, disturbs Meta. To Klopstock, she writes that she does not want her letters to meet the same fate: "Ich weis wie verdrießlich dieses Giseke seyn muß, u: daher habe ich mir vorgestellt, daß es mir mit meinen Briefen auch einmal so gehen könnte. Ich wollte nicht für alle Welt daß meine Briefe an Sie gesehen würden, wenn ich das Unglück erleben sollte daß Sie stürben" [I know how vexed this Giseke must be and thus I have imagined that it could also happen to me with my letters at some time. For all the world I did not want that my letters to you would be seen, if I should experience the misfortune that you die] (98). She asks whether Klopstock has a friend in Copenhagen from whom she can demand back her letters should Klopstock die. If not, she requests, Klopstock should burn her letters. As for letters to her, she has kept them in good order. When she dies, she states, then all her correspondents who want their letters back can ask her sister, who will give them back unread. When Klopstock does not reply, she repeats her request, apologizing for her discussion of death in such as open manner, but stressing the seriousness of her concerns.(102). The discussion in their subsequent exchange turns to one about death, with Klopstock saying that when he dies, she will receive her letters back, sealed (106). Meta Klopstock, like Louise Gottsched, did not outlive her husband, and thus did not have to experience a feared loss of control over the publication of her writings.

Louise Gottsched's letters to Dorothea Runckel and the correspondence that Meta Klopstock held with her sisters, Elisabeth Moller Schmidt and Catharina Moller Dimpfel, and with her friend Eleonore Cruse Giseke are the first extant letters in German depicting sincere friendship between women. Both women are working in the shadows of their famous husbands and thus do not venture too far beyond expressing very positive feelings of love, friendship, and happiness. Between the lines, however, come interjections disclosing fear, loneliness, hesitation, and sorrow—sentiments that did not coincide with the preferred image of the happy wife, supposed to have been instilled with the subservient passivity to love her life.

Although both Louise Gottsched and Meta Klopstock shied away from having their letters published, neither underestimated their talents as letter writers or vehemently denied the possibility that someone could publish them after their death. Because of the foresight of other women, we have access, although not that easy, to these documents. In each case, we must ask what the picture of these women would be like without the letters to women friends. Without Gottsched's letters to Runckel, we would still see a witty, intelligent, curious woman who questions norms, but without sorrow, bitterness, or even anger. Meta Klopstock's letters would lack the private fears she had being a woman in the eighteenth century, as well as signs of her desires to write about her private life and even to publish those writings.

The histories of Louise Gottsched's and Meta Klopstock's letters and their publication intersect with issues of canonization and sexism, as discussed in earlier chapters. As we have seen, the two women's hesitations were not unusual, for a growing publishers' market threatened invasion into one's private life. A woman's reputation could rise and fall according to the decisions of collectors, editors, and publishers, most of them men. As more women entered into the literary market in the late eighteenth century, their influence in the powerful publishing realm opened up networking possibilities among female writers. These networks assumed various dimensions, such as solicitations for contributions to journals, requests for works to translate, or insightful critiques of completed works. In most cases, either because of immobility or etiquette, the letter sustained the literary work. As collectors, editors, even publishers of letters and private documents, women, often in conjunction with male partners, could hope to gain increased recognition.

Perhaps the greatest private collectors of correspondence in the early nineteenth century were Karl Varnhagen von Ense and Rahel Varnhagen, whose collection is now located in the Jagiellonian Library in Krakow. Before 1942, the entire collection was housed in the Rare Manuscript Division of the Prussian State Library in Berlin.[22] In 1942, most of that Division's manuscripts, which also included many original Beethoven and Mozart scores, were relocated to various places in eastern Germany, then believed to be safer. The location of the Manuscript Division remained publicly unknown until the late 1970s. At that point, it was discovered that the Varnhagen Collection, which had been in a monastery in the small town of Grussau in Silesia, had been in the Jagiellonian Library in Krakow since 1946. The fate of the collection has always been unclear: previous demands from the former GDR to return the materials were met with unwillingness on the part of Polish officials, and now German unification has dampened those demands somewhat as Germany seems faced with other financial and political pressures.

Helmina von Chézy's correspondence is one of the most voluminous in the Varnhagen collection. In their letters, the writers Dorothea Schlegel, Fanny Tarnow, George Sand, Charlotte von Ahlefeld, Amalie von Helvig, Elisa von Hohenhausen, Karoline Pichler, Amalie Schoppe, and Amalie Struve formed bonds with Chézy around such hardships as disastrous marriages, ostracism from society, and poverty, all largely due to their socially questionable status as writers. The correspondences show that friendships became the mainstay of the women's professional development, for the writers relied on each other for literary ideas, contributions to projects, constructive criticism of their work, and moral support. In many ways, these early nineteenth-century women carried on the seeds of the literary friendships we observed sprouting from Louise Gottsched's letters to Dorothea Runckel and Meta Moller Klopstock's correspondence with her sisters. Again, the letter nourishes support over time and distance. The later women, however, evoke a greater sense of confidence in their writing and express more appreciation for their epistolary tapestry. Chézy's drive to save letters she received and numerous drafts of letters she wrote affirm her values.

But entries in Karl Varnhagen von Ense's diary reveal that he destroyed more of Chézy's documents than those of anyone else in his entire collection. Before her death, Chézy had asked Varnhagen to help her find a publisher for her memoirs, *Unvergessenes. Denkwürdigkeiten aus dem Leben* [*Unforgotten. Memoirs From a Life*], which, due to blindness in later years of her life, she was dictating to her grandniece, Bertha Borngräber. Chézy had sent Varnhagen many of her correspondences and documents, and Borngräber continued to consult him on publication of the *Unvergessenes* after Chézy's death and to send him documents, which, he at one point states, fill all his chairs, tables, and window sills (27 March 1856).[23] To Varnhagen, the documents are, on the one hand, "ein ungeheurer Wust, ungeordnet, schmutzig, kaum ein Zehntheil erhaltungswerth" [an immense mess, disorganized, dirty, hardly a tenth worth keeping] (28 March 1856). Yet Chézy's documents also incite his fascination for the collection process. His remarks while sorting out the documents disclose a collector aware of the process of revealing one's individual values when selecting what to save and what to discard:

Wunderliche Gedanken, die solcher Nachlaß von Handschriften erweckt. Man erstaunt über die Maßstab der Wichtigkeit, den jeder Mensch für seine Angelegenheiten hat. Helmina von Chézy hat Blätter aufbewahrt, die nicht leicht sonst jemand unter seinen Papieren geduldet hätte! Die Akten zum Beispiel über ihren Gerichtshandel in München, wo ein Arzt sie bei der Polizei wegen liederlichen Lebenswandels, und daß ihre oder ihres Bettes Berührung zwei Kinder syphilitisch angesteckt habe, angezeigt hatte; sie unterzog sich einer gerichtslich-ärztlichen Besichtigung, wo sich denn freilich der Urgrund so schmachvoller Verläumdung ergab,—aber—! Dagegen hat sie alle Briefe von Chamisso verbrannt, und nur Auszüge bestehen lassen, in denen das Du nicht vorkommt; auch von Hammer finden sich keine vertrauliche [sic] Briefe, von Schirges nicht etc.—

[Odd thoughts that such an estate of manuscripts causes. One is astounded by the scale of importance that every person has for his affairs. Helmine von Chézy has saved papers that another person otherwise would not have easily tolerated among his papers. The files, for example, about her court process in Munich, where a doctor reported her to the police because of negligent moral conduct and that her touch or the touch of her bed had inflicted two children with syphilis; she went through a legal-medical examination where the reason for such disgraceful defamation came out,—but—! In contrast, she then burned all letters from Chamisso, and let survive only excerpts in which the familiar form of address was not used; there are also no intimate letters from Hammer, from Schirges none etc.] (29 March 1856)

There is an obvious difference between what Chézy deemed worthy in her life and what Varnhagen did. Whereas the papers she retains help defend her against a scandal that would ruin her reputation as a woman, Varnhagen is upset that she has tampered with her letters to a famous man. He does not wish to read her life as she lived it, but rather as it was lived through a man. With the consent of Börngräber, Varnhagen eventually destroys a third of the papers, as he remarks in his journal on 1 April 1856: "Sie willigt in die Zerstörung der unnützen und widerlichen Papiere, man kann rechnen, daß das Ge-päck dadurch um ein Drittheil erleichtert wird." [She agreed to the destruction of useless and disgusting papers, one can reckon, that the package was lightened by one third]. This destruction was unusual for Varnhagen.[24] Regarding his rumination over what Chézy had saved and not saved, it is obvious what Varnhagen destroyed, for letters from the correspondence with Chamisso still exist, whereas the documents from Chézy's legal proceedings are no longer present.

In the Academy-Archive of the Berlin-Brandenburger Academy of Sciences, located in Berlin, lies another large part of Chézy's docu-ments, a collection of over eight hundred letters, essays, and literary manuscripts.[25] Together with the documents in the Varnhagen Collec-tion, we can piece together a picture of a woman who was also very intrigued by the collection process. In the Academy Archive lie letters to and from women regarding literary activities, many of them re-written several times, some of them, such as letters to George Sand, existing in a form revised for publication. There are also manuscripts of essays, again often in several rewritten versions as if intended for eventual publication, about women authors. In addition, one finds documents, especially correspondence, regarding Chézy's various po-litical and social undertakings, documents whose form also hints at intentions to publish. In her conscious efforts to save documents that a collector such as Varnhagen might consider disorderly and extempo-raneous, the value Chézy placed on letter writing, friendship with women, and women's literary activities strengthens the connection between genre, gender, and historical tradition.

Without the extant letters in the Varnhagen collection and in the Academy Archive, we may never know about the importance that Chézy's friendships with women played in their personal and professional lives, for many of those letters have remained unpublished or unreferenced in Chézy's biographies. Despite Chézy's very prolific oeuvre and her acquaintance with numerous literary, musical, artistic, and political figures of her day, secondary literature on her is sparse, and accessible editions of her works scarce. She, like most of the other women examined in this study, seems to move freely in and out of traditional categories established for women writers. Her poetry and works, which included the libretto for Karl Maria von Weber's opera *Euryanthe* and the drama *Rosamunde*, which Schubert set to music, show images of love, nature, and heartache, which fit into categories traditionally deemed especially akin to the feminine nature. In her autobiography, she places herself in the role of mother to several people; her correspondents also often call her mother. As with many women who had relationships with famous men, scholarship has recognized her most for her correspondence with Adalbert de Chamisso and for her contacts with E. T. A. Hoffmann and Jean Paul.[26] Her wild, independent life and speculation on an illegitimate child she supposedly conceived with Chamisso have caused many to call more attention to her style of life than to her literary and social activities.[27]

In contrast to these conventional portrayals, her biography shows an independent person, divorced once, voluntarily separated from her second husband, and subsequently moving frequently to follow her own needs, often defying traditions others would like her to follow. She actively cultivated contacts with influential people and was engaged in many literary, social, and political activities. The author of the preface to a recent facsimile reprint of her memoir characterizes her as a feminist in the same vein as Germaine de Staël.[28] Indeed, many passages in the memoir suggest a progressive view of women's talents and efforts to dispel prejudices against women writers. She resisted Friedrich Schlegel's advice to publish anonymously or under a pseudonym, wishing instead to follow the French model, in which she saw more women using their own names. Unlike the Germans, Chézy believed, the French promotion of women's works coincides with a larger national pride and harmony (*Unvergessenes* I: 372–73). Her observations on the individual women she knew often extended to bold statements extolling women's writing in general. For example, in *Unvergessenes* she wrote about Dorothea Schlegel: "allein eine denkende Frau wie sie, schwingt sich immer zu einer geistigen Höhe hinauf, welche Männer erst erklimmen und zuweilen versäumen, sie zu besteigen. Dies gilt besonders bei Beurtheilungen des weiblichen Wesens, welches ein Mann nie in seiner ganzen Ausdehnung begreift" [even a thinking woman such as she pushes herself always to an intellectual height that men only begin to climb and occasionally neglect to ascend. This applies especially to the judgment of a female being, which a man in his entire scope never grasps] (I: 318). In all her contradictions, Chézy has been caught in the same bind as many other women writers, as the scholar Susanne Kord has said recently of Caroline Pichler, "not feminine enough for the nineteenth century, not feminist enough for the twentieth."[29]

Helmina von Chézy belonged to the third generation of a matri-archial literary family (her grandmother was Anna Louisa Karsch and her mother was Caroline von Klenke), an anomolous background for eighteenth-century Germany.[30] Although technically noble by birth, neither Helmina nor her foremothers were privileged or wealthy. Confronted with material obstacles to their literary careers, all three women showed how their precociousness could garner infor-mal patronage to help them realize their literary ambitions. In fact, Helmina's own account of her life represents ways to reconcile the poverty she encounters with her aristocratic tendencies. But in each woman's life, the marriage her mother arranged for her proved a major obstacle to a productive literary career. Writing for women was still a domestic activity, and the mother—even though a writer herself—let social ambition overpower development of the daughter's intellect. When Helmina was sixteen, her impoverished mother, Caro-line von Klencke, arranged a marriage with Karl Freiherr von Hastfer, despite Helmina's defiance against the marriage, in the same way that Anna Karsch had arranged Caroline's marriage. But the marriage between Helmina and Karl did not succeed; a year later they were divorced. In 1801, the penniless, eighteen-year-old Helmina went to Paris to join her friend and teacher, the Countess Stephanie Felicité de Genlis.

The Varnhagen collection contains thirteen letters from Madame de Genlis to Helmina von Hastfer written between 1800 and 1803. In the collection are five letters, 1825 and undated from Helmina to de Genlis, and a five-page sketch of de Genlis's work and character.[31] The young Helmina von Hastfer met de Genlis within a circle of other young women, including Dorothea Mendelssohn Veit and Veit's friend Ester Gad, to whom de Genlis was teaching French and offering literary encouragement. De Genlis had undergone a stormy life her-self, having left a disastrous marriage, been expelled from both Paris and Prussia due to political distrust and suspicion, and begun her prolific, successful writing career at the age of thirty-six. When Fredrick William III allowed her to live in Berlin, she prospered and offered a powerful role model for the younger salon women.

In her letters, de Genlis writes about introducing Chézy to different people who would help her find work translating and writing, mostly journalistic articles about French art and literature from the perspective of a German. De Genlis's portayal of the two women's relationship is more one of mother to daughter than one of two friends equal in age and abilities, for she calls her "mon cher enfant" ["my dear child"] and stresses that "the young Helmina" should look to her as a mother. Still, the type of encouragement she gives to Chézy displays characteristics of collegiality and understanding. De Genlis consoles Helmina when her marriage to Baron Hastfer goes awry. She spurs her on to continue her work, to read a lot, to write abstracts of everything she reads, and to keep herself informed. Above all, she advises her to attach herself to moral concerns, thereby making less noise but going far.

Friends would later blame Helmina's friendship with de Genlis for making Helmina "vain and worldly;" subsequent critics blamed Caroline von Klencke for "letting" her daughter follow Madame De Genlis.[32] These accusations are probably founded in part on Chézy's own provocative admittance in her *Unvergessenes* that "Ehrgeiz und Neigung bestimmten mich, eine literarische Laufbahn zu suchen" [Ambition and inclination forced me to look for a literary carrier] (1: 225). Indeed, the relationship between de Genlis and Chézy turned out to be less than idyllic, but perhaps accomplished more for Chézy's own independence than any other she had. Chézy later described in her memoir the stormy turn, based on jealousy from de Genlis's foster son, and de Genlis's own jealousy of Helmina's increasing fame in Paris (1: 177). In fact, she keeps and uses the letters that de Genlis has written to her as proof that the older writer really had presented herself as the warm, caring mentor who had wanted the young Helmina Hastfer to live with her in Paris (1: 229–30). As letters reveal, and as Helmina would later admit, however, without de Genlis's help, the young Helmina would not have survived in Paris. Essays by Chézy show her continual praise for the literary talents of de Genlis along with other French writers. The relationship with de Genlis also represents a lifelong fondness Chézy had for French women writers and their works, including George Sand, Germaine de Staël, and Madame Récamier. Her interests led to translations, essays, and letters.[33]

The eighteen-year-old Helmina von Hastfer's survival in Paris was also due to another friendship with a major woman writer—Dorothea Mendelssohn Veit—and to Veit's partner Friedrich Schlegel, both of whom had moved to Paris from Jena in 1801. Dorothea and Helmina knew each other from Berlin, where both had been under the tutelage of Madame de Genlis.[34] Dorothea's father, Moses Mendelssohn, had also known Helmina's grandmother, Anna Louisa Karsch. From Madame de Genlis's house, Helmina moved in with Friedrich and Dorothea, taking up residence at Rue de Clichy 19, at the foot of the Montmartre. There the two encouraged each other's interests. Through connections with de Genlis and the Schlegels, Helmina was able to support herself in Paris from translation, journalism, and editorial work. Such projects, as Eva Walter points out, were not easy for many German women to acquire.[35] Women's letters, Helmina's notwithstanding, often contain requests for work. If one woman had too much to do, she often passed some on to another or collaborated on a project. Together, Dorothea and Helmina took advantage of the cultural life in Paris, visiting art galleries, the theater, and libraries, looking for new material to contribute to Friedrich's journal, *Europa*, and to his eventual collection of medieval French legends, which he would later publish under his name. Salon gatherings also offered the opportunity to make necessary contacts. In the Veit-Schlegel household Helmina met Anton von Chézy, a professor of Oriental languages, whom she married in 1805, and then supported in his work.

The Varnhagen Collection holds thirty-six letters from Dorothea and Friedrich Schlegel from 1803–35 and two letters from Helmina to Dorothea dated 1812 and 1818.[36] All of the letters are filed in Friedrich Schlegel's folder, a classification that coincides with the subsumation of women's lives under men's. Some of these letters have been published in part or in their entirety in existing editions.[37] Interesting for my study here, however, is a comparison of some of the published versions with original documents. Many letters did not find their way into the first collection of Dorothea's letters, Raich's edition, published in 1881. In 1914, Wieneke published a more complete collection, but even though he includes more letters, he has excerpted many of them. Comparisons between published and original letters reveal that Wieneke cut out most of the comments that show the everyday struggles of the the two women and the way they supported each other, namely financially and through performing small tasks for each other.

When Dorothea and Friedrich Schlegel moved to Cologne in 1804, they both continued to write to Helmina. Dorothea's letters talk about her first impressions of Cologne, which she considers a rather dull city. The Schlegels have continual financial problems; in fact, at one point Dorothea writes about how she is embarrassed because she cannot pay back the money she owes Helmina and admits that her inability to pay Helmina back caused her to put off writing.[38] She relies on Helmina to settle some affairs in Paris, to inform people of her address, and to send her the things she had left behind when they moved. Raich and Wieneke have left out most of these daily concerns in the published letters.[39]

As with the correspondence of Louise Gottsched and Meta Klopstock with female friends, the literary basis for Dorothea's friendship with Helmina is strong. At the end of one letter, in which Dorothea has described in detail the festivities that surrounded Napoleon's visit to Cologne, she offers suggestions should Helmina wish to publish the letter as an article.[40] Several passages in the letters focus on what the women are working on and evidence their collaborative literary endeavors. The evidence of this kind of epistolary networking does not appear consistently in the edited, published letters, due to omissions. Such is the case of a postscript from Dorothea in Paris on 25 August 1804, which reads: "Liebe. Hätten Sie Lust, den dramatisirten Roman von Lacretelle für uns zu übersetzen? es wird Ihnen nicht schwer werden es wäre allenfalls eine Arbeit in Neun Stücken. Wenn Sie ihn wollen, so schicken wir ihn Ihnen sogleich" [Dear. Would you want to translate the dramatized novel by Lacratelle for us? it will not be difficult for you it would be at most a work in nine parts. If you want, then we will send it to you immediately]. Wieneke published the rest of the letter, but, without ellipses, left the postscript out.[41] Dorothea talks about her work in 1804 on "einen alten Roman in Manuscript" [an old novel in manuscript] that she has found and asks Helmina "wenn du also noch Zeit und Lust zum Übersetzen hast, halte dich daran" [if you still have the time and desire to translate, stick to it].[42] In fact, Helmina had helped Dorothea translate and rewrite the story of the Arthurian magician Merlin, published in 1804 when both women were in Paris. In the letter, Dorothea was referring to her work on the story *Lother and Maller,* for which she had discovered an unpublished medieval manuscript and which Friedrich later published in 1805 and then included, along with the Merlin story, in his own collected works (1823).[43] Dorothea continues to ask Helmina about the work she is doing—about translations of novels by the French writer Louise Françoise de Lavaillière (1746–1830), who wrote a biography of Madame de Genlis, and the politician and publicist Pierre-Louis Lacretelle (1751–1824).[44] Helmina relates in her memoirs how Friedrich had always shown skepticism toward her ambitions to write, advising her to publish her works under a pseudonym, advice that she does not follow (1: 248), and even goes so far as to publish her translations under his own name.[45] In contrast, Dorothea offers support that recognizes Helmina's talents more for their own sake. She writes in 1804 how much Helmina's operetta, *Euryanthe*, had pleased viewers, including Friedrich.[46] In later life, Dorothea compliments Helmina on the work she has done and encourages the friend to ensure that someone else will carry it on: "Du hast ein schönes Werk begonnen, andere müssen es wieder führen" [You have begun such a beautiful work, others must carry it on].[47] Wieneke edited this passage out of his edition with the letter. Through Dorothea, Helmina met influential artists and writers such as Novalis and Frau von Krüdener, and gained "eine weite Uebersicht über die Geschichte der Kunst" [a broad overview of the history of art] (*Unvergessenes* I: 250). For Helmina, Dorothea offered a model of a woman who could continue to write the second part of her novel *Florentin*, publish articles in the newspaper *Europa*, translate the Merlin story, engage in extensive correspondence, and remain culturally active, all despite the many required household duties of mending Friedrich's clothes and being his secretary (*Unvergessenes* I: 261).

A main topic of their correspondence is personal health, one that editors in general have had a hard time considering public enough to include in collections of women's letters. One passage that remains conspicuously absent from collections of Dorothea Schlegel's letters is that in which she wittily offers Helmina von Chézy advice about her health:

Es ist sonst mit der Gesundheit der Frauen wie mit der Jungfrauschaft, man erhält sie nicht wieder.—Alles was man thun kann, ist, sich seinen Zustand so erträglich als möglich zu machen, es bleibt nichts anders übrig. Lebe einförmig, weiche heftigen Gemuthsbewegungen aus, man muß immer auch die *unausweichbaren* etwas mitrechnen, beschränke dich selbst, trachte nicht nach Hochmuth, und kleide dich wärmer; was das letzte betrifft, so hoffe ich man wird wenn das Projekt einer National Tracht zu Stande kömmt mit darauf Rücksicht nehmen, und den Frauen verständlich machen, daß sie keine Statuen sind, also auch eines andern Costums bedürfen. willst du oder kannst du von allen diesen Regeln keine befolgen, so mußt du schwache Nerven ertragen und leiden, so giebt keine andre alternative . . .

[Otherwise it is the same with the health of women as with virginity, one does not regain it.—All that one can do is to make one's situation as bearable as possible, there is nothing else. Live simply, dispel strong emotional sentiments, one must also consider the *inevitable*, limit yourself, don't strive for arrogance, and dress yourself more warmly; in relation to the latter, I thus hope that when the project of a national costume materializes, people will take into consideration and make women understand that they are not statues, thus they need another costume. if you do not want or are not able to follow any of these rules, then you must bear and suffer weak nerves, then there is no other alternative . . .]

The very personal nature of the conversation here leads to speculation about why the passage did not find its way into an edition of Dorothea's letters. Concerns about health are not uninteresting or unimportant; more likely, references to women's sexuality embarrassed the editor. Indeed, Dorothea's advice and opinions extend beyond the private realm to confront women's public image. For health reasons, women should demand more sensible clothes. Such passages, in which women display awareness of their sexuality and of the dissonance between public images and personal needs, disclose the letter's role as a vehicle for questioning.

Dorothea's and Helmina's friendship continued congenially until Dorothea's death in 1839. Dorothea consoled Helmina after her divorce from Chézy in 1810. Writing from Vienna, Dorothea offers her a place for refuge, but warns that Vienna is not the most amenable city for literary activities—one needs connections and acquaintances to get ahead (14/15 April 1810; Wieneke 414–19). In 1829, when Friedrich Schlegel dies, Dorothea thanks Helmina for her consolation, saying "Du warst Eine der Ersten die mir in meiner großen Trübsal mit Liebe und Trost entgegenkam, wie sollte ich das wohl vergessen können!" [You were one of the first who offered me consolation and love in my great depression, how would I have been able to forget that].[48] The last letter in the collection is from 1835, in which Dorothea jokes about a brightly colored shawl that Helmina had sent her. Dorothea returns it, asking instead for something less bright—dark blue, green, brown, purple—but not the red that Helmina had sent.[49]

In the correspondence between Dorothea and Helmina, what might seem like a few passages and letters omitted here and there from collections harks back to the same fragmentation that has often occurred when portraying a woman's life and literary deeds. The exclusion of voice points to a larger omission of many women's lives from the dominant culture. The interested scholar must hunt in five different editions to piece together a friendship that lasted over thirty years. Due to the trail of omissions, one is still not sure of having viewed the whole picture. Granted, the hunt for the personal documents of any writer, male or female, can be extremely involved. But more often than not, contacts that women fostered with one another become couched in the lives of men. The chase must often start with looking through editions of men's correspondence. Unfortunately, the contacts women had with one another often get lost in the shuffle.

After her separation from Chézy in 1810, Helmina left France with her two sons and spent the next years traveling around Germany to garner support for care of war invalids and hospital nursing, a patriotic cause she advocated. Later, she also compiled documents on workers in Austria's *Salzkammergut* in an effort to fight their exploitation. Her letters and published works show a solidarity she wished to cultivate betwen women writers. She translated works by Madame de Genlis, wrote a biography of her mother, Karoline von Klencke, published her travel reports, her poetry, with the subtitle "Enkelin der Karschin" [granddaughter of Karschin] (1812), and her short stories, and compiled with Fanny Tarnow a two-volume collection of stories by women entitled *Iduna. Schriften deutscher Frauen gewidmet den Frauen* [*Iduna. Writings of German Women Dedicated to Women*] (1820).

Clearly, in all of her travels and writings, Helmina was greatly influenced by and paid tribute to the many women authors she befriended. Throughout her active life, which led her to live in Heidelberg, Frankfurt am Main, Darmstadt, Dresden, Vienna, Munich, Berlin, and Geneva, she established strong contacts with other women writers, artists, and cultural figures, including Amalie von Helvig, Luise Brachmann, Charlotte von Ahlefeld, and Elisa von der Recke. Her memoirs are filled with praise for several women, whose social circles helped her establish literary, artistic, and musical contacts to further her work. She defends the works of women against criticism from men.[50]

Several of Chézy's epistolary friendships with women demonstrate the inextricable link between politics, literature, and personal lives, including those with the writers Bettine von Arnim and Amalie Struve.[51] In the case of Caroline Pichler (1769–1843), letters show how Chézy turned to her for help for a political cause. Without ever meeting Pichler, Chézy asked if Pichler could sell a volume of poetry whose proceeds were designated to help poor workers in the *Salzkammergut*. Pichler was a successful and prolific author and friend of Dorothea Schlegel, perhaps the main reason Chézy found her so approachable. Her *oeuvre* includes eight novels and three historical works, ten dramas, ten volumes of short stories, numerous poems and idylls, educational treatises and essays, translations, letters, and her memoirs.[52] Her collected works, which she published herself, comprise fifty-three volumes. In her works and her close ties with numerous other women writers, Pichler shares with Chézy a high respect and value of female friendship.[53]

In the Varnhagen collection there are thirty-one letters of Pichler to Chézy, spanning the years 1818 to at least 1840 (many of the last letters are undated).[54] Pichler's first two extant letters document that the collaborative effort to benefit the Salzkammergut workers was successful: Pichler was able to sell books within her circle of women friends in Vienna. In a letter on 18 July 1818, Pichler gives an account of the books she has sold and to whom. What begins as a business endeavor soon moves toward being an extensive epistolary exchange in which Pichler shares with Chézy what she is writing and her ideas on social and political changes she witnesses.

In general, Pichler's literary works have been viewed as archconservative and patriotic.[55] In her letters to Chézy, however, her views are not one-sided. On the subject of women's emancipation, she expresses her hesitations. In reference to criticisms she had voiced against Rahel and Bettina, Pichler writes: "Eben so ist mir das Emancipation ein Ärgerniß, dann würden die Weiber aufhören Weiber zu seyn, und doch keine Männer werden, sondern auch ein krankhaftes Zwittergeschlecht" [Likewise, the emanicipation is an irritation to me, then women would stop being women, and yet not become men, but rather even a pathological hermaphroditic sex] (17 January 1840). This fear that emanication will blur demarcations between the sexes does not mean, however, that she blatantly accepts subservience to any domineering attitudes of men. In another letter, she laments the fact that Alexander Maltitz, a poet and mutual friend, has not entered into any serious love relationship. His sophisticated education, she claims, should make him desirable for many women. But she also sees women as becoming more frivolous, an attitude due mostly to men themselves, who "ziehen sich in allen Gesellschaften von den Frauen zurück, und überlassen sich am liebsten mit der Pfeife im Mund ihrer rohen Bequemlichkeit" [withdraw themselves in all social circles from women, and prefer to leave themselves to their crude comfort with their pipe in their mouth] (6 Feb. 1830). Her fear of erasing any differences between the sexes seems rooted in a fear of a subsequent devaluing of women's roles in general, a dilemma that has followed feminists into the present day. Pichler's emotional and literary ties with many other women, as well as her numerous defenses of women writers whom she believed were misrepresented, evidence her decision to value women's roles, even if that led to polarization. During the cholera epidemic, she laments how hard a time it is for women.[56] In discussing her waning literary production, she cites the required feminine household duties as hindering factors. But those factors lead her to talk about a much more pressing one of conflicting values. She finds it increasingly difficult to combine the way "in der allein ich auch noch künstig arbeiten würde können" [in which I alone would be able also still to work artistically] and "die Erfindungen und Bemühungen der mechanischen, ökonomischen, und polytechnischen Trachtens" [the discoveries and efforts of the mechanical, economical, and polytechnical endeavors] (4 July 1822). Reference to her work as "artistic" contradicts any claims that she was writing merely for financial security, a common excuse women often used to deny ambition. Her statement also questions the ability to combine those values traditionally seen as feminine— concerns over beauty, love, children—with the traditionally masculine ones of economics and technology.

Pichler's initial willingness to support Chézy in her efforts on behalf of oppressed workers evolves into admiration for Chézy's perseverance in fighting for social causes. In 1830 Pichler expresses her respect while admitting her own inadequacies: "Ihren Muth, noch mehr aber Ihre Geduld muß ich bewundern die Ihnen die Mitwirkung bey solchen Geschäften neulich machen. Mich würde zu allererst Unwille u. Indignation zu sehr aufreitzen, wenn ich Unglückliche durch die Form der Gesetze, wider welche freylich nichts einzuwenden noch zu unternehmen ist, erdrückt sehen mußte" [I must admire your courage, but still more your patience, which your participation in such affairs recently afforded you. I would be too aggitated, mostly by unwillingness and indignation, if I would have to see the unfortunate people oppressed by the form of the law against which nothing could be done] (6 February 1830).

Chézy and Pichler finally met in Baden in 1823, where Pichler spent her summers. After Chézy moved to Vienna in 1823, the two women seemed to have regular contact with one another. Pichler's letters talk about meeting each other at the opera and in Dorothea Schlegel's house. They exchange books to read and offer comments; Pichler invites Chézy to perform a reading in her house of *Rosamunde*.

Chézy held the correspondence with Pichler in such high regard that she did not return Pichler's letters to her daughter when she requested them for Pichler's biography. Chézy valued the correspondence as an important mediator between the public concerns and private desires to address those concerns. In her memoirs she admits that a part of her correspondence with Pichler was really intended for a third person, for it treated the workers in the *Salzkammergut*. Along with describing that real situation, so claims Chézy, the correspondence also conveys a sincere image of the two women's integrity and their warm friendship with each other (*Unvergessenes* II, 344).

The extant correspondence from Madame de Genlis, Dorothea Schlegel, Amalie Struve, and Caroline Pichler suggests, for the most part, fruitful, receptive, and warm friendships, although we must also question how much of the existing material was selectively saved by both Varnhagen and Chézy. It would be unrealistic, however, to give the impression that all of Chézy's friendships with women proved unproblematic and thereby imply that in general women writers' relationships with each other were not complicated and diverse. The relationships that developed between Chézy and the writers Fanny Tarnow and Amalie Schoppe display complexities and strife, thus suggesting that solidarity among women did not always materialize nor was it always desirable, given certain conditions.

The Varnhagen collection holds forty-three letters from Amalie Schoppe to Chézy written between 1820 and 1844, nineteen letters from Fanny Tarnow to Chézy from 1818 to 1820, two letters from Chézy to Tarnow, and three from Chézy to Schoppe.[57] Of all Chézy's collected correspondence, Varnhagen seemed to enjoy the one concerning Schoppe and Tarnow the most. In his journal on 28 March 1856, he talks about listening to his niece, Ludmilla Assing, reading the two women's letters aloud: ". . . zu unsrem großen Ergötzen; da wir beide Damen so genau kennen, war uns alles erheblich und bezeichnen" [to our great pleasure; because we knew both women so well; everything was so relevant and significant to us]. On the next day he writes that he and Ludmilla have continued their reading, finding the quarreling, first between Fanny Tarnow and Amalie Schoppe, and then between Tarnow and Chézy "äußerst komisch" [highly strange]. His perception falls back on stereotypes of the jealous, emotional women who are unable to form friendships with one another: "Das Schriftstellerwesen der Frauen erscheint in seiner eigensten Gestalt und Blöße; die weiblichen Leidenschaften, persönliche Eitelkeit und Gefallsucht, leichtes Anschließen und herbe Unverträglichkeit, Tugendstolz und Tugendprahlerei, Neid, aber auch Noth und Bedürftigkeit, Fleiß, guter Wille, alles stellt sich klar an dem Tag" [The character of the woman writer appears in its most particular form and exposure; the feminine passions, personal vanity and craving for admiration, easy agreement and bitter cantankerousness, virtuous pride and virtuous boasting, envy, but also need and neediness, diligence, good will, everything became clear that day]. He sees the years after the Napoleonic wars as "die goldne Zeit dieser Schriftstellerinnen" [the golden age of these women writers]. Drawing on what he sees as a role reversal, he finds that tender, weak men, such as Fouqué, Loeben, Malsburg, and Wilhelm Hensel, were the heroes; the heroines were Amalie Schoppe, Helmina von Chézy, Frau von Hohenhausen, Amalie von Helvig, Frau Schopenhauer, Karoline Pichler, "noch kräftig und hervorragend" [still powerful and distinguished]. Thus, it seems that only in a time when the men were weak and the women strong, could the women become respected writers. Still, that time did not lack strife amongst the women.

Chézy, being a friend to both Tarnow and Schoppe, at first acted as mediator between the two women. According to Schoppe, Tarnow asked her to be a partner in a school for young girls in Hamburg. Upon arriving in Hamburg, Schoppe found out that Tarnow had backed out of the plan and left Schoppe with no economic means to support her family. Schoppe writes about how her high respect for Tarnow had been crushed: ". . . . daß ich diese Fanny so grenzenlos liebte, daß ich mein ganzes Wesen ihr so aufgeschlossen hatte, daß ich ihr Alles. . . . hingegeben hatte!" [that I loved this Fanny so boundlessly that I had opened up my entire being to her, that I had submitted everything to her!] (6 August 1820). Schoppe's letters to Chézy in the 1820s show the former's disappointment turn to anger and then bitterness as she deals with the economic ramifications of the decision. Chézy becomes a sounding board for Schoppe's hardships—her stormy marriage, her responsibilities as a mother of three children, her humiliation as a teacher, and her struggles to write.

The lack of all the letters from Chézy makes it hard to discern her reaction. In her two letters to Tarnow and three to Schoppe that remain, she appears understanding yet diplomatic. The absence of more hostile reactions signals Chézy's possible selective destruction of letters, however, for at the same time as the Schoppe-Tarnow conflict, public documents show that Chézy's friendship with Tarnow was undergoing its own trying times. In her *Unvergessenes*, Chézy spends no good words on Tarnow or her letters, remarking on their deceptiveness: "Ich möchte ihre Briefe, die ich noch besitze, mit einem süßen Saft vergleichen, dessen Bestandtheile man nicht kennt und ohne Untersuchung hinunterschlürft" [I would like to compare her letters, which I still possess, with a sweet juice whose ingredients one does not know and swallows down without examination] (II, 240).

In 1820, Tarnow moved to Dresden, where she continued her contacts with Chézy, and together, using the name "Verein deutscher Schriftstellerinnen," the two women published their two-volume work *Iduna. Schriften deutscher Frauen gewidmet den Frauen.* Through documents in the Varnhagen collection, one can surmise that there must have been public accusations that the friendship between Chézy and Tarnow was falling apart. In an open letter to the editor of the *Bermerker* in 1820, Chézy refutes any rumors that publication of *Iduna* had caused conflict between her and Tarnow. She also questions why the private lives of women writers should continually come up for public judgment, for she does not want the quality of her writing being judged by unfounded rumors concerning her private life. The answer from the editor is vindictive against all women writers; if a woman writer wants to voice her opinion publicly through her works, he states bitterly, then she must learn the consequences of such actions. An unpublished essay dated 18 July 1844 entitled "Ueber Amalie Schoppe geboren Weise u Stellen aus ihren Briefen seit 1819" ["About Amalie Schoppe, born Weise, and Passages From Her Letters Since 1819"] documents Chézy's defense of Schoppe against Tarnow's accusations and thus proves Chézy's ultimate alliance with Schoppe in the matter. Interesting for purposes here is that Chézy uses letters as proof for her arguments.[58]

We still have a lot to explore on the topic of women's friendship. Private correspondences are rich resources for discerning the professional contacts women needed to pursue their literary careers. They also unlock important perspectives on the intersection between women's personal and public lives. The more one explores those perspectives, the more one realizes the large impact friendship had on women's writing and professional opportunities. For those letters with difficult accessibility, such as Louise Gottsched's and Meta Moller Klopstock's, we must rely on editions published within the confines of an ideology that found women writers threatening and their contacts with one another undesirable and unfeasible. For those resources to which we have gained access, a reevaluation of almost each letter unveils another circle of friends who influence each other's writing immensely. Madame de Genlis sponsored Chézy's move to Paris; Chézy wrote biographical reports on de Genlis and translated works by Louise de Lavaillière, who also wrote a biography of de Genlis; Fanny Tarnow and Amalie Schoppe were friends and professional partners; Tarnow and Chézy compiled an anthology of women's writing together. The list of connections goes on, proving the value of networking through letters for women throughout the late eighteenth and early nineteenth centuries.

# 4

## "Thousand Lives, Thousand Forms": Letter Writing and Publication

Mein einziger Wunsch ist, daß ich tausend Leben haben, tausend Formen beleben, alle Verhältnisse durchirren, alle möglichen frohen Empfindungen fühlen könnte, und meine einzige Sorge, daß irgend eine Fähigkeit ungeweckt in meiner Seele schlummern, irgend eine Freude ungefühlt vor mir vorüber rauschen möchte.

[My sole wish is that I have a thousand lives, live in a thousand forms, err my way through all relationships, to be able to feel all possible happy emotions, and my sole worry that any ability would slumber in my soul, any kind of happiness would rush by me unfelt.][1]

READING the eighteenth-century's most well-known epistolary novels—*Pamela, Clarissa, Die Leiden des jungen Werthers, Geschichte des Fräuleins von Sternheim*—and then comparing the correspondence of Meta Moller Klopstock, one wonders why the latter correspondence, too, could not belong to the genre of epistolary literature. The argument that a novel needs an involved, engaging plot is not convincing. After all, as Altman points out, not much "happens" in an epistolary novel; rather, its success depends largely on its ability to carry out themes relating to the psychological workings of an inner self reckoning with forces in the outside world.[2] In fact, in the Klopstock correspondence, a lot does "happen"—Klopstock's unrequited love for his cousin and his reliance on Meta for advice; Meta's busy life in Hamburg; the transformation of their friendship into love; their courtship that Meta's family could not condone; their travels together and apart. As these events unfold, so do the personalities of the two correspondents.

Such speculation leads to further questioning as to whether letters need only serve as documents for biographical facts that support ideas in published works, as they have in many cases. Could letters

112

also be read in conjunction with an author's entire *oeuvre* as texts that contain repeated metaphors and images, insightful reflections, and imaginative narrations? Such a reading would not discount the biographical value of letters. Nor would it state that letters always belong in the class of belles lettres. Rather, this approach suggests a way of divulging, as Leonore Hoffmann describes, "the process of giving shape and meaning with language,"[3] and, to pluralize James Olney's phrase, of constructing "metaphors of selves" to an individual or large audience.[4] Letters can offer women the ability to develop a thousand lives, a thousand forms within a social milieu that seldom provides comparable options. The impact that such a reading could have on the intersection of literature with history warrents further exploration.

The issue of publication pervades any discussion of letter writing. As I pointed out in chapter two, in the eighteenth century a main criterion for whether a letter was good was whether it was publishable. And vice versa, a letter written without intent of publication was deemed more authentic; thus the various rhetorical devices— stories about the "real" letters, notes from editors, and so on—that played with readers' expectations about published letters. In evaluating the literary merit of letters, scholars have attempted to discern signs of the writer consciously corresponding to an eventually larger audience than one correspondent. As we saw in the letters of Louise Gottsched, Meta Klopstock, and Helmina von Chézy, letters of friendship exchanged among women served as a means to promote publication, gain confidence in writing through encouragement, network, find publishers, establish and contribute to journals, and lend money and space for writing.

In describing the role letters have assumed in the literary history of women, recent feminist scholars have often stressed the transition from letter writing to novels, whereby the act of writing letters led to encouraging women to publish in one of the most popular genres of the eighteenth century, the epistolary novel.[5] Lydia Schieth, in her study on eighteenth-century novels by women, questions that assumption, pointing out that very few well-known women letter writers wrote novels (she mentions as examples Meta Klopstock, Dorothea Runckel, Gottschedin, Karschin, Caroline Schlegel, Frau Rat Goethe).[6] Further, the number of epistolary novels by both men and women in the eighteenth century represents a phenomenon that cannot be explained solely by the participation of women in literary production. Rather, particular characteristics of the epistolary form offered a means for writers not confident in other ways of psychological analysis to express the inner emotions of their protagonists.[7]

Schieth's points are well taken, but she dismisses too hastily the importance of the connection between women and letter writing, which Bovenschen and others have observed. First, although Bovenschen's remarks occur in the context of talking about the epistolary novel, she extends the transition from letter writing to all forms of literature in general. The letter is an "entrance ticket into literature."[8] Bovenschen is not denying the fact that men, too, used letter writing as a literary device. She also would probably not disagree with men's and women's common fascination with the epistolary form in other discourse. No scholar has claimed that *only* women write letters, but many have assumed a natural or socialized connection between women and letter writing, as we have seen in the first chapters of this book. Perceptions of that connection as natural relegate women according to their biology to the private sphere. Coupling social conditions with writing reexamines the value of letter writing in relation to other literary productions and the effect of gender norms on writing. Hence, in comparison with men, the quantity and quality of the letters women wrote in relation to their overall literary output is remarkable.

A second problem with Schieth's argument is that it draws on models of women letter writers who have become known mostly through traditional methods of evaluating letter writing. As discussed previously, a woman's connections with famous men, her aberrant personal life, or her literary productivity, and not textual analysis, have usually determined the merits of her letters, as is the case with all the women Schieth cites as examples. As new scholarship on previously unnoticed letter writers appears, on Helmine von Chézy, Therese Huber, and Sophie Albrecht, those criteria need reassessing, as do the actual letters of women who have become known more for other works and deeds than for their epistolary activities.[9] Also, as letters by Louise Gottsched and Meta Klopstock demonstrate, the language in which women often couch hesitation to publish their letters can be ambiguous. Social norms cause us to look at lesser-studied contexts, such as their rapport with other women, to evaluate desires to publish their private writings.

This chapter concentrates on letters by Anna Louisa Karsch (1722–91), Sophie Mereau (1770–1806), and Karoline von Günderrode (1780–1806), three publishing writers during the latter half of the eighteenth century and the early part of the nineteenth century, in order to investigate the relationship between letter writing, publication, and gender. An analysis of their letters with reference to their published works will explore the extent to which letter writing offered them a viable literary mode whereby they used metaphors and narrative techniques while discovering the capablities of their "selves." In the space of this chapter, I cannot present a comprehensive analysis of their correspondence; that would require individual book-length studies in conjunction with historical/critical editions of the letters. My purpose is to bring to the forefront the aesthetic quality of their letters and to challenge the role traditionally relegated to letters as only enlighteners of life histories. My analysis will question Schieth's views while also going further than Bovenschen and others in assessing the literary worth of the three writer's letters. Whereas Bovenschen classifies the letter as a "pre-aesthetic genre" for women, I see it as an aesthetic genre. Karsch, Mereau, and Günderrode coupled their preoccupation with letter writing, with all its advantages and disadvantages, with published experimentations in form and genre. Such a reading does not eliminate the possibility of finding supporting biographical information in letters, but does ultimately complicate use of that information.

Biographies of Anna Louisa Karsch have relied primarily on her own letters for pertinent information, although most of these letters were not published in any accessible form until nearly one hundred forty years after her death, and even then heavily edited.[10] The most well-known of her autobiographical epistles are those she wrote in response to J. G. Sulzer's request to write him her life story as part of a foreword to her collection of poems. Sulzer, a professor of aesthetics, lay the letters aside and wrote his own foreword, which appeared in the 1764 edition of poems.[11] Karschin's daughter, Caroline von Klenke, too, did not consider the letters when she published another poetry collection by Karsch.[12] In 1819 Achim von Arnim published some of her letters to his grandfather, Baron von Labes, and in the 1830s some of the letters to Sulzer were published in the magazine "Zeitgenossen." Various letters about the parade of Friedrichs in Berlin and Goethe's visit had been published in the 1870s. Elizabeth Hausmann's biography in 1933 was the first attempt to publish a collection of Karsch's letters. The volume contains mostly Karsch's letters to Gleim, but still remains the most extensive edition. Unfortunately, the letters are, as Hausmann admits, heavily abridged, and although she assures readers that, despite omissions, the letters remain unchanged, there is no explanation of what she left out or the criteria she used for such omission. Hausmann hints at her desire to paint a picture of Karsch that would illuminate her natural maternal instincts and thus justify her unconventional independence as a woman. When Hausmann points out that nobody had paid much attention to Karsch, even the turn-of-the-century women's movement, she states: "Vielleicht mit Recht. Die Karschin war keine Frauen rechtlerin. O nein, sie war nur eine arme, mutige Frau, die durch die Gabe, die ihr die Natur verliehen, für sich und ihre Kinder und Kindeskinder sorgen wollte und sorgen mußte" [Maybe correctly. The Karschin was no suffragette. Oh no, she was only a poor, courageous woman, who through the talent that nature lent her wanted to take care of and had to take care of herself and her children and her children's children.].[13]

An initial reading of the letters to Sulzer, however, reveals a remarkable life story hardly compatible with conventional norms for femininity in eighteenth-century Prussia. Karsch was born Anna Louisa Dürbach to a lower-class family on a farm near Crossen/Oder in northern Silesia. Her mother had been raised by a noblewoman and then became her maidservant and cook. Her father was an innkeeper, but died when she was six. Shortly before his death, Anna's great-uncle had taken her under his care in Posen, where she learned to read and write. He even planned to teach her Latin, an unusual education for young girls, but her mother, who had remarried, fetched her back to care for the younger siblings. Until the age of sixteen, Anna cared for the children and livestock and voraciously read novels and devotional literature that a neighboring shepherd lent to her. When she was sixteen, her mother selected Hirsekorn, a weaver, to be Anna's husband. It was during this time that she began to compose verse as she sat at the spinning wheel and that she began to recite poems at various occasions. At home, Hirsekorn often beat her and eventually threw her out of the house. After being married eleven years and bearing three children, she became, against her will, the first woman in Prussia to be divorced.

Responding to pressure from her mother, she remarried, this time to the tailor Karsch, and moved to the small town of Fraustadt. Her new husband turned out to be an alcoholic, so she began supporting her children through writing and reciting occasional poems. The type of occasional poetry she produced was not unusual, but the fact that a poor, uneducated woman traveled from place to place in the under-developed eastern areas and produced poems with such rapidity and ease was a wonder. People seemed astounded at her knowledge, recognizing that she was well-read, although not formally educated (Hausmann 79). She was crowned three times as poet (Hausmann 98). Like her granddaughter after her, Karsch secured patronage from local nobles, one of whom illegally arranged for her husband to be inducted into the Prussian army, and another, Baron von Kottwitz, supported her in a move to Berlin in 1861. This is where her epistolary narration to Sulzer stops.

Karsch's letters to Sulzer, begun on 9 January 1762, were meant with publication in mind. They belong to a category of literature that Katherine Goodman has aptly termed "epistolary autobiography," whereby writers illustrate the idea of "constructing the self through the medium of others and emphasize the importance of sociality."[14] Intentions of publication make all the more poignant her emphasis on her striving to learn and recite poetry at the cost of neglecting her duties as a woman. As a young girl, she writes, "meine einzige Zuflucht war das geliebte Buch und schon hatte ich wieder vergessen, daß ich ein Mädchen war" [my sole escape was the beloved book, and I had soon forgotten again that I was a girl] (Hausmann 25). The reprimands she received from her mother and stepfather were strong. Just before her first marriage she recognized that she had not learned everything that a woman should (Hausmann 174). Borrowing books from the neighboring shepherd, reading at the spinning wheel, hiding books under her children's pillows—such were the clandestine ways in which she fed her mania. For a lower-class woman to write about such defiant autodidactic methods in the 1760s, when the ideology of femininity dissuaded any serious book learning, is remarkable. Even more noteworthy is Karsch's persistence in seeing that her own life story appear side-by-side in her first published volume of poetry. She also wanted to see that desire taken seriously. When she saw that Gleim had not written his promised foreword, she reprimanded him by stating that if she did not see his preface soon she would find it necessary to tell the public herself about her upbringing and the unusual path she took to become a poet (Hausmann 201). Recognition of her uncommon life story and the different roles she must assume continued throughout her life, when, for example, she later perceived her life as "Stoff zum Roman" [material for a novel] (Hausmann 271).

There are obvious traits of the epistolary form that Karsch takes advantage of when she writes her life story. Most of all, she creates a personal, unique tale out of an otherwise typical background of a lower-class, eighteenth-century woman. Her letters revolve not around important historical events, but around her marriages, a topic she obviously saw as volatile for her time. In the epistolary form, Karsch creates a dialogue with the recipient through addressing him as "bester Freund" [best friend] (Hausmann 25). She also interjects thoughts directly to her specific reader: "Denn ich muß nicht vergessen Ihnen zu sagen" [For I must not forget to tell you] (Hausmann 32), she writes, or calls on him for reactions: "o stellen Sie sich meinen aufschwellenden Autorstolz vor!" [oh imagine my swelling author's pride] (Hausmann 46). She can describe her own reactions in personal, often modest terms: "Ich bin nicht genug rednerisch, um Ihnen von meinem damaligen Vergnügen eine Beschreibung zu machen" [I am not articulate enough to give a description of my satisfaction at that time] (Hausmann 46). In letting the reader know that she could write at greater length on a certain topic, she also reveals that she has selected information from a large storehouse (Hausmann 50).

Karsch's epistolary autobiography does not end with the letters to Sulzer. After arriving in Berlin, she became friends with the poet Ludwig Gleim, who eventually helped her publish her first collection of poetry in 1764. The small income she received from the publication served her for the rest of her life. Scholars have drawn attention to this relationship as one in which Karsch's love for Gleim remained unrequited and thus weakened her. While it is true that Gleim remained distant to Karsch's initial romantic overtures, she did not swoon, fawn, or lay incapacitated. Instead, she fostered in correspondence a multifaceted portrayal of herself and documented an unusual friendship between an eighteenth-century male and female poet. She remained Gleim's life-long correspondent, often writing to him once a day during her time in Berlin. As Gerhard Wolf justly observes, these letters belong to the most valuable, revealing letters of the time.[15] Readers can still appreciate them today for their historical value and the insights they provide into the process of creating metaphors of selves in letters.[16] She also constantly uses metaphors to stress the importance of the correspondence in their friendship. A letter from him is "theurer als der Schmuck, den mir meine gräfliche Freundin zugedacht und beigelegt hat" [more precious than the jewelry that my friend, the countess, promised and gave to me] (Hausmann 93); or, "die größte Erfrischung, die man mir geben konnte nach einer so beschwerlichen Reise" [the greatest refreshment that one could give to me after such a hard journey] (Hausmann 95); or they are "papierne Zeugen" [paper witnesses] of their friendship (Hausmann 96). As with many women letter writers, however, Karsch recognizes the disparate worth she and Gleim attribute to the correspondence. Whereas her responses are prompt and regular, she must reprimand him for his procrastination in answering her letters (Hausmann 95). The same "Schmuck" [jewelry] and "Erfrischung" [refreshment] can turn into documents written "in Aufwallung von Verdruß" [in the bubbling up of annoyance] (Hausmann 177).

In over fifteen hundred letters to Gleim, Karsch continually reflects on the writing process as a means to create images of herself in connection with other people and events. An example of that process lies in her rereading of the letters to Sulzer and then reporting her observations to Gleim. When she reports that the letters number four, she also admits that the last one is short, for it deals with a happy period in her life. To Gleim she admits: "Sie wissen, daß ich nicht bei Beschreibung des Vergnügens mich zu lange aufhalten kann" [you know that I cannot tarry too long in describing the pleasure] (Hausmann 165). She thus worries about readers who might want a happier image of married life. She asks Gleim to edit the letters for publication, admitting that she has already presented the happiest picture she could of a life of two unhappy marriages:

> Es ist verdrüßlich von zween Männern reden hören und von keinem sagen können, daß er liebte oder ganz geliebt werden konnte. Was wird die Welt von mir urteilen? Ich habe den ersten so viel geschont, als nötig gewesen ist. Mir fehlte nur ein ausgebildeter Verstand und ein wenig von meinem ietzigen Ruhm, an ihm einen besseren Mann zu haben. Aber ich ward in dem Frühjahr unserer Ehe betäubt gemacht, ich war zu weich, ich vergaß in zehn Augenblicken die übelste Begegnung.

> [It puts me in a bad mood to hear gossip about two men and not to be able to say that either of them loved or could be loved wholeheartedly. How will the world judge me? I have treated the former as considerately as was necessary. I was only lacking in an educated mind and a little of my present fame to see him as a better man. But in the spring of our marriage I was numbed, I was too tender, I forgot in ten moments the worst encounter. (Hausmann 165–166)]

As in her epistles to Sulzer, in correspondence with Gleim she stresses the connection between her literary development, her failed marriages, and her inadequate education. The story and fear of her second husband's return keeps coming up (Hausmann 121). Reading and criticizing her earlier poems leads her to think about her former hard life, in which her husband ripped a book out of her hand (Hausmann 147–48). Given the laws that provided no options for women in choosing or divorcing their husbands, rare is the man's autobiography that can identify literary development through recalling such events. As a divorced woman writing to a single man, she also needs to expel rumors that she wants to take Gleim as her third husband. Gleim need have no fears, she reassures him, she wants her peace, freedom, and happiness, and not necessarily another husband. With Gleim, she wants to reach a new level of friendship that need not lead to marriage. She writes to him: "Glauben Sie nur, man kann sehr heftig lieben, ohne jemals an den Punkt des Heiratens zu gedenken" [Believe me, a person can love strongly without ever thinking about the subject of marriage] (Hausmann 166).

As much as Karsch would like to focus on her naïveté and natural talent for composing poetry, she cannot fool her readers. While constantly downplaying her talents, she tries to connect her inadequate education with the style of her poems. Her emphasis on writing from the heart leads her to equate her style with a lesser valued "Weiberart" [women's style] (Hausmann 80). In fact, subsequent critics have been quick to follow suit, making the connection even more limiting in the face of what she produced. But this narrow categorization counters the importance she places on model thinkers from the ancient Greeks (Hausmann 93–94) and Romans (Hausmann 323). Descriptions of her voracious reading and autodidactic learning (Hausmann 139) are supported by her references to Dante (Hausmann 167–68), Cicero (Hausmann 323), the *Iliad* (Hausmann 305), and many other classical works. She compensates for her own lack of formal education by supporting her grandson through university (Hausmann 321). Her regrets that she never was allowed to learn Latin cause her to lament: "Ich habe so viel Philosophie auszuüben, daß ich darüber nicht zur philosophischen Dichterin werden kann" [I have to practice so much philosophy so that for this reason I cannot become a philosophizing poet] (Hausmann 325). She is also constructively and effectively critical of other people's writing, despite apologetic tones and admittance of inadequate education and skills of critical analysis (Hausmann 139). She insists that Gleim continue to use the "Sprache des Herzens" [language of the heart]. She advises her grandson about writing letters that show his heart rather than conscious efforts to write in a formal style (Hausmann 377). Twice she strongly criticizes Klopstock's *Messias* for not moving the heart (Hausmann 153, 246). Her criticism is politely witty: "wenn nicht Klopstock der Verfasser wäre, so würd ich sagen, daß es nur wenig Gesänge darunter gibt, die ich in ihrem ganzen Umfange wünschte gemacht zu haben" [if Klopstock were not the author, I would say that there were only a few songs among them that I would wish to have written entirely] (Hausmann 246). She was, as Gerhard Wolf states, truly ahead of her time in her recognition of the talents of Lessing, Wieland, Herder, Klopstock, and Schiller, which she expressed in correspondence with them.[17] Her knowledge of literary traditions thus supports the idea that she consciously chose the style and content of her writings after much study and reflection.

In the same way that her words do not coincide with her actions in matters of education, so do modesty and self-deprecation counter praise that she relates from others. Why should she accept money for her poems, she asks (Hausmann 111), even though at other times she is ready to defend the worth of her writing. She will create no masterpiece, but she will please her audience (Hausmann 115). She was aware of her worth, as she writes to Gleim: "Doch an einem so erstaunlichen Weibe, wie mich meine Freunde nennen, geschehen lauter erstaunliche Dinge" [Yet to such an amazing woman, as my friends call me, happen totally amazing things] (Hausmann 123). And she was also aware of rhetorical devices with which to pit her self-confidence against humbleness. At one point Gleim questions whether their mutual friend Ramler might have some of her poems for Gleim to read. She doubts it, admitting that she may have talked so negatively to Ramler about her poetry that he might have believed her and considered himself too great to read her poems (Hausmann 229).

An indirect way to give herself the credit she believes she deserves as a poet is through role-playing in letters. In general, letters serve as self-description in various contexts. Her portrayal of herself to Ramler epitomizes how she often pitted what she deemed an ugly physical appearance against a genuine, loving inner self (Hausmann 88). Recognition of the contradictions between her "selves" seems most effective in the letter form, in which she can concurrently ask for opinions, supporting or not. The contrasting distance and personal contact that letters afford encourage her to cite the praise others have given her poems (Hausmann 109), or to relate how well she has recited (Hausmann 113), or to recount that praise indirectly: "Sagen Sie, liebster Freund, meiner ganzen lobsprechenden freundlichen Welt, daß sie aufhören soll, mich ein Wunderwerk zu nennen" [Dear friend, tell my entire praising, friendly world that they should stop calling me a miracle] (Hausmann 155). Adoption of other personae or references to herself in the third person distance her from the source of the praise. From early in her correspondence with Gleim, she calls herself Sappho, taking the initiative from Gleim himself. She labels Gleim Thyrsis, for the wand wreathed in ivy and wine leaves carried by devotees of the Bacchi (Hausmann 104). By placing herself in the third person of Sappho, she can relate the praise that another poet has given her (Hausmann 94; 117). In general, her letters are replete with stories of assumed identities. In one tale, she tells of a man who thinks he recognizes her as the great poet Anna Louisa Karsch, but for the sake of fun she pretends she is not the poet (Hausmann 223–24). Denying her public identity allows her to create a portrait of herself through the eyes of another. Feigning another self, however, can also lead to dissonance. In the end, she admits that she has been taken aback that the man believed her and did not ultimately recognize her (Hausmann 224–25). Anecdotes, storytelling, and character sketches in letters allow her to see parts of herself in other people, for example, the bride who would have her fate (Hausmann 119–21) or another singer who inspires her to create a song in her honor (Hausmann 155–57). As we shall see in Sophie Mereau's letters, Karsch's love of the theater coincides with the penchant toward role-playing (Hausmann 104, 228, 270).

Karsch's discussion of a posthumous publication of her poems propagates her multifarious images and desires. On the one side, she apologetically criticizes the private nature of the poems; on the other side, she recognizes the emotional distance she can take from her subjects. Although she finds little worth in her works, ultimately she does not refuse the offer of publication: "Suchen Sie doch oder lassen Sie vielmehr durch Ihre beyden Nichten auswählen, was etwa unter den Papierhaufen, die Sie von mir haben, brauchbar ist. Wird sich wenig finden" [Look yourself, or better yet, let your two nieces choose for you what is useful among the pile of papers that you have from me. There will be little enough] (Hausmann 313). On the one hand she denies herself any poetic genius and asks Gleim to create for himself a great masterpiece from her poetry (Hausmann 320). On the other hand, she does ultimately identify herself as a poet and demands just rewards. In her dealings with the King about the house he promised to build her, she remains firm in her self-definition as a poet: "Gut wärs allerdings, wenn der König an mir thäte als Dichterin, was er an mancher Person thut" [Naturally it would be good if the King were to treat me as a poet, as he does with many people] (Hausmann 342).

In emphasizing her educational disadvantages and in expressing low self-esteem, Karsch offers a response to critics who harked back to her lack of education when they reviewed her poetry. She was living in an age when women were becoming more and more educated, yet that education was frowned upon if it was perceived to interfere with women's duties as mothers and wives. Criticism against her first collection of poems cites in particular certain neologisms, asking that she learn her language better (Hausmann 212–13). Letters between Sulzer, Bodmer, and Ramler laud her work, but doubt whether she would be capable of greatness; she does not seem to have the "Ruhe" [tranquility] needed for contemplation, nor the formal education (Hausmann 74–75). Reception of her poems also discloses a critical discourse that cannot escape gender stereotypes. Mendelssohn's comments in "Briefe, die neueste Literatur betreffend" on her poem about the battle of Torgau were considered complimentary: some of the stanzas emitted "eine männliche und fast wilde Imagination" [a masculine and almost wild imagination]. There could be no better compliment to mistake a woman's work for a man's, and then wonder at the amount of genius the woman would have to be able to relate without experiencing a battle realistically. Such was the nature of

Mendelssohn's compliment when he writes: "Ich begreife nicht, wie ein unkriegerisches Frauenzimmer auf diese Bemerkung hat zuerst kommen können" [I do not understand how an unwarriorlike woman could be the first to have made this remark].[18] Incongruence between what she experienced and what she wrote caused confusion. Gleim, after learning about the King promising Karsch a house, expresses to Uz his shame, tainted with jealousy, at seeing a woman acquire what two men have not been able to learn: "Müssen wir uns nicht schämen, wir männlichen Dichter, daß wir nichts gemacht haben, das einer solchen königlichen Aufmerksamkeit würdig gewesen ist?" [Shouldn't we be ashamed, we male poets, that we have not done anything that has been worthy of such royal attention?] (Hausmann 201). Goethe's reaction to her letters conveys the whole gamut of her writings: "Schicken Sie mir doch auch manchmal was aus dem Stegreife, mir ist alles lieb und werth, was treu und stark aus dem Herzen kommt, mags übrigens aussehen wie ein Igel oder wie ein Amor. Geschrieben hab ich *allerley*, gewissermaßen *wenig* und im Grunde *nichts*" [Why don't you also send me sometime anything that is improvised, everything that comes sincerely and strongly from the heart is dear and valuable to me, may it otherwise look like a hedgehog or Amor. I have written all kinds of things, that is to say, little, and basically nothing] (Hausmann 277).

Throughout the letters she recognizes the restrictions that come with prescribed gender roles, yet at no time does she couch her professional accomplishments in explanations of how she was able to remain a good mother and wife despite her career. Such explanations were common, one prime example being in Dorothea Runckel's preface to Louise Gottsched's letters, as women conformed their writings to social expectations. Instead, Karsch reverts to calling attention to different, even unequal opportunities between the sexes. When her husband wants to be released from the army, she regrets that she is a woman and not a man who would be able to serve the monarch. (Hausmann 57) Given her unhappy marriage with Karsch, her letter to convince him to stay in the army has personal ulterior motives, and thus it is difficult to assess the sincerity of her wishes. To Gleim she notes her pride as a woman to be counted among his group of male friends: "Ich sehe mich noch so unendlich tief unter Euch männlichen Geistern, daß ich gar nicht einmal wider die Versuchung zum Stolze kämpfen darf" [I see myself still so endlessly deep among you male spirits that I may not even struggle against the attempt at pride] (Hausmann 136). When Gleim is angry over a poem she recites, she identifies the cause of his anger as sexual prejudice and can only laugh about it (Hausmann 236). She agrees to help Hirsekorn get out of the army, while ultimately recognizing that she is submitting to the power of the man over the woman: she reasons that his father was at one point "mein Besitzer" [my owner] (Hausmann 264). In her resignation, she at least admits awareness of the power structures over which she has little control.

Despite, or perhaps because of Karsch's constant moving from one posture to another, epistles represent the ultimate reflective medium to question and justify her life in autobiographical form (Hausmann 112). The interplay between epistolary dialogue and poetry is especially prevalent. The inclusion of poems within the letters points to the tremendous influence the act of letter writing had on her other compositions. Verse within the letters is not merely an added inclusion, but an intrinsic part relating to the correspondence. Playing with forms of address in one letter, she transforms the formal address form of "Sie" into the informal "Du" and then turns that process into a poem (Hausmann 103). She burns a letter Gleim writes to her forbidding her to enter his house while she is visiting. She turns this destruction into a constructive act, however, when she portrays it in a poem (Hausmann 128–29).

Even when her muse fails her in writing in other forms, she claims, she still can write letters: "Briefe kann ich zu allen Zeiten schreiben" [I can write letters at any time] (Hausmann 223). Descriptions of letter-writing activities fill entire letters (Hausmann 230). Reactions to letters employ metaphors to express how much she values them. For example, she responds to the Fürstin von Dessau's letter: "Ein solcher Brief, mein bester Freund, ist angenehmer als ein halb Dutzend Dukaten mit gleichgültiger Miene gegeben oder durch die Hand eines finstern Bevollmächtigten geschickt". [Such a letter, my best friend, is more pleasant than a half dozen ducats given with an indifferent attitude or sent through the hand of an obscure authority] (Hausmann 271). She refers at another point to another letter she has written spontaneously to a guitar player she has seen: "hab ein Epistelchen an ihn geschrieben und wenn ich noch lebe, da bekommen alle Figuren Episteln" [I wrote a little epistle to him, and as long as I still live then every person will receive an epistle] (Hausmann 363). The interweaving of poetry with prose in letters leads her to conclude her preference of the former over the latter. Toward the end of her life (23 November 1790), she exclaims: "Da bin ich nun schon wieder ins Reimen gekommen, als ob ich nicht in Prosa alles sagen könnte, was zu sagen ist; das Reimen ward mir einmal so zur Gewohnheit, ich kanns nicht lassen" [There I came into rhyme again, as if I could not say everything there is to say in prose, rhyme has become such a habit for me that I cannot leave it alone] (Hausmann 371).

But Karsch's own separation of letters from poetry becomes artificial, for she invents her own category for the combination: in letters to Goethe she calls her correspondence "Versbriefchen" [little rhymed letter] (Hausmann 251; 283 [to Goethe]). Her correspondence with Friedrich Wilhelm is remarkable for the adept way in which she combines epistolary prose and verse. In a poem referring to her death day, she writes: Und bis er kommt, laß ich nicht ab/Zu denken und zu dichten" [And until it comes, I will not give up thinking and writing poems] (Hausmann 372). In a poem to Lebbäus Benzler, secretary to Count Stolberg-Wernigerode, she admits: Verse mach ich oft im Schlaf,/Und wird einst mein Geist schon weichen/Aus den Augen merkbarlich,/Läßt die Hand zum Schreiben sich/Noch einmal die Feder reichen:/Dies versichre du dem Herrn . . . ." [I often compose verses in my sleep/And if my spirit should ever retreat/noticeably from sight/Let the hand yet once again /pass the pen for writing/this I assure you, gentleman] (Hausmann 381).

Despite the frequent crossover between public composition of verse and private letter writing, she still shows a hesitation toward publication. Her ambivalence is similar to that of Louise Gottsched and Meta Klopstock. At first, Karsch's *Angst* against entrance into the public sphere applies to all her writings, poetry and letters. The written word contradicts her accustomed medium of oral recitation in front of an intimate audience. To admit a desire to publish would also contradict the impression of modesty she wants to convey. She is cognizant of what many termed the publication mania and thus takes great care to request that poems she sends to Gleim in letters not be published (Hausmann 90). After Gleim and Jacobi published their friendship letters, Jacobi indicated that he might also like to publish Karsch's letters to Gleim. She reacts against the plan, wondering why she should make her platonic love into an object of ridicule. Publication of very private feelings would be something she would bitterly regret later. In fact, she is already sorry for not having destroyed material (Hausmann 232). But the strict tenor of this first refusal soon becomes mitigated by a softer tone that allows for certain qualifications in the publications. In subsequent comments relating to publication of her letters, she seems more concerned about being permitted to proofread the letters first, than about having them published: "Was gedruckt ward, kann nicht widerrufen werden und ich hoffe, daß man wenigstens mir vergönnen wird, meine eigenen Sachen erst zu prüfen, ehe sie der Welt bekannt werden" [What has been published cannot be recalled, and I hope that one would at least allow me to proof my own things before they become known to the world] (Hausmann 233). She talks about the ease with which she can destroy her work, her poems as well as her letters (Hausmann 233). This ease, however, seems to relate more to her modest posture, which she shows when she states that she is not impressed that eight hundred copies of her poems sold at a recent book fair (Hausmann 233). Later, in 1770, she equates her production with other "natural" tendencies that her muse and other women might have (Hausmann 262). In her last years, she recognizes how by refusing to publish her letters she attempted to conform to gender stereotypes. That conformity prevented her as a woman from publishing the intimate correspondence with Gleim. In answer to Gleim's later intention to publish all of Karsch's poems and letters, she writes how she would have published her works earlier, but now she recognizes the barriers that block her: "Man würde die Nase rümpfen über eine Frau, die einer Mannsperson den Gefallen tut, so hinter ihr her zu seufzen . . . Vor 20 Jahren hätte ich alles ohne Bedacht der ganzen Welt geoffenbart. Die Zeit macht klug und scheu" [One would wrinkle one's nose at a woman who allowed a man to do him the favor of mooning after him. . . . Twenty years ago I would have opened up everything to the whole world without consideration. Time makes wise and shy] (Hausmann 313).

In 1763, Karsch received an audience with Friedrich the Great, who promised to have a house built for her. Friederich did not keep his promise, and the letters in verse that Karsch wrote to the King in the following decade are, as Gerhard Wolf comments, pieces of literary history in and of themselves and say more about the situation of poets and artists in Prussia than any other documents of the time.[19] When Friedrich's successor, Friedrich Wilhelm II, finally had the house built in 1789, her situation did not improve drastically. The modest, economical life she led in Berlin comes across in her letters (Hausmann 215; 219; 227). As letters attest, Karsch's poverty-related problems persisted in the last years of her life (Hausmann 305). Even after she received her house, she had to scrape money together for taxes, heat, furnishings, and upkeep, so that her financial and physical condition deteriorated, due to cold and undernourishment. Despite these extenuating circumstances, she recognizes her poetic talents in her autobiographical epistles: "Aber Nahrungskummer weckt mich nach Mitternacht. . . . Gelegenheitsgedichte halfen haus halten, ob sie gleich allerdings keine Ehre brachten. Sie fallen weg und ich kanns Bewußtsein von Schulden schwer dulden. Das war ohne Willen gereimt" [But worries about food wake me up after midnight. . . . Occasional poetry helped the household, even though it certainly brought no honor. They cease and I find it hard to live

with the consciousness of debts. That was not rhymed on purpose]
(Hausmann 361).

In comparison with the many of Karsch's voluminous, witty letters
replete with anecdotes and self-exploration, the letters of Mereau and
Günderrode seem terse and contemplative. Their deliberations, however, signal a crafted prose and a heightened aesthetic consciousness
about writing in general and letter writing in particular. Today, Mereau and Günderrode stand as representatives of a burgeoning group
of middle-and upper-class women who were attempting at the end
of the eighteenth century to succeed at public literary careers without
sacrificing their private lives. Although the form, content, and publication circumstances of their poems differed, both are recognized
today as two of the most well-known women poets of their time.

Mereau holds the distinction of being one of the first women to
have lived financially self-supported from her writings. She was born
Sophie Friederike Schubart in Thüringen in 1770, the second daughter
of the ducal secretary Gotthelf Schubart and his wife Johanna Sophie
Friederike. Along with her sister, she received an education typical of
upper-bourgeois families at that time, which included schooling at
home in modern languages, music, and drawing. In 1793, she married Friedrich Ernst Carl Mereau, a law professor in Jena. The two
had been corresponding for five years before the marriage, which
turned out to be a disaster. After bearing two children, only one of
whom, the daughter Hulda, reached maturity, and living through
long periods of separation, the two were divorced in 1801. The extended correspondence that Mereau held with her lover Kipp and
then Clemens Brentano after 1798 bears witness to the disappoint-
ments she experienced in marriage. After her divorce, Mereau supported herself and her daughter with her writing and editing.
Brentano persisted in trying to persuade Mereau to marry him, but
she continually refused, longing to hold onto her freedom. When she
became pregnant in 1804, she consented to the marriage. In the next
two and half years, Mereau bore three children, all of whom died
in infancy, and had one miscarriage. Concurrently, she completed
translations and wrote short stories and poems. She died while giving
birth on 30 October 1806.

To her contemporaries, her public identity was mostly one of a
poet who had received encouragement, praise, and support from
Schiller. He published her first poems, anonymously, in his *Horen*,
and they were an immediate success, as comments from Goethe and
others prove. She did, however, have many other, often unrecognized
public identities, including a writer of novels and essays, an editor of
literary journals, and a translator. In private, her roles have assumed

more notorious dimensions in the annals of literary history—as an unhappily married wife; the first divorcee in Jena; a mother with a profession; a coquettish saloniere; an unfaithful wife; a lover and then wife of Clemens Brentano. In her public writings, her striving for harmony between independence and social responsibilities, desires and duties, appearances and reality, self-actualization and community building, among others, receives main attention. Hence, categorizing opposing factions into romantic emotions and classical forms, as many scholars have done, simplifies the forces at work. Ultimately, her figures do reach harmony, even if they have to run away from the society that has restricted their freedom, as in *Blüthenalter der Empfindlichkeit*, or the short story "Flucht nach der Stadt." Her diaries, composed of single words that reflect simply the events of the day and her feelings, demonstrate a writer preoccupied with symbolic representation and minimalist forms. Her letters, with their alternating melancholic and elated, shocked and resolute, frustrated and relieved, apologetic and assertive tones, show her struggle to harmonize her desires for freedom and independence with the expectations of a society that did not allow psychological escape as easily as the physical one in her works.

In-depth analysis of her literary works, however, has been rare because scholars have been more interested in her personal life and her relationship with famous men of her day.[20] Only in the past decade have scholars revived and reevaluated her works.[21] No critical edition of Mereau's collected works exists, although she was a prolific author and letter writer, as recent bibliographies of her writings prove.[22] The circumstances of the publication of her correspondence with Schiller mirrored the inadequate way in which women's letters have traditionally appeared. In letters to Sophie Mereau, Schiller offered constructive criticism of her work, praising what he liked and making suggestions for changes, while she showed attempts to reach poetic autonomy. His letters originally appeared in 1808 in Ludwig Achim von Arnim's *Zeitung für Einsiedler* under the title "Auszüge aus Briefen Schiller's an eine junge Dichterin" [Excerpts From Schiller's Letters To a Young Poetess]. Mereau's name was not mentioned, nor were specific details about the correspondence discussed.[23] Arnim published them "um ein belehrendes Beyspiel zu geben, was Critik seyn kann, wenn sie ein frommes Geheimniß zwischen zween, keine feile Oeffentlichkeit ist" [in order to give an educational example of what criticism can be when it is a devout secret between two, no venal publicity] (149). Only in 1984 was the entire extant correspondence first published in Mereau's biography. Until that date, Schiller's name stood first in publications.[24]

Fascination with Mereau's correspondence has categorized it simutaneously as an example of "feminine" writings produced by women and as a model for how women could transcend that femininity. After Mereau sent Schiller the beginnings of her epistolary novel, *Briefe von Amanda und Eduard,* composed from what we now know was the correspondence between Mereau and her lover Kipp,[25] Schiller wrote to Goethe:

Für die Horen hat mir unsere Dichterin Mereau jetzt ein sehr angenehmes Geschenk gemacht, und das mich wirklich überraschte. Es ist der Anfang eines Romans in Briefen, die mit weit mehr Klarheit, Leichtigkeit und Simplicität geschrieben sind, als ich je von ihr erwartet hätte. Sie fänge darinn an, sich von Fehlern frey zu machen, die ich an ihr für ganz unheilbar hielt, und wenn sie auf diesem guten Wege weiter fortgeht, so erleben wir noch was an ihr. Ich muß mich doch wirklich drüber wundern, wie unsere Weiber jetzt, auf bloß dilettantischem Wege, eine gewiße Schreibgeschicklichkeit sich zu verschaffen wißen, die der Kunst nahe kommt.

[Our poetess Mereau has just sent a very pleasant gift for the Horen, and that really surprised me. It is the beginning of a novel in letters, which are written with much more clarity, ease, and simplicity than I would have ever expected from her. In them she begins to free herself from mistakes for which I had believed her totally incurable, and if she continues in this good manner, she will prove to be remarkable. I really am quite astonished at how our women, in a mere dilettantish way, know how to acquire a certain craftmanship in writing that comes close to art.][26]

In 1797, Schiller's comments might have been considered positive for women's emancipation, but today, references to her literary work as dilettante efforts that "come close to being art," come across as backhanded, patronizing praise. As an example of stereotyping the content of Mereau's letters, Karl Varnhagen von Ense remarks in his journal in September 1856:

Ich zwang mich zu einiger Arbeit; las dann in den Liebesbriefen der Sophie Mereau, die sehr liebenswerth sind, ein lebhaftes Bild von ihrer Liebenswürdigkeit und von den Sitten der Zeit geben. In *allen* Zeugnissen, Briefen und Erzählungen von damals findet sich durchaus dasselbe, Vergötterung und Allberechtigung der Liebe, Mißachtung der Ehe, poetische Anerkennung der Sinnlichkeit, Ringen nach Freiheit, Hinblick auf Frankreich. Dies ist alles auch hier.

[I forced myself to do some work; then read in the love letters of Sophie Mereau, which are very lovely, give a lively image of her charm and of the customs of the time. In all extant papers, letters, and reports of that time, I find completely the same adoration and acclaim of love, scorn for marriage, poetic recognition of sensuality, struggling for freedom, orientation toward France. All this is also here.][27]

As for Mereau's other correspondence, only that with Brentano remains entirely published, and then not until over one hundred years after her death. Her other most extensive, and perhaps very revealing correspondence—with Kipp, Charlotte von Ahlefeld, and her sister Henriette Schubart—remains largely unpublished.[28]

Recent research has made strides in rectifying a narrow view of Mereau, and yet the debate over how much of a "feminist" Mereau actually was threatens critical inquiry. In criticizing Gersdorff's biography, Hannelore Schlaffer reduces Mereau to the embodiment of "Koketterie und Schläue" [coquetry and cunning] and deems Mereau interesting mostly for the tactics she used to combine "Verführungskunst und Entschlossenheit, Vergnügungslust und ökonomischen Realismus" [art of seduction and resoluteness, passion for amusement and economic realism] to become "eine vernünftige und gesunde Egoistin" [a sober and healthy egotist].[29] Granted, as already analyzed, Gersdorff's biography has deficiencies that need critical evaluation, but Mereau has many more faces than the subservient ones Schlaffer describes, too. Part of the problem with Schlaffer's viewpoint is that she only makes reference to Mereau's poems. Hence, Mereau's complex method of confronting her literary models through letters has remained until very recently largely unexamined, namely the struggles that she had meeting male standards of classical literature established by Schiller; the aid she gave her sister, Henriette Schubart, in the face of roles restricting women's entrance into the literary realm; her friendship with the poet Charlotte von Ahlefeld, who had entered into an unhappy marriage; the interplay between literary production and letter writing in her exchange with Kipp; and the conflict between boldness and coquettishness she displayed when corresponding with Brentano.

In attempting to use Mereau's letters and diaries as biographical background material for her literary works, most studies point out the discrepancy between her calls for independence as a woman writer, which appear most frequently in private writings, and a certain self-censorship regarding women's emancipation, which surfaces in her novels and poems.[30] Female protagonists in her published works, so several critics have contended, manifest the feminine ideals of virtue, naturalness, and beauty, thus warranting classification as "typically feminine." In Mereau's private life, especially in her unhappy first marriage and in her relationship with Clemens Brentano, she was, according to this dichotomous view of her life, living the oppression against which her fictitious heroines struggled. The image resulting from such a separation of private and public documents contrasts unrealistic emancipated theories with the non-existent outlet for expression of those theories. The use of letters as mirrors for biographical indices also underestimates the letter's power to serve as means for aesthetic experimentation.

Mereau's letters should not, however, be read in such stark contrast to her published works. Such interpretation simplifies the complex process behind her literary production and underestimates the power letter writing held for her. The epistolary form allows Mereau to cross boundaries of style, period, and genre. Hence, she creates what Uta Treder calls a montage effect, which originally provoked criticism against the perplexing inconsistency in her work.[31] From their content, her letters may not include as many passages explicitly describing literary decisions, as scholars such as Christa Bürger would like to see.[32] Instead, Mereau replaces reflection with performance; she creates the literary work in her letters through metaphors, wordplays, and imagining selves that are constantly and provocatively changing, inconsistent, and complex. Bold outbursts against restrictions on her freedom to write accompany a hesitancy to write and apologetic tones. Questions of language and comparisons between published and personal writings signal a welcome opportunity for such discussions. Metaphors of transformation and role reversal reflect a continual process of imaging in public and private.

In order to see how Mereau's style is interactive and responsive, it is most beneficial to look at the correspondence Mereau conducted with Heinrich Kipp and with Clemens Brentano, for in each one letters from both sides have survived. Both sets of correspondence are in the Varnhagen Collection in the Jagiellonian Library in Krakow. The Mereau/Kipp correspondence has not been published in its entirety.[33] The Mereau/Brentano correspondence is now in two major editions, one by Amelung and the other by Gersdorff.[34] My purpose here is not to examine particulars of the relationships, but rather to focus on the lively, productive interchange between the acts of letter writing and literary production.

In the letters between Mereau and Kipp, the reflective process of corresponding inspires artistic imagery. Sophie Mereau and Heinrich Kipp met for the first time in the summer of 1794. Kipp was a student in Jena, and Mereau was in the throes of an unhappy marriage. The two had a love affair for over a year, about which Mereau wrote very little in her diary or other writings. Gersdoff reasons that Mereau's life at this point allowed no documentation "weil sie *lebte,* anstatt zu schreiben."[35] In the summer of 1795, Kipp had to return to his home town, Lübeck, because financial circumstances prevented him from studying in Jena any longer. In the Hanseatic city he found work and family support. The correspondence with Mereau began in early summer, 1795 and continued through mid-November, 1796.

Empowerment through love, lamentations over a loveless marriage, desires for freedom, reflections on France, yes, all those themes are in Mereau's letters to Kipp, as Karl Varnhagen observed when he first read the correspondence. But each theme does not come without its counterpart, without consideration of dualities on all sides. In discussing her marriage with Friedrich Mereau, Sophie at one point attempts to justify her decision not to leave him. "Ich darf nicht ungerecht sein," she writes, "es ist wahr, dass M. sich jetzt vieles gefallen läßt, was wenig Männer tragen würden—u. doch bin ich eben *nur* gerecht gegen ihn" [I should not be unjust, it is true that M. now puts up with a lot, which few men would stand—a. yes, I am *only* just toward him] (27 [July 1795]). Her atonement angers Kipp, who writes back "Aber was will M. Du sagst du bist *nur* gerecht gegen ihn u. ist das nicht genug? Was willst du mehr als gerecht seyn, läßt Liebe sich befehlen?" [But what does M. want. You say you are *only* just toward him a. isn't that enough? What more do you want than to be just, does love let itself be dictated?] (19 [August 1795]). He calls Friedrich Mereau a "Thor" [fool] with neither a head nor a heart. In answering to Kipp's criticism of her husband, Sophie cannot help but portray her decisions metaphorically:

Mein ganzer Umgang mit Dir hat, ich fühle es, etwas in mir befestigt, was mir sonst sehr fehlte—mehr Selbstgefühl und Stolz am rechten Ort. Der Gang meiner Bildung ist der, den die ganze Menschheit nimmt und nehmen muß. Ich war gut ohne es mir bewußt zu sein, aus dunklen Antrieb der Gefühle. Ich wollte Licht. Schon dies Wollen schuf eine Dämmerung, aber Irrthum nahte sich mir und ergriff ihn. Ich verschlimmerte mich, aber ich wußte das daß ich mich verschlimmerte, meine Kräfte übten sich in diesem Kampf. Ich war nicht mehr gut, aber ich fühlte doch das Hohe des Guten. Ich ergriff den Schein für Wahrheit, den Schatten für den Gegenstand. Eitelkeit war mir Größe, Gefallsucht, Liebe, Eigensinn, Freiheit.—Das Licht gieng auf. Der Schein des Bewußtseins strahlte, durch Leiden lernte ich die Wahrheit, und an der Hand der Liebe ging ich mit Bewußtsein wieder zur Natur zum Einfall zurück.

[My entire relationship with you has, I feel, solidified something in me, something that I usually lack—more self-confidence and pride in the right place. The process of my education is one that is and has to be assumed by all humanity. I was good without realizing it, because of the dark impulse of feelings. I wanted light. This desire alone created a dusk, but error approached me and grabbed it. I changed for the worse, but I knew that, that I changed for the worse, my strength was trained in this struggle. I was no longer good, but I nevertheless felt the height of the goodness. I mistook appearance for truth, the shadow for the real thing. Vanity for me was greatness, coquetry, love, obstinacy, freedom.—The light appeared. The beams of consciousness radiated, through suffering I learned the truth, and with love leading me by the hand I consciously returned again to nature to inspiration.] (29 [August 1795])

Her affair with Kipp, her marriage to Mereau, and her adultery are all embroiled in a constant interplay of light and dark, good and bad, truth and illusion, freedom and struggle. Her rationalization of these contrasts as all forming part of her larger "Bildung" mollifies any bitterness or anger. The relationship with Kipp becomes a living fantasy, a condition that brings her to where nature had originally intended. The word "Einfall" in itself is ambiguous, meaning both a collapse and a sudden fancy. One state arises from another, just as the inception of a new idea overcomes or at least coexists with the old.

Fantasy forms a major theme in the letters. In her first letter to Kipp, Mereau writes:

Wie sehn' ich mich hinaus in die freie Welt!—Der süße Wahn, dir irgendwo begegnen zu können, hat alle vorigen Wünsche nach Freiheit wieder in mir aufgeweckt. Wilde Phantasien umschwärmen mich nun!—es ist der sanfte Ton der Empfindung nicht mehr, der, als du noch bei mir warst, im nahen Bezug auf die Gegenwart allen meinen Bildern die lieblichste Beleuchtung verlieh.

[How I long to go out into the free world.—The sweet delusion to be able to meet you somewhere has awakened all previous wishes for freedom in me. Wild fantasies swarm around me now!—the mild tone of feelings is no longer that which, when you were still with me, gave all my images the dearest illumination in relation to the present time.] (17 [June 1795])

Later, she carries on the connection between fantasy and freedom: "Ich hatte diesen Abend viel phantasiert, viel von Sehnsucht nach Freiheit gesprochen" [I had fantasized this evening a lot, talked much about longing for freedom] (27 [June 1795]). She subsequently connects her wishes for personal freedom to the political ones:" . . . oft so ich mich auch nach Dir gesehnt habe, so oft ich gewünscht habe in Freiheit und vorzüglich in Frankreich zu sein" [even though I longed for you, I more often wished to be in freedom and mainly in France] (20 [April 1796].

As Fleischmann remarks, Mereau wrote many poems with themes of mourning, pain, depression, longing, and reflexivity during this year of separation, such as "Vergangenheit [Past]," "Erinnerung und Phantasie [Remembrance and Fantasy]," and "Bergphantasie" [Mountain Fantasy].[36] Whereas the contrast between fantasy and reality is not very demarcated in Mereau's earlier and later poems, it becomes in these poems a viable solution to despair. In the earlier poem, "Schwarzburg," the narrator, does not explicitly give fantastic desire as an answer to distress, but rather queries: "Ist dann die Welt noch eine Sehnsucht werth?" [Will the world still be worth the longing then?][37] In the later poem "Schwermuth," fantasy's possibilities to cure depression are not stated forthrightly, but again as a question: "Wo, wo ist Genuss?—in Phantasieen/ künftiger Freuden?" [Where, where is pleasure?—in fantasies/future delights?].[38] In contrast, in "Erinnerung und Phantasie," a poem Mereau composed during her correspondence with Kipp, the narrator's belief in fantasy's power is much more decisive:

> Entführe du auf deinen muntern Schwingen,
> o Phantasie, mich diesem finstern Harm!
> Schon fühl' ich Kraft durch jeden Nerven dringen,
> und fliehe leichter aus der Schwermuth Arm.

> [Abduct me on your lively swings,
> O fantasy, from this gloomy grief!
> Already I feel strength surge through every nerve,
> and flee more easily from the arm of melancholia.]

The Mereau/Kipp correspondence documents the development of the power that fantasy assumed in Mereau's life and work at this time. In May 1796, almost one year after the correspondence began, Mereau writes about her abilities to fantasize Kipp's closeness more than he can. About the lack of physical closeness between them, she writes: "Ich weiß, wie oft *ich selbst* diesen Mangel fühle, da ich doch weit weniger Herzensbedürfness habe als Du, und mit meiner Phantasie, die allein stete Beschäfftigung verlangt, ja immer nach Gefallen in der Weite mehr schweifen kann" [I know how often I myself feel this lack as I really have less urgent desires than you, and with my imagination, which in itself constantly desires activity, in fact, which can always roam more after pleasure.]

For Mereau, the letters reflect fantasies that do get played out in a certain reality—the reality of her writing. Her correspondence with Kipp offers her not only a forum to discuss the novel she is writing, but also material for that novel. She writes: "Ich schrieb Dir vor einiger Zeit daß ich an einem Roman schrieb" [I wrote you a little while ago that I am writing a novel] (20 [April 1796]). She is referring to her epistolary novel, *Amanda und Eduard*, but does not reveal that it is in large part based on their own correspondence and contains many reworked passages from their letters. "Ich sann auf mancherlei Wendungen und ließ die Schicksale in meiner Phantasie nach Gefallen entstehen und verschwinden, und das lezte blieb mir daß ich meine Helden nach Frankreich gehen ließ. Und das alles harmoniert mit meiner jezigen Stimmung" [I contemplated diverse kinds of turning points and let the destinies in my imagination emerge and disappear at will, and the last thing I came up with was that I let my heroes go to France. And that all harmonized with my present mood] (20 [April 1796]). In practice, it is writing, and not necessarily lived experience, that provides a release from her depressing marriage and an outlet for her otherwise stifled fantasy. The presence of such discussion and then the reworking of material in which the discussion occurs into the novel demonstrates the inspirational role letter writing fulfilled. It also coincides with a continual mixing of forms and dualities prevalent in Mereau's work.

Heinrich Kipp's active participation in the literary process makes the interaction even more dynamic. He asks her to send him poems and her works (10 [July 1795]). He even creates an audience for her works, as when he talks about showing her novel *Blüthenalter der Empfindung* to friends in Lübeck: "Ich hatte dein Blüthenalter mitgenommen, das lasen die jüngern u. ich freute mich herzlich, daß es ihnen allen so gefiel" [I had taken along your *Blüthenalter*, the younger ones read it, a. I was very happy that they all liked it so much] (13 [September 1795]). Given the fact that Mereau was superior to Kipp in her literary expertise, she never falls into an acquiescent role to which a writer such as Louise Gottsched succumbs. Kipp never dominates the discussion with suggestions or reprimands; thus, Mereau never has to apologize for her desire to write and to publicize her works. Instead, she discusses what she is writing, even acknowledging changes she has made based on his suggestions: "Ich feile an dem Gedicht: Schwärmerei der Liebe.—Du kennst es—vielleicht erscheint es in den Horen. Genau habe ich mir die Verse gemerkt, die Du nicht leiden konntest und sie ohne Barmherzigkeit weggestrichen, oder ganz verändert" [I am polishing a poem: Idolization of Love.—you know it—maybe it will appear in the Horen. I remember exactly the verses that you could not stand, and erased them mercilessly, or totally changed them.][39]

In the end, Kipp and Mereau went their separate ways, the reasons for which are varied. Gersdorff sees the role of a second wooer, Georg

Philipp Schmidt, as a cause of jealousy that led to an eventual separation. Schmidt was a Jena student who, both out of affection and security, accompanied Mereau to a secret meeting with Kipp in Berlin from 26 September to 3 October 1796, their last meeting before separating. Hang reasons that the relationship lost its intensity over time and distance, which led to an inevitable breakup. Fleischmann sees the breakup as being Mereau's own choice, a result of a long, inner turmoil between adapting to her roles as mother and wife and finding freedom from a loveless, controlling marriage.[40] Ultimately, her feelings of guilt led her to choose the former.

An important factor in the downfall of the relationship was, however, that Sophie Mereau began writing less and less until the correspondence stopped. Kipp lamented this absence of letters. His final letters to her demonstrate his disappointment. In fact, toward the end, he even equates his being with the letters: "Wenn du so wenig schreibst, dann fürchte ich, liest du nicht gerne, was ich so viel schreibe und möchte aber gerne, gerne von dir gelesen seyn" [When you write so little then I fear you do not like to read what I am writing so much but would very much like to be read by you.][41] To perceive the letters as conveyors of oneself reflects the power that epistolary dialogue can have on the success or failure of a relationship. Certainly, we have seen such power in the correspondence of Louise Gottsched and Meta Klopstock.

Consistency in inconsistency persists in Sophie Mereau's correspondence with Clemens Brentano. The correspondence spans from November 1798 to 24 September 1806. In its periods of intense, long letters and then equally long pauses, it reflects a relationship of alternating passionate love and hesitation, of spontaneity and reflection. Contrasts and incongruities in Mereau's letters connote a writer aware of influential, outside perceptions. Certainly Brentano had his image of Mereau, one that she tried both to accommodate and dissolve. His references to his sister's "Briefchen" as "lesser" accomplishments, his views that women's duties include captivating men and being good mothers, and his reprimand against Mereau as editor of a journal evidence the resistance all the women in his life faced. In his relationship with Mereau, he forbade her to ride horses, wear makeup, and be too social. As in her letters to Kipp, several passages in letters to Brentano display Mereau working through the contradictions in her own mind. At the same time, her plays on language and themes, pitting words and ideas against each other, reflect a need to see the contrasts in relation to, and not always in contradiction to, one another. In reflecting on what kind of letter she could compose, she opts for one that might not conform to standards of a pleasant one: "Ich könnte Ihnen manches Scherzhafte sagen, von goldnen Leiern, und lieblichen Sonnets—aber so lange ich noch den Ernst vermisse, hasse ich den Scherz im Leben, der ohne jenen, hohl ist.—" [I could tell you many things in jest, of golden lyres, and dear sonnets—but as long as I still miss the serious, I hate jesting in life, the one without the other, is hollow] (Brentano/Mereau 86). An end of one letter can initiate another; likewise a beginning can signal an end: "Sie werden nun, hoffe ich, lange nichts von mir hören, und das Erste, was Sie wieder hören werden, soll auf jeden Fall ein Ende sein" [You will now, I hope, not hear anything from me for a long time, and the first thing that you will hear again should in any case be an end] (Brentano/Mereau 86–87). She philosophically tries to map out her own plans while exploring language usage and meaning: "ja! ich habe welche, die einzigen die ich je haben werde—Das Ziel der Ausführung ist gesteckt; ich weiß daß ich dabei mein Leben wage, aber ist es zu viel, wenn man um zu leben, ein Leben wagt, daß ohne dem kein Leben ist?" [yes! I have some, the only ones that I will ever have. The goal of the implementation is laid out; I know that I wager my life in doing such, but is it too much if one risks a life in order to live, that no life exists without it?] (Brentano/Mereau 87). In predicting her own future, she can imagine any extreme: "der nächste Zustand muß Himmel oder Hölle sein" [the next situation must be heaven or hell] (Brentano/Mereau 88).

In the context of Mereau's entire literary output, such inconsistencies also appear as consistent devices. Although, as Kastinger Riley observes, Mereau shows irritation with the slow progress of women's social conditions, that irritation does not come without its accompanying apologies.[42] Moments of elation in overcoming hindrances to her personal satisfaction give way to melancholic assertions about her future. Expressed shock results in an ultimate resoluteness. In the mere venting of frustrations, however, comes relief.

Even the way in which Mereau expresses the possibility that she and Brentano might see each other again after their separation in 1803 is only suggestive, but not totally in concordance with the idea. Through letters, she has definitely felt his pressure to have them lead a life that would conform to expected gender roles. Mereau's brief letter from Weimar in March of that year begins with the poem "Der zurückgekehrte Winter" [The Returned Winter]. In the correspondence with Brentano, this poem is the first of a series that represents Mereau's turning from classical forms, styles, and symbols to strive for her own poetic maturity.[43] The poem's form assimilates a canon in which the first line of every strophe repeats the last line of the preceding strophe, thereby emulating the eternal passing of the seasons. The last stanza unexpectedly breaks the cyclical rhythm, however, by repeating the third line of the first stanza, in the same way that winter returns when spring has already begun. Because there is no trace of a first-person narrator, the poem represents a step away from the separation between empirical knowledge and personal reflection, as found in her earlier poems. Human interaction with nature is there though, woven in by means of the "Erinnrung" [Remembrances] that, like the winter, return again. Mereau's own ambiguous feelings toward a reunion surface in subtle interaction between "Frühlingsdüfte, süßes Wähnen,/laue Lüfte, leises Sehnen" [Smells of spring, sweet illusions/balmy airs, quiet longing] and the lethal Winter, "so mit eisigem Gefieder,/eingehüllt in kalte Flocken" [with such icy feathers, encased in cold flakes]. She substantiates her wavering feelings in the lines to Brentano following the poem. "Es ist nicht unmöglich, daß wir uns wieder sehen;" she writes noncommitantly, "*hier* in Weimar aber niemals. Überlassen Sie es dem Schicksal oder Ihrer Gottheit, wenn Sie eine anerkennen" [It is not impossible that we will see each other again, but never again here in Weimar. Leave it to fate or to your deity, if you recognize one] (Brentano/Mereau 121).

Ironically, despite Mereau's concerted efforts to criticize Brentano for his traditional image of her that stifles her creativity, it is his letters that ultimately convince her to allow him to return to her during their separations. As in the relationship with Kipp, correspondence sustains intimacy along with fantasy. Mereau plays out that fantasy by including in her letters poems that help her deal with psychological crises in her life. Moreover, letters contain tightly woven texts of metaphors, images, and forms that comprise aesthetic units with a conscious message. Her letter from November 1799 provides an apt example of persistent contradictions and the relief she finds in writing them down. She begins immediately with her ambivalence toward writing letters, questioning the conventional view that letters can be substitute dialogues that make up for distances of time and space between friends: "Es ist ein sonderbares Gefühl, sich auf dem Papier jemand nähern zu wollen, und ich habe Ihre Entfernung nie mehr gefühlt als jetzt da ich Ihnen schreiben will" [It is a strange feeling to want to draw close to someone on paper, and I have never felt your distance so much as now, when I want to write to you] (Brentano/Mereau 84). Instead of presence, she sees absence, yet her ambivalence toward letter writing cannot deny its worth:

Ich hasse alle Briefe an vertraute Wesen, ob ich sie gleich um keinen Preis missen möchte.—Ein Brief ist mir immer wie ein Roman,—und ich mag lieber zu wenig als zu viel sagen. Das Papier ist ein so ungetreuer Bote, daß es den Blick, den Ton vergißt, und oft sogar einen falschen Sinn überbringt,—und doch ist selbst der Kampf mit Irrungen besser als die fürchterliche Öde, die kein Ton durchhallt.

[I hate all letters to intimate beings, although I would not want to miss them at any cost.—A letter is always like a novel to me,—and I prefer to say too little than too much. The paper is such a disloyal messenger, that it forgets the glance, the tone, and often even conveys a false sense,—and still even the struggle with errors is better than the horrible dreariness through which no tone resounds.] (Brentano/Merceau 84)

Instead of offering substitute dialogues, the letter has become for her a means of direct expression that will assure an audience. Communication might not be as immediate as theorists had claimed, but the letter has the advantage of offering response and reactions.

Mereau's reflections on letter writing then lead her to analyze her process of writing poetry. She describes the "freie, poetische Stimmung" [free, poetic mood] she has experienced in recent weeks, which is becoming destroyed by "dem kalten Hauch der Notwendigkeit" [the cold breath of necessity] (Brentano/Mereau 84). The often-cited passage that conveys her struggle follows: "Ich kämpfe im Leben einen sonderbaren Kampf. Eine unwiderstehliche Neigung drängt mich, mich ganz der Phantasie hinzugeben, das gestaltlose Dasein mit der Dichtung Farben zu umspielen und unbekümmert um das Nötige nur dem Schönen zu leben" [I am struggling in life a strange struggle. An irreppressible inclination forces me to submit myself totally to fantasy, to engulf amorphous life with the colors of poetry and, unconcerned about necessity, to live only the beautiful (Brentano/Mereau 84). Her metaphorical skiff of life floats "auf keiner spiegelhellen Fläche" [on no clearly reflecting surface], and she has the choice of being driven by a "schmeicheldes Lüftchen" [flattering little wind] or to grasp the rudder. Without the control, however, she will sink: "und ich muß das Ruder ergreifen oder untergehn" [and I must grasp the rudder or go under] (Brentano/Mereau 85).

Whereas the first paragraph brings her away from conventional theories to decide in favor of the advantages of letter writing for her personal desires, the metaphors in the second paragraph lead her to be convinced of the importance of her other duties over her desires. The third paragraph brings her back to her desires. She does not want to complain or rave in her letters: "beides will ich nicht, und ich muß mich daher hüten, die Saite zu berühren, wo alles in mir Klang, Stimme, schmerzhafter Gesang wird—und doch ertönt sie so leicht!—" [I do not want both, and I must restrain myself from touching the string where everything in me becomes sound, voice, painful song—and still it reverberates so easily] (Brentano/Mereau 85). As in the first paragraph, she has come out in favor of releasing her emotions in letters, whether those emotions fit the standards of a happy letter or not. That decision reflects in the rest of her letter, as she praises Brentano for his letters, offering constructive criticism that enjoys a letter that is "herzlich" [cordial] and "wahr" [true], and not only "witzig" [witty]. Her final advice plays with the contradictions she has just analyzed: "Sei stolz und bescheiden. Lebe der Liebe und liebe das Leben" [Be proud and modest. Live love and love life] (Brentano/Mereau 85). Mereau has composed an entire letter around the contradictions and ambivalences she experiences in writing. Yet in merely relating her turmoils she is relieved. The letter, despite the skepticism she has toward it, offers release, just as the composition of *Amanda and Eduard* from correspondence with Kipp presented the opportunity to play out in real life her fantasy.

Fantasy and reality intertwine in prevalent images revolving around the theatrical arena as well. The motif of the theater and the actress as protagonist surfaces in her short story "Die Flucht nach der Hauptstadt," which depicts the theater as both fascinating and deceptive. At the beginning of the story, the narrator is performing in productions her father stages in his own private theater. In doing so, she falls in love with Albino, the actor with whom she acts out love scenes in plays. The fact that the public finds the love scenes so authentic contributes to the play's success as well as blurs the lines between reality and appearances. When her father wants to marry her to an aristocrat, she runs away with Albino. They continue to act together, but are then deceived by a mutual friend, Felix, who turns out to be an actor, too. Felix leads the protagonist to believe that her father has thrown Albino in prison while convincing Albino that the father has locked her up in a cloister. Albino leaves and the narrator stays with Felix. She becomes attracted to Felix when he is on the stage and she thus assumes, as she states, "die Rolle seiner Geliebten" [the role of his mistress].[44] While her talents as an actress bring her fame, her inability to distance herself from role-playing causes her unhappiness. When she discovers Felix's real, tyrannical side, she escapes. A subsequent, brief love affair with an artist ends with his death. Her acting talents bring her eventual happiness, though, when Albino recognizes her in a performance. Their reunion ends happily, with the narrator's final plea for freedom of choice in life and love, "zehnfach zu leben, um uns zehnfach lieben zu können" [to live ten times, in order to be able to love each other ten times.][45]

Besides fictional portrayals of theater life, regular accounts in Mereau's diary display an avid interest in the theater and actual participation in plays. The staging of drama within small circles of friends flourished during the late eighteenth and early nineteenth centuries. The fact that such intimate productions were sustained largely by the participation of women—Mereau also has her companions; Helmina von Chézy, Charlotte von Stein, and Caroline Schlegel-Schelling also talk about participating in plays—suggests an alternative to the precarious material and social conditions under which professional actresses had to live.[46] While actors, too, faced meager wages, nonbinding contracts, and prejudices questioning the intellectual worth of their profession, actresses especially were targets of indictments against their moral integrity, not to mention wage inequities and other disciminatory labor practices.[47] In addition, productions in intimate circles did not have to adhere to censorship restrictions and laws against improvisation that affected playwrights and actors in public institutions. They also granted an audience for pieces whose publication might otherwise have been difficult. The private stagings in which many women were involved also largely coincide with the desires of the bourgeoisie to build their own identity outside the aristocratic world.

Given Mereau's interest in role-playing and the continual dialogue over gender roles in her correspondence with Brentano, the frequent appearance of the metaphor of transvestism seems not coincidental. In her published works, it is often the male figure who can speak out against an inhumane attitude towards women or women who find as men that they can attain independence and freedom in a harmony with society. In *Blütenalter der Empfindlichkeit*, the male narrator asserts ideas on the need for women's freedom in a way that a woman narrator could not. In fact, so adept is Mereau's skill at role reversal that for the first eight pages of the novel, readers are unsure of the sex of the first-person narrator. In her essay on Ninon Lenclos, she lauds the French salonière's belief in equal rights. To that end, though, it seems that only through becoming men themselves will women experience that equality. The challenge women face in accomplishing this task attracted Mereau, for she seems more fascinated with Lenclos's suggestion than condemnatory:

Bald lenkte ihr Hang zur Betrachtung, ihre Blicke auch auf die festgesetzten Verhältnisse der beiden Geschlechter. Sie fühlte die Ungerechtigkeit derselben, und konnte sie nicht ertragen. Ich sehe, sagte sie zu einem ihrer Freunde, daß man an uns die leersten und schaalsten Forderungen thut, und daß die Männer sich das Recht vorbehalten haben, nach dem

Würdigsten und Belohnendsten zu streben, und von diesem Augenblicke an werde ich Mann.

[Soon her tendency toward observation directed her glance toward the ingrained relationships of the two sexes. She felt the injustice of that and could not stand it. I see, she said to one of her friends, that one gives us the emptiest and most resonating demands, and that the men have reserved for themselves the right to strive for the most worthy and most rewarding, and from this moment on I became a man.] (*Kalathiskos* II: 60).[48]

Likewise, Mereau's correspondence employs the metaphor of role reversal in incidents where she wants to stand on equal ground with Brentano. In one extensive passage, she imagines herself following him as a man (Brentano/Mereau 251–52). Clemens calls her "Sophus" in letters. She calls herself his "Freund" (Brentano/Mereau 240). The Klopstocks had also used role reversal, in a manner so that both could experience a oneness in letter writing. More frequently, however, the woman adopted the role of a literary model before her; Meta Moller was "Clarissa" and Anna Louisa Karsch was "Sappho." In adopting these images, the women were in their own right reformulating men's ideas of these foremothers into active role models for subsequent women. Mereau, although she does refer to Brentano's "weibliche Natur," seems to adopt and accept the male character as a window of opportunity to allow her more freedom. Günderrode, too, will adopt the male role. The motif of transvestism plays into larger questions of identity, although Mereau never actually questions or calls attention to the fragmentation of her selves, as we will see Günderrode does.

More often than Louise Gottsched and Meta Klopstock, Sophie Mereau shows confidence in confronting the source of her woes herself, despite her hesitation. Donning a mask or veil, even in letters, mollifies that confrontation. Such is the case when she describes a dream in which she saw Brentano with two other women. She becomes confused as she watches him court the other women, frustrated to see herself in two different roles concurrently: "da ich doch bei diesem Spiel, Spieler und Zuschauer zugleich war" [for in this play I was player and audience at the same time] (Brentano/Mereau 322). The dream serves as a buffer against direct admission of her jealousy. "Genug von Träumen!" [Enough of dreams!] she exclaims, and goes on to talk about her time in Heidelberg. Even though she expresses mistrust in the letter form, her statement equating it with the novel discloses ambiguous feelings about both. The same veil of fiction on which she relies in her published works exists in her letters, too. But close reading of her letters reveals well-crafted pieces whose value lies not only in relation to her published works, but also in their own intrinsic aesthetic merit.

Unlike Mereau and Karsch, Günderrode never published her works under her own name, adopting the pseudonym of Tian or Jon. Born ten years after Mereau, she had less personal interactions with writers of German Classicism and Enlightenment, although scholars have interpreted her works as efforts to harmonize classical ideals with romantic forms. Later, both women came to know many of the same cultural figures of Romanticism—Clemens Brentano, Friedrich Schlegel, Bettine Brentano, and Achim von Arnim. Whereas Mereau became one of the first women to earn her living writing, Günderrode was able to rely on her upper-class background for her main financial support. Although her family was impoverished aristocracy, at least her social class privileged her to live in a cloister founded for women in her situation.

Karoline von Günderrode was born on 11 February 1789 in Karlsruhe. Her mother was a learned woman who had published short essays and poems anonymously and who thus educated Karoline at home. Her father was an advisor for the court and died when Karoline was six years old. In 1797, Karoline went to live at the *Cronstetten-Hynspergisches Damenstift* in Frankfurt am Main, a Lutheran cloister for upper-class unmarried and widowed women. There Karoline read voraciously, studied philosophy and history, and corresponded regularly with her friends Lisette von Nees, Susanne Heyden, Gunda Brentano, and Bettine Brentano. In 1799, she fell in love with the law historian Karl von Savigny and continued to correspond with him after he married Gunda Brentano. In 1801, she met Clemens Brentano and began another intense relationship that ended with his marriage to Sophie Mereau in 1803. In 1804, Günderrode entered into what would become a tragic relationship with Friedrich Creuzer, a classics professor at Heidelberg. Creuzer's decision to return to his wife devastated Günderrode. She committed suicide in 1806.

To interpret her suicide solely in connection with her unrequited love, however, would be to ignore other more profound conflicts in her life. Her letters and writings reveal an irreconcilable contradiction between her desires to study, write, and publish, and the pressure to conform to traditional roles for women. Also, the motif of death recurs, not as a haunting force in her life, but as a site of hope and mystical reunion with mother nature's elements. Unfortunately, not until Christa Wolf's essays on Günderrode and Bettine von Arnim, Wolf's work, *Kein Ort. Nirgends,* and her annotated edition of Günderrode's works and letters have German scholars even remotely considered granting the poet a place in the literary canon.[49]

Regarding the reception and history of their letters as they exist today, Karsch, Mereau, and Günderrode show more similarities than differences. In quantity, their correspondence stands proportionately equal to their published works. As with Karsch and Mereau, Günderrode's letters also caused strong, mixed reactions from readers. After Karoline von Günderrode's suicide, her friend and confidante in the relationship with Creuzer, Susanne von Heyden, burned all of Günderrode's letters to Creuzer. Remains of letters to Creuzer turned up in the Leske family archive, in the form of copies made by the wife Sophie Creuzer. In contrast, Friedrich Creuzer's friends convinced him that his letters to Günderrode could be very important, and thus he requested them back from Heyden. He did not burn them though, in case he ever needed to prove his innocence in the whole affair.[50] Once again, the woman's voice threatened the man's point of view. These letters were published in 1912, but the one-sidedness again eliminates the woman's voice.

Similar to the reception of Karsch and Mereau in secondary literature, the inability to categorize Günderrode's works into any set literary period—in her case, neither Classicism nor Romanticism—has marginalized more than integrated her *oeuvre* within the canon. Like Karsch and Mereau, too, critics have been more interested in her personal life and relationships with famous men of their day than in her works.[51] In recent biographical accounts, the tragic deaths of both Günderrode and Mereau have become examples of women's limited hopes for a long survival under the physical and emotional constraints of the age.[52] Whereas for Mereau, no critical edition of her collected works exists, a historical/critical collection of Günderrode's work finally appeared in 1991, although it only includes letters in the comments about specific works.[53] A separate, more complete, chronological collection of the letters appeared in 1992.[54]

The most extensive recent attempt at thorough analysis of the correspondences is in Margarete Lazarowicz's *Karoline von Günderrode: Portrait einer Fremden*, which looks at Günderrode's correspondences with Karoline von Barkhaus, Friedrich Carl von Savigny, Clemens Brentano, Lisette und Nees von Esenbeck, Bettina Brentano, Susanne von Heyden, and Friedrich Creuzer.[55] These correspondents, contends Lazarowicz, projected their own subjective, fixed ideas when interpreting Günderrode through her letters. Her study thus focuses on analyzing those subjective, outside impressions in the context of the relationships. Lazarowicz rightly suggests that the letters should be studied in conjunction with analysis of Günderrode's literary works. She believes, however, that Günderrode sought and found an outlet for self-expression only in the literary realm. In contrast, according to Lazarowicz, in letters to friends Günderrode was more apt to hold back rather than realize her full self. Thus, the letters act as "mere additions" to literary analysis and not as ends in themselves for their own metaphors.[56]

As with Karsch and Mereau, however, the letter offers Günderrode an aesthetic outlet for creating images of her multifaceted self in relation to her social environment. Both Karsch's and Mereau's fantasies inspire them to create published works from material in their letters and to create a constant interchange between private and public writings. Likewise, their epistolary dialogues are replete with literary metaphors, topoi, and forms that reflect the multifariousness in their lives and works. The letter-writing act has subversive potential: it helps the women writers escape binding social norms at the same time that it can disguise unconventionality. Thus, letters deserve the same keen sense of analysis of images, metaphors, rhetorical devices, and the like, as any other literary work.

As with Karsch and Mereau, Günderrode's letters are replete with images of masking, veiling, and transformation. The most prevalent and complicated is the change in sex roles. The reasons for such a posture are several. For a woman who lacked self-esteem and confidence due to her precarious position as an unmarried writer of the nineteenth-century fallen aristocracy, being a male would allow her to fit in to a society polarized by sex. To Gunda Brentano on 29 August 1801, Günderrode writes about her wish to be a man:

Gestern las ich Ossians Darthula, und es wirkte so angenehm auf mich; der alte Wunsch einen Heldentod zu sterben ergrif mich mit groser Heftigkeit; unleidlich war es mir noch zu leben, unleidlicher ruhig und gemein zu sterben. Schon oft hatte ich den unweiblichen Wunsch mich in ein wildes Schlachtgetümmel zu werfen, zu sterben. Warum ward ich kein Mann! ich habe keinen Sinn für weibliche Tugenden, für Weiberglükseeligkeit. Nur das Wilde Grose, Glänzende gefällt mir. Es ist ein unseliges aber unverbesserliches Misverhältniss in meiner Seele; und es wird und muß so bleiben, denn ich bin ein Weib, und habe Begierden wie ein Mann, ohne Männerkraft. Darum bin ich so wechselnd, und so uneins mit mir.

[Yesterday I read Ossian's Darthula, and it had such a pleasant effect on me; the old wish to die a hero's death seized me with great vehemence it was intolerable to me to continue living, more intolerable to die peacefully and commonly. I had often had the unfeminine wish to throw myself into the midst of a raging battle, to die. Why wasn't I born a man! I have no sense for feminine virtues, for female bliss. I only take pleasure in the wild, great, glittering. It is an unfortunate but incorrigible incongruity in my soul; and it must become and remain so, for I am a woman, and have the yearnings of a man, without a man's strength. For this reason I am so changing, and so at odds with myself.] (*Schatten* 140).

Caught in a world of social constructs based on biological makeup, Günderrode feels the shackles of her female body. Only her physical being stands in the way of letting what she views as her masculine desires free. In the body of a man she could derive the power to integrate her desires with society's expectations. The disunity she feels here will persist in the perceptions she and others have. Clemens Brentano later criticized her first collection of poems because they hovered "zwischen dem Männlichen und Weiblichen" [between the masculine and the feminine] (*Schatten* 190).

A second reason for sex transformation relates to Günderrode's personal friendships. In a triangular relationship, such as that between Günderrode, Savigny, and Gunda Brentano, it is less threatening when the woman who is a friend to the married couple sees herself as a man. The married man and unmarried woman can continue the relationship as merely a friendly, and not an erotic, sexual one. Günderrode writes to Savigny, after Gunda and he become a pair. She asks if she can continue writing, but recognizes that it would be much better if she were male: "Ich finde unser neues Verhältniß sehr schön und frei, aber ich wollte daß irgend ein sichtbares Band mich an Euch bände, wenn ich doch Ihr Bruder wäre, oder Gundelchen's Schwester; ich würde es nicht schöner finden, aber sichrer" [I am finding our new relationship very nice and free, but I would wish that some kind of visible bond would bind us together, if I only were your brother, or Gundelchen's sister; I would not find it more beautiful, but more secure] (*Schatten* 162–63). In correspondence with Savigny and Gunda Brentano, she becomes "der Freund" or even "Günderchen" or "Günderödchen" as a neutered person (*Schatten* 149–50; 153).

Yet in these role changes, Günderrode is not merely conceding to societal expectations. Weißenborn, in her introduction to the recent collection of Günderrode's letters, suggests that Günderrode played just as significant a role in deciding whether she and Savigny and then she and Brentano should marry as the men themselves did. Such an idea challenges the conventional view that the men, threatened by the intense, intellectual feeling she showed toward them, spurned her. Instead, she plays an active role in a mutual decision by rejecting a marriage with them, two men with ideas of a quiet, bourgeois marriage. This union would not fit into the mystical dreams of a larger harmony that unites spirit and nature in a realm removed from the limitations of the prosaic world. This view would also explain her desire to continue a relationship with Savigny after he marries Gunda Brentano. That relationship is now more on her terms, that is, one in which she sees her only possible role as male or gender neutral. This interpretation also coincides with several statements to Savigny that she does not want to marry Creuzer. That she insists on informing his wife of their relationship and at one point even suggests that they live as a threesome together corroborates her desire to form radical relationships outside the boundaries of traditional marriage. For her biography, as with Karsch and Mereau, her life thus becomes a series not of unrequited love relationships, as it has been written, but of attempts to adhere to her own well-formulated ideals.

In her letters to Creuzer, she develops the "Freund" [male friend] character, speaking using the male voice in indirect speech in the third person. In this instance, the character of the male friend can fulfill her fantasy to be with Creuzer:

Der Freund hat mir gesagt, wenn dieser Krieg ihm und seinen Wünschen gefährlich werden sollte, so wollte er, Dir bewußt, Kleidung anziehen, entlaufen und bei Ihnen Bedienter werden. Wegjagen können Sie ihn doch nicht, und er wollte sich so fein verstellen, daß man ihn nicht erkennen sollte. Das wollte er Ihnen gelegentlich alles begreiflich machen. Wollen Sie ihn aber alsdann der öffentlichen Meinung wegen nicht aufnehmen, so wolle er den Tod suchen. Doch was brauche ich das zu schreiben?

[The (male) friend said to me that if this battle should become dangerous for him and for his wishes, then he would want, with you knowing it, to dress up, run away, and become a servant for you. You would not have the heart to chase him away, and he would want to disguise himself so well that no one would recognize him. He would want you to understand that. If you didn't want to take him into your service because of public opinion, then he would want to look for death. But what's the need for writing all this?] (*Schatten* 232)

The fact that she floats back and forth between using the first and third person indicates a more profound reason for creating a new male self in her difficult relationship, a reason founded more on psychological self-analysis than on mere physical desire. The third-person form gives her appropriate distance for reflective questioning. It also allows her to suggest reasons for her own hesitations, such as when she talks about "the friend" not wanting to write: "Der Freund war eben hier; er sagte, oft schon hätte er Ihnen schreiben wollen, aber es sei ihm so unbehaglich, da er das, worum es ihm eigentlich zu tun sei, doch nicht schreiben könne" [The friend [male] was just here; he says that he has often wanted to write to you, but it was so uncomfortable to him in that he could not really write the things he was actually concerned about] (222). Coupled with this hestation to write is the struggle Günderrode fights in her life, that between independence and resignation to norms, as she expresses in the following portrayal of "the friend's" needs:

> Was sein übriges Leben betrifft, so merke ich immer mehr, daß seine heroische Seele sich in Liebesweichheit und Liebessehnen ganz aufgelöst hat. Dieser Zustand ist nicht gut für einen Menschen, der doch für sich allein stehen muß und der wohl nimmer mehr dem Gegenstand seiner Liebe vereint wird. Er kann die Resignation nicht lange ins Auge fassen, er täuscht sich oft darüber; zeigen Sie ihm die Unmöglichkeit, unterstützen Sie mich. Ihre Zuredungen werden am besten wirken. Es ist sonderbar, aber in Gedanken besitzt er seinen geliebten Gegenstand so *ganz*, daß es viele Augenblikke gibt, in denen er meint, man könne nur so gewiß und ausführlich denken, was einmal so wirklich würde, wie man es dächte.
>
> Wenn ein solcher Paroxysmus vorüber ist, wird er immer schrecklich traurig. Sagen Sie mir, wie soll ich mich zu ihm verhalten?"

[Concerning the rest of his life, I notice more and more that his heroic soul resolved itself into love's tenderness and love's longing. This condition is not good for a person who really must stand alone for himself and who probably will never be united with the object of his love again. He cannot apprehend the resignation any longer in his mind, he is deceived often by that; show him the impossibility, support me. Your encouragement will work the best. It is strange, but in thought he possesses his beloved object *totally* so that there are many moments in which he believes one could only so certainly and completely think what at one time would be so possible as one would have thought.

When such a paroxysm is over he always becomes frightfully sad. Tell me how I should behave towards him?] (*Schatten* 222–23)

As in her wish to Gunda Brentano to be a man, the heroic soul fights with his tenderness and longing, the masculine with his feminine desires. When writing to a man now, conveying this struggle through the figure of the male friend makes the attempt at blurring gender constraints less threatening. Placing the reference to being alone within the context of one male friend to another also makes Günderrode's feelings of isolation, resignation, disillusion, and paroxysm less gender-related, and thus less menacing for the male reader. In ending with a question she avoids appearing too forward in her demands.

Through the male perspective she can ask for clarification, which otherwise might seem too bold, such as in the following passage:

Der Freund ist in großer Unruhe, wie Sie die Einsicht in das Unmögliche, die Ihnen die letzten Briefe zeigen, ertragen werden. Sie haben gehofft, er selbst hat es dunkel geahnt, jetzt ist es auf einmal aus auf immer, das holde Licht verlischt auf den letzten Strahl. Wie werden Sie das empfinden? Werden Sie sich nicht wegwenden von einer Aussicht, die sich in trübe Nacht verliert.

[The friend [male] is in great turmoil, over how you will bear the insight into the impossible that the last letters show you. You have hoped, he himself has vaguely forseen it, now it is suddenly gone forever, the lovely light extinguishes to the last ray. How will you feel about that? Won't you turn away from a view that loses itself in the dreary night.] ((*Schatten* 223)

As I have stated before, role-playing is not unusual in women's letters—Meta Klopstock and Sophie Mereau both cultivated exchange of sex roles. In Meta's case, the man participated in the reversal, whereas the men in Sophie's and Karoline's cases merely fostered the change in the women. In all instances, there are certainly practical reasons that the men would allow and even encourage the women to accept male roles. In labeling Mereau "Sophus," Brentano gives her the respect she needed to commit herself to a relationship to him. Savigny could continue his friendship with Günderrode after his marriage if his friend were neuter or of the male sex. For Creuzer, who addresses Günderrode back as the male friend (232; 237), the male disguise offered the necessary mask to conceal their relationship; it was harder for his wife to find out who his lover was. That these early nineteenth-century men did not do as Klopstock had, however, and assign themselves female roles that would complement the women, tells something about the demarcation and valuation of gender roles by the end of the eighteenth century. Many women came increasingly to realize the benefits of being a man and attempted to reap those benefits through role reversal, and increasingly more men seemed to recognize that role reversal for men had few advantages in a society that not only limited career and personal options for women, but also demeaned their restricted roles as mothers and wives. Most blurring of gender roles occurred when women adopted the so-called masculine traits to the benefit of the man.

Like Mereau, who experimented with male and female points of view in both her published works and letters, the sex transformations in Günderrode's letters coincide with similar changing perspectives in her works. Goozé, for example, has analyzed Günderrode's poem "Don Juan," in which female and male voices interchange ("The Seduction of Don Juan"). Goozé claims that Günderrode's use of the third-person male form in letters to Creuzer was both to hide their identities in letters, for the sake of secrecy, and to imagine herself in an equal relationship with Creuzer. Interestingly, many passages reveal a lapse into dreaming and role-playing and point to Günderrode's recognition of the ability to equalize in such fantasies, but also of the impossibility of attainment. Questions, dreams, and subjunctive forms indicate a need to build some kind of utopia that would exist beyond societal constraints. Savigny is a "Schatten eines Traumes" (136). Talking about her depression to Gunda Brentano, she pleads: "laß uns wehnigstens dies fatale Thema mit Träumen umspinnen" [let's at least cover this fatal theme with dreams] (142). Her letters are filled with words such as "Träume" [dreams], "Phantasie" [fantasy], "Zauberwelt" [world of magic] (*Schatten* 142). She relates one such vision to Creuzer:

> Der Freund war eben bei mir; er war sehr lebendig, und ein ungewöhnlich Rot brannte auf seiner Wange. Er sagte, er habe im Morgenschlummer von Eusebio geträumt, wie er ganz mit ihm vereint gewesen und mit ihm durch reizende Täler und waldige Hügel gewandelt sei in seliger Liebe und Freiheit. Ist ein solcher Traum nicht mehr wert als ein Jahr meines Lebens? Wenn ich nur Monate so glücklich und so schuldlos glücklich wäre als in diesem Traum, wie gerne und mit welcher Dankbarkeit gegen die Götter wollte ich sterben!

> [The friend [male] was just here with me; he was very lively, and an unusual red color flamed on his cheek. He said he dreamed of Eusebio in his morning slumber, how he was totally united with him and wandered with him through charming valleys and wooded hills in blissful love and freedom. Isn't such a dream more valuable than a year of my life? If I only were for months so happy and so innocent as in this dream, how happily and with such thankfulness against the gods I would die.] (*Schatten* 235–36)

The combination of relating her dream through the perspective of the male friend and of summarizing the value of the dream for her life in a question again provides an indirect way of confronting constraints.

Perhaps more strongly than Mereau, Günderrode felt herself in constant confrontation with ideals of womanhood from the outside. Karsch recognized at times gender inequities, but handled each situation on its own terms without turning her efforts into a conscious demand for equality. Mereau, as an established writer who had struggled in conventional relationships, was able to remain more ironic in her confrontations and thus not be hurt personally. Her first letter to Clemens reflects her ability to see wittily the human capacity to be many persons at once, as she calls Clemens "*lieber, schrecklicher* göttlicher, unmenschlicher Clemens!*" [*dear, terrible*, divine, inhuman Clemens!] (Brentano/Mereau 75). Günderrode, as a single woman writing in a man's world, stood in more direct confrontation with the ideals of femininity than the men in her closest circle of friends espoused. After first meeting Savigny, she explains to Karoline von Barkhaus her attraction to him, feeling: "wie weit ich von dem Ideal entfernt bin daß sich ein S. erträumen kann" [far removed from the ideal . . . that an S. can dream of] (*Schatten* 134). Savigny's advice to her about the Creuzer affair reflects his view of her as a "passive Natur:" "Etwas recht von Herzen lieben, ist göttlich, und jede Gestalt, in der sich uns dieses Göttliche offenbart, ist heilig. Aber daran künsteln, diese Empfindung durch Phantasie hörer spannen, als ihre natürliche Kraft reicht, ist sehr unheilig" [To love something straight from the heart is divine, and every form in which this divine appears is holy. But to create art out of that, to stretch through fantasy this feeling tighter than its natural strength reaches, is very harmful] (*Schatten* 179). He is happy about the "Ruhe" [calm] she has used in her correspondence with Creuzer, thereby praising her for not undertaking an active pursuit in the love relationship (*Schatten* 177).

In her profession, she encountered disbelief and discouragement. Clemens Brentano cannot believe the poems from Tian are by her, for they reflect an image of her that is incongruent with how he has known her: in real life, she has seemed so "schuldlos, süß" [innocent, sweet], but the poems show "Qual, Schmerz" [torment, pain] (*Schatten* 185). His advice to her is: "sein Sie ein Weib, sein Sie weich, verzeihen Sie mir, sein Sie meine Freundin" [be a woman, be tender, pardon me, be my friend] (*Schatten* 186). His comment that he cannot judge the poems until he knows for sure they are by her reflects his inability to separate the woman from the art work. He is very curious to know why she published her poems, for he sees such publication as a sign that the author has no other listeners for her woes. Such a comment about women's writing is reminiscent of Prutz's remarks that only unhappy women write (189).[57] How could she have hidden her "ernsthaftes poetisches Talent" [serious poetic talent] from him? He criticizes the collection for its inability to fit into definite categories of feminine and masculine and for its learned vocabulary that does not mesh with the whole. He thus implies that he had expected something less learned from her:

Das einzige, was man der ganzen Sammlung Böses vorwerfen könnte, wäre, daß sie zwischen dem Männlichen und Weiblichen schwebt, und hier und da nicht genug Gedichten, sondern sehr gelungen aufgegebenen Exerzitien oder Ausarbeitungen gleicht; dieses erscheint besonders durch einen hie und da hervorblickenden kleinen gelehrten Anstrich, der oft nicht im Gleichgewicht mit dem Ganzen steht, zum Beispiel Worte wie Adept, Apokalyptisch und soweiter als Titel.

[The only thing that one could find fault with in the entire collection would be that you have remained suspended between the masculine and the feminine, and here and there not resemble poems enough, but rather very successfully discarded exercises or compositions; this is apparant especially in the small learned airs that appear here and there, which often do not stand in balance with the whole, for example words such as adept, apocalyptic and so forth as titles.] (*Schatten* 190)

He even questions the originality of her poetry, stating that some poems seem translated from French. After lauding her "Talent zur Versifikation" [talent for creating verse] (*Schatten* 190), he likens her writing to having a wig set upon a dove.

In her relationship with Creuzer, she faces norms that stultify both her personal and professional goals. Based on her poems, Creuzer reports his friends' skepticism toward Günderrode's abilities as a wife. In one letter he recounts how one of his female friends doubts Günderrode's ability to fulfill her duties as a female. In Günderrode's poetry the friend had found "etwas zu kühn, und männlich" [somewhat too bold, and masculine] (*Schatten* 230). Another male friend had disliked the fact that Günderrode had aligned herself with the so-called new school in her poetry and philosophy (230–31). For her time and position, Karoline's response is a strong rejection of such narrow categorization. She first tries to reassure Creuzer that she only wants to please him. But she eventually works up to her main message, which is for him to judge for himself and not let those who do not know her persuade him: "Mein Leben möge mich rechtfertigen, nicht meine Worte." [May my life justify me, not my words] His friends do not know her, she retorts. Regarding her intellectual ideas, she remains strong in her convictions: "Soll ich mich entschuldigen über das, was ich vortrefflich in mir finde? Ich verstehe nicht, in welchem Zusammenhang dies mit meinem gefürchteten Untalent, Sie zu beglücken, steht." [Should I excuse myself for that which I find excellent in me? I do not understand what this has to do with my terrifying untalent to defile you.] Her lapses into masking herself as a friend act as ways to soften her outbursts: "Ich will alles tun, was Sie wollen, wenn nur Sie den Freund nicht verkennen. Haben Sie ihn, seit er Sie liebt, nicht gehorsam, demütig, Ihnen ergeben gefunden? Hat er etwas gegen Sie getan, das nur das kleinste Mißtrauen gegen ihn rechtfertigen könnte? Lassen Sie doch sein Leben reden, nicht Fremde, die es nicht verstehen." [I want to do everything that you want if only you do not misjudge your friend. Haven't you, since he has loved you, found him obedient, humble, devoted to you? Has he done something against you that you are able to justify the slightest mistrust in him? Let his life speak for him, not strangers, who do not understand it.] And yet her final statement cannot help but place her in the active role as speaker of her criticisms: "Meine Liebe können Sie doch nur allein verstehen, und jedes Urteil, das nicht von dieser ausgeht, ist falsch" [You alone can only understand my love, and every judgment that is not based on it is false] (*Schatten* 233). The letter is retort, defense, appeasement, and mollification all in one.

In reacting to a letter from Clemens Brentano in which he quotes something she has said, Günderrode laments that when she rereads her own words she sees herself as if in a coffin "und meine beiden Ichs starren sich ganz verwundert an" [and both my I's stare at each other totally in amazement] (*Schatten* 184). This image is one of the most poignant ones in her letters and acutely reflects her awareness of the ideal images that she and others formulate of her. Weißenborn and Lazarowicz both state that for Günderrode, it did not suffice to express herself only in letter writing.[58] That might be true, but a reading of her letters and a knowledge that the extant correspondence comprises more than four hundred letters proves that her other writings alone also were not adequate for her self-expression. Letters offer her a chance to confront the restrictive images that a gender ideology imposes on her. In writing and reading her letters, she recognizes the importance of her own concerns (*Schatten* 135–36). Corresponding allows her to explore her many faces and to make others understand this aspect about her. That understanding arises during the process of rereading letters: "Gunda Du wirst über diesen Brief lachen; er komt mir selbst so unzusammenhängend und verwirrt vor" [Gunda you will laugh at this letter; it appears so disjointed and confused even to me] (*Schatten* 140). Recognition of multidimensionality cannot come without questions of unity and integrity. In acknowledging other people's disunities, she realizes that the many sides to a person must still be honest to themselves and others. If Gunda does not write to her, she asserts, "so habe ich nichts von Dir als eine Erinnerung, die wahrscheinlich Deinem sogenannten Ich (wenn ich es wiedersehe) gar nicht mehr gleich sieht, denn Du Wandelbare bist doppelt wandelbar, aus natürlichem Hang, und aus Koketterie, die den auch wie Du sagst, Natur ist" [thus I have nothing for you except a memory, which probably does not even resemble your so-called I (when I see it again) any more, for you variable are doubly variable, from a natural tendency, and from coquetry, which, as you also say, is nature] (*Schatten* 141). To her, Gunda is a "wechselnde See," a "Schauspiel . . . ein schönes mannigfaches Spiel" [changing sea, a theater piece . . . a beautiful diverse game] (*Schatten* 139).

Aware of her multifarious "selves," Günderrode explores her need for "truth" in letters and thereby for her own integrity. With a mixture of guilt and frankness, she tells Savigny about her relationship with Creuzer (*Schatten* 174). Her expressed desire not to marry him is coupled with her perception of herself as fragmented: "es war mir wohl als müßte ich mit mir selbst diese Schuld bezahlen, aber Creuzer zu heurathen dazu fand ich in meinem Gemüth keine Möglichkeit, ich war verwirrt und uneins mit mir selber" [it seemed to me as if I had to pay for this guilt with myself, but I found no possibility in my mind to marry Creuzer, I was confused and at odds with myself] (*Schatten* 174–75). Although she cannot come to terms with following conventions, she also recognizes she cannot deny her own feelings either: "was soll ich dann thun, lieber Savingny? Entsagen? ich will gar nicht davon reden was dadurch aus mir wird . . . Ich schreibe Ihnen dies alles lieber Savingny, wie ich es denke und fühle, wenn Du denkst ich irre so sage es mir, aber ich meine nun, es wäre keine gute Handlung wenn ich entsagte, doch traue ich mir selbst nicht recht, weil meine Meinung sich immer sehr nach meinen Wünschen richtet" [what should I do then, dear Savingny? Renounce? I do not want to talk at all about what will become of me then . . . I am writing all of this to you dear Savingny, as I think and feel it, if you think I am wrong, then tell me, but I now think that it would not be a good action if I were to renounce, yet I do not trust myself totally because my opinion always orients itself toward my wishes] (*Schatten* 177–78).

As a person at odds with society's expectations to express herself in ways other than her integrity will allow, she recognizes her own recluse life. To Savigny she describes the "Kämerlein" she has within:

> Ich trage meistens ein stilles Kämerlein in meinem Gemüthe herum in diesem lebe ich ein eignes, abgesondertes, glükliches Leben in dem Interesse und der Liebe zu irgend einem Menschen, einer Idee, einer Wissenschaft, oder einer Kunst und weil ich mich dann gar zu viel in diesem traulichen Winkelchen aufhalte, bin ich blöd und fremd mit der Welt und den Menschen, und bleibe immer zu ungeschikt sie zu behandlen wie man sollte; . . .

[I carry around in me mostly a quiet little room, in this I live my own isolated, happy life in the interest and love of some person, an idea, a science, or an art and because I do stay far too long then in this cosy little corner, I am stupid and strange with the world and people, and always remain inept at treating them as one should; . . .] (*Schatten* 164)

As Christa Wolf asks, when critics accuse Günderrode of being too "unrealistic," too reclusive, whose reality are they relying on? Is it a male-formulated reality in which women play no part anyway? In the face of limited social options, Günderrode's retreat into her "Kämmerlein" becomes one of the few alternatives that she can actually choose to develop. In her real "Kämmerlein"—the small room in the cloister—Günderrode carried on an active life of reading and writing. Here she received guests such as Bettina von Arnim, with whom she planned trips around the world and talked about theories of history and philosophy. Her dreams of dying a hero's death may not have offered a viable solution to the conflicts she faced. Her option to use a secluded space to combat ideological constraints may not seem like the boldest statement against oppression. Still, in formulating both images as the way in which she would like to live her life, Günderrode radically questioned the gender constraints she faced when she walked outside her room.

Within the confines of her room, too, she wrote letters in which she strove for communication and community. In fact, writing seems at times more effective and easier than speaking. To Karoline von Barkhaus, to whom she wants to write about her feelings for Savigny, she admits, "Schriftlich dachte ich wird es leichter sein mich zu ent-dekken, dieser Gedanke ward Entschlus, welcher noch jezt in meiner Seele haftet" [I thought it would easier to reveal myself in writing, this thought became resolution that still now persists in my soul] (*Schatten* 134). At one point she talks about her sister reading Clemens Brentano's *Godwi* aloud to her. Günderrode's remarks on the value of this experience as an unselfish act of giving that connects the personal experience to a larger communal one:

Es ist wunderbar daß alle geistige Genüsse fast durch Mittheilung ver-mehrt werden; da bei Materiellen doch das Gegentheil statt findet. Geben und reicher werden durch geben! es ist höchst wunderbar, ja ich meine es enthält eine Wiederlegung gegen des Materialismus.

[It is amazing that all intellectual pleasures almost multiply through communicating; whereas with material goods the opposite happens. Give and become richer through giving. It is highly amazing, yes, I mean it contains a rebuttal against materialism.] (*Schatten* 139)

When she asks Savigny if they can correspond, she states that her only need "ist mich auszusprechen" [is to express myself] to garner "ein fremdes Urtheil, eines Andern Billigung um wieder froh in mir selbst zu sein" [an outside opinion, the approval of another person in order to be happy again with myself]. She asks sincerely: "mögte immer mit Ihnen sprechen über solche Dinge, und Ihnen darüber schreiben, kann ich das?" [may I always be able to talk with you about such things, and write to about them, can I do that?] (*Schatten* 161–62). Further, she writes to Savigny: "Ich werde Ihnen noch sehr viel über mich schreiben, und sprechen, denn ich bedarf es, ich kann nur heute keinen ordentlichen Gedanken fassen, vermuthlich einer höchst unglüklichen Leidenschaft wegen die mich zu nichts Ernsthaftem kommen läßt" [I will write a lot more to you about myself, and talk, for I need that, only today I cannot think a clear thought, probably because of a highly unfortunate passion that will let me come to nothing serious] (*Schatten* 166).

In answer to Clemens Brentano's question as to why she published her poems, she writes in 1804:

> Wie ich auf den Gedanken gekommen bin, meine Gedichte drukken zu lassen, wollen Sie wissen? Ich habe stets eine dunkle Neigung dazu gehabt, warum? und wozu? frage ich mich selten; ich freute mich sehr, als sich jemand fand, der es übernahm, mich bei dem Buchhändler zu vertreten; leicht und unwissend, was ich tat, habe ich so die Schranke zerbrochen, die mein innerstes Gemüt von der Welt schied; und noch hab ich es nicht bereut, denn immer neu und lebendig ist die Sehnsucht in mir, mein Leben in einer bleibenden Form auszusprechen, in einer Gestalt, die würdig sei, zu den Vortrefflichsten hinzutreten, sie zu grüssen und Gemeinschaft mit ihnen zu haben.
>
> Ja, nach dieser Gemeinschaft hat mich stets gelüstet, dies ist die Kirche, nach der mein Geist stets wallfahrtet auf Erden.

> How I got the idea to have my poems printed, you want to know? I have always had a secret inclination to do so—why? and what for? I rarely ask myself; I was very happy when someone was willing to represent me at the publishers; easily, and not knowing what I did, I have destroyed the barrier that separated my innermost heart from the world; and I have not regretted it as yet, for always new and alive is my desire to express my life in a permanent form, in a shape worthy of joining the most excellent minds, greeting them and sharing their society.
>
> Yes, I have always been drawn to that community; it is the church toward which my spirit is continuously making its earthly pilgrimage.] (*Schatten* 193)[59]

Here is her heroic wish come true—to find the strength to break out of the confines that hold her back. The idea of creating a literary community through her letter writing is significant. When she talks about writing a drama, she defends herself against Gunda's accusations that she is "hochmütig." To Savigny, she asserts:

> ... ich kann es Ihnen nur mit großer Blödigkeit sagen, ich schreibe ein Drama, meine ganze Seele ist damit beschäftigt, ja ich denke mich so lebhaft hinein, werde so einheimisch darin, daß mir mein eignes Leben fremd wird; ich habe sehr viel Anlage zu einer solchen Abstraktion, zu einem solchen Eintauchen in einen Strom innerer Betrachtungen und Erzeugungen. Gunda sagt es sei dumm sich von einer so kleinen Kunst als meine sei, sich auf diesen Grad beherrschen zu lassen; aber ich liebe diesen Fehler, wenn es einer ist, er hält mich oft schadlos für die ganze Welt.

> [... I can tell you only with great stupidity, I am writing a drama, my entire soul is occupied with it, yes, I am putting myself so fervently into it, am becoming so at home in it, that my own life is becoming foreign to me; I have a lot of aptitude for such an abstraction, for such an immersion into a stream of inner observations and productive forces. Gunda says it is dumb to let oneself be controlled to this degree by such a small art as mine is; but I love this defect, if it is one, it indemnifies me for the whole world.] (*Schatten* 167)

Although she publishes under a pseudonym, in her private letters she makes no secret of her need to write. In April 1804 she sends Savigny "Der Kuß im Traume." She also talks later to him about reading history and Schelling, and about working on a new drama: "Mein Leben ist jezt durch diese Dinge erfült, und ich bin zufrieden" [My life is now fulfilled by these things, and I am content] (*Schatten* 171). She admits that her piece "Mohamed" will appear under the title "Fragment." She talks about Nees's reaction and his desire to include a foreword (171). In a letter to Clemens Brentano, she admits the poems by Tian are by her: "Die Gedichte von Tian sind von mir, ich wollte es allen Menschen verbergen, ein Zufall hat es vereitelt ..." [The poems by Tian are mine, I wanted to hide it from everyone, chance foiled it] (*Schatten* 188).

Letters cannot be the permanent form that a published work represents for her. She asks people to burn, tear up, or hide her letters from others (146). Yet through letters she often catches herself adapting dishonestly to norms that could inhibit her self-expression. In the striving for one truth, she encounters moments where there might be many. Yet she continually recognizes her need to maintain her integrity. At one point, she contemplates crossing passages out, as in a letter to Savigny, but decides such action contradicts her striving for truth: "Fast mögte ich das Geschriebene ausstreichen, doch nein, das wäre unwahr" [I almost wanted to strike out what was written, but no, that would be untruthful] (*Schatten* 170). That urge to edit out parts of letters appears not only in her own correspondence, but also in letters she forwards to other people, as Savigny notes about a letter from Gunda (153). Karoline states she doesn't know why she has crossed out a part: "Sie wissen wohl auch wie der Mensch allerlei sonderbare Launen und Einfälle hat [You also well know how a person has all kinds of strange moods and whims] (*Schatten* 156).

Ultimately, through both her epistolary and poetic composition, Karoline did not find the community she desired. As in her drama "Geschichte eines Braminen" with Almor, who procedes through the three stages of development, only the third, in which the individual finds complete harmony with the whole, can there be true fulfillment. It is not enough to complete only the second stage, "Gemeinschaft der Geister," in which bourgeois *Bildung* leads only to learning.[60] She often becomes disappointed when her correspondents do not share her high expectations. When Gunda does not reply, Günderrode feels as if she had fallen in love with her echo, or worse yet, the echo is deaf to all questions and requests, "aber man kann sich doch einbilden eine Antwort von ihm zu hören" [but one can still imagine hearing an answer from him] (*Schatten* 141). Over and over she expresses her need for reply in correspondence. To Gunda Brentano she writes movingly about the monotony of her own voice in an unreplied correspondence: "Die Einseitigkeit unseres Briefwechsels erregt mir auch unangenehme Empfindungen. Ich schlage Töne an und höre nur immer dieselben monotone Klänge, bis zur Ungeduld bringt es mich fast daß nicht neue Töne mit den schon verhallten abwechseln" [The one-sidedness of our correspondence stirs up unpleasant feelings in me. I strike out tones and hear only the same monotonous sounds, it brings me almost to impatience that no new tones alternate with those already sounded] (*Schatten* 142). She compares her thoughts fantasies, and emotions to actors inviting the audience to come behind the curtains, to see the real inner workings of the theater. But without replies to those invitations, without answers to her letters she regrets: "ich muß entweder das Schauspielhaus ganz verschließen, oder auch das innerste entschleiern" [I must either close the theater up completely or else unveil the innermost] (*Schatten* 142). Implicit in her stated need to be loved is a lack of self-confidence in her own worth, caused most likely by the eternal conflict between her selves and the perception of those selves. Again to Gunda Bren tano: "mir scheint es so süß von ausgezeichneten Menschen geliebt zu sein; es ist mir der schmeichelhafteste Beweis meines eignen Werthes" [it appears to me so sweet to be loved by exceptional people; to me it is the most flattering proof of my own worth] (*Schatten* 143). She stresses that "Mittheilung Bedürfnis ist" [communication is need] (*Schatten* 142). That insecurity comes out in her wavering between assertive and apologetic tones. At the same time that she can reprimand Gunda for her nonreciprocity, she can also regret burdening others with her troubles (*Schatten* 135; 136–37; 143).

Letters in general demand that the correspondent place herself or himself in a variety of situations and roles, depending on who the correspondent is and on when the letter is written. Like other forms of personal writings, such as the diary and travel journals, letters are not bound by the pressure for unified plot and characterization.[61] The audience remains varied, the writer can tailor letters directly to the specific listener. Such a variance has caused negative reactions against considering letters as literary works. Without the cohesion of a novel or drama, letters make reading and deciphering difficult, if not impossible, and leave many questions open.

If, however, as scholarship on new historical methods points out, the self exists in a dynamic relationship with social, historical, and cultural factors, then one can speak of aesthetic mediation of selves in autobiographical writings. That concept stands in opposition to rationalist ideas of identity, which postulate a teleological, linear pattern for human development that strives for an autonomous self distinctly separate from an objective outside world. As Friedrichsmeyer points out in her essay "Women's Writing and the Construct of an Integrated Self," in theory, this concept of a unified self, propagated most fully in the Enlightenment's belief in *Bildung* and progress, may have been an ideal postulated for everyone.[62] In practice, however, it served only a small group of privileged males. For women, a major social group that was not able to reach autonomy in the arenas of law, education, or employment, the notion of attaining a harmonious, integrated self-identity remained chimeric. For the woman writer, the dissonance between theory and practice was especially strong. On the one side, early Enlightenment theory had allowed them, in however limited a fashion, a certain authority to speak in public and to write at least for the betterment of themselves and society. On the other side, ideologies of motherhood and wifehood prevented them from stepping too far beyond society's established boundaries. Following limited options became a balancing act. They could remain silent, not writing at all; they could publish under a pseudonym or anonymously; they could write in private genres; or they could adopt what Weigel calls a "cross-eyed glance."[63] Throughout the course of the women's lives, these options were mutable. Many publishing writers continued to engage in long, involved correspondence, the value of which was to try and test new options.

How then are we to interpret the act of creating varying metaphors of selves? Do those selves exist as signs of a fragmented psyche unable to reconcile themselves into a unified person? Do they stand as signs of a flaw in a striving for artistic unity? One way of answering these questions would be to reevaluate the value and attainablity of a unified self as defined within the previously discussed eighteenth-century parameters of the autonomous individual. In this light, the quote from *Amanda und Eduard* presents a radical view on the positive value of ever-changing, ever-varying selves existing concurrently. For women writers, situated within narrow role expectations, the possibilites to be nonstatic and noncategorized could open up immense, previously unexplored avenues.

Regarding the personal and social realms in which the women lived and wrote, focus on multidimensionality should not cause readers to ignore the often painful search for an integral self that goes on in women's letters. The attempt to integrate the multifarious aspects of one's self into one unit surfaces most poignantly in Günderrode's letters. In her correspondence, the reader cannot ignore the search for some kind of unity that can honestly confront restrictive gender ideologies. In this light, her suicide was not just another constructive option she exercised, but rather a tragic example of how detrimental the ideological construct of the feminine could become as an instrument of oppression.

Still, the truths for which Günderrode searches should know no boundaries. Integrity of the self should remain flexible to change and growth. As part of a literary forum, the *oeuvre* of Karsch, Mereau, and Günderrode shows varied experimentation with forms, in which the epistolary form played a major role. Their correspondence teaches us that letters belong to an aesthetic they were trying to achieve in their lives and works. Karsch composed, performed, and published poetry and held extensive correspondence with diverse people. Mereau wrote poems, novels, short stories; she edited a journal and translated dramas, letters, novels; she participated in lectures, salons, and theater scenes. Günderrode wrote poems, dialogues, dramas, aphoristic fragments. Some readers have seen this diversity of forms as an attempt to participate in the general formulaic experimentation of men such as Goethe, Schlegel, Schiller. Considering perceptions that increasingly devalued the aesthetic quality of the letter form, however, we can distinguish an attempt on the part of these three women t challenge gender norms that perpetuate a narrow image of women only in connection with certain genres. Interchange between letter writing and publication occurs as a further challenge to the separation between private and public spheres, a separation that likewise reinforced artificial boundaries for women's creativity. Their letters reflect a growing need to define their own needs in relation to traditional forms of literary expression.

# 5

# An Aesthetics of Letter Writing: Caroline Schlegel-Schelling and Rahel Varnhagen[1]

Oɴ 5 December 1809, Rahel Levin heard rumors that Karl August Varnhagen von Ense wanted to published his correspondence with her. Rahel's brother wrote apprehensively from Hamburg that Varnhagen "seine correspondance mit dir im druck herausgeben [wolle], willst du dagegen nichts thun?" [wanted to publish his correspondence with you, do you want to do nothing against that?][2] On 18 December 1809, Rahel informed Karl August that she had received a packet of letters from her brother Ludwig Robert, from her friend Pauline Wiesel, from the writer Jean de la Motte Fouqué, and from Karl August himself. She then queried:

> Lieber, bester Junge, was ist das? Man schreibt mir, Du würdest Deine und meine Briefe drucken lassen? Woher schreibt sich nur das Gerede? Das sollte auch nicht existiren! Sprich doch nicht mit Menschen von dergleichen; die es bis zu unreinen Menschen hinsprechen! denn das sind doch die gewiß, die es bis zum Theegespräch treiben. Zum Glück besitze ich unsere Briefe.

> [Dear, best boy, what is that? Someone wrote me that you would let your and my letters be published? Where did such a rumor come from? It should not exist! Don't talk with people about such things; those who tell it to impure people! for it is certainly they who bring it to tea conversations. Luckily I possess our letters.][3]

Subsequently, she asked him to return two of her most private correspondences, that with her former lover Don Raphael d'Urquijo and that with her friend Rebecca Friedländer (GW IV. 2: 30). Varnhagen reacted particularly harshly against her request for Friedländer's letters:

> Ja so! wegen der Guten [Rebecca Friedländer] hab' ich noch zu schreiben! Sie soll doch bei Leibe nicht bös werden! Es hat keine Gefahr mit der

Publizität; welche Feder möchte sich auch nach ihrem Roman noch an diese Geschichte wagen! Die Briefe? Gut! vielleicht ließe sich ein druckbarer Auszug daraus machen, aber in 10 Jahren noch nicht. Die dummen Klatschereien gehen immer ihren Gang, diesmal rührt es wohl von Bartholdy her, der eine weitläufige Familie hat. Auf keinen Fall darfst Du der Guten ihre Briefe zurückgeben, hörst Du, Rahel! Sie sind *mein, mein!* und ich will sie behalten. Ich bitte Dich, geliebte Rahel, thu mir nicht ein solches Unglück an, etwas zu verbrennen von diesen Korrespondenzen, die doch einmal mir gehören.

[Yes, so! due to the good one (Rebecca Friedländer) I have yet a lot to write! There is no reason for her to get angry! There is no danger with publicity; whose quill would dare to use this story after her novel! The letters? Good! maybe one could have an excerpt that was worth being printed done, but not for another 10 years at least. The stupid scandalmongerings always go their way, this time it has probably been stirred up by Bartholdy who has an extensive family. Under no condition may you give the good one her letters back, do you hear, Rahel! They are *mine, mine!* and I want to keep them. I ask you, dear Rahel, don't bring such misfortune upon me as to burn something from these correspondences that do belong to me.] (*GW* IV.2: 36)

The vehemence with which Varnhagen expresses ownership of the letters calls attention to the power that editors of personal documents must utilize to carry through with their projects. If indeed possession is nine-tenths of the law, the question of rights over correspondence can become very murky. Rahel had given Karl August her correspondence to read and organize.[4] But Rahel, too, felt possessive about her correspondence and had on many occasions expressed her admiration. Long before she met Karl August Varnhagen, she had even thought about having her letters published. To Frau von Boye in July 1800 she wrote: "Und sterb' ich—such' *alle* meine Briefe—durch List etwa—von *allen* meinen Freunden und Bekannten zu bekommen . . .—und ordne sie mit Brinckmann. Es wird eine Original = Geschichte und poetisch" [And if I die—try to acquire all my letters—through some ruse—from all my friends and acquaintances . . .—and put them in order with Brinckmann. It will be an original = story and poetic] (*GW* I, 208). In a letter from 22 February 1810, Rahel responded to Karl August's suggestion to publish her letters by outlining her own ideas for a future publication of her letters. The passage deserves full citation for its significant statements on truth, history, storytelling, and participation in the editorial process:

Keiner von uns will mehr, daß mein ehrliches Leben auch geschaut werde von solchen, die es selbst sind; und genug findet man immer, unter

Deutschlands Lesern, wenn man nur drucken läßt. Immerfort erzeugt die Erde auch wieder solche. Ich weiß, welche Freude, welches Behagen mir ein Fünckchen Wahrheit in einer Schrift aufbewahrt macht! Nur davon bekömmt die Vergangenheit Leben, die Gegenwart Festigkeit und einen künstlerischen Standpunkt, betrachtet zu werden; nur Empfindungen, Betrachtungen durch eine Historie erregt, schaffen Muße, Götterzeit, und Freiheit; wo sonst nur allein Stoßen und Dringen und Drängen, und schwindliches Sehen und Thun möglich ist; im wirklichen Leben des bedingten beschränkten Tages, wie er vor uns steht! Nicht weil es mein Leben ist, aber weil es ein wahres ist; weil ich auch vieles um mich her oft, mit kleinen unbeabsichtigten Zügen, für Forscher, wie zum Exempel ich einer bin, wahr, und sogar geschicht-ergänzend aussprach. Und endlich, weil ich ein Kraftstück der Natur bin, ein Eckmensch in ihrem Gebilde der Menschheit, weil sie mich hinwarf, nicht legte, zum grimmigen Kampf mit dem, was das Schicksal nur konnte verabfolgen lassen; jeder Kampfgesell der Natur, der größeren Geschichte, ist in einen Geschichtsmoment geworfen, wo er kämpfen muß, wie bei einem Thiergefecht in der Arene; glückliche Veteranen, wirken weiter, zu ihrem und der Menschen Bewußtsein; unglückliche, zerschellen; mich trugen Gedanken und Unschuld, als ich zerschellt schon war, empor, zwischen Himmel und Erde. Kurz, wie es mit mir ist, kann ich nicht sagen; ich will nichts mehr. Kein Plan, kein Bild; es schwankt und schwindet die Erde mit den Lebensgütern; der Lebenschatz ist alles! Sehen, lieben, verstehen, nichts wollen, unschuldig sich fügen; das große Sein verehren, nicht hämmern, erfinden und bessern wollen: und lustig sein, und immer güter! So wie ich war und werde, mögen meine Brüder mich sehen! Ich aber selbst will aus meinen Briefen alles suchen, und verwerfen; und nicht in vierzig, fünfzig Jahren, wie Du der Guten schreibst, sondern viel früher; ich will noch leben, wenn man's liest.

Neither of us wants more, that my honest life will also be viewed by those who are themselves it; and one always finds enough, among Germany's readers, when one only allows publishing. Again and again the earth continues to generate such people. I know what joy, what comfort a little spark of truth in a piece of writing has held for me! Only that gives the past life, and the present shape; and an artistic perspective from which to be seen; only sentiments, observations enlivened by a story create leisure, divine time and freedom; where otherwise only shoving and pushing and squeezing and a dizzy seeing and doing is possible; the real life of a conditioned, limited day as it presents itself to us! Not because it is my life, but because it is a true one; because I often said things, with tiny, unintentional flair, that would represent truth for a researcher, such as I also am, and even things that will supplement history. And finally, because I am a marvel of nature, a corner-person in nature's concept of humanity, because nature threw me, and did not lay me, in grizzly battle with whatever fate found to hound me. Each one of nature's fighters, of greater history's fighters, is thrown into a historical moment in which he must fight, as in battle with an animal in an arena; fortunate veterans continue to affect the consciousness of nature and humans; unfortunate ones are dashed. When I was already dashed, thoughts and innocence elevated me to a position between heaven and earth. In short, I cannot say how it stands with me; I want nothing more. No plan, no image; the earth staggers and vanishes under the goods of life; the gift of life is everything! To see, to love, to understand, not to want anything, to submit in innocence. To exalt being, not to want to hammer, to discover, to improve: and to be cheerful and always gooder! May my brothers see me just as I was and will be! But I myself want to examine my letters and discard; and not in forty, fifty years, as you wrote to the good one [R. Friedlander], but much sooner. I want to live when it is read.] (GW IV.2, 44)[5]

As a potential venue to tell truths, letters recount a good, yet unconventional story that exudes turmoil and struggle and spans the gamut of human emotions. Through its perspective from a "corner-person" of life, the story intersects with history. But that intersection is not always smooth. The story also has no purpose or plan, no teleological structure with a goal and a happy ending. Rahel wants to be alive when her correspondence is published, to stand as witness for the living culture her letters represent. Then, even after her death, the vitality of the letters will live on in interpretation.

The story of Rahel's involvement in the publication of her own letters has occupied scholars for over a century.[6] Rahel did publish some of her letters, but never with her full name.[7] She also helped build one of the most valuable collections of letters in eighteenth- and nineteenth-century Germany. As analyses in the previous chapters show, when talking about publication of women's letters, any references to passages in which women talk about publishing must receive careful wording, considering social restrictions and attempts to break those restrictions. Louise Gottsched and Meta Klopstock couch their reactions to publication in such indirect language as to make what initially seem like refusals ambiguous responses to narrow publication standards. Anna Louisa Karsch wanted her epistolary autobiography to be published, but her publisher did not honor her request. Helmina von Chézy's documents reveal an editor perpetually at work collecting and preparing her correspondence for publication; she exercised her own selective method of saving, which then met another fate at the hands of Karl Varnhagen and others. Sophie Mereau reworked her personal correspondence with Kipp into a novel. Intentions to publish could also waver due to conflicts between a cultural standard for the letter as a public genre and patriarchal norms limiting women's participation in the public forum. Women often distinguished between letters intended for public or private readership. "diesen brief gute Lady lesen Sie allein" [this letter dear lady read by yourself], Rahel writes to Rebecca Friedländer,[8] while at another point she promises that she will write very clearly "so können Sie es Ihren Gästen zu Weihnachten mittheilen" [you can communicate it to your guests at Christmas in such a way] (*Briefe an eine Freundin* 126).

On the issue of publication, Caroline Schlegel-Schelling, another prolific letter writer, remained conspicuously silent, considering Friedrich Schlegel's solicitations and advice that she publish a novel in letters. Many other men urged her to publish, but stipulations always accompanied their encouragements. Novalis sees her artistic potential only in conjunction with a man, as he wrote to her in 1799: "Möchten doch auch Sie die Hände ausstrecken nach einem Roman! Wilhelm müßte die Poesie dazu besorgen. Es könnte ein schönes Doppelwerk werden" [May you also extend your hands to a novel! Wilhelm would have to take care of the poetry. It could be a nice double work.].[9] To A. W. Schlegel in 1802 she relates how Schelling submitted one of her essays for publication in a journal under his name, for "unter meinen Nahmen hätte ich es auf keine Weise thun mögen" [under no circumstances could I have done this under my name] (*Caroline* II: 263). Her reasons are purely pragmatic: she believes the editor will accept it without hesitation if Schelling signs his name to it. She also admits that Schelling eliminated the epistolary form from the original essay and any other "Spur der zarten Hände" [trace of the tender hands] (*Caroline* II: 264).

Besides showing astuteness about editorial authoritativeness, Rahel's and Caroline's comments disclose an awareness of the disparity between the way men and women view the aesthetic value of letters. Reevaluations of late eighteenth- and early nineteenth-century women's letters have referred to their aesthetic quality, defining them as "sensations of an aesthetically mixed form,"[10] in which philosophical conversations, literary reviews, and descriptions of psychological emotions alternate with gossip and chatter.[11] Recent scholarship on Schlegel-Schelling's and Varnhagen's letters aptly stress their worth as illuminators of significant, long-silenced perspectives on the role of women in the early nineteenth century.[12] Evidence of such political consciousness proves Schlegel-Schelling and Varnhagen to be two predecessors of the modern feminist movement. It also has raised continued speculation as to why Caroline and Rahel never published their letters. In light of diverging values placed on the epistolary form at the end of the eighteenth century, the question of publication involves asking more about the nature of the women's nonconformity than about their conformity. In other words, rather than wonder why the two women never published anything and reduce their writings to "just letters," we should ask whether the high value they placed on letters as an aesthetic form precluded publication in accordance with the criteria that they were supposed to meet. Instead of capitulating to conventions that judge the value of a written work only in published form, could women such as Schlegel-Schelling and Varnhagen have been positing an alternative? Could the value they placed on life being art and art life have influenced their decision not to publish their works? What can we enjoy aesthetically from their private letters without having to ask how they would have differed had they been intended for publication?

Such questions have been asked before, but perhaps the contexts in which scholars have set out to answer them need revision. Scholarship has most often looked at the ways in which women refer directly to "great" events, ideas, and works in letters in order to show that their letters do indeed cross boundaries of their allotted private arena and reflect the dominant literary and political ideas of their times.[13] While women's opinions on Goethe, Napoleon, war, political decisions, and the like offer valuable insights from an oppressed social group, the topics they chose as alternatives are just as important. Research still needs more focus on the parts of their letters in which, as Rahel claims, subjective interpretation intersects with truth, storytelling with history, and the individual "Eckmensch" with "great" events. Stories that make the past live through real life, that turn personal lives into catalysts for political actions, these stories, whether true or untrue, trivial or meaningful, malicious or benevolent, sustain intimacy and show faith in the power of giving voice to their own experience.

Assigning the label "Klatsch," or gossip, to define stories about everyday occurances, people, emotions, dreams, and desires has stigmatized most serious study of the private side of women's letters. The term needs reevaluation to eliminate the pejorative connotation it has as a less-significant discourse and a non-literary form. The most relevant study on the analogy between gossip and literature is Patricia Meyer Spacks's book *Gossip*, in which she devotes an entire chapter to the publication of personal letters.[14] Spacks sees a relationship between gossip, which "inhabits the borderlands of socially sanctioned oral discourse," and personal letters, a genre existing on the margins of what culture often deems to call "literature."[15] She founds her argument first on a complex definition of gossip, in which she advocates viewing it as a positive, private form of power that also "subliminally recalls ancient belief in the magic of language."[16] She also distinguishes between malicious gossip and "serious gossip":

whereas the former manipulates power destructively, the latter exists only as a function of intimacy, inspiring interpretations and intensifing human connection. Serious gossip also has the special properties of valorizing the importance of the story and enlarging self-knowledge predicated more on emotion than thought.

Spacks then presents examples from selected letters. In discussing Lady Mary Montagu's letters, she differentiates the personalized news that a tabloid such as *People* purveys from letters such as Montagu's: the latter "dignify small truths rather than trivialize large ones."[17] She continues: "Lady Mary's letters, taken seriously in full detail, can help the reader value the small remark—in life as well as on the page. They do not, like tragedy, for instance, emphasize the grandeur of the human spirit; they insist, rather, on the compelling persistence of personality."[18] Personal letters stress intimate relationships that have continuity, meaning, and effect. Letters act as a preserving agent in that they allow the writer to elevate personal trivia to events worthy of narrative. The reader is allowed to identify with the writer and to judge. The resulting correspondence causes fascination with how much human private lives do intersect with the outside, whether that be political or social, or with one other human being or many. Subsequent exchanges raise the value of personal views in the making of literature and history. As Spacks admits, an academic might hesitate to classify any serious writing as "gossip," but she convincingly argues that any widesweeping condemnation of such talk as meaningless "also excludes the large body of conversation based on personal rather than public values."[19] Her second chapter on the reputation of gossip stresses the traditional connection of gossip with women, which also partially explains the dismissal of its positive qualities. Just as the kind of intimate talk generated by gossip loses respect as a literary form when it is equated with women, so, too, does the epistolary genre engender negative reactions when associated with the female sex, as investigation in chapter two of my study here demonstrated.

In adopting the epistolary form for the bulk of their written work, Caroline Schlegel-Schelling and Rahel Varnhagen elevate it to an aesthetic vehicle that declares the importance of personal experience for the outside world. Their affirmation of letter writing as an act of narration questions the splits between literature and history, fiction and reality, private and public spheres, which narrowly define mutually exclusive types of discourse. Their critical assessment of the culture in which they lived is important for the continual dialogue that feminism promotes. The epistolary aesthetics and poetics they espouse become all the more meaningful because of, and not in spite of, the fact that these women decided not to publish or not to sign their own names to the scant number of letters that were published.

Secondary literature has perpetuated the image of Caroline Schlegel-Schelling's life and epistolary writings as those of the *femme fatale*, or Dame Lucifer, as she was referred to by those in Schiller's circle.[20] She was born Caroline Michaelis on 2 September 1763 as the eldest daughter of the famous orientalist and theologian Johann David Michaelis and his second wife, Louise Philippine Antoinette Michaelis, née Schröder. Her main education came from her father and the intellectual circles that surrounded him in the small university town of Göttingen. As a young girl, she learned French, Italian, and English and read voraciously. She began writing letters at an early age; the first extant letters are from 1778 to her friend Luise Stieler (later Gotter) who remained her lifelong friend and correspondent. Thus, when scholars point out the rivalry between Caroline and other women of the time, they consider only other famous females—mostly Dorothea Veit Schlegel and Therese Forster-Huber—without realizing that her correspondence with Luise Stieler Gotter follows in the footsteps of other unrecognized friendships between women.

Caroline's letters document her active life with much detail and emotion. Passages she writes from Clausenthal during her first marriage to the physician Johann Franz Wilhelm Böhmer disclose her loneliness and her stifled intellectual life in the narrow-minded bourgeois circles of the small town. The letters during her Mainz years, 1792-93, many of them destroyed due to their scandalous nature, reflect her active interest in the political events during the republic established there, as well as the travails of her imprisonment. Correspondence during the years she lived in Jena, after she married August Wilhelm Schlegel and subsequently formed the centerpoint for the circle of Early Romantics residing there, shows her untiring involvement in the literary and cultural undertakings of the famous men around her. Correspondence after her marriage to Schelling until less than a month before her death in 1809 proves her contributions to his work and her unwavering interest in philosophy, literature, and the arts.

Born eight years after Caroline Schlegel-Schelling, on 19 May 1771, into a Jewish family in Berlin, Rahel Levin's background certainly differed from that of Caroline's Christian, academic surroundings. But the two women did have much in common concerning their education and the gender norms that affected many middle-class women. Socializing in the well-to-do bourgeois circles of her father, the wealthy Jewish merchant Levin Markus, and his wife Chaiche, Rahel, like Caroline, was both materially privileged and intellectually deprived. Rahel continually lamented in her letters a lack of formal education, although in her early life and later in her salons she was known for her intellectual prowess, wit, and frankness. Like Schlegel-Schelling, she had immediate access to the necessary materials, which allowed her to read voraciously and learn other languages. She also found in conversation and letter writing fulfilling intellectual and aesthetic vehicles. Some of her first letters were in Hebrew, and her letters in German have been known for their unconventional usage of other languages, orthography, neologisms, and punctuation. Her first salon began in 1789 in the small attic room of her parents' house in Berlin and lasted until 1806, succumbing to Napoleon's defeat of Prussia, rising anti-Semitism, and growing nationalism. With their mixture of nobility, bourgeois, men, women, Jews, Christians, artists, and diplomats, her gatherings earned a reputation for tolerance and unconventionality. From 1819 until her death in 1833 she conducted another salon, not as famous or dynamic as the first. During her twenty-five year relationship with Karl August Varnhagen, whom she met in Spring 1808 and married on 27 September 1814, she collected and organized her correspondence, a task that Varnhagen continued after her death. That correspondence attests to the many friendships she maintained, especially with very controversial women, including the actress and mistress to Prince Louis Ferdinand of Prussia, Pauline Wiesel, and the writer Rebecca Friedländer.

At first reading, the differences in the content and style of Rahel's and Caroline's letters seem obvious. Whereas Rahel's appear more abstract, diffuse, thematically more oriented to the personal and withdrawn from the political, cultural, and historical milieu around her, Caroline's letters reflect a more direct involvement in the public spheres of politics and belles-lettres. Oddly enough though, close reading does not justify so strict a demarcation. As Frederiksen observes, Rahel contemplates more the oppression of women and Jews, relating her own experiences to other injustices she sees around her, a theme one might expect more from the politically astute Caroline. In contrast, Caroline remains ambivalent in matters relating to gender equality, recognizing the restrictive expectations placed on women, without strongly advocating that women—herself and her daughter included—defy that oppression.[21] The letter form enables both letter writers to shift from one role to another as they formulate their various personae as writer, translator, secretary, salonière, political agitant, editor, mother, daughter, wife, and friend in conjunction with their correspondents. On the one hand, those shifts reflect the degree to which Rahel and Caroline were able to mediate their desires with an ideology that limited their literary expression. On the other hand, expression of their multifarious selves could be a liberating act against the static categories of that ideology as long as they could maintain some structural integrity of the self. Their entire epistolary *oeuvre* suggests such an integrity in that it displays a need for constancy and continuity in personal relationships and interactions with the world.

Indeed, the two share a search for unity that will not deny variety in their selves and writing. Constant talk about the significance of correspondence fills their epistles. For Caroline, a letter is "ein Blitz von Glück" [a lightning bolt of happiness] (*Caroline* II, 4). In depressing times, correspondence offers what she calls a "Ziel für meine Imagination" [goal for my imagination] (*Caroline* I, 208). Letters are her main connection with the outside world: "Jede Mittheilung, welche mir Freude machte und meinen Kopf beschäftigen könte, hab ich nur durch Briefe" [Every communication that gives me pleasure and is able to occupy my head I have only from letters] (*Caroline* I, 208–9). To her correspondents, Caroline is an inspiration for continued dialogue, as her sister Lotte Michaelis writes: "Meine Correspondenz mit Dir hat eine ganz eigne Art—so völlig wie eine unterredung, so alles, was mir in den Kopf komt, was mich Intreßirt, mir gefält, muß meine Caroline wißen, in rheim oder Prosa, lustig und traurig, wen ich was schönes höre oder lese, so ist mein erster Gedancke, Du must es vor Carolinen beschreiben" [My correspondence with you has a totally unique way—so much like a conversation, everything that comes into my head, what interests me, pleases me, my Caroline must know, in rhyme or prose, happy or sad, when I hear or read something beautiful, then my first thought is, you must describe it for Caroline] (*Caroline* I, 135). And Caroline recognizes her own worth; when reprimanding a correspondent for not being very responsive, she queries: "ist eine Correspondentin wie ich nicht besseres werth?" [is a correspondent such as I not worth more?] (*Caroline* II, 286)

Rahel constantly appreciates other people's letters. To Brinkmann on 9 January 1808 she writes: "Lieber Freund, schreiben Sie mir aber: Sie glauben gar nicht, welche Nahrung und Beschäftigung Ihre Briefe für mich sind. Sogar (dummes Sogar!) der Witz ist abgestorben. Wenn Sie nur wüßten, wie ich Sie mir täglich auffrische, wiederhole, und um mich herstelle!" [Dear friend, write to me: You do not believe what nourishment and preoccupation your letters are for me. Even (dumb even!) the wit has died off. If you only knew how I recall you, repeat you, and imagine you around me!] (*GW* I, 332) Her discourses are not limited to thanks and praise, but assume theoretical dimensions, such as when she observes the difference between conversation and letter writing. At times she favors neither one nor the other means of communication. To Rebecca Friedländer she declares: "Obgleich Sprechen u. Schreiben zu gar nichts hilft, so sollte man gar nicht aufhöhren zu sprechen u. zu schreiben!" [Although speaking and writing do not help anything, one should not stop speaking and writing] (*Briefe an eine Freundin 206*). Again to Friedländer, she couples writing with speaking in her encouragement: "Schreiben Sie nur, und sprechen Sie heraus! dies thut dem Geiste, Körper, Seele, u. dem Herzen gut" [Just write and express yourself! This is good for the spirit, body, soul, and the heart] (*Briefe an eine Freundin* 222). At other times, she opts in favor of writing letters. When she converses, as she admits to Alexander von der Marwitz, she adapts her assertions according to the reactions of the speaker, beginning with talk about herself and then having the subject conform to what interests her listener. In letters, she can remain more reflexive: "Nur in Briefen ist das anders. Wo kein Gegenstand meinen Blick trifft, kein fortschreitendes Verhältnis mich auffordert und in Anspruch nimmt, da bin ich nur mir selbst gegenüber, und schaue immer nur in mein Inneres . . ." [Only in letters is that otherwise. Where my glance does not meet an object, no approaching relationship summons me and claims me, there I only face myself, and always look only into my inner self] (*GW* I, 540). Being true to one's inner self is much more gratifying than the pretension that comes with trying to please others. The dualistic portrait of the inner self in confrontation with the outer world, of the need to satisfy one's own wishes instead of another person's, joins with an appreciation of letters as potential bearers of truths. To lifelong friend Pauline Wiesel she revels in the honesty of her own letter: "Ist dieser lange Brief, in Gewitterluft, und mit gräßlichen Nerven, nicht ehrlich?" [Is this long letter, in stormy air, and with hideous nerves not honest?].[22] Search for truth sustains the continuity in her correspondence with Pauline Wiesel, as we shall see later.

Coupled with reflections on letter writing and reading is a recognition that through letters the writer can meet the challenge of combining art and truth. Friedrichsmeyer has pointed out how Caroline Schlegel-Schelling consciously rejects other modes of writing available to women at the time, including diaries and novels.[23] In her requests for reading material, Schlegel-Schelling prefers biographies, memoirs, or histories, something "amüsant und wahr" [amusing and truthful] (*Caroline* I, 151). Again, truth in self-expression and letter writing collaborate, as in the following quote from one of her first extant letters:

Glaub es nur, ich bin keine Schwärmerinn, keine Enthousiastinn, meine Gedanken sind das Resultat von meiner, wens möglich ist, bei kalten Blut angestellten Überlegung. Ich bin gar nicht mit mir zufrieden, mein Herz ist sich keinen Augenblick selbst gleich, es ist so unbeständig, Du must das selbst wißen, da Dir meine Briefe immer meine ganze Seele schildern.

[Believe it, I am no passionate person, no enthusiast, my thoughts are the result of my, if it is possible, deliberations arrived at in cold blood. I am not at all content with myself, my heart is never the same at any moment, it is so inconstant, you must know that yourself, for my letters always portray my whole soul to you.] (*Caroline* I, 7)

Like Karoline von Günderrode, Caroline Schlegel-Schelling is aware of the multifarious parts of her soul. Schlegel-Schelling's insatiable interest in the theater, which she shared with Mereau and Karsch, also verifies her preference for forms in which dialogue and human interaction are prominent. Through letters Schlegel-Schelling was able both to adapt to the ideological framework in which she lived and to avoid monotonous life experience or static, categorical interpretation of the world around her. Her letters vary, depending on her epistolary partner and the particular role she played at different times in her life. She identifies August Wilhelm's letters as "materiellen, das heißt materienvollen" [material, that means full of material] (*Caroline* II, 63), or "raisonnabeln" [reasoning] (*Caroline* II, 188). As a result, her letters to him are brimming with informational material, stories about life in Jena during his absence, reviews of literary works and theatrical performances, reports on his literary business as she performed secretarial duties, and summaries of her other correspondence, topics that many might view as gossip in a trivial sense, but which exalt the breadth of her daily life. With Schelling, she begins to recognize the control he wants to have over her letter writing, as she ends a letter to Meta Liebeskind in 1804 with "Er will nicht, daß ich noch länger schreiben soll" [He does not want for me to write any longer] (*Caroline* II, 393). In fact, Caroline becomes his tireless secretary and manager, answering his own personal and business letters when he had no time because he was working on literary projects (*Caroline* II, 397). She also identifies herself more than once as his mother (*Caroline* II, 6; II, 42; II, 65), or the brother of her child, as in a mythical, even mystical union "gleich der Jungfrau, die Mutter ist, und Tochter ihres Sohnes, und Braut ihres Schöpfers und Erlösers" [similar to the virgin, who is mother, and daughter of her son, and bride of her creator and savior] (*Caroline* II, 61). Still, other letters reveal her to be a colleague, as she critiques his work and on numerous occasions asks him to send her his works in progress (*Caroline* II, 5; II, 57; II, 71–77). In letters to others she also discloses her own contributions to Schelling's work, such as when she tells A. W.

Schlegel about an essay she has written and to which Schelling would sign his name (*Caroline* II, 263–64). And then there is the letter to her sister-in-law on 4 August 1805, in which Caroline admits that she cannot write many personal letters because she has been working so much on Schelling's publications (*Caroline* II, 408).

In a letter to David Veit on 16 February 1805, Rahel Varnhagen places herself with poets and philosophers, a passage scholars often quote to prove her recognition of her own intellectual self-worth. The passage surfaces within the context of her questioning what sustains their correspondence and why Veit sometimes does not write to her. She thus projects an awareness of being able to present variation of the self through the epistolary form. She has "die gewaltige Kraft, mich zu verdoppeln, ohne mich zu verwirren. Ich bin so einzig, als die größte Erscheinung dieser Erde. Der größte Künstler, Philosoph oder Dichter, ist nicht über mir. Wir sind vom selben Element. Im selben Rang, und gehören zusammen" [the powerful strength to double myself, without confusing myself. I am as unique as the greatest appearances on this earth. The greatest artist, philosopher or poet is not above me. We are of the same element. On the same level, and belong together] (*GW* I, 266). Concerning her literary talents as a letter writer, she exclaims to Gentz on 23 November 1831, toward the end of her life: "Mit den größten Schriftstellern finde ich mich überein. Komme zu ihnen auf ihren hohen Sternen; aber auf meinem Weg: oder durch einen glücklichen Aufschwung" [I find myself united with the greatest authors. I come to them on their high stars, but in my own way: or through a lucky flight] (*GW* III, 541). She praises her own letters, as when she ends a letter to Rebecca Friedländer with the assessment: "Ein sehr guter Brief; trotz seines volumes!" [A very good letter; despite its volume!] (*Briefe an eine Freundin* 117); or when she writes to Pauline Wiesel: "Verwahren Sie meine Briefe, weil sie hübsch sind" [Keep my letters because they are cute] (Varnhagen/Wiesel 72).

The high value both women place on the capabilities of letter writing to be authentic and truth seeking while at the same time reflective of the diversity in life experiences stands as a reaction against views that letters by their very subjective manner cannot convey truths. This is not to say that letters receive only efferent worth in the two women's transmission of objective facts and figures. Instead, Rahel and Caroline promote the authenticity of the epistolary form as a means to convey human emotions, to look at those parts of lives that written, factual history has excluded, and to portray the individual plunged into the sweep of history. Rahel's most vehement assertions of truth in the face of social falsehood surface in her letters to Pauline Wiesel, her closest friend and most devoted correspondent. Pauline Wiesel was born Pauline Cesar in 1779 in Berlin. Her marriage to Friedrich Ferdinand Wiesel, as her letters to Rahel reveal, resulted in dissatisfaction and eventually in divorce. Because of her extramarital love affair with Prince Louis Ferdinand and her later radical style of living, she was ostracized from Berlin society. She felt at ease in Varnhagen's salon, a neutral meeting ground for men and women of various classes, religions, and occupations. After the Prince was killed in battle against the French in 1806, Wiesel did not want to take up her comfortable, bourgeois, domestic life with her husband again, but opted instead to lead a bohemian existence. She lived with men and women until she remarried in 1828. Rahel Varnhagen's friendship and correspondence with Pauline Wiesel was one of the longest in Varnhagen's life, lasting over twenty-five years.

The correspondence between Rahel and Pauline shows that the salon gatherings and personal meetings alone could not offer opportunities enough to devise an alternative to the deception they saw around them. Rahel's comment to Karl August Varnhagen on 25 September 1815 after receiving a letter from Pauline emphasizes a sustained truth in the two women's correspondence: "So eben hab' ich Paulinens Brief noch Einmal gelesen. Der ist *Millionen* werth. Diese Götterworte, diese Ansicht, diese Wahrheit, diese Orthographie" ([I have just read Pauline's letters once again. It is worth *millions*. These godly words, this perspective, this truth, this orthography] *GW* VI.1: 31). But Rahel was also aware of the powers that letter writing has to mediate a self with the outside world. She, like Karsch, Mereau, and Günderrode, realized that writing was an active process that involved reading and rereading. That process could also be very terrifying in its truthful exposure of another unrecognizable self. In her writing journal, Rahel records the same kind of alienation that Günderrode experienced when she reread her letters: "Oft les' ich in diesem Buche; und dann ist mir, als wär' ich todt, und ein Anderer liest es" [I often read in this book; and then it seems to me as if I were dead, and another person is reading it] (*GW* I, 280). For Rahel, the stability of words threatens a desired spontaneity in thoughts and actions. Again in her writing journal, she admits her own striving for *le mot juste* to express authenticity at the same time that these conscious attempts disgust her:

> So ekle ich mich auch, das Meiste, wenn es mir schon Einmal entfahren ist, zu sagen oder in gutgesetzten Worten aufzuschreiben. Mich dünkt, es ist so wenig; und es wird zu nichts, zu kalt, wenn man's erst schreibt, und gar denkt, ich will es schreiben. Darum kann ich auch gar nicht

schreiben, obgleich ich solche Liebhaberei an schöner Sprache und gutem
Ausdruck habe.

[Thus I am also disgusted to say or to write most things in well laid-out
words when they have already happened to me once. It seems to me, it
is so little; and it will come to nothing, too cold, when one actually writes
it down, and even thinks, I want to write it. For that reason I also cannot
write at all, although I have such a love of beautiful language and good
expression.] (*GW* I, 280)

Reification of experience into words creates a horrifying feeling of
loss: "Auch kommt's mir vor, hätt' ich eine Stimmung ausgedrückt,
in Prosa, oder Versen, ich könnte sie nun nie wieder haben, nie mehr
mit Ehren von ihr sprechen: ich hätte ihr in das zarte Gesicht geschla-
gen" [Also it occurs to me that if I had expressed one mood, in prose
or verse, I would never be able to have it back again, never be able
to speak with honor about it: I would have hit it in the tender face]
(*GW* I, 280–81). She must strive to live her experiences out in writing,
to reach a balance between her love of well-constructed, beautiful
language and the immediacy of the moment. She must also try to
maintain a critical distance from her work without losing intimacy
and immediacy in a dialogic exchange. Poets, she states, mould their
contemporary worlds with emotion and immediacy, but distance and
time allow successive generations to interpret and appreciate those
reformulations.

Rahel's correspondence with Pauline Wiesel comes closest to realizing the balance between unwavering truths and flexible selves, between conscious creation and spontaneity. The two combine life
experience with truthful language, immediacy with reflexivity and
critical distance. Rahel builds a strong bond that confirms to the two
women their resolve to maintain integrity with their own truths:
"Und wir sind geschaffen, die Wahrheit in dieser Welt zu leben" [And
we are made to live the truth in this world] (Varnhagen/Wiesel 13).
Yet by remaining integral, Varnhagen feels as if the two women inevi-
tably become outsiders in a society based on deception: "Wir sind
neben der menschlichen Gesellschaft. Für uns ist kein Platz, kein
Amt, kein eitler Titel da! Alle Lügen haben einen: die ewige Wahrheit,
das richtige Leben und Fühlen, das sich unabgebrochen auf einfach
tiefe Menschenanlagen, auf die für uns zu fassende Natur zurückfüh-
ren läßt, hat keinen!" [We are outside of human society. For us there
is no place, no position, no vain title! All lies have a place: but the
eternal truth, the true life and feeling, that can continuously be re-
traced to the simple profound human facilities, to the nature that is
all too comprehensible to us, has none!] (Varnhagen/Wiesel 13). The

thought of being an outsider, however, does not weaken Rahel's refusal to compromise herself with falsehoods: "Und somit sind wir ausgeschlossen aus der Gesellschaft, Sie, weil Sie sie beleidigten. (Ich gratuliere Ihnen dazu! so hatten Sie doch etwas; viele Tage der Lust!) Ich, weil ich nicht mit ihr sündigen und lügen kann" [And thereby we are shut out of society, you because you insulted it (I congratulate you on that! thus you really had something; many days of pleasure!) I, because I cannot sin and lie with it] (Varnhagen/Wiesel 13). She would rather suffer the consequences that society imposes on those who rebel than be dishonest, as she expresses even many years later: "Die Dolche in mein armes weiches Herz will ich ertragen: die Lüge kann ich nicht ertragen: die muß immer wieder hinaus, so oft auch der Lebenslauf sie heranschwemmt" [The daggers in my poor, tender heart I want to bear: the lie I cannot bear: it must always come out again, as often as the course of life washes it ashore] (Varnhagen/ Wiesel 48).

Rahel Varnhagen and Pauline Wiesel never produced any published work together, never traveled together, never lived together, despite their expressed desires to do all three. Such communal undertakings would not have been unusual for two women who already lived on the fringes of their respective societies. Over and over, Pauline tries to coax Rahel into traveling with her, only to have Rahel refuse or make up some excuse. Rahel's refusals indicate larger beliefs in the power of community bonds that travel could sever.[24] Travel becomes a kind of escape away from places or activities most receptive to those bonds, such as in her salon and in her correspondence. The correspondence thus does not represent a mere substitute for communal living, a medium conditioned by social factors that might have hindered their mobility or living conditions. The exchange of letters allows them to elevate a friendship that one otherwise might consider ordinary and uneventful to one that sustains human life. Truth exists in presenting the turmoil and individual struggle. "Teures Herz! Einzige Pauline! die leben bleiben muß! sonst bin ich in meinem Grab, so einsam! Nur eine ist, die weiß wer ich bin. Sie, Sie, Sie! Niemand wird es glauben: ich weiß es." [Dear heart! Unique Pauline! who must stay living! otherwise I will be in my grave, so lonely! There is only one person who knows who I am. You, you, you! Nobody will believe it: I know it] (Varnhagen/Wiesel 63). Their letters often assume poetic dimensions as they call for a means to realize the desires that family and culture denied them. Rahel writes with what she labels "Herzensblut anstatt mit Tinte" [blood of the heart instead of ink] (Varnhagen/ Wiesel 63). Dismayed with standards of language that they saw as too restrictive and non-expressive, they invented their own language, a "green" one. In 1818 Rahel writes:

> Teure Pauline! hätten wir uns vor Wiesel gekannt, so hätten Sie eine Freundin gehabt, die Ihnen nicht wie eine Pedantin hätte vorkommen können, und die Ihnen doch sanft, Ihre Natur anerkennend, hätte rathen können! Diese Freundin wär' ich gewesen. Welch Leben! . . . Solche wie Sie, hätte mein Nachdenken, meine Vorsicht, meine Vernünftigkeit haben müssen! Solche wie ich, Ihren Lebensmut, und Ihre Schönheit. Sonst haben wir vollkommen was eine begabte Menschennatur beglücken kann. Sinn, Sinne, Verstand, Laune, empfindliches Herz, Kunst- und Natursinn—das heißt auf unsere Sprache, "wir lieben Grünes".—

> [Dear Pauline! if we had known each other before Wiesel, then you would have had a friend who could not have appeared like a pedant to you, and who could have tenderly advised you, recognizing your nature. This friend would have been I. What a life! . . . Such people as you should have had my musings, my circumspection, my rationality! Such people as I your courage, and your beauty. Otherwise we have completely what makes a talented human nature. Sense, senses, intellect, humor, sensitive heart, sense for art and nature—that means in our language, "we love greenness.—"] (Varnhagen/Wiesel 33)

In their correspondence, Rahel and Pauline defy not only socialized gender norms. In their urgency to express a range of powerful emotions and their valorization of those emotions in a consciously created alternative language, they achieve a strength of expression fully equal to any work framed in the conventions of accepted literary forms. Rahel sees the recounting of her emotions and stories as the basis of human drama. Overwhelmed by the wish to describe everything, she apologizes to Pauline Wiesel for not having written sooner: "denn Ihnen möchte ich alles, jeden fliehenden Tag mit seinen fliehenden Minuten beschreiben; wie er mir das Leben in den Busen einkerbt" [for I would like to describe everything to you, every fleeting day with its fleeting minutes; as it notches life into my bosom] (Varnhagen/ Wiesel 59). Her correspondence with other people is also filled with various expressions to create an intimate meeting place for the inner selves and to reveal the multidimensionality of mundane experience. To Rebecca Friedländer she admits: "nur Kleinigkeiten; kleine Momente von Ewigkeiten existieren für mich.—" [only trivialities; little moments of eternities exist for me] (*Briefe an eine Freundin* 205). She encourages Friedländer to vent her pains, her sorrows, implying that no subject is too small, no complaint too unworthy: "Es existirt ein Wesen, das den ganzen stand Ihres herzens kennt; jeden nur kom-

menden Zustand begreift. Keine nuance, kein Schmerz, kein Liebens-
hauch geht verlohren. _Klagen_ sie! Klagen Sie mir; die ich davon
gestorben bin" [There exists a being that knows the entire state of
your heart; grasps every imaginable upcoming condition. No nuance,
no pain, no breath of love is lost. _Lament!_ Lament to me; the person
who has died of that] (_Briefe an eine Freundin_ 158). She reassures
Gustav von Brinkmann in a letter dated 8 January 1808 about the
importance of everything he has said: "Glauben Sie wenigstens, lieber
Freund, daß kein Wort in Ihren vier himmlischen Briefen verloren
ging; Spaß, Ernst, Trauer, alles ging nach seinem Orte in meiner
Seele" [Believe me at least, dear friend, that no words of your four
heavenly letters got lost; fun, seriousness, grief, everything went to
its place in my soul] (_GW_ I, 329). Taking pleasure in the macrocosmic
worth of microcosmic emotions and events, she praises in Brinckmann's letter "Ihren rührenden Scherz, die gütige Kinderlaune, die
ehrwürdige, liebende Jugend, den freundlichen Ernst, das komische
Gehenlassen, die ewige feste sittliche und tief von mir verehrte Sicher-
heit! [Your moving jest, the kind childish disposition, the venerable,
loving youth, the friendly seriousness, the funny nonchalance, the
eternal, stable, moral and profound security that I admire!] (_GW_ I,
332). Where others might put an exact date, Rahel writes just the day
of the week or is very explicit about the time, the weather, and her
state of mind. Every topic is legitimate, every emotion significant.

Schlegel-Schelling uses the words "schwatzen" and "Gechwätz" [to
chat; chatter, gossip], to recall the connection between gossip and
literature that Spacks makes, to describe the act of writing and the
content of her letters (_Caroline_ II, 550). In over four hundred extant
letters, Schlegel-Schelling hardly ever expresses a note of apology or
regret for what she writes, unlike the frequent apologies in Karoline
von Günderrode's and Sophie Mereau's letters. She only apologizes
when she has not been able to write, due to sickness or lack of time,
which implies an admission of the importance of her letters for
others. Her letters engage topics that many editors of collections of
letters have traditionally considered too personal—childbirth, infant
death, recipes, fashion, financial hardship. In shaping the mundane
into topics worthy of narrative reflection, she implicitly challenges
categories of greatness. Her letters achieve narrative significance and
challenge stereotypes of literariness.

Caroline's depictions of her divorce from August Wilhelm Schlegel
exemplify the way in which a personal event gains importance as a
subject of artfully constructed narration. Caroline's letters show also
how the narration of that event must assume different shapes within
various spheres of discourse. She talks about the divorce in letters to

August Schlegel and Julie Gotter, the daughter of Caroline's lifelong friend, Luise Gotter. She also most probably wrote the letter to the administrating duke Herzog, in which she requests the divorce. She implores August Wilhelm Schlegel and her closest friends not to talk about the divorce to anyone else (*Caroline* II, 339) and assures them that she, too, has kept the utmost discretion to prevent "irgend ein Geschwätz hin" [some kind of gossip] (*Caroline* II, 341). Although divorce was not uncommon—Caroline had witnessed the divorces of Therese Forster, Dorothea Veit, and Sophie Mereau—it nonetheless often meant ruin to a woman's reputation, financial situation, and relationships with her children. For example, Dorothea Veit Schlegel's first husband, Simon, stipulated that their oldest son Jonas live with him after the divorce; the younger son Philipp, then five, could stay with his mother, but if she remarried, Veit insisted, she would lose custody of Philipp and all visitation rights to Jonas. The letter to the administrating duke Herzog asking for Caroline's divorce, most likely composed by Caroline herself, considering her urgency, was carefully worded to conceal the freedom she had enjoyed for the few years of separation from Schlegel, any unhappiness she had experienced in the marriage, or any professional ambitions she had that were connected with her husband. Instead, she attributed the cause of the divorce to Schlegel's literary work and her own illness and need of rest and peace (*Caroline* II, 342–44).

In contrast, in letters to Julie Gotter, her reasons are not as simple nor has her part in making the decision been so passive or easy. Unbound by convention, she takes consolation in being able to tell her friend, without "das geringste Bedenken" everything "wie alles der Wahrheit nach und in meinem Herzen steht" [the slightest deliberation; as everything stands according to the truth and in my heart] (*Caroline* II, 353). She begins by talking about traveling to a spa in Swabia, then to Italy, to spend the winter in Rome. Whereas before she had shunned the idea of traveling (*Caroline* II, 332), she now admits her divorce was meant to bring about freedom to do as such, a reason not appearing in the letter to the duke (*Caroline* II, 353). The letter to Julie Gotter, however, is not all happiness: it also conveys pain and loss of stability in her life: "Ich habe nun alles verlohren, mein Kleinod, das Leben meines Lebens ist hin" [Now I have lost everything, my jewel, the life of my life is gone] (*Caroline* II, 354). Over and over, feelings of guilt conflict with remorseless self-justification. Conventional reasoning that causes her to blame herself for the divorce confronts the assertion of self. Schlegel deserved more, but she could no longer be everything for him, she states. She believes her health prevented her from bearing him children, which might have made him happy, but with children, she admits, the divorce would have been impossible. She should have been more careful in her decision to marry him in the first place, but her mother had insisted. Schlegel should have remained just her friend, but she believes she was honest with him from the beginning. She states she has no guilt, no remorse, and she asks Julie directly: "glaubst Du, daß er der Mann war, dem sich meine Liebe unbedingt und in ihrem ganzen Umfange hingeben konnte?" [do you believe that he was the man to whom my love could devote itself unconditionally and to its entire extent?] (*Caroline* II, 355). She must do "was für mich das Rechte und Wahre ist, und auch ganz und gar nicht danach zu fragen, wie das nach außenhin aussehn mag, was an sich gut ist" [what for me is just and true, and also absolutely not question how it may look like from the outside, what is basically good] (*Caroline* II, 355–56). After all the contestation, argumentation, and confrontation, she attains peace of mind: "Ich kann Dir nicht ausdrücken, wie ruhig ich seit dem Moment bin, wo wir uns entschieden hatten, ich bin fast glücklich zu nennen, und meine Gesundheit hat beträchtlich gewonnen" [I cannot express to you how peaceful I have been since the moment when we decided, I could almost be called happy, and my health has gained considerable] (*Caroline* II, 356). She is ready to ignore all the slander (*Caroline* II, 356). Not asking anyone to defend her, she requests only that her loved ones judge her in the context of the life she now leads with literary figures and not by her past political life (*Caroline* II, 356). She ends her letter in the fashion to which she and her readers are accustomed—the promise of recounting hundreds of other funny things, finding comedy in the society around her (*Caroline* II, 358).

Passages in other women's letters in which they describe their feelings after dissolving unsatisfying marriages support Caroline's dual senses of guilt and relief. In her autobiographical letters, Anna Louisa Karsch reflects on her two divorces as both traumatic and welcome turning points in her life, for they forced her (especially the first divorce, which she did not want) to earn her own living from her talents as a singer of occasional poems. Dorothea Veit writes after her divorce to Carl Gustav von Brinkmann in 1791 from the desk he has given her, one of the few material things she has salvaged from her marriage, which she calls a "Schiffbruch, der mich von einer langen Sklaverei befreit" [shipwreck that freed me from a long slavery].[25] Her losses are nothing though, she contemplates, compared to the freedom she has gained, and her letter is a venue to defend her actions as well as formulate the importance of that freedom. Sophie Mereau, whose divorce in the summer of 1801 offered a model for the legal expedience that Caroline Schlegel-Schelling wanted, also expresses both relief and trepidation in letters to Clemens Brentano after her divorce.[26] Mereau, like Karsch, was one of the first women who dared to live on money from her own literary accomplishments. Her future turns more uncertain, as she writes shortly after to Brentano: "Meine Gegenwart ist eine dumpfe Stille und die Zukunft steht vor meiner Seele wie eine Wolcke, von der ich nicht weiß, ob sie wohltätigen Schatten oder verheerenden Sturm gebiert—ich bin im Fegfeuer, der nächste Zustand muß Himmel oder Hölle sein" [My present condition is a gloomy silence and the future stands in front of my soul like a cloud, of which I don't know whether it bears a benevolent shadow or a devastating storm—I am in purgatory, the next condition must be heaven or hell] (Brentano/Mereau 88). In each of these instances, what would usually be a topic for much malicious gossip—as Caroline hints at the beginning of her letter to Julie Gotter—has achieved status as a theme for narrative reflection. Not only have Caroline and others provided information on the perspectives of women toward loveless marriages and the aftermath of their dissolution; by placing it in writing, they reveal the topic in a depth that resists categorization as trivial. The care with which they choose their words reflects a posturing devised to confront restraining social expectations, as we see especially in Caroline Schlegel-Schelling's three letters on her divorce. Here is the subject out of which novels are born. The artful way in which the women convey the complexity and ambiguity of their psychological turmoil deserves recognition.

Another problematic theme in Varnhagen's and Schlegel-Schelling's letters is sickness, a theme that has also caused many scholars to criticize the letters as a litany of banal complaints. Accounts of personal illness, however, portray the persistent maladies that affected women—headaches, chest pains, exhaustion—and cause readers to look at reasons for their ill-health. The fact that Caroline often had eighteen to twenty-five people at her table for lunch in Jena, ran other affairs in the household, contributed to literary reviews, and acted as personal secretary for Friedrich Schlegel, August Wilhelm Schlegel, and then Friedrich Schelling, adds dimension to the perception that all she did was write letters. The sickness she suffered, like that mentioned by Louise Gottsched, Karoline von Günderrode, and Rahel Varnhagen, appears to have been the price talented women paid for trying to be active and creative while having to perform the duties expected of them by the famous men in their lives.

In her study, *The Female Malady*, Elaine Showalter makes a case against romanticizing women's bouts of illness as subversive forms of rebellion and refutes any essentialist equation between femininity and illness. Rather, representations of illness communicate women's powerlessness.[27] A careful historical study of women's illness should recognize in a particular cultural context the importance that gender plays in defining and treating disorders. In the letters of Rahel and Caroline, dual forces of powerlessness and empowerment are at work. The openness and frequency with which they express in letters their complaints have profound bearing on the constraints under which women could express themselves. Illness, like divorce, defied aesthetic criteria established for a "good" letter, to recall Gellert's promotion of model letters full of wit and good humor. In Meta Moller's premonitions about death before her childbirth, in Karoline von Günderrode's observations of her self as lying within a coffin, in Caroline Schlegel-Schelling's extensive, moving descriptions of the deaths of her nephew and then her own daughter, and in Rahel Varnhagen's frequent mention of her sicknesses and menstruation, the women find in the exchange of letters aesthetic ways of talking about their illnesses by revealing the illness as part of a matrix of experience. Personal letters also encourage women to couch their criticisms of society at large within discussions of physical symptoms. In a description to David Veit on 22 March 1795, Rahel's self-analysis of her immediate illness helps her find a key to larger feelings of oppression. She asserts: "Ich bin krank. Nun sag' ich's selbst" [I am sick. Now I say it myself] (*GW* I, 131). In investigating the cause, she must look at her entire environment "durch gêne, durch Zwang, solang ich lebe; ich lebe wider meine Neigung, wenn ich auch nur immer dagegen handeln seh'" [through gêne, through force, as long as I live; I live against my inclination, even if I also always see acting against that] (*GW* I, 131). Her observations on her smallness refer not only to her physical stature, but also her psychological state: "Mein ewiges Verstellen, meine Vernünftigkeit, mein einziges Nachgeben, welches ich selbst nicht mehr merke, und meine Einsicht, verzehren mich" [My perpetual acting, my sensibility, my continuous relenting, which I myself do not notice, and my insight, consume me] (*GW* I, 132). Her analysis leads her to realize that only she can help herself: "Ich bin krank: und ich muß mir selbst helfen" [I am sick: and I must help myself] (*GW* I, 132). She poses solutions—go to the country, to a spa, relax—all with the intention of getting away from the stifling society in which she gets "Ennui's- und Anstrengungs-Schmerzen" [pains of ennui and exertion] (*GW* I, 133). Physical pains have turned to psychological ones, or rather intertwine, as a letter to Varnhagen on 7 March 1812 asserts: "Ich fühlte mich eben so krank, daß ich es nicht mehr zu scheiden wußte, wer den anderen erst so gemacht hatte, Gedanke oder Körper" [My sickness was such that I no longer knew how to distinguish which had caused the other, thought or body] (GW IV.2, 263). She tries to comfort Rebecca Friedländer with the reasoning that physical pain can have a larger unidentifiable cause: "Seyn Sie nicht so ängstlich! Selbst Physischen Schmerz halte ich für Verwirrung in die wir nicht einzudringen vermögen" [Don't be so anxious! Even physical pain I take for confusion that we are not able to penetrate] (*Briefe an eine Freundin* 275). This reassurance takes pressure off the victim as a cause for the illness.

Rahel's focus on her illness as having social causes bridges the personal with the public. At one point, absence of illness clarifies the cause of her depression. To Rebecca Friedländer she writes that despite the fact that she has slept well and has no headache, she still feels unwell. She traces her feelings to anxiety due to pressures from her milieu:

> Ich weiß auch die Ursache. Es ist die Angst—-Angst sage ich—-über den Jammer: die mich zu allem Schreklichen in mir zurükführt. Meine Umgebungen sind zu drükend u. ich vermag ohne ihnen zu entfliehen, auch kein Stäubchen daran zu verändern. *Hier* wird mir *Alles* zu Rahel! das heißt, zur infamsten Situation! *Nie* erscheine ich die die ich bin; ewig nimmt mich Einer aus den Andern hand. Und in der Verzweiflung laße ich's dabey; Anstrengung um sich darzustellen ist auch Tollheit; u. der höchste Ekel!

> [I also know the cause. It is fear—fear I say—about the misery: which leads me back to all the horror inside me. My environments are too stressful and I am not able to change one speck of dust in them without fleeing from them. *Here everything* becomes Rahel for me. That is, to the most infamous situation. I *never* appear as the person I am; someone perpetually takes me from the other hand. And in my despair I let it be; exertion to represent oneself is also craziness; and the highest disgust.] (*Briefe an eine Freundin* 228–29)

Faced with living up to a reputation as "Rahel," she constructs an environment that places undue pressure on her identity. As in her correspondence with Pauline Wiesel, the expectations that society places on her defy moments of self-truth. She sees herself adapting and anguishes over her weakness.

In letter after letter, both Caroline and Rahel recognize the impact that personal actions can have on the social and political realms. Their call for authenticity and truth in private letters implies hopes for ramifications in the public domain. Varnhagen and Wiesel really believed that their friendship together could establish the utopia they envisioned in a free, independent, "green" life that challenged more traditional living structures. For Rahel to defy narrow categorization of herself and her world was for her to exert counterpressure against the social parameters of her existence. In letters, Varnhagen and Schlegel-Schelling seize the opportunity to comment on social injustices and the political climate. As Friedrichsmeyer observes, referring to Caroline Schlegel-Schelling: "Her choice of epistolary art was in the widest sense a function of her engagement in the world around her."[28] On a trip to Münden, Caroline comments on how the aristocracy in Münden has exploited the people only to be able to build the beautiful castles in Cassel (*Caroline* I, 62). As if unshackled from marital restraints, her political engagement becomes much stronger in her letters after Böhmer's death. In one letter to F. L. W. Meyer, a writer with whom she exchanged letters for many years in the 1790s, she draws the connection between political and literary interests. Were Meyer in Paris, she speculates, he could write to her about the King's unsuccessful escape and the people's freedom chants; she, in exchange, would write about literary events and people such as Schiller and Schlegel (*Caroline* I, 225). There might be a hint of irony in her statement, considering Meyer's conservative, royalist sympathies and Caroline's eventual falling out of favor with Schiller and Schlegel. Her first extant letter from Mainz to Luise Gotter, 20 April 1792, exemplifies the artful way in which she weaves her private life, centered around children and tea circles, with her insatiable urge to observe and eventually relate historical events:

An meiner Kleinen hab ich mehr Freude wie jemals. Kurz, ich kan Dir sagen, es ist alles wie ich erwartete. Wir können noch sehr lebhafte Sceenen herbekommen, wenn der Krieg ausbrechen sollte—ich ginge ums Leben nicht von hier—denk nur, wenn ich meinen Enkeln erzähle, wie ich eine Belagerung erlebt habe, wie man einen alten geistlichen Herrn die lange Nase abgeschnitten und die Demokraten sie auf öffentlichen Markt gebraten haben—wir sind doch in einem höchst interreßanten politischen Zeitpunkt, und das giebt mir außer den klugen Sachen, die ich Abends beym Theetisch höre, gewaltig viel zu denken, wenn ich allein, in meinen recht hübschen Zimmerchen in dem engen Gäßchen sitze, und Halstücher ausnähe, wie ich eben thue.

[I am having more joy with my little one than ever before. In short, I can tell you that everything is how I had expected. We can still receive lively scenes if the war should break out—I would not go away from here for my life—just think, when I describe to my grandchildren how I experienced a siege, how the long nose of an old clergyman was cut off and the democrats burned it in the public market—we are really in a highly interesting political era, and that, outside of the clever things that I hear in the evening around the tea table, gives me an enormous amount to think about, when I sit alone in my nice small room in the narrow little alleyway and do needlepoint neckerchiefs, as I am accustomed to doing.] (*Caroline* I, 250)

The modern reader might find Caroline's portrayal of the horrors of war as "lively scenes" too reductive. Within her world, confined by rigid gender stereotypes, however, her expressed need to move beyond the restrictions is progressive. Also significant here is her desire eventually to be storyteller to her grandchildren, an aspiration that elevates the narrative act into a significant part of the making of history. She persists in writing letters in political turmoil, even though she admits that the correspondence could be considered "high treason" (*Caroline* I, 274). She resists Meyer's warnings not to write during wartime, demanding: "So gehorch ich nicht—ich will schreiben" [Thus I will not obey—I want to write] (*Caroline* I, 278).

Not only do Caroline's letters emphasize the influence of personal actions on the political realm; they also show the impact of political actions on the personal sphere, implying that politicians must also think of the personal consequences of their political actions. That she viewed her private life as embroiled in her surrounding world, first political, then literary, is evident in her observation on how people will view her divorce from A. W. Schlegel. To Louise Gotter she writes:

Sonderbar ist es, daß, Einmal in die Stürme einer großen Revolution verwickelt mit meinen Privatbegebenheiten, ich es gleichsam jetzt zum zweitenmal werde, denn die Bewegung in der literarischen Welt ist so stark und gährend wie damals die politische. Die Schufte und ehrlosen Gesellen scheinen eben die Oberhand zu haben.

[It is strange that, once embroiled in the storms of a great revolution with my private affairs, I am again thus so for a second time, for the movement in the literary world is so strong and fermenting as the political at that time. The scoundrels and honorless fellows seem to have the upper hand.] (*Caroline* II, 356)

It is difficult for her to separate her present literary world from her former revolutionary one, although she knows she will be judged simply by the more polemical of the two. She knows that she can alternate between the two, but others will have a hard time understanding the connection. In characterizing herself as "a good woman, and no heroine," she prioritized her private role over any public one. Her remarks to Pauline Gotter in August 1807 about Napoleon's expansion reflect her awareness of his power and the people's powerlessness: "Für mich ist er immer nur noch das personnificirte Schicksal gewesen, das ich nicht hasse und nicht liebe, sondern abwarte, wohin es die Welt führt" [For me he has been, as always, still only the personified destiny that I don't hate and don't love, but rather wait out to see where the world will take it] (*Caroline* II, 504).

Still, she is not paralyzed into ineffectiveness. Living during a turbulent time in Germany and having very little stability in her personal life, letters become for her a form of political newspaper, not only for information on battles and encroaching armies, but mainly to remain personally connected to those events. She relies on correspondence to learn how the personal lives of her friends and relatives have been affected by the changes. For her, newspapers prove inadequate sources for relaying messages on the effect political events had on people's everyday existence. She asks her sister to tell her news of Germany that the newspapers would not report (*Caroline* II, 377). To Luise Gotter in Gotha she inquires from München in November 1806 about events in Jena, asking mostly about Luise's personal situation and those in their circle of friends: "Alles, was mir näher angehört, ist mehr oder weniger in diesem Umsturz begriffen" [Everything that belongs closely to me is more or less seized in this revolution] (*Caroline* II, 476). Caroline sees her own letters as newspapers, too, as she instructs her sister to pass her letters around (*Caroline* II, 376). Her observations on how the political climate affects university life and Schelling's ability to find a job center also on personal hardships. From Würzburg in December 1805 she tells Julie Gotter about groceries becoming expensive and the fears they have of the continual encroachment of the Prussian army against the French (*Caroline* II, 419). As French troops come to Würzburg though, she remains skeptical about Napoleon's belligerence. She does not see the battle as black and white, but rather as one provoker against another, with Napoleon being: "der König der Könige, dem der Herr aller Herren doch gnädiglich bald den Hals brechen möge" [the King of the Kings, whose neck the lord of all lords may mercifully break soon] (*Caroline* II, 423). To her sister she expresses her appreciation for any news she can send and for the letters she has received from others. She reports on other letters she and Schelling have had from Jena and Weimar and then compares those letters with reportages in the newspapers. Such is the case when she writes about Goethe's experiences: Goethe wrote personally to Schelling about their fears and the shortages of money and goods during the occupation, whereas the papers reported more anecdotally on rumors that he had proposed to Christiane Vulpius on the day of the battle in order to form a close bond at a time when such bonds seemed impossible (*Caroline* II, 478).

Caroline's letters are filled with observations about the effect of war. From Munich in March 1809 she talks about devastation in the city from the war. On a trip to Maulbronn she describes evidence of war along the way (*Caroline* II, 561). She expresses her opinion on the political tenor of the war, blaming Prussia for having made mistake after mistake (*Caroline* II, 480). Still, in her own descriptions of the events, she realizes the importance of human communication in recounting the public events. When talking about the Kaiser's visit to Stuttgart she complains to Meta Liebeskind that she cannot trust the newspapers to report accurately on the event. To compensate for this lack of reliable information, she asks Meta Liebeskind to describe the Kaiser's visit to Munich "im historischen Styl" [in historical style]. She also asks her to report on anything she might have heard about the Tyrol, commenting that she has read nothing in the newspaper during the last fourteen days that she does not already know (*Caroline* II, 562).

Two long letters by Caroline to Huber about his scathing critique of the *Athenäum* in the *Allgemeine Literaturzeitung* draw on the inevitable exchange between the personal and the political within the scope of artistic creation. She sees the impact of his review on the reactionary forces, but also questions how those forces have had an impact on him. As Friedrichsmeyer comments, these two letters "convincingly document the extent to which she believed in romantic art in general, and in letters in particular, as the means for bringing about political change."[29] The letters are her own formulation of a politics inseparable from the private realm and irreducible to black and white. Caroline makes clear from the beginning that her response is hers alone, as A. W. is picking up Auguste, who has been away for eight weeks. She first talks about the *Allgemeine Literaturzeitung* as a journal for the masses, implying that Huber has compromised his integrity by submitting his critique to such a magazine. Others have already criticized the *Athenäum*, she states, to make the point that the issues are not as black and white as Huber might think. His own thinking is too compensatory:

> Es bildet sich jetzt ein allgemeiner Kampf des Guten und Schlechten, Sie kennen revoluzionäre Zeiten, und sollten an der Weise nicht kritteln. Was Sie wollen, nennt man im Politischen halbe Maaßregeln, ich gestehe, ich halte Sie, auch im politischen, für zu friedliebend, zu genau abwägend, darum haben Sie eine größere Wirkung verfehlt, die Ihnen sonst gewiß zu Gebote stand.

> [A general battle of the good and the bad is now forming, you know revolutionary times and should not find fault with the method. What you

want are called half-measures in political terms, I admit, I consider you, also politically, too peaceloving, too painstakingly balancing my options, for this reason you have failed at having a larger effect, which otherwise certainly stood at your command.] (*Caroline* I, 578)

Gender issues arise in her defense as she admits her own part in compiling the journal, but also her own willingness to submit to the decisions of the male editors (*Caroline* I, 578–79). She cannot uphold a separation of the professional from the private life. In reaction to Huber's defense of Wieland as a writer against the *Athenäum's* criticism, she queries: "Ist nicht Wielands Poesie Wielands Person? Es ist nur thörichte Weisheit beide hinterher noch trennen zu wollen" [Isn't Wieland's poetry Wieland's person? It is only crazy wisdom to want to separate the two] (*Caroline* I, 579). She also criticizes Huber's double standard in saying that Schlegel was not manly enough to sign his own name to the Wieland critique when Huber himself did not sign his own name to his own reviews (*Caroline* I, 579–80). In the process of combining art and politics, she defends *Lucinde* as a novel before its time, which should have been published fifty years later (*Caroline* I, 580). Regarding rumors that even members of the Jena group had argued amongst themselves over the journal and the aesthetic program, she recognizes the importance of disputes and arguments, so as to dispel any notion that they merely flatter one another. Again, the personal situation mirrors the surrounding revolutionary tenor of the time: "Keine Revoluzion ohne Faction, das wissen Sie, oder sind Sie plözlich so modéré geworden?" [No revolution without faction, that you know, or have you suddenly become so modéré?] (*Caroline* I, 581). In publishing his critique at a time when Napoleon's rise to power promises to incite significant political revolution, Huber's criticism only helps consolidate conservative forces. He is naive if he believes that literature can be separated from politics:

> Und glauben Sie denn, daß in die Sache der schlechten Schriftsteller nicht auch die hohen Häupter gemischt werden? Es ist alles geschehen, um den Herzog aufzuwiegeln, und was der nicht that, oder nicht thun konnte, wurde ihm angelogen. Und alle dies Volk wird sich nun ausgelassen über Ihre Rezension freuen et vous avés bien merité de la patrie! Die Redaktoren fügen sicher noch die Anmerkung hinzu, daß sie von einem Freund Schlegels sey.

> [And do you really believe that the important figures are not beings drawn into the affairs of the bad authors? Everything happened to stir up the duke, and what he didn't do or couldn't do was lied to him. And all these people will happily rejoice about your review and vous aves bien merité

de la patrie! [You have truly deserved the homeland!] The editors will certainly add the remark that the review is by a friend of Schlegel.] (Caroline I, 581)

She accuses him of taking on the review for personal reasons, and not because of his own knowledge, for he knows no philosophy, poetry, and Greek (*Caroline* I, 584). Instead of relying on his knowledge as his main qualification for writing the review, Caroline claims, he has depended on the strength of his own character (*Caroline* I, 584). She, too, cannot separate the political from the personal, the literary life from her own private relationships. At the end of the first letter and in the second letter, she breaks off her friendship with him. He will regret the consequences, she warns, as she writes: "Das war recht dumm von Ihnen, lieber Huber" [That was really stupid of you, dear Huber] (*Caroline* I, 586–87).

Within the context of other opinions that Caroline expresses on her political involvement, these letters to Huber also show that interpretations of subjectivity must consider the powerful act of representation that goes on during letter writing. In efforts to view their individual roles within the larger picture, women such as Schlegel-Schelling and Varnhagen felt torn over the decisions they made and the images they projected. In letters from prison, Caroline Schlegel-Schelling admits that her sufferings are very hard on her as a woman. Still, she does see herself as a martyr for a cause, for it is her connections with suspect people, and not anything she has done personally, that has brought on the charges of treason against her (I, 282). In scorning the great people of history, she also realizes her acquiescence, as she writes to Gotter: "ich lache die Großen aus, und verachte sie, wenn ich tief vor ihnen supplicire, aber ich bin wahrhaftig nur eine gute Frau, und keine Heldin. Ein Stück meines Lebens gäb ich jezt darum, wenn ich nicht auf immer, wenigstens in Deutschland, aus der weiblichen Sphäre der Unbekantheit gerißen wäre" [I laugh at the greats and despise them, when I supplicate profoundly in front of them, but I am truly only a good woman, and no heroine. I would now give part of my life if I were not forever, at least in Germany, ripped out of the feminine sphere of anonymity] (*Caroline* I, 293). She has no qualms about staying in her allotted feminine sphere. To Meyer she asserts: "Ich bin ja niemals eine unnatürliche Heldin, nur immer ein Weib gewesen [I have certainly never been an unnatural heroine, only a woman] (*Caroline* I, 296). While recognizing that motherhood might have saved her from harsher treatment in prison, she also states that she knows of no man from whom she would ask protection (*Caroline* I, 298). To allay any anxiety her conservative friend Meyer might have about her political actions, she writes: "denk, ich sey dieselbe Frau geblieben, die Du immer in mir kantest, geschaffen um nicht über die Gränzen stiller Häuslichkeit hinweg zu gehn, aber durch ein unbegreifliches Schicksaal aus meiner Sphäre gerißen, ohne die Tugenden derselben eingebüßt zu haben, ohne Abendtheurerin geworden zu seyn" [think, I have remained the same woman whom you knew in me, created not to go beyond the boundaries of quiet domesticity, but by an unfathomable fate ripped from my sphere without having forfeited the virtues of such, without having become an adventuress] (*Caroline* I, 299). The common person cannot help but touch the nebulous forces of history, as Rahel, too, remarked in her wishes to publish her own letters.

Caroline projected these images of acquiescence mostly during times when political turmoil jeopardized her life. In contrast, in her political letters to Huber, Caroline makes the lines between the quiet domestic sphere and the turbulent adventures of the outer world indistinct. What comes across as reluctance to confront stereotypical roles does not necessarily confirm those roles, either. As Friedrichsmeyer observes, Caroline categorically rejects the act of sacrifice that could make her a heroine.[30] Passages that reflect submission to standard gender norms thus seem less statements of conformity than measures to conceal the subversive tasks she undertook.

Caroline's letter teaches us that those who characterize personal letters as too subjective or apolitical must carefully define their terms. In general, most of what becomes identified as politics relates to males insofar as it covers national and international diplomacy, laws, and wars. Focus on local changes, where women and their issues are most likely represented, are ignored or undervalued.[31] Moreoever, women held no legal place in the public world of the early nineteenth century. As Hannah Arendt postulates in *The Human Condition*, the notion of the private realm is etymologically related to the word deprivation. Under this rubric, the private becomes that which the public excludes, that which should be hidden due to shame or incompleteness. Instead, we should begin to identify the private with the activity or aspect of a person's life that that person wishes to exclude from others, as Iris Marion Young asserts in a recent article on feminist politics. The agent therefore becomes the individual who opts to withdraw through his or her own volition rather than suffer exclusion at the hands of others. In adopting the slogan "the personal is political," the contemporary feminist movement has made public issues out of many ideas claimed too trivial or private for public discussion. This is what Caroline Schlegel-Schelling and Rahel Varnhagen do in their letters.

A second tenet of this redefinition is that no person, action, or aspect of a person's life should be forced into the private or public sphere without his or her consent. A major concern thus becomes how much power the common woman can have over determining her destiny and identity. This concern lies implicit in Caroline's statements, or lack thereof, about the publication of her letters, as it does in Rahel's ideas for her own edition of her correspondence. Karl Varnhagen's declaration that Rebecca Friedländer's letters belonged to him turned ownership into domain. Rahel wanted to honor Rebecca's request with her own insistence that the letters be preserved in one place. The same was true of her correspondence with Pauline Wiesel: Rahel requested in her last will and testament that Pauline Wiesel's letters be returned to her, the only such request in her will.[32] Rahel's ideas on the publication of her letters and Caroline Schlegel-Schelling's silence on the issue indicate a grappling with the paradox that faces any literary production: how to remain true to oneself faced with the prospect of being published. For the letter writer, the question remains this: how to maintain spontaneity and authenticity in the face of publication? For these two women, offers to publish their letters seemed to become threats, not only because that process would reveal innermost feelings publicly. On the contrary, those were the emotions after which they strived. The vigor with which Karl Varnhagen von Ense and Friedrich Schlegel step into the publication process suggests a possible abrogation of any control the women could have over their own writings. That loss of control over the final form of their life's work could lead to an exclusion of parts of their lives that were significant. The fact that publication is not a primary motivation for Caroline's and Rahel's letter writing suggests an aesthetic agenda that promotes an ongoing exchange of emotions and ideas, which publication threatens to finalize.

Caroline witnessed such defeat in her male colleagues' attempts to mold her epistolary poetics into another form. Rahel ultimately saw that defeat when her friend Rebecca Friedländer publicized their relationship in a form that did not reflect a constant, immutable friendship with each other. Rahel's correspondence with Friedländer shows how the demarcation between private and public could complicate and eventually destroy hopes to eliminate that dichotomy. Friedländer and Varnhagen exchanged letters frequently and regularly from 1805 to 1810. Even though both women lived in Berlin, often only a few blocks from each other, Rahel wrote sometimes daily. The reasons for her letters were often to say she would not be visiting that day, due to sickness, headaches, the weather, menstruation pains, or depression. Like Caroline Schlegel-Schelling's final letters, their correspondence brings readers through one of the most volatile times in German history.

Rebecca Friedländer was born in 1783 as Rebecca Salomon to a well-to-do Jewish family (her father was a jeweler in the Prussian court in Berlin). Married at the age of eighteen to Moses Friedländer, she divorced her husband soon thereafter and turned to writing. Her first novel in 1808 was poorly received. She later converted to Christianity and assumed the pen name of Regina Frohberg, but did not remarry. All that remains of the correspondence are Rahel's letters, whose originals are in the Varnhagen Collection in Krakow and have been recently published by Deborah Hertz. Rebecca's letters no longer exist: after Rahel's death she requested them back from Karl August, stating that she wanted to burn them. The five years that mark their friendship was a turbulent period in both women's lives. Rebecca lived alone in an apartment in the house of a mutual friend in Berlin and was experiencing stormy love relationships and isolation from her family and friends. Rahel underwent two unhappy love affairs, one with Karl von Finckenstein and the other with Don Raphael d'Urquijo. More devastating was the dissolution of her beloved salon and the growing antisemitism amongst her friends and in Prussia.

The introductions that Hertz writes to each section of the letters between Rahel Varnhagen and Rebecca Friedländer exemplify how interpretations of letters can become caught in the split between diplomatic, military history and the social history of the two women. In beginning each section with accounts of negotiations, relations, and battles between the French and Prussian, Hertz bestows a higher importance on the military. When she states that Rahel's worries in 1805 were those of a very privileged woman and thus do not include the impending battles and the impact of the diplomatic and military changes on the two women's lives, Hertz implicitly undervalues the importance of Rahel's social milieu for the larger political arena (*Briefe an eine Freundin* 74). Rahel herself seemed aware of the representative role that her microcosm played within the macrocosm. In 1805, she wrote to Gustav von Brinckmann: "Wenn ich 'kleinen Kreis' sagte, so meine ich damit die große Welt" [When I said 'small circle,' then by that I mean the large world] (*GW* I, 264).

As with interpretation of Caroline Schlegel-Schelling's letters, instead of looking solely at the way in which external politics find meaning in the private sphere, Rahel's letters teach us the significance of personal observations as vehicles for more complete understanding of widesweeping public changes. For example, Rahel's reference to Alexander Humboldt and his sister-in-law, Caroline von Humboldt, wife of Wilhelm, as liars, comments on the burgeoning antisemitism of her close friends. She extends that small circle to encompass a larger one, though, as she writes: "Heute waren wieder unendliche Lügen von allen Seiten. Sie kennen meinen Kopf: ich haße sie nicht. Ich fühle nur—u. das immer schmerzhaft—*daß* welche sind. der Pflanzenkönig [A. Humboldt] log, das Weib, alle" [Today there were again endless lies from all sides. You know my head: I don't hate them. I only feel—and that always painfully—*that* these are some. The plant king (A. Humboldt), the woman, everyone] (*Briefe an eine Freundin* 160). In addition, Rahel's comments and silences on her Jewishness point to an ambivalence that many Jewish women had toward assimilation. Hannah Arendt interprets Rahel's Jewishness in the context of Rahel viewing herself as a pariah in her society, but happy to be in that position. Hertz, in contrast, finds a complete desire for assimilation in Rahel's and Rebecca's constant push to belong to non-Jewish circles and to nurture relationships with gentiles. Hertz even points out that flattery and submissiveness were deemed necessary for acceptance. A more varied reading of Rahel's letters unveils a middle point that recognizes the turmoils of her Jewishness and the general desire that every human has to belong to a larger whole. In an undated letter, she is frustrated over a prejudicial remark someone has said to her. While blaming her Jewish heritage, she also recognizes that the hate from her surrounding society pressures her unduely to conform: "Gott! Soll ich denn ewig Schutt räumen, den Andere mir laßen? Was ist es garstig sich immer erst legitimieren zu müßen! darum ist es je *nur* so *ekelhaft* eine Jüdin zu seyn!!" [God! Should I clean up the perpetual rubbish that others leave for me? What is it loathsome always to have to legitimate oneself! thus it is at any time *only* so *disgusting* to be a Jewess] (*Briefe an eine Freundin* 286).

The letters to Friedländer also bring to the forefront controversies over publication, ownership, and power. In one letter in 1807, Rahel proclaims that she could do a better translation than one of a book she has just read. She imagines a dialogue with herself in which she questions the worth of her talents and her ability to bring them to fruition through publication. She concludes that she has talent, but lacks certain abilities:

hier ist die Geschichte: meine Uebersetzung ist beßer: ich habe also Tallent. Soll ich es üben? und etwas verdienen? Ach Gott! ich kenne mich schon! Manche Anlage; u. so wie ich sie ausbilden will unmöglich! *Diese* zur Ausbildung fehlt mir. Natur hat innerlich viel für mich gethan; die anderen Götter sind aber alle bey meiner Wiege ausgeblieben.

[here is the story: my translation is better; I thus have talent. Should I exercise it? and earn something? Ah, God! I know myself well! Much investment; and the way I want to develop it impossible! I lack *this* for development. Nature has done much for me internally; the other gods, however, were all absent at my cradle.] (*Briefe an eine Freundin* 155)

From this statement, in which Rahel accepts her own incapacities, Hertz concludes that Rahel's individual temperament, and not a self-conscious rejection of the translation medium, contributed most to her decisions not to publish. Given the immense and varied body of work Rahel produced, however, such an interpretation based on one citation seems too narrow. Stipulations, desires, wishes change from letter to letter, from day to day, from correspondent to correspondent. Acknowledgment of her talent in the above statement, for example, contradicts a later statement in which she recognizes the difference between genius and talent, the latter of which one must have to write books: "*Genie?!* ist zu bücherschreiben gar nicht nöthig: Tallent muß man haben: u. sehr großes, wenn Genie nicht gradzu dies Tallent hemmen soll. Ein Paradox, der nächstens ein Gemeinplatz seyn wird! Wie es mit Göttlichem beystand allen Wahrheiten gehen wird!" [Genius! is absolutely not necessary to write a book. One must have talent: and a very great one, if genius should not hinder this talent. A paradox, which will soon be a commonplace! As it will happen with divine assistance to all truths] (*Briefe an eine Freundin* 251). This latter exertion of free will coincides with Rahel's fluctuations. The time, the context, the place must be right. Although such an interpretation might sound confusingly relativist, it avoids generalizations that can present too static a picture. It also corroborates a reworked definition of the private and public spheres.

Rebecca Friedländers's book *Schmerz der Liebe* thus seems to have provided a main impetus for severance of the corresondence and friendship, as both Hannah Arendt and Barbara Hahn conclude.[33] The novel, a *roman à clef* about Berlin society, was first published anonymously in 1810 and then appeared again in 1815 under the name of Regina Frohberg. Told through the eyes of a certain Gräfin Aarberg, the novel depicted Rahel in a poor light as Baronin Charlotte von Willingshausen. Characterized as hard and cold, she also was portrayed as incapable of friendship with men or women. The book could have upset Rahel for the negative portrayal she received in it as the complaining salonière, as Arendt claims, but that reason seems secondary in light of what she writes to Friedländer. Most disturbing seems to be the fact that Friedländer caused their relationship to become part of a public forum. Rahel's outbursts in the correspon-

dence indicate that she was most disappointed that the book incorpo-
rated none of the dialogic exchange after which they had striven in
letters.[34] In reaction to a statement made by the character who represents Rahel in the book, Rahel conveys her paralysis at seeing her
words on the printed page: "Was soll ich wohl sprechen, nach dem
Sie mir meine eigenen Worte angeführt haben 'daß mich nur ein Koch
u. eine Equipage rühren'. mit welchem Zutrauen kann ich sprechen
wenn Sie mich so, nicht aus bosheit, aber im Ernste auslegen" [What
should I really say after you have cited my own words to me 'that
only a cook and an equipage stir me!' with what trust can I speak
when you interpret me in such a way, not out of malice, but in
seriousness] (*Briefe an eine Freundin* 252). Fearful of the license that
readers now have to interpret her words, she writes: "Ein Mensch
wie ein buch, kann dem Sinne nach zerrißen werden, u. dann kann
man alles draus machen" [A person just like a book can literally be
torn up, and then one can make everything out of it] (*Briefe an
eine Freundin* 252). The net of pain will cover not just her, but also
Friedländer and their relationship, too: "Ist aber das herz davon nicht
zu reinigen, so muß die unbezwingliche Neigung zu mir neben ve-
rachtung u. _solcher_ Mißbilligung ewig nur wieder Schmerzen machen: Ihnen, u. mir" [Is, however, the heart not to be purified from
such, thus the unrestrained inclination towards me, plus despise and
_such_ disapproval, must perpetually only cause pain again: to you and
to me] (*Briefe an eine Freundin* 252). When Rahel tries to forgive
Rebecca and even encourage her to publish the book despite harsh
criticism from its initial readers, Rahel attempts to distance herself
from the published version. The book, she asserts, has nothing to do
with their relationship; in fact, Rebecca should consider it a stranger,
"einen fremden." Rahel asks that Rebecca come visit her, which would
be better than worrying about expenses of retracting the book (*Briefe
an eine Freundin* 253–54).

Rahel's attempts at reconciliation through separating her private
life from its representation in the published version eventually fail,
however. Ultimately, she sees an impingement on her personal life, a
decision that she has not made, but that Rebecca forced upon her
through the publication process. Rahel reports how others want her
to retaliate; thus her attempts to separate their private relationship
from the public fail due to the expectations of others as well:

Ihr buch macht mir viel Verdruß. Alle bekannte fallen über mich her, wie
Sie mich so haben können an Pranger stellen; u. wollen Rechenschaft *von
mir*. Und wie ich sie noch sehen könnte; u. etc: etc:! es nimmt nie ein
Ende. Viel sprechen kann ich noch nicht. Ich sagte; wie schon ein bogen

gedrukt war, hätten sie mir angebothen, es mit 260 r[eichs]t[haler] kosten zurüknehmen: ich habe aber gesagt, das druken laßen könnte mir nicht schaden. da sagen sie wieder; Sie hätten's hinter meinem Rüken wegnehmen sollen. Manche wollen es rezensiren, dagegen schreiben. Ich sage ein Spiel der Phantasie sey erlaubt: u. wenn ich es mir gefallen ließe, so müßten es alle. Aber der Vorfall ist verdrüßlich.

[Your book causes me much annoyance. All acquaintances talk badly about me, how you could have put me in the stocks; and want justification *from me*. And how I still could see them; and etc: etc:! There is no end. I still cannot talk much. I said; as soon as a sheet was printed, they had offered to rescind it with 260 R[eichs] T[haler]: I, however, said the printing could not harm me. They say again; you should have taken it away behind my back. Some want to review it, write against it. I say a game of fantasy is allowed: and if I don't object to it, then nobody should. But the incident is annoying.] (*Briefe an eine Freundin* 259)

She now has disillusions about intimacy: "Ein Gewißen ist so etwas intimes, daß nichts anderes, als es selbst mitsprechen kann, wo von ihm die Rede ist" [A conscience is something intimate, that cannot speak along otherwise as itself, where one is talking about it] (*Briefe an eine Freundin* 262). At one point, she forgives Rebecca, but still cannot understand the motives:

das ist unsere größte Lebenszeit; aber auch ich kann ein fait nicht ändern; höchstens, die handlung nicht begehen, die mir meine Gefühle darüber diktirten: u. das will ich, u. thue es. Sie sagen aber selbst, sie mußten Ihrem herzen Luft machen; wodurch Liebe?—wenn Sie mich in der baronin *nicht* schilderten; u. thaten Sie es, so bin ich doch getroffen!

[That is our greatest time of life; but I also cannot change an act; at most, not commit the action that dictates my feelings about it: and that I don't want, and do so. You say, however, yourself that you must let your heart air itself; how so, Dear?—if you didn't portray me in the Baron; and you did it, thus I am affected.] (*Briefe an eine Freundin* 262–63)

In one of her last letters in the relationship, her questions revolve around Rebecca's personal feelings for Rahel:

Hier springt mir eine frage vor's Gesicht die gar nicht hierher zu paßen scheint: was lieben Sie denn an mir? So heißt sie—bald sind Sie böse auf mich, bald sehnen Sie sich nach mir. Noch nie habe ich diesen wiederspruch bewirkt. Am häufigsten bin ich nicht beachtet worden, viel verachtet, lange, lange nicht geliebt: gehaßt oft; geliebt uebernatürlich selten, von Geliebten äüßerst kurtz, von ein paar freunden nur; von freundinen sehr ernst u. sehr lange. Aber auf solche doppelte Weise wie bey Ihnen, lebt' ich noch in keiner brust. Eine Zeile Ärger, eine Zeile Sehnsucht, eine Stolz eine demuth. bin ich an diesem Wechsel Schuld. Ueberlegen Sie's: ich gebe mich ganz Ihrem Ansspruch.

[Here a question jumps out at me, which does not seem to belong here at all: what do you love about me? Thus it means—soon you will be mad at me, soon you will long for me. I have never brought about this contradiction before. Mostly I have not been paid attention to, have been despised a lot, not been loved for a long, long time; often been hated; seldom loved supernaturally, utmost briefly by lovers, only by a couple friends; by women friends very seriously and for a long time. But in a double way as by you have I never lived in any breast. A line of anger, a line of longing, a pride a humility. am I guilty of this change. Consider it: I give myself totally to your claim.] (*Briefe an eine Freundin* 269)

Rahel has aptly characterized their relationship as reflected in all her letters to Friedländer—double-sided, ambiguous, volatile, inconstant. At one point Rahel confesses her love for Rebecca: "Sie sind die erste frau deren brief mir solche Emozion gegeben als ihr heutiger—dies kenne ich nur bey Liebe—Und ich habe schon frauen so geliebt als Sie" [You are the first woman whose letter gave me such emotion as yours today—this I know only in love—and I have already loved women in the same way as you] (*Briefe an eine Freundin* 279). At another point she acknowledges her anger and frustration: "Sie sind das erste u. einzige Weib das mich argert. Jetzt schlagt mir wieder mein herz vor beleidigung" [You are the first and only woman who makes me mad. Now my heart pounds again out of insult] (*Briefe an eine Freundin* 288). At many times she praises Rebecca for her letters, encouraging her to write more: "Ihr brief hat mich sehr gerührt. Er ist so edel: *Sie* waren so affinirt. Er ist ein paar Mal so schön geschrieben: die Worte kamen aus tiefer Miene! Ich liebe Sie" [Your letter stirred me much. It is so noble: You were so refined. It is written so beautifully a couple times: the words came from a deep mien. I love you] (*Briefe an eine Freundin* 149). She even praises the honesty of their friendship, as well as the potential for veracity in Rebecca's letters, as she had in Pauline's: "Sie sollen ewig wahr gegen mich seyn; denn Sie können es" [You should be perpetually truthful with me; for you can do that] (*Briefe an eine Freundin* 156); or at another time: "Auch in Ihrem brief hat mir die Wahrheit u. das Zutrauen am besten Gefallen" [Also in your letter the truth and the trust please me the most] (*Briefe an eine Freundin* 183). Yet, unlike in any letters to Pauline Wiesel, Rahel frequently also admonishes Friedländer about the inauthenticity of her letters and points out misunderstandings. She corrects statements that might make their relationship mean more than it does:

> *Meine* Wahrheit—nicht Wahrheit überall—können Sie nicht verdauen: Sie bilden dinge daraus die mir unvermuthet sind. Ich habe nicht gesagt: daß ich nicht ohne Sie leben kann—u. noch nie sagte ich's einem Weibe—-Sie haben es zu mir gesagt: als ich gehen wollte u. es zur that kam, wollten Sie ohne anzugebende Ursache nicht mit.

> [*My* truth—not truth everywhere—you cannot digest: You form things from it that are unforeseen to me. I didn't say: that I cannot live without you—and I have never said that to a woman—you said that to me: when I wanted to go and it came to the action, you did not want to come along, without stating a reason.] (*Briefe an eine Freundin* 243)

In recommending that Friedländer write more openly about her problems, Varnhagen also implies a certain lack of forthrightness in Rebecca's letters (*Briefe an eine Freundin* 222; 224; 226). She comments on the veils that cover Rebecca's letters: "Auch von Ihren briefen ist ein Schleier genommen eine Abhäutung könnt' ich's nennen. Sie glauben nicht wie mich Ihr billet in die Seele hinein freut: u. der wahre Antheil—den recht echt Geistigen—den ich an Ihnen nehme, geht erst nun an" [Also from your letters a veil has been removed, a shedding, I could call it. You do not believe how your ticket made me happy to the soul: and the true sympathy—the truly authentic spiritual one—that I show to you, begins from now on] (*Briefe an eine Freundin* 138).

It is difficult to judge one writer's letters in isolation from responses, as is the case with Rahel's letters to Friedländer; thus, a comparison with the correspondence between Wiesel and Varnhagen, in which there are extant letters from both sides, seems hardly fair. Still, as Hahn analyzes in Rahel Varnhagen's and Pauline Wiesel's correspondence, the spinoff of phrases and ideas from one letter to the next creates a continual interplay.[35] This mutual exchange appears lacking in Rahel's letters to Friedländer. The intimacy that Rahel and Pauline sustain over a long period of time proves the deep-seated need for continuity in human relations. Unlike in the correspondence with Friedländer, in which Rahel's final outbursts question the changed nature of Rebecca's friendship, Pauline and Rahel affirm their constancy. Pauline links her own immutability with Rahel's profound understanding of her character, as she writes on 14 December 1808: "Gott! Gott! warum ändern alle Menschen, und warum ändere ich nicht; warum sehe ich besser, deutlicher, natürlicher,—und warum kennt mich keiner, wie Sie und ich mich kennen!" [God! God!

why do all people change, and why do I not change; why do I see better, more clearly, more naturally—and why does nobody know me, as you and I know me?] (Varnhagen/Wiesel 8). Pauline understands her changes only in outer appearances, not in her inner self. She writes on 5 October 1815:

> Liebe beste Engels Ralle: Sie lieben mich noch immer, und ich bin es auch noch währt *Wenn ich es jemals währt wahr* denn ich bin in nichts verändert, nur die Umstende und Umgebungen um mich herum, ich denke und fühle und Sehen so richtig als sondst, Aber es macht Auf Andere nicht mehr den Eindruck, die Jugend ist nur noch in meine innerste, Aber von Ausen füld Sie, und die Menschen wollen die Augen geschmeigeld haben; *sehr Verzeihlich* uns gefäld ja auch Vieles nur durg die augen.

> [Dear best angel Ralle: You love me still, and I am still worth it *If I was ever worth it* because I have not changed at all, only the conditions and environments around me, I think and feel and see as correctly as always, But it does not make an impression on others any more, youth is only still in my interior, But from the exterior you and people want to have the eyes yielding; *very forgivable* we really like a lot through the eyes.][36]

After a lapse in their friendship, Rahel begins a letter in 1822 reassuring Pauline of her unwavering feelings: "Theure freundin geliebte, von mir einzig gekannte Pauline! diese Zeilen sollen Ihnen blos sagen daß meine Sehnsucht nach ihnen die alte ist, und *mit* mir nur neue Gestalt annimmt. daß frühling ist, und sie auf's höchste gesteigert ist" [Dear beloved friend, Pauline, only dearly known by me! these lines should only tell you that my longing for you is the same old one, and *with* me only takes on a new form. That it is spring, and it [the longing] has risen to the highest].[37] New beginnings hold the promise of resuming old bonds. Within the renewal process letters hold them together. Rahel draws together the same contrasting images of spring and the past to end the letter: "Goldtaube! Ich habe alle deine briefe. Aber ich war so erdrükt und erstokt daß, ich's Schreiben für nichts hielt für unmöglich. Nun aber ist ein frühling: und er löst mir das herz und dies grüßt Sie, Schreiben Sie mir."[38] Rahel stresses the eternal nature of their friendship when she writes on 8 June 1826: "Einzige Pauline: immer und ewig! Diese Worte allein wären genug und ein Brief für Sie" (Varnhagen/Wiesel 59).

Ultimately, Rahel fails to see the same consistency in her relationship with Rebecca Friedländer, as she writes in one of her final letters to Freidländer:

> Ich, u. meine briefe, u. alle meine äußerungen, müßen immer sehr "verschiedene Empfindungen" in Ihnen hervor bringen. Es ist in mir noch

ein für Sie unverdauliches Ingredienz. Es wird Ihnen dereinst dessto beßer schmeken, u. bekomen. Meine einmalige Mischung—trempe—ist nicht zu ändern. u. wenn man sie karakterisieren wollte, muß man dies von ihr sagen.

[I and my letters and all my remarks must always bring forth very "diverse emotions" in you. Inside me there is an ingredient that is not yet digestible for you. It will one day taste better to you and be more agreeable for you. My unique mixture—temper—cannot be changed. and if one wants to characterize it, one must say this about it.] (*Briefe an eine Freundin* 263)

Rahel realizes how the multiple reactions that her letters invoke in Rebecca are unavoidable, especially in an epistolary exchange that involves continual assertion and response. Rahel wants, however, to have Rebecca recognize constancy in that multidimensionality. In turn, Rahel appreciates her own abilities to provoke multiple reactions as part of her unchangeable nature. Rebecca's publication has muted what Rahel considers immutable, that is, her consistent desire to remain non-static. Rahel wrote only three more letters to Rebecca after this one, very turbid, admonishing letters that reflect also her disappointment and confusion over Rebecca's actions.

Constancy for Rahel lay in the never-ending pushing and shoving of the individual human story into the historical moment of the time, of the unplanned representation of the friction and fissures on the wayward, yet integral path of life experience. As with other women in this study, the letters of Caroline Schlegel-Schelling and Rahel Varnhagen resist in many ways the parameters of their cultural world. Schlegel-Schellings's letters to Luise and Julie Gotter and Rahel Varnhagen's correspondence with Pauline Wiesel and Rebecca Friedländer substantiate the complexities of friendship among women, an unimaginable subject for many men in the late-eighteenth and early nineteenth centuries. Their correspondence also withstands the doubts that many men at the end of the eighteenth century and the beginning of the nineteenth century were having against the letter's capabilities as an aesthetic medium and women's abilities to write. Schlegel-Schelling's and Varnhagen's exaltation of the mundane, everyday, social concerns contradicts future editors' shunning of the banal in letters. In their admiration of the letter's potential to convey truth and authenticity, the two women counteract the growing preference writers were giving to other forms that appeared more objective. Their perceptions of the letter as a forum to weave social and political commentary into the narrative challenge traditional notions of the public and the private in which the private becomes a deprived arena and the public a privilege for women. Defiance does not come without contestation and turmoil, though, as the women grapple with ideas within a politics that has excluded them.

In a way different from the correspondence of the other women, however, Rahel Varnhagen's and Caroline Schlegel-Schelling's letters inspire characterization of an aesthetics that did not need, or even desire, publication in order to come to fruition. Caroline's ignoring of the subject of publication altogether, despite prodding from male colleagues, prevents detraction from spontaneity in her storytelling art. Rahel's ruminations on publication make her an agent of her own destiny in deciding case by case which matters to make public and which to keep private.

# 6

## Storytelling and Poetry in Letters: Bettine von Arnim's *Goethes Briefwechsel mit einem Kinde* and *Die Günderode*

Of all the letter writers in this study, Bettine von Arnim is perhaps the most famous and infamous. For few others—Rahel Varnhagen and Caroline Schlegel-Schelling are exceptions—has the connection between genre and gender been so prominent. And for few others have critics drawn that connection so pejoratively. Indeed, negative reactions advise caution about including Bettine von Arnim in any tradition of women's letter writing for fear of essentializing women's experiences under one generic rubric. Despite the almost two-century-old interest in von Arnim, opinions in secondary literature and personal accounts by her contemporaries are fraught with contradictions, prejudice, and backhanded praise. When comparing Bettine to other females, many scholars have traditionally portrayed her as either possessing traits that have stereotyped all women, or else as standing above other women as an anomaly. To equate the "Ewig-Weibliche," or the "eternal feminine" in her works with emotions lacking rational thought harks back to a value system that undermines women's works within a restrictive gender ideology.[1]

Elevating Bettine von Arnim's individuality above other women writers can also fall prey to unfair prejudice. Many of Bettine's own contemporaries categorized her works and deeds outside those of which they believed women capable and thus cleanse her of what Elisabeth Lenk refers to as the "blemish of femaleness."[2] Behind critics' praise of Arnim's works as being outstanding for her sex often lies great bias against women writers in general.[3] Such opinions reflect the common nineteenth-century attitude that females should not exhibit literary ambitions, especially in regard to the display of private emotions in public.[4] Setting her apart from others has also led to character analyses that classify her vaguely as "das wunderliches Kind" [the strange child],[5] "eine Pythia",[6] "eine gaukelnde Sylphide" [a deceptive sylph],[7] or "Kobold der Romantik" [imp of Romanticism].[8] As with other women writers, many studies base her greatness on her relationship with famous men, drawing attention to her roles as Goethe's correspondent, Achim von Arnim's wife, and Clemens Brentano's sister.[9] In continuing to publish her private writings, so contends Touallion in her entry on women's writing in Merker-Stammler's *Reallexikon*, Bettine von Arnim relegated herself to one of the "secret artists" whose personalities are greater than their works.[10]

The 1980s, with 1985 being the bicentennial of Bettine's birth, showed a flourishing interest in Bettine von Arnim as a gifted woman writer.[11] Reprints and new critical editions of her works have appeared, as have publications of her correspondence.[12] Book-length studies and dissertations present modern feminist perspectives on her works and deeds.[13] Recent studies reevaluate Bettine von Arnim's place within the annals of literary history, either by concentrating on her later political works in the context of her cultural milieu,[14] by demystifying her projected child image in *Goethes Briefwechsel mit einem Kinde*,[15] or by elucidating problems of language and intertextuality in her works.[16] Since 1987, the Bettina-von-Arnim-Gesellschaft in Berlin has been producing a newsletter, organizing symposia, and publishing an international yearbook along with individual specialized studies on Bettina's life and works. Interest is due mostly to the incredibly diverse primary material that is available. Besides publishing four epistolary works, Arnim wrote books and letters criticizing censorship, the living conditions of Germany's poor, and the oppression of Jews, Hungarians, and Poles. She was very actively involved in the events of her day and had an extraordinary network of personal contacts. In her daily life, she corresponded with over two hundred people, was the focal point of a circle of famous personages, and was instrumental in publishing Achim von Arnim's works after his death.

In an attempt to place Bettine von Arnim's works into her cultural milieu, various studies classify the epistolary form she employs in the majority of her works as Romantic, growing out of a time when individuality, subjectivity, fragmentariness, and formlessness were emphasized in literature.[17] Recent scholars also recognize the socio-historical importance of letters for early nineteenth-century German women and the development of women's literature.[18] In reaction to the abundant attention given to Bettine's correspondence with men in contrast to that with women, some fine studies have looked at the relationship between Bettine von Arnim and Karoline von Günderrode as the realization of a utopian exchange of ideas in a teaching and learning situation.[19] To date, however, few reexaminations have placed Bettine von Arnim's works in relation to the complex development of other German women's epistolary activities.

Bettine von Arnim's epistolary writings display motifs similar to correspondence of the women letter writers discussed thus far in my study while also maintaining their own individuality. Besides affording her the opportunity to present a woman's perspective on her interactions with famous men of her day, publication of her correspondence permitted her to explore her bonds with influential women and to pay tribute to those bonds. In a society that stressed contacts with famous men, the portraits that von Arnim gives of her relationships with Elisabeth Goethe in *Goethes Briefwechsel mit einem Kinde* and Karoline von Günderode in *Die Günderode* especially provide singular insights into an obscure part of cultural history. Within those relationships, the epistolary form functioned as a means to express the multidimensionality of her self and her experience in the world.

The confidence Arnim takes in publishing her own works, however, brings a new dimension to the development of women's letter-writing practices. Her letter-books teach us that the active agent as correspondent and editor cannot be divorced from the texts she writes or from the way in which those texts become historicized. The letter form allowed her to challenge the increasing tension between the selves and the surrounding world, between literature and history, and between various genres; the epistolary form provided her the chance to question traditional boundaries of genre, content, social spheres, and process. Through writing, editing, and publishing private correspondences, she placed a heightened value on narrative techniques, especially those that link the letter with storytelling and the dramatic. Our twentieth-century perspective can now see how canonical scholarship has devalued these forms by relegating them to the feminine. Publication does not necessarily mean we should assign a higher value to her works than to the unpublished letters of other women. To the contrary: the publishing process, as reflected in the changes Bettine von Arnim made when revising her works, emphasizes the diversity of purpose that coincides with individual needs and historical conditions.

First, it is important to review the skepticism characterizing the initial reception of Bettine von Arnim's works because it demonstrates the roots of theoretical problems that continue into the present day. Although critics were eager to place *Goethe's Briefwechsel*, Bettine von Arnim's first work, in the same category as Theodor Mundt's memorial to Charlotte Stieglitz, *Charlotte Stieglitz: Ein Denkmal* (1835), and Karl Varnhagen von Ense's collection of his wife's letters, *Rahel: Ein Buch des Andenkens für ihre Freunde* (1834), readers of *Goethes Brief-*

*wechsel* remained puzzled about its form. The titles of the other letter collections by Varnhagen and Mundt, as well as those of other contemporary letter editions by Pückler-Muskau (*Briefe eines Verstorbenen*), Goethe (*Der Briefwechsel zwischen Schiller und Goethe*, "Solgers nachgelassenen Schriften und Briefwechsel"), and Schlegel (*Lessings Gedanken und Meinungen aus dessen Schriften*), immediately established certain expectations for the reader. The editions were presented as memorials to famous people or as literary or travel correspondences. The letters in these editions had all been collected and edited by a person who was not the subject of the book. (In the case of Pückler-Muskau's book, the editor was fictional, but this fact nonetheless gave the impression that the letters were written by someone other than the person who decided to present them to the public), and published for historical and cultural reasons. By publishing letters by another person, the editor assured the reader that the letters were not written for publication. Separation of editor and author of the private letters reinforced the sincerity of the thoughts in the letters, a factor that seemed intrinsic to the epistolary form.

The title of Arnim's first book implies that her work is a correspondence, and, in fact, the earliest commentators on the work refer to it as a "Briefwechsel," or correspondence.[20] But, for those who were drawn to the correspondence to discover more about the famous person Goethe through his letters, they found that Goethe, by the mere scarcity of his own letters in the book, was not the main correspondent.[21] Although some early reviews classified the work using established literary terms such as a novel and a poem, many still had reservations about the success of her endeavors. The writer Gutzkow, for example, was especially perturbed about the anecdotal quality of many passages.[22] Critics also allowed their personal attitudes towards Goethe and his writings to play an essential part in evaluating Arnim's works.[23]

*Goethes Briefwechsel mit einem Kinde* undoubtedly instigated controversial debate about genre and gender. Theodor Mundt described the heated debate that ensued over the work in Berlin in 1835.[24] Many people questioned the work's literary value, emphasizing the difference between letters and other private documents, and a work of art. These initial reactions sound much like the debate over the literary value of letters, as discussed in the beginning chapters of this book. Those who argue against the perception of letters as artworks claim that letters are not imbued with the same consciousness and autonomy that usually characterize the production of an artwork. Definitions of literature as a conscious creation of a work intended for the public echo those expressed by other scholars who fail to consider the value of the piece in and of itself. The contrast of objectivity and subjectivity, and the extent to which an author's real life should become involved in the completed work, also continued to play an important role in critics' attempts to determine the literary quality of Arnim's books.[25]

Bettine's personality, as manifested in the image of the child, in contrast to the old Goethe, caused much approbation in early reviews. This was especially true in those articles from authors and critics who knew her personally. Readers frequently referred to the childlike character that Bettine creates through her letters, and not the person Bettine von Arnim, as the "author," the "Dichterin" (in some cases it is the masculine "Dichter"), of the work. This same tendency to blur author, editor, and letter writer into one character marks the discussion of her later works as well. Bettine is referred to as "das Kind," [the child] "die jüngere Freundin" [the younger girlfriend] (in *Die Günderode*), "die jüngere Schwester" [the younger sister] (in *Clemens Brentanos Frühlingskranz*), or as mother to the younger aspiring poet Phillip Nathusius (in *Ilius Pamphilius und die Ambrosia* ). While it is difficult not to place her into such roles, as her works are very strongly autobiographical, to confine her character so rigidly to prescribed functions ignores structural and thematic purposes that the character Bettine serves within the works. The persona of the child that she assumes in *Goethes Briefwechsel mit einem Kinde*, for example, does not merely play into the infantilization of women in the patriarchal ideology. Rather, her portrayal of herself as child and muse demonstrates her attempts to maintain or revisit an untrammeled and imaginative self, an idealistic age of simplicity and spontaneity. Moreover, defining Bettine the person and Bettine the character frequently in terms of very stereotypical relationships—explicitly to a man, as sister, child, mother, lover, as is done with three of her works—does not clarify the very complex and varied dimensions these relationships assume. Further, this undifferentiated mix of fiction with reality, and narrator with the narrated character, and with events in Bettine von Arnim's epistolary works caused further complications in categorization.

The largest controversy in the history of the reception of Bettine von Arnim's works has been that of the alterations she made to the original letters when preparing the published version. One of the first critics to call public attention to the changes she made in Goethe's letters was Friedrich Wilhelm Riemer in his *Mittheilungen über Goethe* in 1841. Riemer had lived in Goethe's house from 1803 until 1812 as a personal secretary and tutor for Goethe's son August. To him, Bettine's visits to Goethe during this period were always impositions.[26]

Contesting the validity of *Goethes Briefwechsel*, he states that the reader must carefully separate "the genuine, real, possible from the false, contradictory, impossible, absurd, yes the mad and crazy."[27] Other reviewers soon followed in their criticism, such as the Goethe-biographer G. H. Lewes in his biography *Life and Works of Goethe*, published in 1855.[28] By the time Moritz Carriere's positive portrayal of Bettine von Arnim's works, personality, and deeds appeared in his *Lebensbilder* in 1890, it was an accepted fact that "not everything in the works was factually correct."[29] But, Carriere still valued her works as literary examples of the "melodic voice of the time" and they remained, for him "landmarks of the history of the soul of our people."[30]

In fact, in 1879, Gustav von Loeper had published some letters from the original correspondence between Goethe and Bettine in his book , concentrating mostly on letters that Goethe wrote to Bettine.[31] He delineated the changes that were made in one letter from Bettine and fourteen from Goethe in *Goethes Briefwechsel*. This study was later updated when Reinhold Steig published the original letters, as well as the descriptions of the enclosures, from both Bettine and Goethe, in 1922.[32] The reprints of the 1927 second edition of these letters appeared in the fifth volume of Bettine von Arnim's *Werke* in 1961.[33] In regards to the other works, there was less research done on the original letters. In 1892, Reinhold Steig published one original letter of Karoline von Günderrode, which Bettine had revised for *Die Günderode*, and an undated letter from Clemens Brentano, likewise altered for *Clemens Brentanos Frühlingskranz*.[34] This lack of information on the other works is due in part to scholars' more intense interest in the relationship of Bettine to Goethe than in her relationship to the other correspondents, and, consequently, to their unwillingness to consider Arnim's books works of art to be studied on their own merit. The Arnim family also persistently denied access to the manuscripts.[35]

My study, too, cannot ignore Bettine von Arnim's editing process. In criticizing editors for omitting passages from women's letters and then justifying Bettine's reworking of her correspondence, I do not mean to promote a double standard. The context of the accusations against Bettine seems particularly important as does an understanding of the aesthetic agenda she appears to put forward in her works. Editors such as Karl Varnhagen and Theodor Mundt claim mostly biographical and historical worth in the women's letters they edited for the public, and that ultimate purpose continues to justify the omission of concerns deemed too trivial and private in editions of women's letters. In contrast, Bettine von Arnim assigns a definite aesthetic purpose to her publications, a purpose that elevates the personal to be worthy of public attention. In the preface to *Goethes Briefwechsel*, she deliberately anticipates criticism against the work for its inauthenticity, but counters with accusations that these critics fail to see "eine höhere Idealität" [a higher ideality] in the work.[36] That ideal, as we shall see in the following textual analysis, derives from the process of self-representation through interactions with others as well as the intricate weaving of the private person with the public image. As the century progressed, the extent to which Arnim edited the original letters became a major question, mostly to determine whether her works belonged to the historical or literary realms. Her works incited a debate over the role of private forms of writing in the public forum as critics grappled over how to fit the books into one of the neat literary categories scholars saw essential to studying published works. The main polemical issue lay in where to draw the distinction between art and reality, between fictionality and nonfictionality, between those writings that were destined for the public eye, and thus written as autonomous literary creations, and those that were to remain within the private sphere.

When, in 1905, Waldemar Oehlke published his extensive study of the changes that Bettine von Arnim had made between the original letters and how they appeared in her published works, late-nineteenth-century scholars had already begun, in a very positivistic way, to determine the extent of Bettine's editing.[37] The documents that Oehlke had at his disposal were not complete.[38] When Oehlke did not have original letters to compare, he based his conclusions about the alterations on facts about dates he gleaned from old record books. Through contrasting similar events that Bettine refers to in *Goethes Briefwechsel*, *Die Günderode*, and *Frühlingskranz*, Oehlke posited the ways in which she had changed the chronological order of letters within each work. From anaylses of her style, and the manner in which it changed over the years, he speculated on those passages that may have appeared in the original letters and those she may have written later when she revised. Through comparing Bettine's style with that of her correspondents, Oehlke also surmised which passages she could have added in the correspondent's letters for the published works, and which were actually written by the correspondent. Much of Oehlke's study on the three later works is based on this speculative method, and thus is not as valid as Oehlke leads us to believe. Although Oehlke's study is very thorough, it also exemplifies a positivistic attempt to discover "facts and figures" in Arnim's works, with little analysis of the effect and consequences of the alterations.

Despite the shortcomings of Oehlke's work, his study represents one of the first secondary works to define Arnim's epistolary books as works of art. Oehlke's designation of the works as "Briefromane" [letter or epistolary novels] in the title of his study demonstrates his desire to call attention to the fictionality of the works. For most scholars, however, the term "Briefroman" was inappropriate. Not everyone has agreed with Oehlke's implication that fictionality was the main factor to classify a work as a novel. Opposers state that Arnim's works, alterations and editing considered, were not novels because of their lack of an overall connecting unit between the letters, such as a plot or a theme.[39] Likewise, to base a categorization of her works as novels on the question of fictionality is not effective because Bettine's method of rewriting the original letters much later in her life placed her works "on the margins of fictionality" in which historical documentation becomes fused with fictional renditions.[40] Similarly, the commonalities between her works and poems, which are based on Bettine's very lyrical style, are disputable because these stylistic characteristics are not unique to the epistolary form.[41] To equate her letter books to a drama, a common equation for letters based on their very dialogic nature,[42] is also invalid because it ignores the drama's factor of theatrical performance not shared by the letter.

One of the ways in which scholars have attempted to classify Bettine von Arnim's highly subjective narrative style in combination with the poetic license she took in revising the letters to publish has been to call her works autobiographies, usually in the tradition of Goethes *Dichtung und Wahrheit*.[43] Certainly, a study of any or all of Arnim's works should not ignore their autobiographical nature. Knowledge of Bettine von Arnim's life, works, and reception immediately conjures up comparisons with her writings. Those friends who knew her in real life perceived in her works traits that they had noticed in her character. And those, such as Gutzkow, who received a certain impression from her works had that impression confirmed with they met Bettine.[44] Unlike Goethe, who was aggravated that readers of Werther wanted to know what was real and what was fictional in the work, Bettine did not publicly deny the model of the child she presented in *Goethes Briefwechsel*.

To consider Bettine's works as autobiographies, however, demands that we understand the complexities of the term. Both the autobiography and the epistolary work share the commonality of being written in the first-person narrative form. That form may be most likely to engender certain themes, such as the quest for self, the striving for authenticity, and the relationship between fictionality and reality. They differ, however, in the themes surrounding the the actual writing process, such as the act of collecting materials, the condition of writing, the particular discourse situation, the relationship of reader to writer, and the publication of the finished product. For example, classifying Arnim's books as autobiographies limits discussing the intricate narrative levels she handles. In the act of writing a letter and an autobiography, the "narrator's present," or the time at which the narrator records the experiences, and the "narrative past," or the time about which the narrator writes, can vary significantly.[45] The narrator in the latter usually gains a certain critical distance due to the time lapse between experience and recording the events. In contrast, the letter writer is usually still involved in the narrated action, mostly because he or she writes a letter to report on an event in the present, in the immediate past, or with anticipation for the future. In revising her early letters much later in life, Arnim worked on two planes of narration: employing letters written "to the moment" in her younger years while looking back from a new and distant perspective. She hoped to preserve the immediacy of the original circumstance while having the perspective of the later moment. The reader can detect signs of her grappling with this dilemma. The theme of letter writing runs constantly through her works and leads to specific questions regarding the writing process: Why does she write letters? Under what circumstances are the letters written? What effect does rereading the letters have on her process of compiling the letters? What effect do the changes in the original letters have on the overall published work?

The parallel with Goethe's autobiography, *Dichtung und Wahrheit*, as Katherine Goodman convincingly shows in her study of German women's autobiographies, immediately sets certain criteria that do not usually apply to women's works.[46] *Dichtung and Wahrheit* has set the model for a particular concept of the autonomous, individual "self" and the teleological view of history that sees great personalities as representatives of human consciousness. Women confront the narrowness of this tradition when writing and being evaluated, for they have not obtained equivalent status as "great people in history" and have experienced difficulty in expressing a "self" that is not fragmented and dispersed. An equation of the letter with autobiography under such a model ignores specific structures and historical developments that characterize the epistolary form and women's participation in writing in that form. Letters of friendship prove in practice the long-disputed capabilities of women to form bonds with other women revolving around professional contacts and exchange of ideas. Moreover, several women found in letters a means for spontaneous expression that did not require adherence to rigid structures of form, the rules for which they had been denied access to anyway. Prolific letter writers made practice into an art form at a time when the separation of art and reality in literature was becoming increasingly more demarcated. The authenticity of epistolary communication avoided abstraction and impersonality in writing. These women were able to speak directly through their letters without another mediating agent. The process of self-actualization occurring while writing letters was especially important during a period of increased social pressure on women to remain within the private sphere and not to venture into the public literary market. For Bettine von Arnim, whose biography demonstrates protective, patriarchial familial attitudes towards her education and artistic development, finding a personal means to express her individuality gains heightened significance.

Goodman analyzes letters by Rahel Varnhagen and Bettine von Arnim in her study on women's autobiography. In answer to the questions she raises about genre classification, however, she arrives at the term "epistolary autobiography" to discuss Varnhagen and Arnim, a term that also applies to Anna Louisa Karsch's letters to Sulzer, which she had intended as the preface to her collection of poems. The epistolary autobiography, as Goodman states and as I discussed with Karsch, challenges not only traditional genre distinctions but also "philosophical assumptions upon which the very idea of autobiography has been based: the superior truth of a unifying perspective and the very notion of what it means to be an individual."[47]

The joint term "epistolary autobiography" also addresses the wish for spontaneity, authenticity, and immediacy that women such as Rahel Varnhagen and Caroline Schlegel-Schelling wanted. The act of two people directly exchanging letters has long been equated with conducting a dialogue. Since Greek and Roman times, letters have been devices for developing rhetoric as well as a conversational bridge during times of separation.[48] In the eighteenth century, Gottsched stressed: "Ein Brief ist die Rede eines Abwesenden, von denjenigen Angelegenheiten, die ihm am Herzen liegen" [A letter is the speech of an absent person, about those affairs that are pressing].[49] The formal characteristics of the letter allow such an association. Discourse, or the relationship between the "I" speaker and the "you" spoken to, occurs in letters, as in dialogues, between two people who stand in a direct and reciprocal relationship. The letter writer addresses his or her discourse to a particular reader and formulates the letter accordingly. The letter writer is also allowed to have a conversation with himself or herself under this dialogic exchange; witness, for example, Rahel Varnhagen and Karoline von Günderrode when they claim to be talking to the different sides of their selves when they reread their own letters and letters others have written to them. The recognition of a specific reader who stands distinct from the letter writer is one factor often absent from the discourse of the diary writer, for example, who usually perceives himself or herself as the sole reader and writer. In addition, the position of the letter writer vis-à-vis his or her reader contrasts with that of the writer of works destined for the public, either fictional or autobiographical, who cannot know with certainty who will read the work, where and when. Just as important as the letter writer's image of the reader in epistolary discourse is the expectation that the reader will reply; thus the reader performs an important part in the correspondence.[50] Indeed, the etymology of the word "correspond," originating from "com" meaning "together, mutually," and "respondere," meaning "to respond," emphasizes reciprocal exchange. Conversation assumed a major role in Bettine's letters; it comes as no surprise that the correspondences she portrays as most reciprocal were with people who were also partners in dialogue, such as Elisabeth Goethe and Karoline von Günderrode.

To assign the term "epistolary autobiography" to writings by Anna Louisa Karsch, Rahel Varnhagen, and Bettine von Arnim, however, still does not speak to the main difference of approach between the three authors, namely, the final editing and publishing process. One of the most puzzling aspect of Arnim's four epistolary works still remains the fact that she published her correspondence herself as creative works. One solution to the problem of categorization is to break from the notion that her works must be classified under the traditional literary categories of the novel or autobiography. Instead of representing an end product with closure of plot and character development, her works stress the value of a continual interpretive process accomplished through rereading and rewriting. I have chosen to use the terms "epistolary books" or "letter works," which accord somewhat with the German terms "Briefbücher" or "Briefwerke." These rather neutral terms circumvent problems of fictionality, plot construction, and representation of a single self to the outside world, but, as another scholar contends, they also challenge such problems.[51] The designation "epistolary book" characterizes the amalgamation of written and oral discourse, of prose and poetry, of fiction and nonfiction, of art and life, and of author, narrator, and character found especially in Arnim's correspondence and work.

The process whereby she altered letters is a creative act. The worth of the published works should not be based solely on comparisons with the original documents and vice versa. The rest of this chapter will examine some significant changes that Bettine von Arnim made when she published her correspondence with Elisabeth Goethe in

*Goethes Briefwechsel mit einem Kinde* and with Karoline von Günderrode in *Die Günderode*. Understanding her alterations as part of a work that fused the biographical, historical person with his or her literary talents prevents condemnation of the changes as deception and thereby leads toward a more productive appreciation of her aesthetic program. In these two works, Bettine von Arnim views letters as a means to depict the diversity of her own life and experiences. In this context, the letter books represent autobiographies. In using the epistolary form as a basis, however, Arnim portrays self-development only in a constant dynamic with people and events around her. By incorporating various processes, genres, and interactions into the published product, she makes correspondence the quintessential form to convey to the public the multifaceted dimensions of the relationships to her correspondents. She also reworks the traditional image of Elisabeth Goethe and Karoline von Günderrode from one in which the women retreat into their own private concerns to one of two women engaged intellectually with the world around them.

After using the foreword of *Goethes Briefwechsel mit einem Kinde* to defend the work against those who might defame it as risqué and to describe the emotional process of editing her correspondence with Goethe, Bettine von Arnim surprises readers by beginning the *Briefwechsel* with the correspondence between her and Katharina Elisabeth Goethe, the so-called Frau Rat (Councillor's Wife), rather than that between her and Goethe. In fact, Elisabeth Goethe figures prominently as Bettine's main correspondent in the first part. In comparison with the exchange between Bettine and Goethe in the second part, the letters between Frau Rat and Bettine show significantly more reciprocity. Even though Bettine's letters to Goethe dominate the second part, the voice of Frau Rat continues to speak in the form of stories and anecdotes that Bettine relates second-hand about the Rätin's life and Goethe's childhood.

Despite the ubiquity of Elisabeth Goethe throughout the *Briefwechsel*, most studies have allowed her significance to be overshadowed by the greatness of her son, portraying her instead either as a temporary surrogate mother to Bettine or as merely an intermediary between Bettine and Goethe.[52] Such treatment underestimates the female-centered friendship and mentoring process between the two women. Elisabeth Goethe's relationship to Bettine, in fictional and real-life context, demands a more thorough treatment, for that relationship plays a major role in Bettine's development as a storyteller. The major changes Bettine made when she reworked the original letters into published form demonstrate Bettine's reassessment of the merits of oral storytelling and letter writing, two means of self-expression that form a vital part in women's history, but that have been undervalued in a literate society.

In 1806, Bettine began to visit Frau Rat Goethe in Frankfurt. Bettine foresaw problems in her friendship with Karoline von Günderrode and explains to Karoline, in a letter of June 1806, her turning to Frau Rat for friendship (*Werke und Briefe* V, 204). Clemens Brentano, Bettine's brother, describes, in letters to the authors Sophie Mereau and Achim von Arnim, Bettine's visits to Frau Rat, stating that she sought the Rätin's companionship not only to hear her stories, but also to transpose the oral stories into written words, for she brought a notebook with her on her visits and wrote down the stories the Rätin narrated.[53] Bettine also alludes to her intended biography of Goethe, based in part on these oral stories, when she writes to Clemens about her first visit with Goethe in Weimar (*Werke und Briefe* V, 176).

Katharina Elisabeth Goethe was born in 1731, nine years after Anna Louisa Karsch and three years after Meta Moller Klopstock. Her first extant letters begin in 1774 and continue until shortly before her death in 1808. The over six hundred printed pages of witty stories told with unconventional orthography, dialectical nuances, and unorganized thoughts and ideas make her one of the most remarkable letter writers of the eighteenth and early nineteenth centuries. Like many other letter writers, however, her writings are incomplete, for we know that her son Johann Wolfgang von Goethe burned all her letters before 1792, most probably, as Ulrike Prokop speculates, in order to propagate a specific image of the Rätin as cheerful mother and wife.[54] It is possible that Katharina Elisabeth did not show those characteristics in earlier letters, for only to her son did she remain the dedicated mother, while her relationship with her only living daughter, Cornelia, remained distant.[55]

Born into a bourgeois family, her father being the village mayor in Frankfurt, Katharina Elisabeth Goethe, née Textor, did not receive a formal education. In contrast to the educated circles that surrounded her, she was exposed to the culture of what Prokop calls the world between the public discourse of the domestic sphere, which included fairy tales, biblical readings, servants' gossip, and her mother's and grandmother's stories.[56] At seventeen, she was married to Johann Caspar Goethe, whom she hardly knew and who was twenty-two years older than she. In thirteen years she bore eight children, only two of whom survived. Until her death, she continued to participate with active fascination in art forms that held marginal status within high culture. After bearing her last child, she began following the ideas of mysticism in the circle of Susanna von Klettenberg; she socialized with actors and actresses and took great interest in the theater; and she wrote letters in which she advised authors to write readable texts, called for democracy and freedom for oppressed social groups, and lamented the ineffectiveness of the written word to reproduce her thoughts.

One of the lesser recognized talents for which circles in Frankfurt did admire Elisabeth Goethe was that of good oral storytelling. In 1776, Klinger tells of the many captivating hours he spent, "nailed to the chair" listening to her telling fairy tales.[57] In letters, Elisabeth Goethe alludes to her role as storyteller and entertainer among the young people in Frankfurt, describing, for example, in 1777, how eight young girls had visited her and listened to her "Mährgen" ["Märchen;" fairy tales] together.[58] In fact, her letters demonstrate how she placed her own talent as an oral storyteller above her letter-writing abilities, for she frequently apologized for her inept writing, wishing instead that the correspondent could hear her narrate a story rather than read her written version.[59]

The problem with assessing Elisabeth Goethe's talents as an oral storyteller lies in the inability to document her repertoire. Although visitors to her house admired her gift of storytelling and conversation, scholars have not regarded these talents as particularly artistic or literary. Titles of the numerous biographies that continually refer to Katharina Elisabeth Goethe as Goethe's mother prove that scholars have preferred to study her merely as the mother of the great poet, and not on her own merits. Another reason for the dearth of extensive documentation or in-depth studies of Elisabeth Goethe's storytelling art is that conversation and other forms of oral transmission, as Patricia Spacks postulates, inhabit the "borderlands," of "what our culture agrees to call 'literature'" and, because they rarely belong to any generally accepted canon, are difficult "to assess in orthodox critical terms."[60] Proof of this lower status can be found when Elisabeth Goethe repeats apologies for her ostensible inability to write letters and expresses her preference for the spoken word. As we have seen in the association of the oral, conversational tradition with women's letter writing, this "borderland" has become, since the Middle Ages, often negatively associated with women. In a "devocalized world," as Walter Ong refers to post-Gutenberg society,[61] in a society where literacy and the written word have come to assume higher value over orality, the conversational tone of many women's letters, essays, and novels has unfortunately also become undervalued. This is not to say that male oral storytellers and letter writers, too, have not also suffered similar neglect. But men, having access to an educational and professional world that encouraged them to experiment in many different genres and tones, could find other avenues to express their ideas, whereas letters and other dialogic, domestic forms of expression became the most convenient and socially accepted ways in which women in the eighteenth and nineteenth centuries could express themselves.

Bettine von Arnim's turn toward Elisabeth Goethe came at a time when the younger writer was exploring questions of form and writing, while wondering about her future as a twenty-two-year-old, single, talented woman. She was living with her older brother Franz, a very authoritarian figure who saw in his sister a wild, young woman who needed taming. He deemed "weibliche Arbeit" [feminine work] and the "Besorgung des Hauswesens" [cares of the domestic creature], the "einzigen Balsam" [sole balsam] for Bettina's "Leichtfertigkeit" [frivolity].[62] Likewise, her brother Clemens, who encouraged her to write, also foresaw no professional future for her as a woman writer, as his correspondence with her indicates. The fact that she took her notebook with her on her visits suggests that she was searching for a role model to aid her own storytelling. Also, as the scholar Konstanze Bäumer postulates, in expressing the interest to write down stories about Goethe's childhood, Bettine was formulating an exact writing plan that would give her a necessary purpose in life.[63] This purpose seems especially critical at a time when the main options for a gifted woman like Bettine lay primarily in the domestic or religious sphere, or those that would accord with her so-called natural female propensities. Although Elisabeth Goethe's status as mother of the revered poet must greatly have influenced Bettine's choice of her as a model, and although Elisabeth Goethe's maternal pride made her eager to relate stories about her son, one can also infer that Bettine was attracted to Elisabeth Goethe as a talented, stimulating person in her own right. The high value that Bettine placed on her contact with the older storyteller surfaces in a letter to the Chancellor von Müller on 24 August 1833 in which Bettine wrote about her plans to order her correspondence with Elisabeth Goethe. She stated that she possessed twenty letters from the "Rätin," as she called her, and was interested in publishing those letters on their own merit in order to formulate a portrait of Elizabeth Goethe's unique, as yet undocumented character.[64]

The problem with Bettine's statement to Müller, however, is that no clear evidence proves that she possessed twenty letters from Frau Rat. In actuality, only four letters that Elisabeth Goethe wrote to Bettine Brentano exist (*Gesammelte Briefe* 511–14, 544–45; Köster), and, unless many have been lost, one may assume that Elisabeth Goethe did not write as many as Bettine claims. Two letters are dated

19 May 1807 and 13 June 1807, and the other two are undated, but Köster has dated the last one as 28 August 1808. The first part of *Goethes Briefwechsel*, in contrast, contains nine letters from Frau Rat, sixteen letters from Bettine, and two additional narrative stories by Bettine, one about Bettine's trip to Köln [Cologne], dedicated "für meine liebste Fr. Rat beschrieben," [described for my dear Fr. Rat] and the other is the story of Karoline von Günderrode.

One may rightly assume then, as other scholars have, that Bettine wrote the letters from Frau Rat that appear in *Goethes Briefwechsel*, and that many of the letters that appear as Bettine's in the work were never read by the Rätin.[65] Bettine has taken on the job of editor and of main writer in the correspondence. Whatever role Frau Rat may have played in Bettine's life, either as surrogate mother, storyteller, or friend, that role changes immensely in the published work, as a comparison of the existing original letters with the published ones shows. In her original letters, Elisabeth Goethe concentrates on Goethe and refers to Bettine only in relation to the great poet. In the work, Bettine, by altering her own and the Rätin's letters, transforms the Rätin into a guide whose storytelling significantly encourages and draws attention to Bettine's spontaneous narration.

In the few original letters from Frau Rat to Bettine, Elisabeth Goethe's role as intermediary between her son and Bettine becomes clear. The Rätin recognizes her own outstanding talent as a conversationalist, writing to Bettine on 13 June 1807 that she is looking forward to their "Schwatzen" [chatting] together, for she is a "Meister" [master] in conversation while in letter writing she is "Tintenscheu" [ink shy] (*Gesammelte Briefe* 513). During her storytelling hours with Bettine, Frau Rat seems to have talked mostly about her son, and told fairy tales, as she explains in a letter to her daughter-in-law Christiane von Goethe in 1807.[66] The positive role that Elisabeth Goethe assigns to the orality and the fiction of the stories divulges the power she bestowed on the storytelling act.

In *Goethes Briefwechsel*, Bettine has omitted passages from the actual letters and chronologically rearranged and rewritten them so as to reverse roles with Elisabeth Goethe and to place herself in the position of storyteller. Already Bettine's first letter in the *Briefwechsel*, a letter that has no original counterpart, introduces the reader to her spirit of adventure. From Cassel she writes about her wild ride on Rothschild's notoriously savage horse and about how her endurance earns her the name of "l'héroïne" from the French there (*Werke* 2: 15). Adventure, heroism, encounters with famous people, and love are themes introduced in this first letter that will pervade all of Bettine's works.

Bettine later admitted that she had embellished this letter to please and impress Frau Rat. To Meusebach she contended in 1836 that she had invented this story "um die Frau Rat zu amüsieren" [to amuse the Frau Rat] and that this letter began a series in which she told other "extravagante Abenteuer und Geschichten" [extravagant adventures and stories].[67] Although scholars have never had evidence of this letter or the subsequent ones to which Bettine refers, the passage to Meusebach suggests that she deliberately fabricated stories so as to place herself in the role of storyteller and entertainer to Elisabeth Goethe and, we may conclude, to her readers of the *Briefwechsel*.

In fact, the original letters from Elisabeth Goethe suggest that Bettine did not tell as many stories in real life as in the published letters. After Bettine's visit to Weimar in 1807, in the letter to Bettine of 19 May 1807, Frau Rat writes that Christiane Goethe has informed her about Bettine's visit in Weimar and praises Bettine for the pleasure that her visit caused.[68] In her next letter to Bettine, dated 13 June 1807, Elisabeth Goethe begins by warmly accepting Bettine as her daughter and as Goethe's brother and friend, based on the heartfelt reception that Goethe gave her in Weimar.[69]

In the published *Goethes Briefwechsel*, in contrast, Bettine informs the Rätin herself of the visit from its first inception instead of relying on the daughter-in-law in Weimar to relay *post factum* the pleasure that her visit has caused. She writes to the Rätin in March 1807 of her plans to visit Goethe. In an imagined dialogue, she poses questions and answers about preparations for her trip in order to excite the Rätin's curiosity about how she will execute the journey. She then divulges her plans to travel in men's clothing with her sister and her brother-in-law to Weimar on the way to Berlin (*Werke* 2: 17).

In addition to hearing beforehand about the Weimar trip from Bettine in the published *Briefwechsel*, Frau Rat learns directly from Bettine, and not from those in Weimar, the results of the trip. Bettine composes a letter especially for the published work in which she becomes storyteller to Frau Rat. Of course, Bettine may have narrated her story to Frau Rat during one of their storytelling hours together in Frankfurt, but as the letters from Elisabeth Goethe prove, such a narration could only have happened after Elisabeth Goethe heard from her daughter-in-law in Weimar.[70] The published narrations show how reordering and rewriting help Bettine build up her own role in the work and advance her own storytelling talents. By placing herself in the position of relating to Elisabeth Goethe the initial plans and then the journey to Weimar, Bettine is no longer the outsider listening to stories by Goethe's mother about Goethe. She is now in the privileged position of possessing knowledge about Goethe.

In *Goethes Briefwechsel* the Rätin assumes the role of listener, but she also encourages Bettine to write and gives her advice on narrative technique. After Bettine has visited Goethe, she is so elated that she cannot immediately write about her visit. She can only explain her reaction metaphorically, exclaiming: "Mein Herz ist geschwellt wie das volle Segel eines Schiffs, das fest vom Anker gehalten ist am fremden Boden und doch so gern ins Vaterland zurück möchte" [My heart has swelled like the full sail of a ship that is held fast by an anchor on foreign soil and yet would like so much to return to the fatherland] (*Werke* 2: 18). In Elisabeth Goethe's reply, a letter that, as we can discern by comparing the published with the original letter, has been interpolated by Bettine, the Rätin admonishes her for the fragmentary description:

> Was läßt Du die Flügel hängen? Nach einer so schönen Reise schreibst Du einen so kurzen Brief, und schreibst nichts von meinem Sohn, als daß Du ihn gesehen hast; das hab ich auch schon gewußt, und er hat mir's gestern geschrieben. Was hab ich von Deinem geankerten Schiff? Da weiß ich soviel wie nichts. Schreib doch, was passiert ist.

> [Why do you let the wings hang? After such a beautiful trip you write such a short letter, and write nothing of my son but that you have seen him; I already knew that, and he wrote that to me yesterday. What do I have from your anchored ship? I know as much as nothing about that. Do write what happened.] (*Werke* 2: 18)

By demanding that Bettine tell her objectively the facts of "what happened" in a chronologically ordered narrative form, Elisabeth Goethe assigns Bettine a new role in the work. Bettine is now the mediating storyteller between Frau Rat and her son. Frau Rat, lamenting that she has not seen her son in eight years, asks Bettine to tell her some concrete information about him (*Werke* 2: 18). The letter ends with a variation on the passage in which Frau Rat bestows on Bettine the title of daughter to her and of friend and sister to Goethe.[71]

In the epistolary work, Bettine has the Rätin prod her to explain, in her own words, the events in Weimar. In her role as advisor, however, Frau Rat expects a different kind of letter than what Bettine writes. In the published work, the Rätin becomes exasperated with Bettine's spontaneity and her metaphorical imagery of love and emotions, preferring instead an orderly letter: "schreib ordentliche Briefe, in denen was zu lesen steht," she advises, "schreib, was Euch begegnet, alles ordentlich hintereinander. Erst, wer da ist, und wie Dir jeder gefällt, und was jeder anhat, und ob die Sonne scheint, oder ob's regnet, das gehört auch zur Sach" [write proper letters in which there is something to read, write what you encounter, everything properly one after the other. First, who is there, and how you like each one, and what each one has on, and whether the sun is shining, or whether it's raining, that also belongs to the telling] (*Werke* 2: 28). In a subsequent letter, she admonishes Bettine for running her thoughts together: "ohne Komma, ohne Punkt [without comma, without period] (*Werke* 2: 36). Bettine tries to follow this advice by writing about everyday events, but she becomes disappointed in her mundane life and worries that such a structured narrative style will not convey her emotions adequately. She perceives her unordered, emotional letters as true expressions of her feelings: "denn ich schwelge in einem Überfluß von Gedanken, die meine Liebe, mein Glück ausdrücken, wie es Ihm erquicklich ist. Was ist nun Geist und Klugheit, da der seligste Mensch, wie ich, ihrer nicht bedarf?" [for I revel in the abundance of thoughts that express my love, my happiness, as is refreshing to him. What then is intellect and wisdom, since the most blissful person, as I, does not need them?] (*Werke* 2: 30).

Frau Rat's criticism of Bettine's epistolary style and Bettine's own defense in *Goethes Briefwechsel* become all the more unusual when considering the fact that, as far as the existing original letters disclose, the passages that contain the two women's contrasting views on style have been devised totally by Bettine. Under the guise of Frau Rat, Bettine is interjecting self-criticism and self-reflection, but she also anticipates reactions to her style and creates an opportunity to defend herself. Although at times playing Frau Rat's insistence on order against Bettine's spontaneity makes the latter seem all the more ebullient, it also helps to bring both arguments into focus. Nobody seems right or wrong; instead, each storyteller becomes drawn to the other through a process of reciprocal exchange.[72]

The first part of *Goethes Briefwechsel* provides readers with Bettine's construction of Katharina Goethe's role as inspirational friend to the younger writer. That role becomes even more pronounced in the subsequent stories that Bettine retells to Goethe about his life and in von Arnim's later social, dialogic works, *Dies Buch gehört dem König* (1843) and *Gespräche mit Dämonen* (1852), in which Frau Rat is the main conversant who questions members of the clergy and government on individual freedoms and institutional hierarchy. In all these works, we may read Bettine von Arnim's personal tribute to her mentor as well as a reconstruction of a woman storyteller intellectually engaged in the creative act.

But the creation of the two personae, Bettine and Frau Rat, in the *Briefwechsel* also shows the writer Bettine von Arnim's acute powers of ironic self-reflexivity, with which Bettine develops herself into a storyteller who becomes the possessor of knowledge and the power of speech. In reactions to Frau Rat's feigned criticisms, Bettine demonstrates a heightened sense of her audience and develops methods of questioning and spontaneous interaction that do not stress chronological or objective narration. Instead, emotional response and personal involvement mark her character for the rest of the work, and her other works as well. That personal development could not have come without the aid of Elisabeth Goethe's responsiveness in their relationship both in real life and in Bettine's reconstructed portrayal. Biography and artistic representation stand in a dynamic interplay.

Bettine's second work, *Die Günderode*, appeared in 1840, thirty-four years after Karoline von Günderrode's death and five years after *Goethes Briefwechsel*. In the eyes of many critics, the book was not as successful as *Goethes Briefwechsel*.[73] Whereas nineteenth-century literary historians devote extensive space in their studies to Bettine's correspondence with Goethe, little mention is given to *Die Günderode*.[74] This malaise is most likely due to the nature of the subjects involved: Goethe, being the great and revered poet, captured the interest of reviewers more than Günderrode, who was relatively unknown and unread.

In contrast to scholars who condemned *Goethes Briefwechsel* as a falsification, reviewers who wrote about *Die Günderode* were less accusatory. Surely, there were those such as Geiger who characterized the work as "völlig unhistorisch" [totally unhistorical], and who were disappointed to find that Karoline von Günderrode was not the main character of the work, as the title suggested.[75] Still, critics were much more willing to recognize *Die Günderode* as an art work than they had been in the case of *Goethes Briefwechsel* and seemed generally less perplexed about the form of the work. And while there was still concern for the authenticity of the letters in the book, despite the scant research material that remained, *Die Günderode* was not aesthetically devalued, as *Goethes Briefwechsel* had been.[76]

*Die Günderode* follows in the tradition of *Goethes Briefwechsel* in that it is also based on original letters that the two women exchanged from 1804 to 1806. At this time, Karoline was living in the *Damenstift* in Frankfurt, and Bettine was at her grandmother's residence in Offenbach. Although the two young women saw each other often, they corresponded with one another when they were apart, even for a day. When their friendship began to wane, due mostly to a conflict between Bettine and Karoline's married lover, Friedrich Creuzer, Bettine demanded her letters back from Karoline.[77]

The significant process of rereading and revising the letters for publication surfaces again, as it had in the creation of *Goethes Brief wechsel,* in private letters. In a letter to Clemens on 2 April 1839, Bettine describes her "research" on the letters to Günderrode:

> Ich habe in einem verborgnen Schrank einen Teil der Papiere von Günderode und mir, von Arnim sorgfältig verpackt und eingesiegelt, vorgefunden, an 30 Briefe der Günderode, noch mehrere von mir, aus Offenbach, aus Schlangenbad und Marburg und Kassel. Ich hab vor vier Monaten, wo ich in Gießen bei einem vertrauten Bekannten der Günderode forschte, und in Frankfurt noch allerlei Rudera philosophischer Studien, Briefe von mir pp zusammen gefunden, ich bin entzückt darüber, ich schwimme in Genuß, während ich sie ordne.

> [I have found in a concealed cupboard a part of the papers by Günderode and me, carefully packed away and sealed up by Arnim, about 30 letters of Günderode, even more by me, from Offenbach, from Schlangenbad and Marburg and Cassel. I found four months ago, when I researched in Gießen at a well-known acquaintance of Günderode, and in Frankfurt still all sorts of packs of philosophical studies, letters from me, pages together, I am delighted about them, I am swimming in pleasure, while I put them in order.] (*Werke* 5: 187)

That the composition of the book was a task both stimulating and arduous comes to light in Bettine's letters to Philipp Nathusius, which appeared in Bettine's fourth epistolary work *Ilius Pamphilius und die Ambrosia.* She is unable to meet her planned completion date of 1839 because she cannot decide which letters to include. The correspondence "ist liegengeblieben, die Verwirrung in meinem Gedächtnis wird zur totalen Niedergeschlagenheit, wenn ich mich mit dem befassen will, was mir das Liebste ist" [has remained lying, the confusion in my memory is becoming total depression, when I want to concern myself with what is most dear to me] (*Werke* 2: 530). In letters to Nathusius she often quotes from her letters to Günderrode, praising their relevance to her own life and their beauty (*Werke* 2: 537). She contemplates deeply the relationship with Günderrode while she is revising (*Werke* 2: 599). Her final sigh of relief in February 1840 demonstrates what a difficult task she has completed:

> Du kannst mir Glück wünschen, gestern habe ich nach einer Reihe von Tagen, die mit angestrengter Arbeit überfüllt waren, die *Günderode* beendet.—Ich habe mich diesen Morgen aufs Sofa gelegt und gestreckt. Gestern abend umschwärmten diese Erinnerungen mich so, daß ich wie ein Trunkner noch hin und her wankte, bis beinahe drei Uhr in der Nacht.

> [You can wish me luck, yesterday, after a series of days that were filled with strenuous work, I finished the *Günderode.* I laid down and stretched

on the sofa this morning. Yesterday evening these memories swirled around me in such a way that I swayed back and forth like a drunk until almost three o'clock at night.] (*Werke* 2: 677–78)

While early reviewers saw the correspondence as one in which the ideas and writings of Bettine figured more prominently than those of Karoline (Geiger 137), recent studies have recognized *Die Günderode* as the most communicational of Arnim's four epistolary books.[78] Conversational and epistolary intercourse interact with each other continuously. Karoline's and Bettine's letters to one another often resume the profound conversations about religion, philosophy, and history that they had had together in Frankfurt. In addition, as Edith Waldstein has observed, accounts of conversations that the two women hold with other people are also plentiful, for example, Bettine's talks with her mathematics tutor (*Werke* 1: 498–99; 440), with the nurse (*Werke* 1: 378–79), and with "St. Clair" Sinclair (*Werke* 1: 312–17).[79] Aside from numerous letters relating to conversations, there are also conversations about letters. That is, both women write frequently about letters that they have received from and written to a third party: Bettine discusses letters from Clemens with Sophie von LaRoche (*Werke* 1: 312); Karoline converses with St. Clair Sinclair about a letter that Bettine had written to her father (*Werke* 1: 309); Bettine describes a letter that she has just read from Goethe to Jacobi (*Werke* 1: 510); and Karoline talks about letters from Clemens (*Werke* 1: 481).

In *Die Günderode*, Karoline hesitates to write letters, which is corroborated by many passages in her own extant letters. Instead, she prefers to express herself in the more "permanent form" that she had found in poetry. In fact, Bettine cites the same passage that Karoline had written to Clemens Brentano in which she refers to her letters as corpses, "Leichen," and talks of her immense fear when she rereads her letters (*Werke* 1: 492). The inclusion of Günderrode's poems and prose pieces throughout *Die Günderode* thus allows Karoline to "talk" using the form with which she feels most comfortable and with which she comes better to understand herself. As she states in a letter to Bettine in *Die Günderode:* "Ich suche in der Poesie wie in einem Spiegel mich zu sammeln, mich selber zu schauen und durch mich durchzugehen in eine höhere Welt, und dazu sind meine Poesien die Versuche" [I search in poetry as in a mirror to focus myself, to recognize myself and through myself to walk through into a higher world and to this end, my poems are attempts] (*Werke* 1: 465). Further Günderrode equates poetry with conversation because both represen true and direct means of communicating one's innermost feelings

"Das Wichtige an der Poesie ist, was an der Rede es auch ist, nämlich die wahrhaftige, unmittelbare Empfindung, die wirklich in der Seele vorgeht" [The most important thing about poetry is also the same for speech, namely, the truthful, direct sensation that really goes on in the soul] (*Werke* 1: 467).

Hence, the poems that Bettine includes in the body of the work and in the appendices are not merely haphazard additions that relate very little to the overall work. In the first place, many of the writings from Karoline in *Die Günderode* are written in a dialogue form.[80] The prose pieces "Die Manen" and "Ein apokalyptisches Fragment," in the I-form, as well as the drama "Immortalita," present a dialogue between two or more people. Even most of Karoline's poems that Bettine publishes in the work are actual dialogues, such as "Wandel und Treue," "Des Wandrers Niederfahrt," "Die Pilger," and "Der Franke in Aegypten"; other poems use the first-person narrative form addressed to a second person "du," for example, "Darthula," the untitled poem "Liebst du das Dunkel," "An Clemens," "Ist alles stumm und leer," "Lethe," and "Der Kuß im Traum." Only two of Karoline's pieces that appear in *Die Günderode*, "Don Juan," and "Mahomets Traum in der Wüste," are in the third person.

In the second place, the themes that are so prevalent in Karoline's poetry, such as the aesthetics of death and beauty, questions of time and historical continuity, and the relationship of the individual to the *Weltall*, are recaptured in her letters. For example, "Die Manen," the first piece that appears in *Die Günderode*, a dialogue in prose that deals with the theme of transitoriness, is preceded by two references to death in letters by the two women. The second part of Bettine's first letter to Karoline recalls a conversation about death that the two women had had in Frankfurt together. Likewise, Karoline's first letter to Bettine, the one that includes "Die Manen," opens with a dream in which Bettine dies.

In addition to the poems by Karoline in the book, Bettine also includes three poems she has written herself (*Werke* 1: 379, 456, 471–72). These poems do not function as fillers, though, but rather, arise directly from a personal situation and hold their own special place within the work. One untitled poem that she sends to Karoline, for example, is inspired by a particular poetry reading that Bettine attended in Frankfurt. In fact, Bettine is so impressed by the reading that she notices the influence of poetic words on her everyday language and thus becomes inspired to compose poetry. Feeling herself filled with poetry, she enthusiastically shares her accomplishment with Karoline. The fact that the poem has arisen from a personal situation also lends the sense of immediacy and intimacy to its creation.

It is now a generally accepted fact, of course, that Bettine vastly interpolated many of the letters in *Die Günderode,* or else wrote many letters later than 1806, the final year of the original correspondence.[81] In the few original letters that do exist, the extent of the revisions is quite evident. One noticeable change is the fact that Bettine has Karoline discuss her ideas and writings more in *Die Günderode* than Karoline did in her real letters. An immediate and verifiable example, for which both the original and revised letter exist, is found in the letter in which Bettine evaluates Karoline's verse in dialogue, "Wandel und Treue."

In the original letter, Bettine has just read Karoline's piece and quotes mostly out of a letter from Clemens in order to review the poem for Karoline. She only very apologetically presents her own opinions of the poem. In *Die Günderode,* she has Karoline explain her own poem in a letter to her. In the rewritten letter, Karoline equates the two figures in the poem, Narziss and Violetta, to Bettine and herself respectively. Not only does such an explanation that Bettine places in the mouth of the actual poet add authenticity to interpretation; it also places Bettine in a close relationship to the creation of the poem. By planting the poem in a situation that relates directly to the friendship between the two women, and thus to the epistolary work, Arnim attempts to make a smooth transition between the creation of art and a personal friendship.

In fact, the poems in *Die Günderode* are not merely added for embellishment. They often provoke a detailed discussion of writing, language, poetry, and philosophy in the letters. Because of the very dialogic nature of many of the pieces, and because Karoline ostensibly encloses her poems in letters to Bettine, Bettine often interprets Günderrode's poems as being directed towards her specifically and tries to identify the poems' themes with the women's friendship. Although Bettine did probably read some of Günderrode's pieces, as verified from the above quote, and could have participated in their conception, the nature of many of the poems makes such an identification unjustified. In fact, Bettine is sometimes frustrated when the poems do not mirror her perceptions of their relationship. For example, Günderrode includes her "Apokalyptisches Fragment" in a letter to Bettine. The theme of this poem parallels many of the frustrations that Günderrode expresses in her other works and letters. The "I" narrator in the "Fragment" is trying to grasp the meaning of the many contrasts in life, namely, the ethereal vs. the ephemeral spheres; the past vs. the present vs. the future; and an intense longing for freedom vs. a relentless need for boundaries. As "Wandel und Treue" does, so does "Apokalyptisches Fragment" extol the beauty in death because death returns humans to a natural state and replaces the confinements of the body with the unlimited soul. About the consequences of death, the narrator in the fragment exclaims in the twelfth paragraph: "Da dachte ich, meine Sehnsucht sei, auch zurückzukehren zu der Quelle des Lebens" [Then I thought my longing was also to return to the source of life] (*Werke* 1: 233).

Bettine is extremely affected by this poem and cannot comprehend why Karoline has sent it to her. First she states that she cannot understand the poem and blames her own immaturity: "Dein apokalyptisch Fragment macht mich auch schwindeln; bin ich zu unreif, oder was ist es, daß ich so fiebrig werd, und daß Deine Phantasien mich schmerzlich kränken" [Your apocalyptic fragment also makes me dizzy; am I too immature, or what is it that I become so fevery and that your fantasies hurt me] (*Werke* 1: 235). To her, it contradicts her image of the two women's friendship. Bettine accuses Karoline of ignoring their closeness and coldly wishing to terminate this bond in death. She cannot imagine the spiritual relationship between two people referred to in the poem. Instead, she recognizes a friendship with roots in everyday reality:

> In diesem Fragment lese ich, daß Du nur im Vorübergehen mit mir bist, ich aber wollte immer mit Dir sein, jetzt und immer, und ungemischt mit andern; erst hast Du geweint im Traum um mich, und nachher im Wachen vergißt Du alles Dasein mit mir, ich kann mir nichts denken als nur ein Leben, wie es grad dicht vor mir liegt . . . ich kann keine Fragmente schreiben, ich kann nur an Dich schreiben. . . . Zeit und Ewigkeit, das ist mir alles so weitläufig, da fürcht ich Dich aus den Augen zu verlieren. . . .

> [In this fragment I read that you are only with me temporarily, but I wanted to be with you always, now and forever, and not mixed in with others; first you cried in the dream about me, and afterwards in waking you forget all existence with me, I cannot think of anything but only a life, as it lies just closely in front of me. . . . I can write no fragments, I can only write to you. . . . Time and eternity, that is all so elaborate to me, for this reason I fear losing you out of my eyesight.] (*Werke* 1: 235)

Bettine cannot imagine the satisfaction after death that Karoline can, especially regarding the possibilities for their friendship. She wants their friendship to remain within the ethereal realm for as long as possible. She is frustrated with the kind of impersonal communication that Karoline expresses in her fragment. Unable to identify her position with that in Karoline's fragment, she prefers to write letters to Karoline that relate more to their individual situation.

All of the poems published in *Die Günderode* are intrinsic to the text, and within the scope of Bettine's compilation, they play a major role in the friendship between the two women. Bettine's conversation with the Herzog Emil August von Gotha about Karoline's drama "Immortalita" prompts her to recount the encounter to Günderrode in a letter and to enclose the Herzog's comments written on the manuscript of the piece. Likewise, Bettine includes "Don Juan" and "Darthula" in the appendix after mentioning to Karoline that she has sent this poem to the Herzog (*Werke* 1: 273; Appendix *Werke* 1: 401 and 397 respectively). Bettine incorporates verses of Karoline's "Darathua" in a letter, as she remembers its origins in a real life situation, that is, while Bettine was braiding Karoline's hair. A footnote makes a reference to the complete poem in the appendix. Each poem becomes integrated into the epistolary text after it has been an integral part of the two women's everyday conversations.

Reflecting back on the multidimensionality of Günderrode's entire *oeuvre*, as described in chapter four of this study, the reader should not find Bettine von Arnim's intertwining of Günderrode's epistolary writings with her other works so unusual. In fact, this mixed form appears entirely apropos in the context of Günderrode's many letters, dialogues, verse, dramas, and proposed novel. In including poetry with letters, not only does Arnim combine two of the most accepted genres in which they as women living in the late eighteenth and early nineteenth century were encouraged to write; she also supports the variety of styles that Günderrode demonstrates in her works. As in Günderrode's works, the use of a form that is not easily categorized ultimately explodes the boundaries of genre and gender. Once again, in amalgamating the private letter with pieces that had appeared in public, Arnim places the self in an ongoing dynamic relationship with its literary and cultural context.

*Die Günderode* thus acts as a tribute to a writer whose works had appeared over thirty years previously. By 1840, when Arnim published *Die Günderode*, Karoline Günderrode's works were probably known only by a small group of friends who had also known her during her lifetime. The editions of her poetry that had appeared in 1804 and 1805 had not been reprinted. The first set of her collected works was not published until 1857. In fact, the death of the poet probably loomed more closely in the public's minds than her talents. By republishing Günderrode's poems, even in an altered form, with her letters, Bettine von Arnim was resurrecting a side of the poet that had long been lost, if it had even been recognized or appreciated before.

Still, one cannot ignore the most controversial aspect of Bettine von Arnim's inclusion of Karoline's poems with the letters in *Die Günderode*, and that is the fact that Bettine changed Karoline's original phrasing and diction in many pieces for the published epistolary work. This revising seems even more strange when one considers that most of the poems that Bettine reprinted in *Die Günderode* in 1840 had appeared previously in the collection of Karoline's works in 1804 and 1805.[82] Bettine must have known that many readers would have access to the original collection and could readily compare her edited version with the actual pieces. In the book she gives no indication that she is publishing any original, unedited versions that Karoline would have given to her specially.

While one cannot ignore Bettine's act of appropriating Günderrode's works for Bettine's own purposes, one cannot also deny the radical nature of the published epistolary work within its literary, social, and cultural context. In its final form, *Die Günderode* establishes a community of two female writers and readers who create a work from a complex, continual, evolving process of exchange. The correspondence between Karoline von Günderrode and Bettine von Arnim parallels the literary networking that Louise Gottsched and Dorothea Runckel, Meta Moller Klopstock and her sisters, and Helmina von Chézy and her several correspondents achieved. Yet Bettine brings the process of community building one step further by showcasing to a public readership the creativity that such exchanges can make possible. Bettine's changes to Günderrode's pieces result in new renditions that might not have belonged to the original intent. By letting the reader know the dialogic context in which the pieces arose, however, Bettine makes clear the origin of the seeds that have matured into the final product.

Bettine's changes to Karoline's poems are minimal, whereas her revisions of the dramatic and prose pieces are very marked. Renditions of "Die Manen" show vast changes. This is the first piece Karoline sends to Bettine. It is a dialogue between a teacher and pupil. The themes that arise, namely, the fusing of the past, present, and future through remembering, as well as the student-teacher relationship between the two characters, are directly related to themes in *Die Günderode* and to the relationship between the two women. Many of Bettine's changes to the dialogue do not modify these themes, but show signs of grappling with the piece's dialogic quality.

As an explicative introduction to the poem, Bettine has Karoline write in her letter:

Auf meiner Heimfahrt von Hanau hab ich das Gespräch gedichtet, es ist ein bißchen vom Zaun gebrochen.—Ich wollt, die Prosa wär edler, das heißt: ich wollt, sie wär musikalischer; es enthält viel, was wir im Gespräch berührt haben. Du schreibst mit mehr Musik Deine Briefe, ich wollt, ich könnt das lernen.

[On my return trip from Hanau I composed the conversation, it is a little bit of a quarrel.—I wish the prose were more refined, that is, I wish it were more musical; it contains a lot that we touched on in conversation. You write your letters with more music, I wish I could learn that.] (*Werke* 1: 224–25)

In this paragraph, most probably written by Bettine herself, as Oehlke observes, Bettine provides clues as to how she has changed the text.[83] In the first place, Karoline has been inspired to write the dialogue by the two women's conversations together, and thus, the prose originates from a real-life, conversational, situation. But Karoline wishes that such a prose piece composed of dialogue could be stylistically more elevated, that is, more like music, which combines both tones and words, and which, through melody, is flowing and smooth. Bettine's letters, so the writer believes, are exemplary for the musical tone for which prose should strive. Bettine's revisions to "Die Manen" suggest attempts to heighten this fluidity while maintaining the melodious qualities of the piece.

Karoline's original version of "Die Manen" begins with the following words from the pupil:

SCHÜLER: Weiser Meister ! ich war gestern in den Katakomben der Könige von Schweden. Tags zuvor hatte ich die Geschichte Gustav Adolphs gelesen, und ich nahte mich seinem Sarge mit einem äusserst sonderbaren und schmerzlichen Gefühl, sein Leben und seine Thaten gingen vor meinem Geiste vorüber, ich sah zugleich sein Leben und seinen Tod, seine große Thätigkeit und seine tiefe Ruhe in der er schon dem zweiten Jahrhundert entgegen schlummert. Ich rief mir die dunkle grausenvolle Zeit zurück in welcher er gelebt hat, und mein Gemüth glich einer Gruft aus welcher die Schatten der Vergangenheit bleich und schwankend herauf steigen.

[Wise master! yesterday I was in the catacombs of the Kings of Sweden. A day before I had read the history of Gustav Adolph, and I approached his coffin with an extremely strange and painful feeling, his life and his deeds went through my mind, I saw his life and his death at the same time, his great activity and his deep tranquility in which he is already slumbering toward the second century. I recalled the dark cruel time in which he lived, and my soul resembled a tomb from which the shadows of the past arose pale and staggering.][84]

Bettine revises this passage into:

SCHÜLER: Weiser Meister! ich war in den Katakomben der Schwedenkönige, ich nahte mich dem Sarg des Gustav Adolf mit sonderbarem schmerzlichem Gefühl, seine Taten gingen an meinem Geist vorüber, ich sah zugleich sein Leben und seinen Tod, seine überschwengliche Tatkraft und die tiefe Ruhe, in der er schon dem zweiten Jahrhundert entgegenschlummert; ich rief mir die grausenvolle Zeit zurück, in der er lebte, mein Gemüt glich einer Gruft, aus der die schwankenden Schatten der Vergangenheit heraufsteigen.

[Wise master! I was in the catacombs of the Swedish Kings, I approached his coffin with an extremely strange and painful feeling, his life and his actions went through my mind, I saw his life and his death at the same time, his exalted energy and the deep tranquility in which he has already slept into the second century. I recalled the cruel time in which he lived, and my mind resembled a tomb from which the shadows of the past arose.] (*Werke* 1: 225)

By eliminating the expressions of time, such as "gestern" [yesterday] and "Tags zuvor" [the day before] from the original, Bettine generalizes the text and makes it more timeless. To her, it is not important that the pupil has read the history of Gustav Adolph, and thus she omits this fact as well. Instead, the pupil's words immediately concentrate on his own emotional feelings when he encounters the coffin. The pupil no longer sees the life and deeds of the king pass before his eyes, but only the deeds, and "seine große Thätigkeit" [his great activity] hyperbolized into "seine überschwengliche Tatkraft" [his exalted energy].

Bettine frequently eliminates the conjunctions "und" [and] and "aber" [but]. The resulting long, uninterrupted sentences, which are broken up by slight pauses of commas or semicolons, are characteristic of Bettine's writing style. In this first passage, she has combined Karoline's three opening sentences into one. Other omissions seem to simplify, such as the elimination of "sein Leben und seine Taten" [his life and deeds] "bleich und schweigend heraufgestiegen" [ascended pale and staggering]. The same simplification of wording occurs when Bettine combines the three-word genitive construction into one, such as "der Könige von Schweden" [of the Kings of Sweden] into "der Schwedenkönige" [of the Swedish Kings]. This combined genitive construction is one of Bettine's frequent changes to Karoline's pieces, as evidenced in the subsequent passages in "Die Manen." Bettine either makes one word from two: "Geräusch der Welt" [sound of the world] becomes "Weltgeräusch" [world sound]; "Sprache der Welt" [language of the world] becomes "Weltsprache" [world language]; "Täuschung der Sinne" [illusion of the senses] becomes "Sinnen-täuschung" [senses' illusion]; or else she combines the adjective with the noun, as in "Entwicklung des innern Sinns—innere Entwickelung der Sinne" [development of the inner sense—inner development of the senses]; Erscheinung des Innern—innere Erscheinung [appearances of the interior—interior appearances]; Auge des Geistes—das geistige Auge [eye of the spirit; the spritual eye]; die seltenste Individualität—die individuellste Seltenheit" [the rarest individuality—the most individual rarity].

Not all of Bettine's genitive reconstructions create an overall simplified version of Karoline's words, for example, when Bettine places the genitive object before its subject, such as when she writes "sagte ich mir, sind dies des grossen Lebens Früchte alle?" [I said to myself, are these all the great life's fruits?] as opposed to Karoline's original: "sagte ich mir selbst, sind das alles Früchte eines grossen Lebens?" [I said to myself, are those all the fruits of a great life?]; or, when she replaces "der Vergangenheit Schoss" [the past's womb] with "Schoss der Vergangenheit" [womb of the past]. In the other prose pieces, reversal of genitive object and subject is even more prevalent. For example, in "Immortalita," Bettine writes "des Unglaubens Herrschaft" [the disbelief's dominion] in place of Karoline's words "die Herrschaft des Unglaubens" [the dominion of disbelief]; and "des Urhimmels Kräfte" [the original heaven's powers] for "die Kräfte des Himmels" [the powers of heaven]. In "Apokalyptisches Fragment" she changes "um den Bogen des Himmels" [around the arch of the heaven] to "um des Himmels Bogen" [around the heaven's arch] and "im Schosse dieses Meers" [in the womb of this sea] to "in dieses Meeres Schoss" [in this sea's womb].

Condensation usually simplifies. Compare, for example, Karoline's rendition of the teacher's explanation in "Die Manen" of the ephemeral quality of the present and the importance of remembrances. Karoline writes:

> LEHRER : Die positive Gegenwart ist der kleinste und flüchtigste Punkt; indem du die Gegenwart gewahr wirst, ist sie schon vorüber, das Bewußtseyn des Genusses liegt immer in der Erinnerung. Das Vergangene kann in diesem Sinn nur betrachtet werden, ob es nun längst oder so eben vergangen, gleichviel.

> [The positive present is the smallest and most evanescent point; by the time you become aware of the present it is already over, the consciousness of pleasure always lies in memory. In this sense, the past can only be observed, whether it is long or just passed, all the same.][85]

Bettine's rendition reads:

LEHRER : Gegenwart ist ein flüchtiger Augenblick; sie vergeht, indem Du sie erlebst; des Lebens Bewußtsein liegt in der Erinnerung; in diesem Sinn nur kannst du Vergangenes betrachten, gleichviel ob es längst oder eben nur vorging.

[The present is an evanescent moment; it passes in the time you experience it; life's consciousness lies in memory; in this sense you can only observe the past, no matter whether it passed long ago or just now.] (*Werke* 1: 225)

Not only has Bettine simplified the text through omissions and less abrupt punctuation; she has also generalized the statement by leaving out the qualifying adjective "positive." For her, all the present is fleeting. Instead of retaining the passive construction in the concluding part, Bettine has the teacher address the student directly, with the "Du" becoming active. Replacement of the adverb "nur" changes the meaning of the last part. Whereas in Karoline's version the past could "only be observed," that is, not relived, in Bettine's rendition the past can be observed only when the present is viewed as a fleeting moment.

Bettine eliminates adjectives, such as removing "dunkle" [dark] from Caroline's phrase "die dunkle grausenvolle Zeit" [dark cruel time], or "ein bleiches" [a pale] from "ein bleiches Schattenleben" [a pale shadow life]. Substantives are also frequently suppressed, as well as adverbs, verbs, and articles. Sometimes a term may be replaced by one that is simpler, clearer, and not so foreign. Once again, in "Die Manen," "große Tätigkeit" [great activity] becomes "überschwengliche Tatkraft" [exalted energy]; "kein Wunsch" [no wish] is "kein Sehnen" [no longing]; "Homogenes" [that which is homogenous] appears as "Gleichartiges" [that which is similar]; "harmonieren" [harmonize] as "zusammenstimmen" [concur]; and "afficirt" [moved] as "angeregt" [stimulated].

Bettine's preference for conciseness is verified by her changes in the other prose pieces as well, especially in "Immortalita" and "Apokalyptisches Fragment." In fact, in the latter prose piece there is hardly any phrase left unchanged in Bettine's version. The condensation of phrasing prevalent in "Die Manen" is noticeable in these other two pieces as well. For example, in the original "Apokalyptisches Fragment" stands: "mein Puls floh nicht schneller, meine Gedanken bewegten sich nicht rascher" [my pulse did not flee more quickly, my thoughts did not move more swiftly],[86] while in *Die Günderode* the sentence reads: "mein Blut, meine Gedanken bewegten sich nicht rascher" [my blood, my thoughts did not move more swiftly] (*Werke* 1: 233). Inverted word order causes change in emphasis, such as in the beginning statement "Apokalyptisches Fragment." The original: "Ich stand auf einem hohen Felsen im Mittelmeer" [I stood on a high cliff in the Mediterranean],[87] becomes "Auf hohem Fels im Mittelmeer stand ich" [On the high cliffs in the Mediterranean I stood] in Bettine's version (*Werke* 1: 232). Drawing the emphasis away from the speaker and instead laying stress on the dramatic vastness of Nature in front of the speaker seems to convey the idea of human transitoriness and helplessness more powerfully.

The style and tone resulting from Bettine's changes is consistently direct and concise. In making Karoline's philosophical style more simple and straightforward, Bettine is following her own desire to bring philosophy within the reaches of human comprehension, a desire that she stresses throughout all of *Die Günderode*. As she later states to Karoline: "Philosophie müsse nur durch die Empfindung begriffen werden, sonst sei es leeres Stroh, was man dresche, man sage zwar, Philosophie solle erst noch zur Poesie werden, da könne man aber lange warten" [Philosophy must only be grasped through sensation, otherwise it is empty straw that one threshes, although some claim that philosophy should become poetry first, but one would have to wait an awfully long time for that] (*Werke* 1: 278).

In fact, Bettine responds somewhat indifferently to Karoline's dialogue "Die Manen." She finds Karoline's letter much more melodic than the dialogue piece and quotes from the letter to prove her point. In order for Bettine to understand a work and to interpret its meaning, that work must contain elements that can be quickly grasped through the emotions. If a work is not "melodic," that is, if it does not directly mediate between thought and the senses, then it cannot be true, she believes:

> Dein Brief ist ganz melodisch zu mir, viel mehr wie Dein Gespräch. *'Wenn Du noch nicht bald wieder zu uns kommst, so schreibe mir wieder, denn ich habe Dich lieb.'* Diese Worte haben einen melodischen Gang. . . . Der musikalische Klang jener Worte äußert sich wie der Pulsschlag Deiner Empfindung, . . . ich meine, man kann kein Buch lesen, keins verstehen oder seinen Geist aufnehmen, wenn die angeborne Melodie es nicht trägt, ich glaub, das alles müßt gleich begreiflich oder fühlbar sein, wenn es in seiner Melodie dahin fließt. Ja, weil ich das so denke, so fällt mir ein, ob nicht alles, solang es nicht melodisch ist, wohl auch noch nicht wahr sein mag.

> [Your letter is totally melodic to me, much more than your conversation. *"If you do not come again to us soon, then write me again, for I am fond of you."* These words have a melodic course . . . The musical sound of these words makes itself known, like the pulse of your sentiments, . . . I

mean, one cannot read a book, cannot understand one or receive its spirit when the innate melody does not carry it, I believe, all that should be immediately comprehensible and perceptible, when it flows in its melody. Yes, because I think that, thus I realize whether everything, as long as it is not melodic, might not yet also be true.] (*Werke* 1: 228–29)

Those whom she finds most at fault for writing incomprehensibly, and thus without truth, are the philosophers, who impose rigid structures on language that stifle naturalness and spontaneity. Bettine resists against reading the writings of philosophers such as Schelling and Fichte, whose works Karoline von Günderrode recommends to her, because they divorce their thoughts from their emotions. In fact, Bettine claims that reading Schelling and Fichte has made her physically ill:

> Dein Schelling und Dein Fichte und Dein Kant sind mir ganz unmögliche Kerle. Was hab ich mir für Mühe geben, und ich bin eigentlich nur davongelaufen hierher, weil ich eine Pause machen wollt. Repulsion, Attraktion, höchste Potenz. . . . Glaubst Du, ein Philosoph sei nicht fürchterlich hoffärtig?—Oder wenn er auch einen Gedanken hat, davon wär er klug?—O nein, so ein Gedanke fällt ihm wie ein Hobelspan von der Drechselbank, davon ist so ein weiser Meister nicht klug. Die Weisheit muß natürlich sein, was braucht sie doch solcher widerlicher Werkzeuge, um in Gang zu kommen, sie ist ja lebendig?

> [Your Schelling and your Fichte and your Kant are in my opinion totally impossible fellows. What pains I have taken, and I really have only run away to this place because I wanted to take a break. Repulsion, attraction, most extreme power. . . . Do you believe a philosopher is not terribly arrogant?—Or even if he has a thought, he would be clever from it?—Oh no, such a thought falls from him like a planed chipping from the turn bench, from that such a wise master is not clever. Wisdom must be natural, why does it need such disgusting tools in order to come into motion, it is indeed living?] (*Werke* 1: 229)

Language should be clear and comprehensible. Philosophers who try to complicate their ideas, either out of arrogance or vanity, contribute nothing to wisdom and truth. Instead of writing to explain and discover, they are flaunting their ability to confuse. Overall, the changes that Bettine makes to Günderrode's letters and literary pieces suggest adherence to an aesthetic program that favored spontaneity and emotional response over abstract expression of ideas. That program did not reprimand Karoline as being too masculine, as Savigny's advice had asked Karoline to be "weich" [tender] and "weiblich" [feminine]. Instead, within the dichtomy of gender roles, Bettine's advice leads to a reversal of the hierarchy of values that berate outward expression of emotion as too feminine and elevate abstract, philosophical to be characteristically masculine.

To some readers, Bettine's appropriations of another women's works might also seem apprehensible, especially considering that Günderrode could not offer her immediate response in the dialogue. *Die Günderode* does not portray Karoline von Günderrode as a lovesick, suicidal author, a static view that much secondary literature continued to promote. The tribute that Bettine pays to Karoline brings both writers into a dynamic relationship in which they each create from the other's creations. Günderrode has not only given her works to the world, but she has also had a profound impact on the next generation of writers. In the same way that Bettine von Arnim ironically appropriates Elisabeth Goethe's storytelling talents as a means to show her gratitude toward the older letter writer, so, too, does Bettine's appropriation of Günderrode's poems come across as laudatory and not malicious. Her changes do not suppress sides of Günderrode's life and works, as editors of women's letters so often felt the liberty to do, but rather make important strides toward painting a more complete picture.

The alterations also mirror Bettine's desire to display her aesthetic appreciation for letters. In one very central letter, she relates to Karoline her fascination for the letters she found at her grandmother's house in Offenbach. Most of the letters in the intriguing boxes of yellowed papers she finds in the dusty library had belonged to her deceased grandfather, the Chancellor Michael von LaRoche. To Karoline, Bettine retells Sophie von LaRoche's detailed reminiscenses about her deceased husband, Bettine's grandfather. Chancellor von LaRoche had possessed a very humanitarian interest in the welfare of the peasants. His efforts to lower the taxes for the poor eventually resulted in an altercation with the Elector and the Chancellor's subsequent resignation. The entire incident sparked an avid and prolific correspondence between the Elector and the Chancellor, which Sophie von LaRoche had preserved. Recognizing Bettine's interest in the whole story, Sophie von LaRoche offered to give her the coat of arms that the peasants had bestowed upon the Chancellor for his resistance to the taxes. But Bettine would rather have the correspondence between the two officials. She explains to Karoline:

Das Wappen wollt sie mir aufheben und mir vor ihrem Tod noch schenken, ich hätte lieber den Briefwechsel gehabt.—Ich glaub, zu so etwas hätt ich Verstand, es einzuleiten und zu bereichern für den Druck, da wollt ich wohl noch viel hinzufügen; mir kommt immer nur der Verstand, wenn ich von andern angeregt werd, von selbst fällt mir nichts ein, aber wenn ich von andern großes Lebendiges wahrnehme, so fällt mir gleich alles dazu ein, als sei ich aus dem Traum geweckt. . . . Erfinden kann ich gar nichts. Aber ich weiß gewiß, wenn ich diese Briefe des Großpapa durchläse, es würde mir alles einleuchten, was dazu gehört, ich weiß noch so viel von ihm, und die Großmama würde mir noch manches erzählen. . . .

[She wanted to save the crest for me and present them to me before her death, I would have preferred to have the correspondence.—I believe I would have an understanding for such a thing, to introduce it and to enrich it for printing, thus I would still want to add a lot; understanding only comes to me when I am stimulated by others, by myself I don't have any ideas, but when I see others in great animation, then I'm inspired immediately, as if I were awoken from a dream. . . . I cannot invent anything. But I know for sure, if I were to read through these letters of Grandpa, everything that relates to that would become clear to me, I still know so much about him, and Grandma would tell me some more.] (*Werke* 1: 434)

This statement adds perspective to Bettine's wishes to alter and publish her correspondence with Elisabeth Goethe and Günderrode. Correspondence fulfills her wishes to identify herself with whatever she reads and writes. Bettine places great worth on the response that letters draw out of her, and thus values publication for further reworking that response. Various scholars have pointed out that Bettine's family viewed her letters as literature and that Bettine herself gave a few subtle hints that she perceived her letters as literary documents.[88] Although there is no existing evidence that the above passage was part of an original letter, the problems of self-expression and insecurity in writing she addresses here were present in many of her earlier original letters, and especially in those to Günderrode. Publication thus assumes a dual function. For her personal edification, it inspires and empowers her to bring her aesthetic program into praxis. In their revival of "great" people, such as Elisabeth Goethe and Günderrode, Bettine von Arnim's letter books allow readers to view the deceased writers and their works within an eternally living, responsive, and communicative culture. That revisitation is especially significant for women writers whose works and deeds tend to be forgotten.

# 7

## Corresponding with the World: Letters and Women around the 1848 Revolution[1]

In 1849, the writer Fanny Lewald devoted an entire four-part series of articles in the respected daily literary journal *Blätter für literarische Unterhaltung* to Bettine von Arnim's works. Most interesting about the series is its form: it is written as a letter addressed to Bettine. Lewald concentrates on Arnim's last epistolary work, *Ilius Pamphilius und die Ambrosia*, lauding Bettine as a "fremde, schöne, seltene Wunderblume unter uns" [strange, beautiful, rare flower of wonder among us].[2] Like many men and women before her, Lewald also does not escape stereotyping Arnim as "das Ideal der weiblichen Natur" [the ideal of feminine nature].[3] Seeing in her "den heiligen Cultus, den tiefen selbstverleugnenden Liebesdienst der Frauenseele" [the sacred cult, the profound self-denying service of love of the women's soul], Lewald defends the open love that Arnim exhibits in *Ilius Pamphilius* against anticipated attacks of those who might view the work as a "Gipfel der Unweiblichkeit" [height of unfemininity].[4] Yet at the end of the series, Lewald thanks Arnim for the inspiration that her will and courage give to Lewald personally and to women of her time in general:

> Es sind mir Stunden ernster Sammlung, wahrhafter Erbauung gewesen, die ich Ihnen danke. Ein Mensch der uns zeigt was man erreichen kann wenn man es erreichen will, der uns die Möglichkeit eines Gelingens, einer Vollendung darstellt, hilft uns, begeistert uns mehr als dicke Bücher voll moralischer Maximen.

> [These are hours of serious contemplation for me, true edification, for which I thank you. A person who shows us what one can achieve when one wants to, who shows us the possibility of success, or perfection, helps us, inspires us more than thick books full of moral maxims.][5]

Fanny Lewald's open letter to Bettine von Arnim brings the epistolary connection between women into a new generation of political activists. Lewald knew Bettine personally, probably having met her through her later husband, Adolf Stahr, friend of Bettine since the publication of *Goethes Briefwechsel* and collaborator in the publishing of Bettine's later works. Lewald mentions Bettine somewhat cursorily in her *Lebensgeschichte*[6] and corresponded with her briefly. In one letter dated 5 November 1847, now located in the Goethe-Schiller Archive in Weimar, Lewald refers to their shared interest in the "Proletariat."[7] Aesthetics meet politics in a circularity invoked by the epistolary form.

In the previous three chapters I have drawn particular attention to the aesthetic value of women's letters and the creation of an art of self-representation whereby the women can formulate diverse patterns of life experience and expression. That emphasis comes largely in response to the patriarchal denial of women's creativity and follows the theories of many recent studies that focus on the autobiographical act as one that allows writers to assume a multiplicity of forms in their lives and works.[8] In this chapter I would like to pick up on discussions in the introduction and chapters one, two and three to demonstrate how women use letters as a means to show how their life, self, and writing remain constantly engaged with and in the world around them. This is not to say that a discussion of the aesthetics of letter writing totally divorces itself from culture and history. On the contrary, besides including in their letters frank commentary on the cultural, historical, and political *Zeitgeist*, women redefined the public sphere through posing alternative criteria for friendship, authenticity in writing, narrative art, genre, and publication. Helmina von Chézy's letters on behalf of wounded soldiers in Prussia and the poor in the *Salzkammergut* and Bettine von Arnim's political writings exemplify how women maximized the qualities of the epistolary form to question on their own terms the powers that be.[9] Through constant interplay between the inner self and the outside world their letters straddle the theoretical polarization of the autonomous individual and cultural determinism. The letters under study in this final chapter are those by women actively participating in the 1848 Revolution. While the space I have allotted here will in no way do justice to the amount and diversity of material I use, I wish to suggest ways in which the association the women writers in the mid-nineteenth century drew with their predessors and successors link their past, present, and future in an intricate web of historical modeling.

My analysis looks at some writings by Mathilde Franziska Anneke (1817–1884), Louise Aston (1814–1871), Emma Herwegh (1817–1904), and Fanny Lewald (1811–1889), all who either through participation or observation publicly commented on events in the 1848

Revolution. Using war as a common historical experience may disturb revisionist historians who prefer to diminish the significance of such events in favor of following the lived fissures and ruptures experienced in everyday life. As Paul John Eakin opines in his book on autobiography, however, for better or worse, war still functions as the most recognizable symbol of our collective experience: "Wartime propaganda promotes this identification between the individual and society: to enlist is to enlist in history, to participate in a global movement of some kind."[10] For women in nineteenth-century Germany, their unlegitimized participation caused them to experience their individuality and the collective with a triple gaze, if you will:[11] as accessories to the male-dominated struggle, defiers of the gender norms of the larger society, and subversive cohorts with other women. During such times, the form they adopt to connect their personal experiences with those of the larger whole must employ artistry and political savoir faire.

Male reactions to women's political epistles and works constantly reminded them that they were overstepping the boundaries of the traditionally female private sphere and impinging upon the male-centered public domain.[12] In responses to Bettine von Arnim, for example, Friedrich Wilhelm characterized her method of defending the Polish independence fighters as typically "feminine" for its lack of objective evaluation, ignorance on political issues, and emotionalism.[13] His advice to von Arnim when she asks him to allow Xavière Mazurkiewicz to visit her brother, the Polish insurgent Ludwig von Mieroslawski, in prison demonstrates the passive, subservient attitude that men expected women to have toward politics: "Rathen Sie Frau von Mazurkiewicz, sich *der Ordnung zu fügen, kein Auffsehen zu machen oder zu veranlassen.* Dies ist ein echt weiblicher Rath in so unweiblicher Zeit als die Jetztzeit" [Advise Frau von Mazurkiewicz to adhere to order, to make or cause no scene. This is truly feminine advice in such an unfeminine time as now].[14] The King's attempt to suppress women's participation reflects an epistemological dichotomy that views political expression as intellectual, systematic, and thus masculine, whereas personal concerns are emotional, unsystematic, and feminine. As we saw in analyzing Rahel Varnhagen's and Caroline Schlegel-Schelling's attempts to redefine the demarcations between public and private, in the male-dominated dichotomy, privacy becomes defined only in opposition to the public and political, that is, as that which the public and the political have the right to suppress and censor.[15] The King demands submission and silence under the auspices of "feminine advice," using his power as a public man to exclude the private emotions of a woman.

The "unfeminine time" of social and political unrest in the mid-nineteenth century was characterized not only by open protests and battles, which were traditionally men's activities, but also by the formidable control that men possessed to restrict women's public participation. Legally, women had no voting rights, and thus no official say in any policy-making decisions.[16] As we saw in the opening chapters of this study, cultural stereotypes of women as mothers, virgins, and housewives psychologically censored them from participating in any activities that defied those roles.[17] If a woman did engage in political action, she was not supposed to display any self-initiative or desire to participate for the sake of making herself a public figure.[18] Women could legitimize their actions by stressing that either loyalty to be at their husbands' sides, an altruistic desire to help others, or the need to enhance familial or cultural life had drawn them into political service.

The letters and diaries of the salonière Clotilde Koch-Gontard (1813–1869) stand as testimony to the burning interest several women did have in politics as countered by the limited access they had for active engagement . As a first-hand observer to the Frankfurt Parliament in 1848–49, Koch-Gontard also conducted a lively salon frequented by famous politicians and cultural figures. Many respected her advice and opinion, and she enjoyed her participation, however limited, at the parliamentary meetings. While taking full advantage of the opportunities allowed her, she disputes the conventions that exclude her from the political arena. In reaction to news reports and letters she receives, she writes to Karl Mittermaier on 19 March 1848:

Doch ich höre Sie sagen: Es ist mit dem Weibergeschwätz wieder kein Ende, in die Kinderstube und an den Strickstrumpf gehört die Frau, der Mann nur ist berufen zum Handeln nach außen. Jetzt weniger als jemals noch mag ich meine Stellung in dieser Beziehung begreifen, und es macht mir recht viel Mühe, die Küche als den Hauptschauplatz meiner Tatkraft anzusehen

[Yet I hear you say: There is still no end to women's gossip, the woman belongs in the children's room and should be knitting socks, only the man has a calling for public action. Now less than ever can I understand my position in this relationship, and I have a lot of trouble seeing the kitchen as the main place for my energy.][19]

Later in that year, to her friend Josefine Buhl, she scorns the rules that obviate her defense of the moderate position she and her friends held: "Ich habe es in den letzten Zeiten recht schmerzlich empfunden, nur eine Frau sein zu müssen, die das Zusehen hat, und doch mit

Gefühl und Tatkraft im Leben begabt ist" [I recently found it quite painful to have to be only a woman whose hands are bound, but whose life is nevertheless endowed with feeling and energy.][20] Koch-Gontard's resentment, however, has its consequences, for more than once she recognizes her deviance from traditional roles and admits her guilt about letting herself as a woman get caught up in politics.[21] Still, she consciously defies the limits, expressing her opinion even though others might perceive her as a fool;[22] promising a friend that she will come visit her, even though her husband has forbidden her to ride on the train;[23] and breaking the law that forbids women access to the parliament, sneaking in to hear Mittermaier's closing speech.[24] Koch-Gontard's letters epitomize the inner workings of an individual consciousness embedded in its cultural milieu as she struggles to combine the two in a world that prefers to divide them.

Koch-Gontard hints at publishing her letters along with those of Heinrich von Gagern. She speaks about organizing the documents, and then when Gagern sends her a copy of his memoir, she envisions her diaries and correspondence as a sequel.[25] Abnegations of her talents, however, prevent her, and she ends up burning her earlier writings before 1843. The measures she takes to meet restrictions—whether they be giving private discourse public meaning in letters, diaries, salons, or acquiescing to social constraints—evidence how women needed to build strategies of persuasion in the political realm.

Despite the restrictions Koch-Gontard relates, several women did become politically outspoken in the 1830s and 1840s, using the revolutionary call for democratic representation in government and for elimination of all human oppression to defend their own equal political rights.[26] The strategies they adopt for their participation do not differ all that much from those of Koch-Gontard. Although I certainly cannot give extensive treatment to all these women's writings here, brief treatment of some instances of how they use the epistolary form in their political works introduces yet another way women took full advantage of the connections between literature, history, and gender that the letter form allowed. In incorporating the letter form into published observations, they tread the fine line between historical and aesthetic representation of their lives and desires, between understanding and eventually coming to terms with their individual identity within the larger historical picture.

As Gerlinde Hummel-Haasis remarks, changes in women's personal lives often instigate their participation in political action.[27] In the case of Mathilde Franziska Anneke, she become involved in social issues after divorcing her first husband and becoming ostracized from society. She turned to writing and political activity in part to support her and her child, but also to challenge the discrimination she witnessed due to her precarious status. In Münster, she received the title of "Kommunistenmutter" [Communist Mother]. After marrying her second husband, Fritz Anneke, she moved to Cologne in 1847, where she immediately published *Das Weib im Conflict mit den socialen Verhältnissen* [*Woman in Conflict with the Social Conditions*] one of her first feminist productions. When he was imprisoned, she became editor of the *Neue Kölnische Zeitung*, whose title she changed to *Frauen-Zeitung* [*Women's Newspaper*] to avoid censorship. The couple's participation in the Baden-Pfalz battle in 1849 led to their exile in Switzerland and eventually the United States. She relates her revolutionary experiences in her *Memoiren einer Frau aus dem badisch pfälzischen Feldzuge 1848/49)* [*Memoirs of a Woman From the Baden-Palatinate Campaign 1848/49*] (1853), which she began in Baden, but then published herself in Newark, New Jersey. In the United States she became an active member of the American women's movement, founding a "German Women's Newspaper," traveling widely to present speeches at national conventions, and establishing a girls' school in Milwaukee.[28]

Novelist, editor, and insurgent Louise Aston was born in Gröningen as the daughter of a church administrator. Her marriage to a wealthy Magdeburg factory owner turned into a disaster when he began to abuse her. She divorced him and, like Anneke, turned to politics after this turn in her personal life made her a social outcast. She moved to Berlin and, in an attempt to prove women's equality with men, she often assumed attire and mannerisms that resembled those of George Sand. Aston wore pants, smoked cigars, expounded on religious and sexual freedoms in public, and frequented local taverns alone. Her unconventional behavior led to her eventual banishment from Berlin, an experience she related in her book *Meine Emancipation, Verweisung und Rechtfertigung* [*My Emancipation, Expulsion, and Vindication*] (1846). Subsequently, she joined the democratic rebellion, became the editor of a short-lived newspaper called *Der Freischärler* [*The Insurgent*] (1848), and wrote two novels, *Lydia* (1848) and *Revolution und Counterrevolution* (1849), which tell about events of 1848 from the perspective of a politically engaged woman.[29] As a supporter of the 1848 Revolution, she participated in the Schleswig-Holstein campaign. After marrying in 1850, Aston retreated from public, political life, and traveled with her husband, who was a doctor on special missions. Her reputation as a rebel lived on, though.

Born on 10 May 1817 into a Jewish family who had converted to Protestantism, Emma Herwegh was raised to defend democratic principles in a unified Germany. She married in 1843 to the well-known author and agitator against the monarchy, Georg Herwegh, and she continued to support the revolution. When both Emma and Georg were expelled from Prussia in 1842, they spent their exile in Zürich and Paris. Emma Herwegh accompanied her husband's armed troops in their effort to support the 1848 Revolution in Germany from Switzerland. In exile, she contributed to his history of the battle and translated works by Italian and French activists, including Garibaldi. Her extensive correspondence with famous men and women of her day and her writings on the German democratic legion attest to her important role in the campaign. Her *Geschichte der deutschen demokratischen Legion aus Paris* [*History of the German Democratic Legion from Paris*] appeared in 1849 and then again in the edition of letters, *Briefe von und an Georg Herwegh*, in 1896.[30]

Fanny Lewald was born Fanny Markus to a middle-class Jewish family in Königsberg. She received an excellent education compared to other women of her time and social status, but still she continued to lament the fact that it was inferior to that of her brothers. In 1828, she converted to Christianity and assumed the surname Lewald. She refused to marry the man her parents had chosen for her. In 1841 she began to write, but anonymously, as her father would allow her to publish only under those circumstances. She was soon able to support herself financially. Eventually she became a prolific writer of novels, travel literature, and short stories, whose early writings criticize women's restricted social situation, especially in marriages of conveniences, and advocate less-stringent divorce laws. Lewald, too, was an enthusiastic supporter of the 1848 Revolution and traveled around, writing reports and letters on its progress. In her *Erinnerungen aus dem Jahre 1848* [*Memoirs from the Year 1848*] (1850), she presents her observations on the Revolution while in Paris. She later became a monarchist, a complex turn that can be considered from several viewpoints—the influence of her conservative husband, the general Jewish political discussion, and the dialectics of bourgeois rationality that both encouraged and restricted her utopian thinking.[31] Her subsequent writings, *Osterbriefe für die Frauen* [*Easter Letters For The Women*] (1863) and *Für und wider die Frauen* [*For and Against The Women*] (1870), still promote equal opportunity for women in education and employment, in conjunction with the program of the bourgeois women's movement.

One of the most familiar, convenient ways these women used to comment on political events and their role in those events was by adopting the epistolary form in their personal writings and by including authentic letters in their published writings.[32] Fanny Lewald's

*Erinnerungen aus dem Jahre 1848* [*Memoirs from the Year 1848*] was, as she states in the introduction, originally letters to her friend Therese (von Struve) von Lützow, to whom the book is also dedicated. Louise Aston incorporates her letters to the King into her book, *Meine Emancipation, Verweisung und Rechtfertigung* [*My Emancipation, Expulsion, and Vindication*], to defend her free, liberated actions after her 1846 expulsion from Berlin. Mathilde Anneke's and Emma Herwegh's autobiographical accounts of their activism converge with the epistle in the form of an introductory, dedicatory address to a reader or a direct invocation of a specific reader throughout the work. Anneke addresses her *Memoirs of a Woman from the Baden-Pfalz Campaign* to "You women at home."[33] Herwegh directs her *Zur Geschichte der deutschen demokratischen Legion aus Paris. Von einer Hochverräterin* [*On the History of the German Democratic Legion From Paris. By A Traitor*] (1849) to the prisoners taken captive during the uprising in Baden, as she corrects what she believes have been false accounts of her escape with Georg Herwegh at the conclusion of the battle.

Granted, each of these works differs from one another in subject matter and political intent. Aston's vindication has as its sole political agenda her bitter defense, and thus represents the most rebellious perspective on women's individual freedoms of all four. Both Anneke and Herwegh portray frontline revolutionary action from their personal perspectives as participants; yet Anneke recognizes herself as a focal point of developments in her memoir, whereas Herwegh strives for a more documentary account that centers on the whole troop's actions. In contrast, Lewald, as observer of events, produces a report that is more in the style of journalistic travel literature than the others.

Despite their differences, these texts, in their appropriation of the letter, still depict women's repeated return to the epistolary form as a means to assert their desire to become involved in public events. Widespread use of the letter form seems to be a direct consequence of the previously discussed paradox between, on the one hand, a gender ideology that limited women's access to the public sphere, and, on the other hand, revolutionary demands that tolerated women's call for equality as part of the general protest against oppression. The letter, often penned from inside the writer's own personal space and yet assuming the presence of an outside addressee, offered women a viable link between the public and private spheres. As an act that did not appear self-initiated, and thus evoked no air of ambition or fame, but rather responded to an issue or concern coming from another person or outside source, letter writing enabled women to feign subordination to norms of the feminine while voicing their opinion. In letter writing, women could adopt various strategies whereby they could internalize patterns of normative behavior while satisfying their need for political expression.

Virginia Woolf best explains the significance of the letter's double-edged quality for women, writing: "The art of letter writing is often the art of essay-writing in disguise. But such as it was, it was an art that a woman could practice without unsexing herself. . . . without exciting comment, anonymously as it were, and often with the pretense that it served some useful purpose."[34] Besides allowing women to interject subversive comments into what might be perceived a harmless, private text, the "disguise" of the letter also permitted them to challenge the hegemonic system of formal discourse and gender norms. Recently, the scholar Anne Hermann, in her study of epistolary essays by Virginia Woolf and Christa Wolf, points out how the letter form has allowed women to stress their historical exclusion from full participation in society and their isolation from more canonized forms of rhetoric in the male-dominated literary world.[35] Women letter writers, by working within a traditional form of female rhetoric, and from outside more conventional forms of patriarchal discourse, are still able, under the letter's pretense, to criticize authoritarian power structures.

As disguised protest then, the letters of the politically active women, like those of the publishing writers Anna Louisa Karsch, Sophie Mereau, and Karoline von Günderrode, often show ambivalence and hesitation, demonstrating women writing as gendered subjects as they reformulate the authoritarian political system that has excluded them. In an attempt to comply with the androcentric dichotomy assigning women to the private sphere, the four women often refute any implications that their political writings and deeds might be publicly oriented. In the introduction to her *Recollections From the Year 1848*, Fanny Lewald stresses that friends have cajoled her to publish her letters, even though she doubts the public worth of her personal views.[36] Louise Aston opens her defense of her unconventional appearance and way of life in a letter that expresses her disapproval of women who publish merely for the sake of self-exposure, accusing them of vanity. Instead, the most legitimate reason why women should publicize their private life is out of self-defense, that is, as response to a situation inflicted from an outside source; her own work reflects the latter motive:

Eine Frau, die ihre Privatangelegenheiten vor das Forum der Öffentlichkeit bringt, muß entweder grenzenlos eitel sein oder von der *äußersten Notwendigkeit* zu diesem Schritte gezwungen werden, einer Notwendigkeit, gegen welche sich aus falschem Schamgefühl zu sträuben, ebenso feig als ehrlos wäre. In diesem letztem Falle befinde ich mich.

[A woman who brings her private affairs in front of the general public forum must be either boundlessly vain or forced out of the *utmost necessity* to take this step, a necessity at which to balk because of false shame, would be cowardly as well as dishonorable. I find myself in the latter situation.][37]

In a similar manner, Emma Herwegh cautions readers directly against interpreting her history as the work of a professional author, for she would never want to increase "die Zahl der schrifstellerischen Frauen (mit dem technischen Ausdruck *bas-bleus* genannt)" [the number of women who write (called by the technical expression *bluestockings*.][38] Instead, she denies any ambition or talent in her work. In addition to renunciations of self-interest, Herwegh states that she has fought for the democratic cause not to seek her own fame, but to accompany her husband.[39] Likewise, Mathilde Franziska Anneke, in the introduction to her memoir, pleads belief in the Revolution along with loyalty to her husband to justify her fighting in Baden and the Palatinate. She advises her female readers to understand her actions:

Seid milde, Ihr Frauen, ich appelire an Eure schönste Tugend, seid milde und richtet nicht; wisset, nicht der Krieg hat mich gerufen, sondern die Liebe,—aber ich gestehe es Euch—auch der Hass, der glühende, im Kampf des Lebens erzeugte Hass gegen die Tyrannen und Unterdrücker der heiligen Menschenrechte. Mit der Liebe bin ich dem Manne meines Herzens gefolgt, dessen kräftiger Arm dem Kampf der Rache gegen diese Tyrannen geweiht ist.

[Be gentle, you women, I appeal to your most beautiful virtue, be gentle and don't judge; you know, the war did not call me, but rather love,— but I admit to you—also the hate, the glowing hate that the struggle of life begets against tyrants and oppressors of the sacred human rights. W..h love I followed the man of my heart, whose powerful arm is dedicated to vengeance against these tyrants.][40]

One might be inclined to believe these women's modest claims to political innocence and thus question how we may consider these strategies of political persuasion. Remarkable in each case, however, is the incongruence between the initial justifications and what follows in the rest of the text, the word and the action. While Lewald may have originally written her account of the 1848 Revolution as letters to her friend as spontaneously as she claims she did, the final, published version is so highly stylized and well organized that the reader cannot help but surmise that she edited the "letters" carefully before publication. Instead, her "letters" seem to be well-planned, conscious attempts to temper politically motivated events—such as her visits to Heine and Georg Herwegh and to political clubs in Paris, and her reports on the Parliament sessions and the assassination of Prince Lichnowsky in Frankfurt—with less-controversial cultural affairs, such as visits to museums, the opera, and fancy restaurants.

Similarly, Aston outlines in her preface only two options available for women who wish to publish, neither of which allow for independently motivated self-expression. Yet Aston's own career is a poor model for her observations: as the author of numerous critical poems, articles, and novels, many with autobiographical tendencies, Aston relied many times on the public arena to voice her personal opinions on female emancipation and the revolution. Anneke and Herwegh, too, in their introductions, contend that they did not partake in political activities independently from their husbands. But they use the autobiographical form to display the many activities that they did undertake and to state their views on a wide variety of contemporary issues. Neither woman was submissive or passive: Herwegh acted many times as a messenger between the German Legion in Paris and their leaders in Baden, as the former waited for orders to cross the Rhine; Anneke, too, was a messenger for the troops during the Baden-Palatinate battles. Both women also comment freely on the state of the revolution, criticizing problems of disorder among the rebels and pointing out conflicts between the people and the revolutionaries.

Each woman initially negates any political motivation behind writing her political epistle, but then publishes it. The letter serves as a shield between the self and public in that the women refute any demands for attention in writing while actually receiving that attention. The text represents the subversive activity of writing that the woman alleges she would never attempt and actually offers a pretext for assertions. Moreover, the letter form directly addressing a reader personalizes the statements and thus leads the reader to believe claims to näiveté. Under this veil of intimacy, women can adeptly assert their opinions or portray their rebellious actions.

In the four women's appropriations of the letter form for political causes, the reader can thus discern two specific tactics—conscious conformity to the norm that women should not be involved in politics and deviation from it. Such ambivalent expressions enable the women activists to interpret the restrictive political system and to assert their views within accepted boundaries of female discourse. Their interpretation becomes most interesting when they write, as Virginia Woolf states, "without unsexing themselves," that is, by calling particular attention to their gender and thus allowing readers to view the controversial intersection between the sexual and the political. In such instances, subversive messages become couched in statements that affirm their femininity, a strategy other women use to clarify their motives. Anneke, for example, was a large, muscular woman who rode horseback to deliver messages and to fight in battle. Men opposed her actions by satirizing her masculine dress. In her memoir, Anneke argues how a newpaper portrayal of her wearing men's clothes is a lie: "Ein wuchtiger Schleppsäbel, ein Hirschfänger, Muskete und Männerkleidung sind die Requisiten, die sie [die "Kölnische Zeitung"] aus ihrem Lügenschrein auch für mich in Bereitschaft gehalten, und womit sie mich, zu dieser gelegenen Zeit, ausgerüstet hat" [A massive cavalry sabre, a hunting-knife, musket, and men's clothing are the requisitions that the "Cologne Newspaper" also kept ready for me in their box of lies, and with which they equipped me at this opportune time.][41] She counters these accusations of masculinity by describing how she stood instead: "unbewaffnet und in meiner gewöhnlichen Frauentracht die nur durch ein leinenes Beinkleid zu einem Reitanzuge complettirt wurde, den Feldzug an der Seite meines Gatten mitgemacht habe" [unarmed and in my regular women's attire that was made into a riding suit only by a linen trouser, participating in the campaign at the side of my husband].[42] Anneke asserts her femininity by clarifying that she only conveniently wore trousers underneath woman's clothing, and by emphasizing once again how she was not fighting independently of her husband. Behind Anneke's justification, however, lurks a harsh criticism of how male reporters had concentrated more on her masculine clothing than on her rebellious intents.

Even Louise Aston, one of the most adamant defenders of women's rights to untrammeled action and speech, uses a letter to the King, which she includes in her published defense, to stress her feminine nature. Unlike Anneke, however, who espouses feminine traits to clarify and validate her actions, Aston does not apologize for her behavior per se. Instead, she tries to take advantage of her presumed disadvantaged situation as a woman in order to convince the King merely to allow her to stay in Berlin. Locating herself in a traditionally "feminine," defenseless position in society, she turns to the King as a "helpless" woman, "without protection and refuge,"[43] pleading: "Ein Mann findet sich schnell in eine neue, von seiner frühern ganze verschiedene Lage, oder hat die Kraft seine neuen Verhältnisse selbst seinen Bedürfnissen gemäß zu gestalten; einem Weib wird das unendlich schwer" [A man finds himself quickly in a new situation that is totally different than his previous one, or has the strength to shape his new relationships himself according to his needs; that becomes endlessly difficult for a woman.][44]

By promoting the "feminine," personal quality of their political intents, the women echo the patriarchal view that female-instigated political action is harmless.[45] Women, however, could have stood to gain from presenting their political requests in this manner. As Christa Wolf comments, marginalization can also work in women's favor: "In serious times it can be a protection not to be taken seriously."[46] In fact, nineteenth-century women's writings were often excused as being "hysterical" outpourings of the weaker sex and therefore could be allowed more poetic license than men's works. Fanny Lewald's observations concur, as she remarks in her *Recollections From the Year 1849*, that her early provocative stories might have been published because she was a woman, and therefore considered to be "extravagant" and unthreatening to the male order.[47]

In the case of Aston, however, women could not always elude the male persecutors by affirming their femininity. The helplessness that Aston promotes in her letters to the King is severely undermined by adamant demands throughout the rest of the pamphlet for free speech and action for women. Aston's reputation as a woman of strong, independent beliefs overrode her perceived defenselessness, for she was eventually banned from Berlin.

If women could not conceal their determination by conforming to standards of femininity, they opted instead to disengage their own individual political activities from those of other women. In such instances, the private, solitary act of writing letters reinforces the harmless picture of isolation that the women try to paint. The wish for separatism is apparent, on the one hand, in Louise Aston's defense, when she denies accusations that state she is an "emancipated woman" because she smokes, wears men's clothes, frequents local taverns, and talks publicly about politics and religion.[48] On the other hand, women often try to transcend their sex, attempting to locate their endeavors in a gender-neutral realm. In her letter to her readers, Emma Herwegh contends that her history of the Democratic Legion in Paris is only the work of a person whose "Gefühlsnerven etwas über den Kreis seiner Privatverhältnisse hinausreichen" [emotional nerves reach somewhat beyond the circle of one's private relationships.][49] Wary that readers might attribute sex-linked traits to this characterization, however, she states: "Diese Eigenschaft dünkt mich, ist weder eine ausschließlich männliche noch weibliche—sie gehört beiden Geschlechtern an, soweit sie sich eben mit Beibehaltung der ihnen eigentümlichen Auffassungsweise zu *Menschen* emanzipiert haben" [This characteristic seems to me neither a completely masculine nor feminine one—it belongs to both sexes, insofar as they have emancipated themselves, with maintaining their own specific ways of perception, to be *people*.][50]

To interpret the four women's persuasion tactics as either embracing feminine norms to their own advantage or rejecting their female nature at the expense of women's solidarity would be too simple. Along with efforts to transcend gender, it is important to recognize these women shared with one another politically an awareness of the influence that confining norms of femininity exerted on their political expression. In ambivalent sentiments toward their sex, Louise Aston, Mathilde Anneke, Emma Herwegh, and Fanny Lewald realize that the reception of their political works is based more on the fact that they are women than on their actual political beliefs or innate powers of reasoning. Apologies for writing, denial of ambition or legitimate claims to authority, stress on the personal connections that led them to political activism, and disavowal of any relations with organized women's movements contrast with their strong desire to assert themselves and thus indicate how they have interpreted their precarious position as politically active females.

Such contradictions signal viable strategies to deal with a world markedly divided along the lines of public/private, male/female domains. The anthropologist Mary Catherine Bateson, in her examination of the lives of five contemporary women, suggests that the ambiguities rooted in the social patterns of so many women's lives can, in fact, be positive in the overall schema of viewing life as a work in progress. She writes: "Women have not been permitted to focus on single goals but have tended to live with ambiguity and multiplicity. It's not easy. But the rejection of ambiguity may be a rejection of the complexity of the real world in favor of some dangerously simple competitive model."[51] By appropriating the letter form to claim a public role for what they define as their own private concerns, the four politically active German women question the right that men have had to force certain issues into privacy. In using this private means to deal with public concerns, they reformulate politics as a field that demands personal interaction. By bridging inner struggles with outer ones, they question the innate strength of the dichotomy established and maintained by men; by developing the essay-letter genre, they open a third sphere of discourse, one that challenges the division between public/private, political/personal, male/female, even as it acknowledges the boundaries that safeguard and define the dichotomy. Most of all, by showing an awareness of the boundaries limiting women's political involvement, they ask that freedoms be a right and not a privilege of only one gender.

In her essay on the revival of the epistolary form in the early twentieth century, Ebrecht argues that the function of letter writing had changed from earlier centuries. Instead of presenting a way to enter the public sphere, she contends, letters offered a means to preserve a private world threatened by impinging public discourse. What Ebrecht fails to see is that for women the threat of the split between private and public in general had existed long before the early twentieth century. Their use of private correspondence to challenge such demarcations is now centuries old. And women's reliance on and fascination with the epistolary form does not end with 1850 or even with the early twentieth century. I think particularly of Margaret Fuller's praise of Bettine von Arnim's *Die Günderode* for its dissolution of the well-defined boundary between the private and the public sphere: "Here the pure products of public and private literature are on a par."[52] The letters between Bettine and Karoline represent those of two people who ". . . write in the spirit of sincerity, write neither to the public nor the individual, but to the soul made manifest in the flesh." [53] Helene Stöcker (1869–1943), active collaborator in the radical wing of the bourgeois women's movement, also took an interest in Arnim. She wanted to write her dissertation on Arnim but was refused by her advisor, Erich Schmidt, because she could not gain access to the Wiepersdorf archives. For Stöcker, as she writes in a 1929 article, Bettine's work transcends time and place, for she was more than a Romantic writer; she was at the same time "leader, prophet, fighter."[54] Gertrud Bäumer, a leader of the less-radical wing of the bourgeois women's movement, also esteemed Arnim's works highly in her essay on women's history. The interest in women letter writers continues into the present day with writers and artists such as Ingeborg Drewitz, Sarah Kirsch, Margarethe von Trotta, and Christa Wolf rediscovering the patterns of epistolary discourse while producing their own.[55] In most cases, their writings show interdisciplinary qualities that combine fiction with autobiography, politics with literature, autobiography with biography.

Changes did occur around 1850, however, but not necessarily changes in quantity or quality. Rather, with increasingly more women finding in their predecessors models to emulate, the process whereby they learn skills of letter writing and self-consciously employ the form to explode the boundaries of genre, historical period, and gender figures more prominently. In using the epistolary form for political gains, the strategies women adopted around the 1848 Revolution seem very consciously enacted. They show awareness of both the power and threat the epistolary form can engender. By tracing the threads of the means whereby the women establish confidantes and confidence, we see patterns emerging and ever evolving. To talk of a women's epistolary tradition, however, does not refer to an innate, biological propensity.[56] Historically, women letter writers have worked against a double standard: their letters are "too personal" to count as political documents and "too unconsciously created" for the canon of fictional literature. In response, they craft a medium that makes valid and valuable their lives and their multifaceted roles, ever borrowing from, developing, altering, and adopting those of their foremothers. We should listen to their many souls corresponding to themselves and the world.

# Notes

## Introduction

1. Jeannine Blackwell and Susanne Zantop, ed., *Bitter Healing: German Women Writers 1700–1830* (Lincoln, Neb.: University of Nebraska Press, 1990).

2. See: Naomi Bliven, "Books: Old Pros," review of *Bitter Healing, The New Yorker* (25 March 1991), 86–88; and the reviews in "International Bookshelf," *MS* (Nov./ Dec. 1990), 57.

3. Katherine R. Goodman and Edith Waldstein, ed., *In the Shadow of Olympus: German Women Writers Around 1800* (Albany, N.Y.: State University of New York Press, 1992). See also Ruth-Ellen B. Joeres and Mary Jo Maynes, ed., *German Women in the Eighteenth and Nineteenth Centuries: A Social and Literary History* (Bloomington: Indiana University Press, 1986). The term "German-American Germanist Feminism" is taken from Ruth-Ellen B. Joeres, who, on the back of Goodman's and Waldstein's volume offers the following review of the book: "There is a good balance here between established scholars and quite new scholars. This group represents an emerging trend in 'German-American Germanist Feminism'—a growing group who often publish in German. It is essential that colleagues in other disciplines have feminist scholarship available to them in a language they can read."

4. For a partial list of recent works by these women, see the bibliography under each woman's name. For more complete bibliographies see *Bitter Healing: German Women Writers 1700–1830* and Elke Frederiksen, ed. *Women Writers of Germany, Austria, and Switzerland: Annotated Bio-Bibliographical Guide* (New York: Greenwood Press, 1989).

5. Elaine Showalter, "Feminist Criticism in the Wilderness" in her *The New Feminist Criticism: Essays on Women, Literature and Theory* (New York: Pantheon Books, 1985), 243–70.

6. I rely here on Anne Hermann's discussion, in the context of analyzing Christa Wolf's and Virginia Woolf's epistolary essays, of Lacan's, Derrida's, and Johnson's responses to the *Purloined Letter*. Anne Hermann, "Epistolary Essays by Virginia Woolf and Christa Wolf," *New German Critique* 38 (1986): 161–80. For complete texts of the responses, see *The Purloined Poe: Lacan, Derrida, and Psychoanalytic Reading*, ed. John P. Muller and William J. Richardson (Baltimore: Johns Hopkins UP, 1988).

7. Theoretical examinations of the letter in the German-speaking realm also point out different meanings of the word "Brief," or letter, and the ramifications those meanings have, although not always drawing the connection between linguistics and psychoanalysis that poststructuralist studies in English have done. See Wolfgang Kessler, "Brief und Briefwechsel im 18. und 19. Jahrhundert als Quelle der historischen Kulturbeziehungsforschung," Alexandru Dutu, Edgar Hösch, and Norbert Oellers, ed., *Brief und Briefwechsel in Mittel-und Osteuropa im 18. und 19. Jahrhundert. Brief und Briefwechsel im 18. und 19. Jahrhundert als Quellen der Kulturbeziehungsforschung* (Essen: Hobbing, 1989): 341–48; Eva Meyer, "Briefe oder

die Autobiographie der Schrift," *Manuskripte* 94 (1986), 18–22; and Norbert Oellers, "Der Brief als Mittel privater und öffentlicher Kommunikation in Deutschland im 18. Jahrhundert," in *Brief und Briefwechsel in Mittel-und Osteuropa*, 9–36.

8. Barbara Johnson, *The Critical Difference: Essays in the Contemporary Rhetoric of Reading* (Baltimore: Johns Hopkins UP, 1980), 141.

9. For the sake of conciseness, I have here, as well as in the following descriptions, simplified the issues surrounding "French" and "Anglo-American" feminist theories. For an anthology of texts and introductory explanations concerning the various feminist theories, see Robyn R. Warhol and Diane Price Herndl, *Feminisms: An Anthology of Literary Theory and Criticism* (New Brunswick, N.J.: Rutgers University Press, 1991). Many critics make a clear point of the fact that geographical location plays no role in determining whether someone is an "Anglo-American" or a "French" feminist. Inherent in the labeling, however, is a split whose boundaries are not always clear, as Diana Fuss's book on use of the term "essentialism" in feminist theories points out. See Diana Fuss, *Essentially Speaking: Feminism, Nature and Difference* (New York: Routledge, 1989).

10. See Anne K. Mellor, "On Romanticism and Feminism" in her *Romanticism and Feminism* (Bloomington: Indiana University Press, 1988), 3–9; and Toril Moi, *Sexual/Textual Politics: Feminist Literary Theory* (London: Methuen, 1985).

11. See particularly the essays in Elizabeth Goldsmith, ed., *Writing the Female Voice: Essays on Epistolary Literature* (Boston: Northeastern University Press, 1989). In German Studies, see Elke Frederiksen, "Die Frau als Autorin zur Zeit der Romantik: Anfänge einer weiblichen literarischen Tradition," in *Gestaltet und Gestaltend: Frauen in der deutschen Literatur*, Marianne Burkhard, ed., vol. 10 of *Amsterdamer Beiträge zur Germanistik* (Amsterdam: Rodopi, 1980), 83–108; Barbara Becker-Cantarino, "Leben als Text: Briefe im 18. Jahrhundert," in *Frauen Literatur Geschichte. Schreibende Frauen vom Mittelalter bis zur Gegenwart*, Hiltrud Gnüg and Renate Möhrmann, ed., (Stuttgart: Metzler, 1985); and Doris Starr Guilloton, "Rahel Varnhagen und die Frauenfrage in der deutschen Romantik: Eine Untersuchung ihrer Briefe und Tagebuchnotizen," *Monatshefte für deutschen Unterricht* 69 (1977): 391–403. Two most recent collections of essays also take largely historical approaches: *Die Frau im Dialog. Studien zur Geschichte und Theorie des Briefs*, edited by Anita Runge and Lieselotte Steinbrügge (Weinheim, Basel: Beltz, 1990); and *Brieftheorie des 18. Jahrhunderts*, edited by Angelika Ebrecht, Regina Nörtemann, and Herta Schwarz (Stuttgart: Metzler, 1990).

12. For an example of a reading that relies on French feminist theories, see Mary Jacobus's chapter "Reading Correspondences" in her book *Reading Woman: Essays in Feminist Criticism* (New York: Columbia University Press, 1986), 278–92. In German, see Eva Meyer's article "Briefe oder die Autobiographie der Schrift."

13. My summary of the essentialist/constructionist debate borrows from an example from Diana Fuss. The side on which one stood in this debate, Fuss states, would be revealed in an answer to Ernest Jones's question: "Is woman born or made?" An essentialist such as Jones would say woman is born, not made; an anti-essentialist such as Simone de Beauvoir would state women is made, not born (Fuss, *Essentially Speaking*, 3).

14. See particularly Moi's book, *Sexual/Textual Politics* for a critique of feminist studies until the mid-1980s.

15. Hermann, "Epistolary Essays by Virginia Woolf and Christa Wolf;" Ruth-Ellen B. Joeres, "'That girl is an entirely different character! Yes, but is she a feminist?': Observations on Sophie von la Roche's *Geschichte des Fräuleins von Sternheim*" in Joeres and Maynes, *German Women in the Eighteenth and Nineteenth Centuries*, 137–

56; Sigrid Weigel, "Der schielende Blick: Thesen zur Geschichte weiblicher Schreib-praxis," in Inge Stephan and Sigrid Weigel, ed., *Die verborgene Frau: Sechs Beiträge zu einer feministischen Literaturwissenschaft*. Argument Sonderband 96 (Berlin: Argument Verlag, 1983), 83–137.

16. Fuss, *Essentially Speaking*, 119.

17. The term "new historicism," coined rather inadvertently by one of its original proponents, Stephen Greenblatt, now seems to have become officially recognized as such. For a history of the movement and its name in English literature see H. Aram Veeser's introduction to *The New Historicism* (New York: Routledge, 1989). For comments on the involvement of German Studies, see Klaus Berghahn, "New Historicism: Editorial Introduction," *Monatshefte* 84.2 (Summer 1992): 141–47. The fact that one major periodical in German literature—*The German Quarterly* (Spring 1989)—included several articles on new historicism and that another—*Monatshefte*-(Summer 1992) recently made "New Historicism" the special topic for an issue adds to official recognition of the name for German scholarship. The fact that scholars still do not agree on whether to capitalize the term or not contributes to its theoretical openness.

18. Peter U. Hohendahl, "Interdisciplinary German Studies: Tentative Conclusions," *German Quarterly* 62.2 (Spring 1989): 231.

19. Judith Lowder Newton, "History as Usual? Feminism and the New Historicism," in Veeser, ed., *The New Historicism*, 152–67.

20. Anton Kaes, "New Historicism and the Study of German Literature," *German Quarterly* 62.2 (Spring 1989): 213.

21. Clifford Geertz, *The Interpretation of Cultures* (New York: Basic Books, 1973).

22. Newton, "History as Usual?"; Sara Friedrichsmeyer and Jeanette Clausen, "What's Missing in New Historicism or the 'Poetics' of Feminist Literary Criticism," *Women in German Yearbook* 9 (1993): 253–58.

23. See articles by Sara Lennox, "Feminism and New Historicism," *Monatshefte* 84.2 (Summer 1992): 159–70; and Newton, "History as Usual?"

24. I refer here to Lennox, "Some Proposals for a Feminist Literary Criticism," *Women in German Yearbook* 7 (1991) edited by Jeanette Clausen and Sara Friedrichs-Meyer (Lincoln: University of Nebraska Press, 1991): 91–97; Leslie Adelson, "Racism and Feminist Aesthetics: The Provocation of Anne Duden's *Opening of the Mouth*," *Signs* 13,2 (Winter 1988): 234–52; and Peter U. Hohendahl, "Interdisciplinary German Studies: Tentative Conclusions," *German Quarterly* 62.2 (Spring 1989): 227–34.

25. Lennox, "Some Proposals for Feminist Literary Criticism."

26. Susan Faludi, *Backlash: The Undeclared War Against American Women* (New York: Doubleday, 1991).

27. Joeres, "That Girl Is An Entirely Different Character!," 137–38.

28. Joan Kelly, "The Social Relations of the Sexes: Methodological Implications of Women's History and Theory," *The Essays of Joan Kelly* (Chicago: University of Chicago Press, 1984): 1.

29. Newton has borrowed the term "cross cultural montage" from Dominick La-Capra, as quoted by Ellen Pollak in her article "Feminism and the New Historicism: A Tale of Difference or the Same Old Story?," *The Eighteenth Century: Theory and Interpretation* 29.3 (Fall 1988): 281–86. See Newton, "History as Usual?," 152 and 166, note 3.

30. Louis A. Montrose, "Professing the Renaissance: The Poetics and Politics of Culture" in Veeser, *The New Historicism*, 23.

31. Ibid., 23–24.

32. For details of these criticisms, see Frank Kermode, "The High Cost of New

History," review of *Forms of Nationhood: The Elizabethan Writing of England* by Richard Helgernson, *The New York Review of Books* 39.12 (25 June 1992): 43–45; and Edward Pechter, "The New Historicism and Its Discontents: Politicizing Renaissance Drama," *PMLA* 102.2 (1987): 292–303.

33. Anton Kaes, "New Historicism and the Study of German Literature," 213.

34. Clifford Geertz, *The Interpretation of Cultures*, 449.

35. Ibid., 451.

36. See the essays in de Lauretis' book on power, and especially that by Tania Modleski, "Feminism and the Power of Interpretation: Some Critical Readings," *Feminist Studies/Critical Studies*, Teresa de Lauretis, ed. (Bloomington: Indiana University Press, 1986): 102–20.

37. Marilyn French, *Beyond Power: On Women, Men, and Morals* (New York: Ballantine, 1985). I thank Diane Young for her discussion of French's book and her eloquent, succinct way of expressing French's argument.

38. For a description of the issues surrounding new historical methods and a tradition of women's literature, see Lennox's articles, "Feminism and New Historicism" and "Some Proposals for Feminist Literary Criticism." Hannelore Schlaffer strongly argues against positing a female historical and literary tradition, stating that what she calls the mediocrity of women's cultural productions has created no continuity: Hannelore Schlaffer, "Weibliche Geschichtsschreibung–ein Dilemma," *Merkur* 445 (März 1986): 256–60.

39. Elizabeth Fox-Genovese, "Culture and Consciousness in the Intellectual History of European Women," *Signs* 12.3 (1987): 529–47.

40. Schlaffer, "Weibliche Geschichtsschreibung," 256.

41. See footnote 11 above.

42. Sara Lennox, "Feminist Scholarship and *Germanistik* ," *German Quarterly* 62.2 (Spring 1989): 165.

43. Susman, for example, accuses women of leaving little behind besides a few insignificant letters: Margarete Susman, *Frauen der Romantik* (1929; reprint, Cologne: Metzler, 1960): 77. Bovenschen sees women's timidity to speak out as a conformity to social norms and an inability to break with conventions: Silvia Bovenschen, *Die imaginierte Weiblichkeit : Exemplarische Untersuchungen zu kulturgeschichtlichen und literarischen Präsentationsformen des Weiblichen* (Frankfurt a.M.: Suhrkamp, 1980): 41–42.

# Chapter 1. Reclamation of the Sources and Genre

1. In Gottfried Keller, *Gesammelte Briefe*, Carl Helbling, ed., 4 vols. (Bern: Verlag Benteli, 1951), 2: 128. For this reference, I am indebted to Barbara Hahn in her *"Antworten Sie mir!": Rahel Leven Varnhagens Briefwechsel* (Stroemfeld: Roter Stern, 1990), 219, although she misquotes the passage and miscites the page number in the original volume.

2. Hermann Kletke, ed., *Auserwählte Briefe deutscher Männer und Frauen* (Berlin: Hasselberg, 1860), III–IV.

3. Friedrich Gundelfinger, ed., [Friedrich Gundolf], *Romantiker-Briefe* (Jena: Eugen Diederichs, 1907), xvii.

4. Heinrich Finke, ed., *Der Briefwechsel Friedrich und Dorothea Schlegel: 1818–1820 während Dorotheas Aufenthalt in Rom* (Munich: Josef Kösel & Friedrich Pustet, 1923), XXXII.

5. See in particular Hahn's study, *"Antworten Sie mir!...."*

6. Werner Vortriede, ed., *Bettine von Arnim and Achim von Arnim. Achim und Bettina in ihren Briefen*, 2 vols. (Frankfurt a. M.: Insel, 1981), 945.

7. Rainer Brockmeyer, "Geschichte des deutschen Briefes von Gottsched bis zum Sturm und Drang" (Ph.D. diss, Münster, 1959), 258.

8. Emil Burger, ed., *Deutsche Frauenbriefe aus zwei Jahrhunderten* (Frankfurt a. M., Berlin: Moritz Diesterweg, 1908), 4.

9. Ernst Wasserzieher, "Einleitung," *Briefe deutscher Frauen* (Berlin, Bonn: Ferd. Dümmlers Verlagsbuchhandlung, 1925), V.

10. Angelika Ebrecht also points out how the use of "deutsch" in titles of collections at the beginning of the twentieth century became widespread in response to growing nationalist ideology, and thereby also placed women in the role of "mothers and wives for the fatherland." It is noteworthy, however, that the connection between women's letter writing and love or other personal emotions has persisted in other historical periods and places, continuing into the present day. See: Angelika Ebrecht, "Brieftheoretische Perspektiven von 1850 bis ins 20. Jahrhundert," in *Brieftheorie des 18. Jahrhunderts: Texte, Kommentare, Essays*, Angelika Ebrecht, Regina Nörtemann, and Herta Schwarz, ed. (Stuttgart: Metler, 1990): 239–56. Witness the titles of two recent anthologies published in Germany: *Briefe über die Liebe: von Frauen in Haft und Verbannung* [*Letters About Love: From Women in Prison and Exile*], Julia Wosnessenskaja, ed. (Munich: Roitmann, 1987); and *Briefe einer grossen Liebe: die private Korrespondenz aus dem Nachlass der Herzogin von Windsor* [*Letters of A Great Love: Private Correspondence From the Estate of the Duchess of Windsor*] (Munich: Droemer Knaur, 1986).

11. For examples, see Elsie Gotsmann, ed., *Deutsche Briefe der Liebe und Freundschaft* (Berlin: Kiepenheuer, 1937); and Kletke's *Auserwählte Briefe deutscher Männer und Frauen*.

12. Helga Haberland and Wolfgang Pehnt, *Frauen der Goethezeit in Briefen, Dokumenten und Bildern. Von Der Gottschedin bis zu Bettina von Arnim* (Stuttgart: Reclam, 1960).

13. Louise Adelgunde Kulmus Gottsched, *Briefe der Frau Louise Adelgunde Victorie Gottsched gebohrnen Kulmus*, 3 vols. (Dresden: Joh. Wilh. Harpeter, 1771–1772).

14. Schiller's letters to Sophie Mereau were printed in *Zeitung für Einsiedler*, ed. Clemens Brentano and Achim von Arnim (Heidelberg: Mohr und Zimmer, 1808). Only in 1958 did Mereau's letters appear in: Friedrich Schiller, *Werke: Nationalausgabe* (Weimar: Böhlau, 1972), vols. 31; 35; 36/I; 37/II; 38/I. As far as I know, the letters that Fräulein von Schönfeld wrote to Gellert have not been published.

15. See volumes 24, 29, and 30 of Friedrich Schlegel, *Kritische Friedrich-Schlegel-Ausgabe*, ed. Ernst Behler with the assistance of Jean-Jacques Anstett and Hans Eichner (Paderborn, Munich, Vienna: Verlag Ferdinand Schöningh; Zürich: Thomas-Verlag, 1958—).

16. See the following passages in: Johann Wolfgang von Goethe, *Werke. Herausgegeben im Auftrage der Großherzogin Sophie von Sachsen*, 133 vols. in 142 books (Weimar: Hermann Böhlau, 1891), 1. Abt., 42, 1. Bd., 183 ff.; 1. Abt., 41, 2. Bd., 269 ff.

17. Quoted in Günter Jäckel, ed., *Frauen der Goethezeit in ihren Briefen* (Berlin: Verlag der Nation, 1964), 43.

18. Karoline von Günderrode, *Der Schatten eines Traumes: Gedichte Prosa, Briefe, Zeugnisse von Zeitgenossen*, ed. with an essay by Christa Wolf, 3rd ed. (Darmstadt: Luchterhand, 1983), 277.

19. Margarethe Susman, *Deutung einer grossen Liebe: Goethe und Charlotte von Stein* (Zürich: Artemis Verlag, 1951), 7–10.

20. See Katherine Goodman "The Sign Speaks: Charlotte von Stein's Matinees," in

*In the Shadow of Olympus: German Women Writers Around 1800,* ed. Katherine R. Goodman and Edith Waldstein (Albany, N.Y.: State University of New York Press, 1992).

21. "Über Goethe. Bruchstücke aus Briefen," ed. Karl A. Varnhagen von Ense, in *Morgenblatt für gebildete Stände,* 1812, Nr. 161: 641–43; Nr. 162: 647–48; Nr. 164: 653–54; Nr. 168: 671; Nr. 169: 674–75; Nr. 176: 702. See Hahn's *"Antworten Sie mir ..."* for a bibliography of Rahel's publications during her lifetime (223–24).

22. See Varnhagen's comments in his edition of Rahel's letters in: Rahel Varnhagen, *Gesammelte Werke,* ed. Konrad Feilchenfeldt, Uwe Schweikert, and Rahel E. Steiner (Munich: Matthes and Seitz, 1983), 1: 580.

23. My source for this information is Deborah Hertz, "The Literary Salon in Berlin, 1790–1806: The Social History of an Intellectual Institution" (Ph.D. diss., University of Minnesota, 1979), 157.

24. In this context, the entire quote from Lewald's autobiography is especially interesting: "Meine Worte und Gedanken sahen mich auf dem weißen Papier mit den schönen schwarzen Lettern, und in Gesellschaft mancher bekannten Schriftstellernamen, fremd und vornehm an. Es war mir, als befände ich mich plözlich in kostbarer, mich verschöender Kleidung in einem prächtigen Saale, von verehrten Menschen gütevoll empfangen. Es tat mir äußerst wohl. Aber wie ich es mir damals noch keineswegs beikommen ließ, mich für ein Talent zu halten, so hatte ich noch viel weniger den Mut, meinen Vetter anzufragen, ob er mir ein solches etwa zutrauen würde." [My words and thoughts appeared strange and distinguished to me on the white paper with the beautiful black lettering and in the company of some well-known authors. It was as if I suddenly found myself in costly, embellished clothes in a magnificent room, warmly received by honorable people. I felt really good. But as there was no way that I could make myself recognize my own talent then, I thus had even less courage to ask my cousin whether he would give me the credit for such.](Fanny Lewald, *Meine Lebensgeschichte,* ed. and intro. Gisela Brinker-Gabler (Frankfurt a. M.: Fischer, 1980), 184–85.)

25. Jeannine Blackwell, "Anonym, verschollen, trivial: Methodological Hindrances in Researching German Women's Literature," *Women in German Yearbook: Feminist Studies and German Culture* 1 (1985), ed. Marianne Burkhard and Edith Waldstein, (Lanham: University Press of America, 1985): 39–59.

26. Barbara Hahn, "'Weiber verstehen alles à la lettre:' Briefkultur im beginnenden 19. Jahrhundert," in *Deutsche Literatur von Frauen,* Gisela Brinker-Gabler, ed. (Munich: C. H. Beck, 1988), 2: 20.

27. Gert Mattenklott, Hannelore Schlaffer, and Heinz Schlaffer, *Deutsche Briefe 1750–1950* (Frankfurt a. M.: S. Fischer, 1988).

28. Annette Kolodny, "Some Notes on Defining a 'Feminist Literary Criticism,'" *Critical Inquiry* 2 (1975): 92.

29. The series is: Norbert Heinrichs and Horst Weeland, ed., *Briefe Deutscher Philosophen (1750–1850): Microfiche-Edition* (Munich: K. G. Saur, 1990) The accompanying index includes the introduction, a list of the volumes by title, and an alphabetical index of recipients and senders.

30. Katja Behrens's collection of Romantic women's letters contains many ellipses: Katja Behrens. ed., *Frauenbriefe der Romantik* (Frankfurt a. M.: Insel, 1981). Subsequent editions of Caroline Schlegel-Schelling's letters have had to rely on cuts made by Schmidt, for the original letters are lost: Caroline Schlegel-Schelling, *Caroline. Briefe aus der Frühromantik,* Erich Schmidt, ed., revised and enlarged by Georg Waitz, 2 vols. (Leipzig: Insel, 1913). A subsequent collection of Schlegel-Schelling's letters is: *"Lieber Freund, ich komme weit her schon an diesem frühen Morgen":*

*Caroline Schlegel-Schelling in ihren Briefen*, Sigrid Damm, ed. (Darmstadt: Luchterhand, 1980).

31. Susmann, for example, writing in 1929, clearly implies that subjectivity inheres in the female being. Hence, she concludes that Rahel Varnhagen was "[g]anz Frau—denn das Leben und Wissen Rahels nicht weniger als das Carolinens strömte ja einzig aus dem innersten Mittelpunkt ihres persönlichen Daseins hervor; . . ." [totally woman—for Rahel's life and knowledge, no less than that of Caroline, poured solely out of the innermost middlepoint of her personal existence] (*Frauen der Romantik*, 85). In Susman's estimation, Bettine von Arnim also possesses "ein romantisches Frauendasein" [a romantic woman's being] (106). Tanneberger, who concerns herself more with Arnim's political deeds, attributes Arnim's courage to a certain feminine compassion, placing her activities within those realms considered traditionally feminine and dictated by emotions of the heart: Irmgard Tanneberger, *Die Frauen der Romantik und das soziale Problem* (Oldenburg: Schulzesche Hofbuchdruckerei und Verlagsbuchhandlung, 1928), 74.

32. Georg Steinhausen, *Geschichte des deutschen Briefes: Zur Kulturgeschichte des deutschen Volkes* (1889, Dublin, Zürich: Weidmann, 1968).

33. Hahn, "*Antworten Sie mir*," 217.

34. Steinhausen, *Geschichte des deutschen Briefes*, 395.

35. Karl von Holtei, ed., *Briefe an Ludwig Tieck*, 4 vols. (Breslau: Trewendt, 1864), 2: 224.

36. Of the beginning and middle of the eighteenth century, Steinhausen praises women's letters as some of the most beautiful writings in the development of the German letter (*Geschichte des deutschen Briefes*, 267). About the Age of Sentimentality, he also calls attention to the worth of women's letters (*Geschichte des deutschen Briefes*, 296). Even in the first half of the nineteenth century, when, as Steinhausen claims, the letter lost its importance and its aesthetic quality, women still continued the tradition of admirable letter writing (*Geschichte des deutschen Briefes*, 406–7).

37. See especially: Gustav Hillard, "Vom Wandel und Verfall des Briefes," *Merkur* 23 (1969): 342–51; and Georg Jappe, "Vom Briefwechsel zum Schriftwechsel," *Merkur* 23 (1969): 351–62. The studies by Hillard and Jappe contribute little to the existing scholarship on letters, mostly because they supply very few examples to corroborate their assertions, and because the evidence presented is not well-documented. Various lexica and dictionaries of literary periods have also glossed over letters in their treatment of the nineteenth century, beginning with Romanticism. Wilhelm Grenzmann, for example, the author of one of the more extensive articles on the letter that appeared in Merker Stammler's *Reallexikon*, apologizes for the entry's shortcomings, especially concerning the Romantic period: Wilhelm Grenzmann, "Brief," *Reallexikon der deutschen Literaturgeschichte*, ed. Paul Merker and Wolfgang Stammler, 2nd ed., rev. and enlgd. by Werner Kohlschmidt and Wolfgang Mohr (Berlin: Walter de Gruyter & Co., 1958), 1: 186–93. For examples of other lexical entries that laconically touch upon the role of the letter beyond the eighteenth century, see: Otto F. Best, *Handbuch literarischer Fachbegriffe: Definitionen und Beispiele* (Frankfurt a.M.: Fischer, 1978), 44–46; and Gero von Wilpert, *Sachwörterbuch der Literatur*, 5th ed. (Stuttgart: Alfred Kröner, 1969), 102–4. It is interesting to note that the *Lexikon deutschsprachiger Schriftstellerinnen 1800–1945* omits letter writers: *Lexikon deutschsprachiger Schriftstellerinnen 1800–1945*, ed. Gisela Brinker-Gabler, Karola Ludwig, and Angela Wöffen (Munich: dtv, 1986). Frederiksen's bio-bibliographical guide rectifies this omission: Elke Frederiksen, *Women Writers of Germany, Austria, and Switzerland: An Annotated Bio-Bibliographical Guide* (New York: Greenwood Press, 1989).

38. Jappe, *Vom Briefwechel zum Schriftwechsel*, 357.

39. Jappe, 358; Hillard, *Vom Wandel und Verfall des Briefes*, 344.

40. Margo Culley, "Women's Vernacular Literature: Teaching the Mother Tongue," in *Women's Personal Narratives: Essays in Criticism and Pedagogy*, Leonore Hoffmann and Margo Culley, eds. (New York: The Modern Language Association of America, 1985), 14–15.

41. Ibid., 15.

42. Albert Wellek, "Zur Phänomenologie des Briefes," in *Witz, Lyrik, Sprache: Beiträge zur Literatur- und Sprachtheorie mit einem Anhang über den Fortschritt der Wissenschaft* (Bern, Munich: Francke, 1970): 43–67; Gottfried Honnefelder, *Der Brief im Roman. Untersuchungen zur erzähltechnischen Verwendung des Briefes im deutschen Roman* (Bonn: Bouvier, 1975).

43. Peter Bürgel, "Der Privatbrief. Entwurf eines heuristischen Modells," *Deutsche Vierteljahrschrift für Literaturwissenschaft und Geistesgeschichte* 50 (1976): 281–97.

44. Wellek, 65.

45. Ibid., 63–64.

46. Ibid., 55.

47. Ibid., 58.

48. Since 1960 it has been known that Beethoven did, in fact, write three letters to Arnim, a fact that Wellek, writing in 1959, could not have known. See Gertrud Meyer-Hepner, "Bettina in Ost und West," *Neue Deutsche Literatur* 7,1 (1959): 152–54.

49. Wolfgang G. Müller, "Der Brief," in *Prosakunst ohne Erzählen: Die Gattungen der nicht-fiktionalen Kunstprosa*, Klaus Wiesenburger, ed., Konzepte der Sprach- und Literaturwissenschaft 34 (Tübingen: Niemeyer, 1985), 67–87.

50. Wolfgang Frühwald, ed., *Probleme der Brief-Edition: Kolloquium der Deutschen Forschungsgemeinschaft, Schloß Tutzing am Starnberger See, 8.-11. September 1975* (Boppard: Boldt, 1977).

51. Three of the papers in this volume deal with general editing concerns. The other papers treat unique problems that have arisen during publication of letters by specific persons or during specific periods. The remaining five articles present problems specific to published letters of G. W. Leibniz, J . H. Wichern, and Fontane and the correspondence between Goethe and Schiller and between Alfred Mombert and Stefan George.

52. Dutu, Hösch, and Oellers, ed., *Brief und Briefwechsel* (see Introduction, n7).

53. Norbert Oellers, "Der Brief als Mittel privater und öffentlicher Kommunikation in Deutschland im 18. Jahrhundert," in Dutu, Hösch, and Oellers, 22.

54. See footnote 31 above.

55. Tanneberger, 2.

56. Susmann, 77.

57. Richard Brinkmann, ed. *Romantik in Deutschland* (Stuttgart: Metzler, 1978); Paul Michael Lützeler, ed., *Romane und Erzählungen der deutschen Romantik: Neue Interpretationen* (Stuttgart: Reclam, 1981); Paul Michael Lützeler, ed., *Romane und Erzählungen zwischen Romantik und Realismus: Neue Interpretationen* (Stuttgart: Reclam, 1983); Klaus Peter, ed., *Romantikforschung seit 1945* (Königstein/Ts.: Verlagsgruppe Athenäum-Hain-Scriptor Hanstein, 1980).

58. Fritz Schlawe, *Die Briefsammlungen des 19. Jahrhunderts. 1815–1915. Bibliographie der Briefausgaben und Geszwitregister der Briefschreiben und Briefempfänger*, 2 vols (Stuttgart: Metzler, 1969).

59. Heinrichs and Weeland, ed., *Briefe deutscher Philosophen* (see footnote 29 above); Jens Haustein, ed. *Briefe an den Vater: Zeugnisse aus 3 Jahrhunderten* (Frankfurt a.M.: Insel, 1987). Some titles in the series *Briefwechsel mit Autoren* include:

*Briefwechsel mit Autoren: Rudolf Goerg Binding und Thomas Mann*, ed. Hans Wysling (Frankfurt a.M.: Fischer, 1988); *Briefwechsel mit Autoren: Gottfried Bermann Fischer und Brigitte Bermann Fischer*, ed. Reiner Stach with assistance from Karin Schlapp and introduction by Bernhard Zeller (Frankfurt a.M.: Fischer, 1990); *Briefwechsel mit Autoren: Samuel Fischer und Hedwig Fischer*, ed. Dierk Rudewald and Corinna Fiedler with introduction by Bernhard Zeller (Frankfurt a.M.: Fischer, 1989).

60. Wolfgang Kessler, "Brief und Briefwechsel im 18. und 19. Jahrhundert als Quelle der historischen Kulturbeziehungsforschung," in Dutu, Hösch, and Oellers, 341–48.

61. Louise Rosenblatt, *The Reader, the Text, the Poem: the Transactional Theory of the Literary Work* (Carbondale: Southern Illinois University Press, 1978), 22–47. Susan S. Kissel, "Writer Anxiety versus the Need for Community in the Botts Family Letters," in Hoffmann and Culley, *Women's Personal Narratives*, 53–55.

62. Guilloton shows her preference for reading letters "efferently" over "aesthetically" in her article on Rahel Varnhagen; here Guilloton sees Rahel as more interested in the theme of women's emancipation than in aesthetics: Guilloton, "Rahel Varnhagen und die Frauenfrage" (see Intro., n11). Damm, too, lays a higher value on the historical worth of letters than on their aesthetic worth: Sigrid Damm, ed., preface to *"Lieber Freund ...,"* 13 (see footnote 30 above). The title of Becker-Cantarino's study of the eighteenth-century European epistolary culture and women's role within that culture—[Life as Text: Letters as Means for Expression and Understanding in the Epistolary Culture and Literature of the 18th Century]—emphasizes the relationship between the letter and women's cultural and historical experiences: Becker-Cantarino, "Leben als Text: Briefe als Ausdrucks- und Verständigungsmittel in der Briefkultur und Literatur des 18. Jahrhunderts" (see Introduction, n11). Eva Walter uses letters as the main source of information about women's lives, including such topics as household chores, living arrangements, sexuality, pregnancy, birth, fashion, writing, views on politics and culture, and relationships with children, partners, and friends: Eva Walter, *"Schreib oft, von Mägde Arbeit müde:" Lebenszusammenhänge deutscher Schriftstellerinnen um 1800—Schritte zur bürgerlichen Weiblichkeit* (Düsseldorf: Schwann, 1985).

63. Within the past decade scholars have begun to explore the possibility of an aesthetic value in individual Romantic women's writings. Some examples include Frederiksen, "Die Frau als Autorin zur Zeit der Romantik" (see Introduction, n11); Sara Friedrichsmeyer "Caroline Schlegel-Schelling: 'A Good Woman, and No Heroine," in Goodman and Waldstein, *In the Shadow of Olympus*, 115–36; Katherine Goodman, "Poesis and Praxis in Rahel Varnhagen's Letters," *New German Critique* 27 (1982): 123–39; essays by Consolina Vigliero ("'Mein lieber Schwester-Freund'. Rahel und Ludwig Robert in ihren Briefen"), by Barbara Hahn, ("'Nur wir sind gleich bey der Ungleichheit'. Der Briefwechsel von Rahel Levin Varnhagen und Pauline Wiesel"), by Klaus Haase, ("'Laß dies mein Epitaph sein'. Zur Selbstdarstellung in Rahels Briefen") and by Liliane Weissberg ("Selbstbeschreibung als pädagogischer Diskurs: Rahel Varnhagens Briefe"), all in Barbara Hahn and Ursula Isselstein, ed., *Rahel Levin Varnhagen: Die Wiederentdeckung einer Schrifstellerin*. Zeitschrift für Literaturwissenschaft und Linguistik Beiheft 14 (Göttingen: Vandenhoek and Ruprecht, 1987); Hahn, *"Antworten Sie mir:" Rahel Levin Varnhagen's Briefwechsel* ; and Liliane Weissberg, "Turns of Emancipation: On Rahel Varnhagen's Letters," in Goodman and Waldstein, *In the Shadow of Olympus*, 53–70. These studies provide new insights into the value that letters played in various women's lives and the experimentation of style, content, and language the letters show. Of all these studies,

however, only Frederiksen's has attempted a comparative study of the styles and themes in letters by different women.

64. See also articles by Brigitte Leuschner on Theresa Huber as a letter writer and by Uta Treder on Sophie Mereau's reworking of her correspondence with Kipp for her novel *Amanda und Eduard:* Brigitte Leuschner, "Therese Huber als Briefschreiberin," in *Untersuchungen zum Roman von Frauen um 1800*, Helga Gallas and Magdalene Heuser, ed., Untersuchungen zur deutschen Literaturgeschichte 55 (Tübingen: Niemeyer, 1990), 203–12; Uta Treder, "Sophie Mereau: Montage und Demontage einer Liebe," in Gallas and Heuser, 172–83. Magdalene Heuser's articles on women's letters in the eighteenth century, which deal with original texts with difficult accessibility, are also noteworthy: Magdalene Heuser, "'Das beständige Angedencken vertritt die Stelle der Gegenwart.' Frauen und Freundschaften in Briefen der Frühaufklärung und Empfindsamkeit," in *Frauenfreundschaft-Männerfreundschaft: Literarische Diskurse im 18. Jahrhundert*, Wolfram Mauser and Barbara Becker-Cantarino, ed. (Tübingen: Max Niemeyer, 1991): 141–65; and Magdalene Heuser, "Das Musenchor mit neuer Ehre zieren. Schriftstellerinnen zur Zeit der Frühaufklärung," in Brinker-Gabler, *Deutsche Literatur von Frauen*, 1:293–313.

65. I refer here to: Karoline von Günderrode, *"Ich send Dir ein Zärtliches Pfand": Die Briefe der Karoline von Günderrode*, Birgit Weißenborn, ed. (Frankfurt a. M.: Insel, 1992). It is interesting to note that the new three–volume historical/critical edition of Günderrode's works does not contain her letters, due to constraints of time and finances. See: Karoline von Günderrode, *Sämtliche Werke und ausgewählte Studien: Historisch-Kritische Ausgabe*, ed. Walter Morgenthaler with assistance from Karin Obermeier and Marianne Graf, 3 vols. (Stroemfeld: Roter Stern, 1990). I thank Karin Obermeier for kindly responding to my inquiry about this omission.

66. Gert Mattenklott, *Jüdische Intelligenz in deutschen Briefen 1619–1988* (Frankfurt a. M.: Frankfurter Bund für Volksbildung, 1988).

67. See footnote 11 of introduction.

68. See footnote 11 of introduction.

69. Becker-Cantarino raises this criticism in her essay "Zur Theorie der literarischen Freundschaft im 18. Jahrhundert am Beispiel der Sophie La Roche," in Mauser and Becker-Cantarino, *Frauenfreundschaft-Männerfreundschaft*, 51–52, note 11.

70. Dagmar von Gersdorff, *"Dich zu lieben kann ich nicht verlernen": Das Leben der Sophie Brentano-Mereau* (Frankfurt a. M.: Insel, 1984). See also Chapter 4, n28 below.

# Chapter 2: Letters, History, and Gender

1. Several scholars have cited theories stating that women's creativity was inferior to men's and thus that women's duties lay in the domestic sphere and not in the cultural realm. See: Patricia Herminghouse, "Women and the Literary Enterprise in Nineteenth-Century Germany," in Joeres and Maynes, ed., *German Women in the Eighteenth and Nineteenth Centuries*, 78–93; and Elke Frederiksen, "German Women Writers in the Nineteenth Century: Where Are They?" *Beyond the Eternal Feminine: Critical Essays on Women and German Literature*, Susan L. Cocalis and Kay Goodman, ed. (Stuttgart: Akademischer Verlag Hans-Dieter Heinz, 1982), 177–201.

2. Steinhausen, *Geschichte des deutschen Briefes*, 6–12.

3. Walter Ong, *The Presence of the Word: Some Prolegomena for Culture and Religious History* (Minneapolis: University of Minnesota, 1981), 241–55.

4. Ibid., 250–51.

5. See especially Barbara Becker-Cantarino's study *Der lange Weg zur Mündigkeit: Frauen und Literatur (1500–1800)* (Stuttgart: J. B. Metzler, 1987); and her article "Frauen in den Glaubenskämpfen: Öffentliche Briefe, Lieder und Gelegenheitsschriften," *Deutsche Literatur von Frauen*, Gisela Brinker-Gabler, ed., 1, 149–72.

6. Becker-Cantarino, "Frauen in den Glaubenskämpfen," 156.

7. Virginia Woolf, "Dorothy Osborne's Letters," *Collected Essays*, 4 vols. (London: The Hogarth Press, 1966–1967), 3:59–65.

8. Ibid., 3:60.

9. Ibid., 3:60.

10. Jürgen Habermas, *Strukturwandel der Öffentlichkeit: Untersuchungen zu einer Kategorie der bürgerlichen Gesellschaft* (Darmstadt: Luchterhand, 1982), 67.

11. See Steinhausen, *Geschichte des deutschen Briefes*, 323. The exact quote from Gellert's letter reads "Sie haben mir wieder einen Brief geschickt, der bis zum Druck schön ist" [Again you have sent me a letter that is beautiful enough to print] (letter #38, 17 March 1760, page 106).

12. See Natascha Würzbach, ed., *The Novel in Letters: Epistolary Fiction in the Early English Novel 1678–1740* (London: Routledge & Kegan Paul, 1969), xiv.

13. Rolf Engelsing, *Der Bürger als Leser: Lesergeschichte in Deutschland 1500–1800* (Stuttgart: Metzler, 1974), 296–338. Helga Brandes, in her study of eighteenth-century women's journals, shows how the moral weeklies at the beginning of the eighteenth century began addressing women, thus showing their increasingly active participation as readers. Quoting from Engelsing's study *Analphabetum und Lektüre*, page 49, Brandes cites that only 5–10 percent of children and adolescents, mostly males, could read at the beginning of the century. By the end of the century, critical warnings against women's "*Lesewut*" [reading fury] as well as the number of journals addressed specifically to women, signify the growing literacy rate among women (Helga Brandes, "Das Frauenzimmer-Journal: Zur Herausbildung einer journalistischen Gattung im 18. Jahrhundert," *Deutsche Literatur von Frauen*, Brinker-Gabler, ed., 1: 452–55).

14. For a study of the relation between the growing epistolary cult, the bourgeois class, and a national literature in eighteenth-century Germany, see Regina Nörtemann, "Brieftheoretische Konzepte im 18. Jahrhundert und ihre Genese," Ebrecht, Nörtemann, and Schwarz, ed., *Brieftheorie des 18. Jahrhunderts*, 211–24.

15. Louise Adelgunde Kulmus Gottsched, *Briefe* 1:8.

16. I thank Matyáš Bečvárov for this observation.

17. Reinhard M. G. Nickisch, *Stilprinzipien in den deutschen Briefstellern des 17. und 18. Jahrhunderts*, Palaestra 254 (Göttingen: Vandenhoeck & Ruprecht, 1969), 175–76.

18. Christian Fürchtegott Gellert, *Werke*, Gottfried Honnefelder, ed., 2 vols (Frankfurt a. M.: Insel, 1979), 2: 164.

19. Nickisch, *Stilprinzipien*, 176.

20. Gellert, *Werke* 2: 168.

21. In his *Stilprinzipien*, Nickisch provides an extensive bibliography of the more than two hundred letter-writing manuals of the eighteenth century, including a breakdown of each manual by chapter. The list includes manuals written expressly for women and manuals that contain chapters to instruct the female letter writer specifically.

22. Engelsing also discusses letters from women in Bremen at the turn of the century to brothers or male friends in which women repeat their lessons, ask for further reading suggestions, and talk about the books they have been studying (*Der Bürger als Leser*, 328–29).

23. See Wolfdietrich Rasch, *Freundschaftskult und Freundschaftsdichtung im deutschen Schriftum des 18. Jahrhunderts: Vom Ausgang des Barock bis zu Klopstock* (Halle/Saale: Max Niemeyer, 1936), 81–111, 222–63.

24. Reinhard M. G. Nickisch cites four such collections of letters between male friends that appeared in the 1750s (*Die Stilprinzipien*, 187).

25. Gellert, *Werke* 2: 134.

26. Ibid., 134.

27. See Meta's letter to her sister, E. Schmidt, on 4 and 5 April 1756 in: *"Es sind wunderliche Dinger, meine Briefe:" Briefwechsel 1751–1758*. Bibliothek des 18. Jahrhunderts, ed. Franziska and Hermann Tiemann (Munich: S. H. Beck, 1980), 348–49; and her letter to Richardson on 14 March 1758 (*"Es sind wunderliche Dinger, meine Briefe,"* 433–35).

28. Mary Poovey, *The Proper Lady and the Woman Writer: Ideology as Style in the Works of Mary Wollstonecraft, Mary Shelley, and Jane Austen* (Chicago, London: University of Chicago Press, 1984), 37–38.

29. Gellert's praise of women's letter-writing abilities is most prevalent in his letters to Demoiselle Lucius. In response to one of her letters he replies in 1760: "In der That kann ich mich nicht erinnern, daß ich jemals einen so lachenden und doch natürlichen Brief von einem Frauenzimmer erhalten hätte; von einer Mannsperson will ich garnicht sagen; denn unser Witz ist nicht fein genug zu dieser Schreibart" [In actuality, I cannot remember ever having received such a mirthful and yet so natural letter from a woman; from a man I do not even want to say; for our wit is not fine enough for this style of writing]: Christian Fürchtegott Gellert, *Briefwechsel Gellerts mit Dem Lucius. Nebst einem Anhange . . . Sämmtlich aus den bisher meist noch ungedruckten originalen*, Friedrich Adolf Ebert, ed. (Leipzig: F. A. Brockhaus, 1823), 4. And in 1761 he writes: "Es ist stets mein Grundsatz gewesen, daß die Frauenzimmer, die gut schreiben, uns in dem Natürlichen übertreffen, und dieses wollte ich durch Ihren Brief erweisen" [It has always been my principle that women who write well surpass us in naturalness, and I wanted to prove this through your letter] (*Briefwechsel mit Demoisells Lucius*, 15).

30. Sally Winkle, *Woman as Bourgeois Ideal. A Study of Sophie von La Roche's "Geschichte des Fräuleins von Sternheim" and Goethe's "Werther"* (New York: Peter Lang, 1988).

31. Silvia Bovenschen, *Imaginierte Weiblichkeit: Exemplarische Untersuchungen zu kulturgeschichtlichen und literarischen Präsentationsformen des Weiblichen* (Frankfurt a.M.: Suhrkamp, 1980), 164.

32. Eva Walter, *"Schreib oft, von Mägde Arbeit müde:" Lebenszusammenhänge deutscher Schriftstellerinnen um 1800—Schritte zur bürgerlichen Weiblichkeit* (Düsseldorf: Schwann, 1985). The "new motherly love," according to Walter, manifested itself in the turn toward nursing one's own child and not employing a wet nurse, in an increased display of pride in one's child, in open display of worry and sorry over losing a child, and especially in an unprecedented interest in pedagogical methods and using those methods in educating one's own child (139–58).

33. Elisabeth Badinter, *Mother Love: Myth and Reality: Motherhood in Modern History*, forward by Francine du Plessix Gray (New York: Macmillan, 1980).

34. Winkle analyzes Sophie von LaRoche's *Sternheim* and Goethe's *Werther* as transitional works for this shift in the formation of the bourgeois feminine ideal. In conjunction with her literary analysis, she discusses Rousseau's writings, especially *Emile*, as playing a major role in this shift. Whereas LaRoche emphasizes women's ability to acquire education and self-esteem through social means, all within the boundaries of patriarchal structure and social convention, Goethe adheres much

more closely to the notion of woman's role as naturally determined and to her innate character as sentimental and passionate.

35. Bovenschen, *Imaginierte Weiblichkeit*, 220.

36. Gellert, *Werke* 2: 167–68.

37. For an examination of the role of women as readers of the eighteenth-century *Moralische Wochenschriften* see the chapter "Das lesende Frauenzimmer" in Wolfgang Martens's book *Die Botschaft der Tugend: Die Aufklärung im Speigel der deutschen Moralischen Wochenschriften.* (Stuttgart: J. B. Metzler, 1968): 520–42.

38. Reinhard M. G. Nickisch, "Die Frau als Briefschreiberin im Zeitalter der deutschen Aufklärung," *Wolfenbütteler Studien zur Aufklärung* 3(1976): 29–65.

39. Ibid., 58.

40. Herder writes to Caroline Flachsland in 1771 about LaRoches' *Fräulein von Sternheim:* "Welche Einfalt, Moral, Wahrheit in den kleinsten Zügen, und alle werden interessant!" [What simplicity, morality, truth in the smallest characteristics, and all are interesting!] Merck's review in the "Frankfurter gelehrten Anzeigen" is equally as praising: "Allein alle die Herren irren sich, wenn sie glauben, sie beurtheilen ein Buch—es ist ein *Menschenseele*, einen gar zu großen Hang zu guten Werken." [Thus, all the men are mistaken when they believe they are judging a book—it is a *human soul*, a much to great tendency toward good works.] For reviews of *Geschichte des Fräuleins von Sternheim* see Barbara Becker-Cantarino, Afterword, *Geschichte des Fräuleins von Sternheim,* by Sophie von LaRoche (Stuttgart: Philipp Reclam jun., 1983): 363–76.

41. Bovenschen, *Imaginierte Weiblichkeit*, 211.

42. Christian Fürchtegott Gellert, *Briefe, nebst einigen damit verwandten Briefen seiner Freunde,* Johann Adolf Schlegel and Gottlieb Leberecht Heyer, ed. (Leipzig: Weidmanns Erben und Reich, 1774): 243. The belief that subjectivity inheres in the female nature was endorsed by many of the well-known and influential pedagogues of the late eighteenth and early nineteenth century. See Elisabeth Blochmann, *Das "Frauenzimmer" und die "Gelehrsamkeit"* (Heidelberg: Quelle & Meyer, 1966): 63–86.

43. For a description of women's opportunities during the fifteenth and sixteenth centuries, see Barbara Becker-Cantarino, *Der lange Weg zur Mündigkeit: Frauen und Literatur (1500–1800)* (Stuttgart: J. B. Metzler, 1987).

44. Friedhelm Neidhardt, *Die Familie in Deutschland: Gesellschaftliche Stellung, Struktur und Funktionen*, Beiträge zur Sozialkunde 5 (Opladen: Leske, 1966): 30.

45. R. Dahrendorf, "Demokratie und Sozialstruktur in Deutschland," *Gesellschaft und Freiheit: Zur soziologischen Analyse der Gegenwart* (Munich: R. Piper, 1961).

46. Fox-Genovese discusses the ideology of separate spheres in Europe and the historical debate on the influence of capitalism on that ideology. In doing so, she gives good bibliographical sources for women's history in Europe: Fox-Genovese, "Culture and Consciousness," 542, note 42 (see Introduction, n39). For a discussion on Germany see Becker-Cantarino's study *Der Lange Weg zur Mündigkeit.*

47. Karin Hausen, "Die Polarisierung der Geschlechtscharaktere—Eine Spiegelung der Dissoziation von Erwerbs- und Familienleben," *Sozialgeschichte der Familie in der Neuzeit Europas,* Werner Conze, ed. (Stuttgart: Klett, 1976): 369–70.

48. Richard Sennet, *The Fall of Public Man* (New York: Knopf, 1977): 18. I thank Patricia Meyer Spacks for her reference to this quote in her book *Gossip* (Chicago: University of Chicago Press, 1985), 6.

49. See, for example: Barbara Duden, "Das schöne Eigentum: Zur Herausbildung des bürgerlichen Frauenbildes an der Wende vom 18. zum 19. Jahrhundert," *Kursbuch* 47 (1977): 125–43; and Bärbel Becker-Cantarino, "Priesterin und Lichtbringerin. Zur Ideologie des weiblichen Charakters in der Frühromantik," *Die Frau als*

*Heldin und Autorin: Neue kritische Ansätze zur deutschen Literatur,* Wolfgang Paulsen, ed. (Bern, Munich: Francke Verlag, 1979).

50. Ulrike Prokop, "Die Einsamkeit der Imagination: Geschlechterkonflikt und literarische Produktion um 1770," Brinker-Gabler, ed., *Deutsche Literatur von Frauen,* vol. 1, 325–65.

51. For a discussion of the categorization of *Frauenliteratur* and *Trivialliteratur* see: Lydia Schieth, *Die Entwicklung des deutschen Frauenromans im ausgehenden 18. Jahrhundert* (Frankfurt a.M.: Peter Lang, 1987).

52. Mohr's article provides a more detailed account of the debate between Körte and Voß and Jacobi: Heinrich Mohr, "'Freundschaftliche Briefe'—Literatur oder Privatsache? Der Streit um Wilhelm Gleims Nachlaß," *Jahrbuch des Freien Deutschen Hochstifts* (1973): 14–75.

53. Ibid., 53–54.

54. For statistical evidence of the growing book market at the end of the eighteenth century, see Helmut Kiesel and Paul Münch, *Gesellschaft und Literatur im 18. Jahrhundert als Quelle der historischen Entstehung des literarischen Markts in Deutschland* (Munich: Verlag C. H. Beck, 1977): 180–203.

55. Cited from Günter Jäckel, ed., *Frauen der Goethezeit in ihren Briefen* (Berlin: Verlag der Nation, 1964): 275.

56. Ibid., 293.

57. Helga Brandes, "Das Frauenzimmer-Journal: Zur Herausbildung einer journalistischen Gattung im 18. Jahrhundert," Brinker-Gabler, ed., *Deutsche Literatur von Frauen,* vol. 1, 452–68.

58. For a discussion of "Das Allgemeine Landrecht der Preußischen Staaten" in relation to women's legal rights, see: Hannelore Schröder, "Das 'Recht' der Väter," *Feminismus: Inspektion der Herrenkultur: Ein Handbuch,* Luise F. Pusch, ed. (Frankfurt a.M.: Suhrkamp, 1983): 479–82; and Ute Gerhard, "Dokument 17," *Verhältnisse und Verhinderungen: Frauenarbeit, Familie und Rechte der Frauen im 19. Jahrhundert: Mit Dokumenten* (Frankfurt a.M.: Suhrkamp, 1978): 396–442.

59. For reprints of those paragraphs in the "Preußisches Vereinsgesetz" that applied to women's rights, as well as reactions and consequences of this law see Gerhard, Ibid., Document 18, 443–50.

60. Blochmann gives insights into perceptions on women's education in the late eighteenth and early nineteenth centuries (footnote 42 above). For a description of the reception that Dorothea Schlözer, the first woman granted a Doctor of Philosophy, received, see the biography: Bärbel Kern and Horst Kern, *Madame Doctorin Schlözer: Ein Frauenleben in den Widersprüchen der Aufklärung* (Munich: Verlag C. H. Beck, 1990).

61. Virginia Woolf, *A Room of One's Own* (New York, London: Harcourt Brace Jovanovich, 1929), 54.

62. Goodmann points out how scholarship on Rahel Varnhagen in the nineteenth century, as well as comments from Rahel's contemporaries, described Rahel's salon as a "womb" and praised her for not publishing: Katherine Goodman, "The Impact of Rahel Varnhagen on Women in the Nineteenth Century," Burkhard, 146–47.

63. See, for example, Becker-Cantarino's article, "Priesterin und Lichtbringerin," and studies by Duden (footnote 49 above), Hausen (footnote 47), and Barbara Fass, *'La Belle Dame Sans Merci' and the Aesthetics of Romanticism* (Detroit: Wayne State University Press, 1974).

64. Friedrich Schlegel, *Kritische Friedrich-Schlegel-Ausgabe,* ed. Ernst Behler with the assistance of Jean-Jacques Anstett and Hans Eichner (Paderborn, Munich, Vienna: Verlag Ferdinand Schöningh; Zürich: Thomas-Verlag, 1958—), 1:92. (Cited as KFSA).

65. Becker-Cantarino, Priesterin und Lichtbringerin;" and Sara Friedrichsmeyer, *The Androgyne in Early German Romanticism: Friedrich Schlegel, Novalis and the Metaphysics of Love* (Bern, New York: Peter Lang, 1983).

66. Friedrich Schlegel, *Werke in zwei Bänden*, ed. Nationale Forschungs-und Gedenkstätten der Klassischen Deutschen Literatur in Weimar, 2 vols. (Berlin, Weimar: Aufbau Verlag, 1980): 2: 105. (Cited as *Werke*.)

67. See, for example, Bärbel Becker-Cantarino, "Schlegels *Lucinde*: Zum Frauenbild der Frühromantik," *Colloquia Germanica* 10 (1976–77): 128–39.

68. In a chapter entitled "Die Frau als Pflanze—Theorie des Vegetabilischen," Winfried Menninghaus has compiled a comprehensive collection of quotes from Schlegel's fragments in which the analogy between woman and "das Vegetabilische," and man and "das Animalische" or "Mineralische" is clearly stated: Winfried Menninghaus, Afterword, *Friedrich Schlegel: Theorie der Weiblichkeit* (Frankfurt a.M.: Insel, 1983), 135–40.

69. See Menninghaus's epilogue in his edition of Friedrich Schlegel's theories on femininity for comparative views of other men's views on women (Ibid., 217–23).

70. Sara Friedrichsmeyer, "Romanticism and the Dream of Androgynous Perfection," *Deutsche Romantik and English Romaniticism*, ed. Thomas G. Gish and Sandra G. Frieden, Houston German Studies 5 (Munich: Wilhelm Fink, 1984), 69–70; and Friedrichsmeyer, *The Androgyne in Early German Romanticism*.

71. Friedrich Hölderlin, *Hyperion*, vol. 3 of *Sämtliche Werke*, ed. Friedrich Beissner (Stuttgart: Kohlhammer, 1957), 90.

72. Ortner's essay on women's position between culture and nature still offers a good introduction to the topic: Sherry B. Ortner, "Is Female to Male as Nature Is to Culture?" *Women, Culture, and Society*, Michelle Zimbalist Rosaldo and Louise Lamphere, ed. (Stanford: Stanford University Press, 1974), 67–89. For a critical explanation of Rousseau's, Schiller's, and Humboldt's views on women (as well as those of other eighteenth-century male intellectuals) see Bovenschen, *Die imaginierte Weiblichkeit*.

73. Novalis, *Schriften: Die Werke Friedrich von Hardenbergs*, Paul Kluckhohn and Richard Samuel, ed., 4 vols. (Stuttgart: Kohlhammer, 1960–1975), 2: 160.

74. Clemens Brentano and Sophie Mereau, *"Lebe der Liebe und liebe das Leben": Der Briefwechsel von Clemens Brentano und Sophie Mereau*, Dagmar von Gersdorff, ed. (Frankfurt a. M.: Insel, 1981), 104. (Cited as Brentano/Mereau).

75. Clemens Brentano, *Das Unsterbliche Leben: Unbekannte Briefe von Clemens Brentano*, Wilhelm Schellberg and Friedrich Fuchs, ed. (Jena: Diederichs, 1939), 287.

76. Caroline Schlegel-Schelling, *Caroline. Briefe aus der Frühromantik* (see Chapter 1, n30; cited as *Caroline.*)

77. See, for example, Waitz's introduction (Ibid., xi–xii); Damm, Foreword, *"Lieber Freund*, 37; 48 (see Chapter 1, n30); and Gisela Dischner, *Bettina von Arnim: Eine weibliche Sozialbiographie aus dem neunzehnten Jahrhundert* (Berlin: Klaus Wagenbach, 1977).

78. Cited in Damm's edition of Caroline Schlegel-Schelling's letters, Ibid., 9.

79. Various quotes in the letters of Dorothea Schlegel prove the domestic role that she and Caroline assumed in the Jena circle. When Dorothea first moves to Jena in 1799, she praises Caroline's talent as a cook and hostess in a letter to Rahel Varnhagen, as if Caroline is managing the whole house; cited in Behrens, ed., *Frauenbriefe der Romantik*, 343 (see Chapter 1, n30). In a letter to Rahel Varnhagen on 10 April 1800, Dorothea is frustrated that she has not been able to work because she has assumed the main responsibility of caring for Caroline and the household while

Caroline has been sick. Most distracting to her is the fact that her privacy is not respected (Behrens, *Frauenbriefe der Romantik* 346).

80. Ludwig Jonas and Wilhelm Dilthey, ed., *Aus Schleiermacher's Leben In Briefen*, 4 vols. (Berlin: Georg Reimer, 1860–63), 3:83.

81. Joseph von Eichendorff, "Die Deutsche Salon-Poesie der Frauen," *Schriften zur Literatur*, vol. 3 of his *Werke*, 4 vols (Munich: Winkler Verlag, 1970), 87–101.

82. Karl Gutzkow, *Ausgewählte Werke*, Heinrich Huber Houben, ed, 12 vols. (Leipzig: Max Hesse Verlag, 1908), 3: 100.

83. Goodman, "The Impact of Rahel Varnhagen," 146–147.

# Chapter 3. "Let us rather exchange letters of friendship:" Women's Friendship in Letters

1. Louise Gottsched to Dorothea Runckel, 24 March 1754, in Louise Adelgunde Kulmus Gottsched, *Briefe der Frau Louise Adelgunde Victorie Gottsched gebohrnen Kulmus*, 3 vols (Dresden: Joh. Wilh. Harpeter, 1771–1772), II: 216. Cited as *LAKGB*.

2. Woolf writes: "Suppose, for instance, that men were only represented in literature as the lovers of women, and were never the friends of men, soldiers, thinkers, dreamers; how few parts in the plays of Shakespeare could be allotted to them; how literature would suffer!" (Virginia Woolf, *A Room of One's Own* (New York, London: Harcourt Brace Jovanovich, 1929), 87) Heilbrun lists men who talk of friendship—Plato, Aristotle, Plutarch, Montaigne, Rousseau, Emerson, Thoreau, etc. But, she concludes, the rare friendships among women that occur, "intrude into the male account the way a token woman is reluctantly included in a male community" (Carolyn G. Heilbrun, *Writing A Woman's Life* (New York: W. H. Norton & Co., 1988), 99).

3. Sylvia Bovenschen, "Vom Tanz der Gedanken und Gefühle. Die unaufhörliche Berührung von Tiefe und Oberfläche, Alltag und Ewigkeit. Über die Freundschaft," *Frankfurter Allgemeine Zeitung* , 25 January, 1986, Supplement, n. p.; Wolfram Mauser and Barbara Becker-Cantarino, *Frauenfreundschaft—Männerfreundschaft: Literarische Diskurse im 18. Jahrhundert* (Tübingen: Max Niemeyer, 1991).

4. Recent scholarship shows exception to this traditional view. Examples are: Deborah Hertz, "Inside Assimilation: Rebecca Friedländer's Rahel Varnhagen," in Joeres and Maynes, 271–88 (see introduction, note 3); Christa Wolf, "Nun ja! Das nächste Leben geht heute an," *Die Günderode* by Bettine von Arnim (Frankfurt a.M.: Insel, 1983), 545–84; and other recent research on Bettine von Arnim that discusses the friendship between Bettine von Arnim and Karoline von Günderrode, including Edith Waldstein, *Bettine von Arnim and the Politics of Romantic Conversation*, Studies in German Literature, Linguistics, and Culture 33 (Columbia, S.C.: Camden House, 1988); and Marjanne Goozé, "Bettine von Arnim, the Writer," Ph. D. diss., University of California, Berkeley, 1984. Hertz, however, in her book on Jewish society in Berlin, writes "Except for de Genlis, salon women rarely provided each other with practical aid or even intellectual inspiration either in or out of the salon setting" (Deborah Hertz, *Jewish High Society in Old Regime Berlin* (New Haven: Yale University Press, 1988), 171). Hertz is referring to a large group of salon women, Helmina von Chézy included.

5. German literary historians point out the rivalry between Caroline Schlegel-Schelling and Dorothea Veit Schlegel, and between Rahel Varnhagen and Henriette Herz. For recent examples of such scholarship, see Konrad Feilchenfeldt, "'Berliner Salon' und Briefkultur um 1800," *Juden in der deutschen Literatur* I, special issue of

*Deutschunterricht* 36.4 (1984): 87; and Eva Walter, "*Schreib oft, von Mägde Arbeit müde*," 172–78 (see Chapter 2, note 32).

6. Becker-Cantarino examines theories on friendship while analyzing the patriarchal society in her essay "Zur Theorie der literarischen Freundschaft im 18. Jahrundert am Beispiel der Sophie La Roche," Mauser und Becker-Cantarino, 47–74. (note 3 above)

7. Bovenschen, "Vom Tanz der Gedanken und Gefühle."

8. Dorothea Henriette von Runckel, *Moral für Frauenzimmer nach Anleitung der moralischen Vorlesungen des sel. Prof. Gellerts und anderer Sittenlehrer* (Dresden: Runckel, 1774) (cited as *Moral*); Carl Friedrich Pockels, *Versuch einer Charakteristik des weiblichen Geschlechts. Ein Sittengemählde des Menschen, des Zeitalters und des geselligen Lebens*, 4 vols (Hannover: Ritschersche Buchhandlung, 1798) 2: 168–232. (Cited as *Versuch*).

9. I am indebted to notes in the book *Brieftheorie des 18. Jahrhunderts*, edited by Ebrecht, Nörtemann, and Schwarz, for information on Runckel's life (see intro., note 11). The preface to Runckel's work is on pages 137–38 of *Brieftheorie*.

10. Magdalene Heuser compares Runckel's work *Sammlung freundschaftlicher Originalbriefe, zur Bildung des Geschmacks für Frauenzimmer* with letters by Louise Gottsched and Marianne Ziegler while investigating the connection between letter writing and women's friendship. The fact that the letters in Runckel's collection appear anonymously and with very few dates suggests the intention to generalize through nonspecific models. The letters encourage women to write and build friendships. Although the friendships relate mostly to those between men and women, passages disclose the letter's ambiguous functions, both as an emancipator from the confines of the home and as a private, disciplinary method of education (Magdalene Heuser, "'Das beständige Angedencken vertritt die Stelle der Gegenwart.' Frauen und Freundschaften in Briefen der Frühaufklärung und Empfindsamkeit," Mauser and Becker-Cantarino (note 3 above), 141–65.

11. Several examinations in the English-speaking realm have described women's friendships as resulting from a specific sociohistorical context consisting of these so-deemed female rituals. A pioneering article is: Carroll Smith-Rosenberg, "The Female World of Love and Ritual: Relations Between Women in Nineteenth-Century America," *Signs* 1.1 (1975): 1–29. Later studies include: Nancy F. Cott, *The Bonds of Womanhood* (New Haven: Yale University Press, 1977); Laurie Crumpacker, "Letters to a Friend: Feminism and Politics in the Correspondence of Four Eighteenth-Century Women," *CEA Forum* 15.4 (1985): 7–9; Lillian Faderman, *Surpassing the Love of Men: Romantic Friendship and Love Between Women from the Renaissance to the Present* (New York: Morrow, 1981); Pauline Nestor, *Female Friendships and Communities: Charlotte Brontë, George Eliot, Elizabeth Gaskell* (Oxford: Clarendon Press, 1985); and Leila J. Rupp, "'Imagine My Surprise': Women's Relationships in Historical Perspective," *Frontiers* 5.3 (1980): 61–70.

12. See Madgalene Heuser, "Das Musenchor mit neuer Ehre zieren: Schriftstellerinnen zur Zeit der Frühaufklärung," Brinker-Gabler, *Deutsche Literatur von Frauen*, vol. 1: 293–313; and Reinhard M. G. Nickisch, "Briefkultur: Entwicklung und sozialgeschichtliche Bedeutung des Frauenbriefs im 18. Jahrhundert," Brinker-Gabler, *Deutsche Literatur von Frauen*, vol. 1: 389–409. Entire essays and works devoted to Gottsched are: Richard Critchfield, "Beyond Luise Gottsched's *Die Pietisterey im Fischbein-Rocke oder die Doctormäßige Frau*," *Jahrbuch für Internationale Germanistik* 17.2 (1985): 112–20; Veronica C. Richel, *Luise Gottsched: A Reconsideration* (Bern: Peter Lang, 1973); and Ruth Sanders, "'Ein kleiner Umweg:' Das literarische Schaffen der Luise Gottsched," *Die Frau von der Reformation zur Romantik. Die Situation*

*der Frau vor dem Hintergrund der Literatur und Sozialgeschichte,* Barbara Becker-Cantarino, ed. (Bonn: Bouvier, 1980).

13. Bovenschen calls Gottsched the "Sachverwalterin der Theorie ihres Mannes" [manager of her husband's theory] (Bovenschen, *Die imaginierte Weiblichkeit,* 136) and "eine Schriftstellerin wider Willen" [an author against her will] (137).

14. See Nickisch, "Briefkultur," and Heuser, "Das Musenchor mit neuer Ehre zieren."

15. Elke Frederiksen, *Women Writers of Germany, Austria, and Switzerland: An Annotated Bio-Bibliographical Guide* (New York: Greenwood Press, 1989), 86.

16. Biographical information on Louise Gottsched's life comes from Becker-Cantarino's entry in Frederiksen's *Women Writers of Germany, Austria, and Switzerland* (see Introduction, note 4), and Heuser's article "Das Musenchor mit neuer Ehre zieren" (302–7).

17. In the next section, on Gottschedin, all passages from Gottschedin's correspondence with Runckel will be cited by volume and page number (see note 1 above). I prefer also to refer to her as "Gottschedin" to avoid confusion with her husband, when necessary.

18. Biographical information on Meta Moller Klopstock comes from the chapter "'Es sind wunderliche Dinger, meine Briefe:' Randbemerkungen zur Schreibweise Meta Klopstocks" in Marianne Schuller's book *Im Unterschied: Lesen/Korrespondieren/Adressieren* (Frankfurt a.M.: Verlag Neue Kritik, 1990); and Ulrike Prokop's article "Die Einsamkeit der Imagination: Geschlechterkonflikt und literarische Produktion um 1770," Brinker-Gabler, *Deutsche Literatur von Frauen,* vol. 1, 325–65. I refer to Meta Klopstock by her first name, again so as not to confuse her with her husband.

19. Klopstock, Meta geb. Moller. *Briefwechsel mit Klopstock, ihren Verwandten und Freunden* ed. and with commentary overseen by Hermann Tiemann. Vol. I Bd. I: 1751–1754; 2: 1754–1758; 3: Erläuterungen. Mit einem Beitrag von Erich Trunz (Hamburg: Maximilian-Gesellschaft, 1956).

20. Meta Klopstock, *"Es sind wunderliche Dinger, meine Briefe:" Briefwechsel 1751–1758.* Bibliothek des 18. Jahrhunderts, ed. Franziska und Hermann Tiemann (Munich: S. H. Beck, 1980). All citations will come from this edition.

21. Ibid., 492.

22. Ludwig Stern's book *Die Varnhagen von Ensesche Sammlung in der königlichen Bibliothek zu Berlin* (Berlin: Behrend & Co., 1911) documents the original contents of the collection. Nigel Lewis's book *Paper Chase: Mozart, Beethoven, Bach ... The Search for Their Lost Music* (London: Hamish Hamilton, 1981) describes the search for the lost material. Deborah Hertz's article "The Varnhagen Collection is in Krakow" provides a shorter report: *American Archivist* 44 (1981): 223–28.

23. Quotes from Varnhagen's journals are taken here from original manuscripts in the Jagiellonian Library in Krakow. I thank Dr. Gerhard Ziegengeist for calling these passages to my notice. I also thank the Jagiellonian Library, and especially Elżbieta Burda, the curator of the manuscript department, for access to and help with the documents in the Varnhagen Collection.

24. I thank Dr. Gerhard Ziegengeist, who has done much work on Varnhagen's diaries, for this insight.

25. I thank the Akademie-Archiv for help in accessing the documents, and especially Dr. Klaus Klauß, the Director, for ensuring that I received copies of documents.

26. See the edition *Adelbert v. Chamisso und Helmina v. Chézy: Bruchstücke ihres Briefwechsels,* Julius Petersen and Helmuth Rogge, ed., Mittheilungen aus dem Literaturarchiv in Berlin, N.S. 19 (Berlin: Literaturarchiv-Gesellschaft, 1923); and René Riegel, ed., *Correspondance d'Adalbert de Chamisso: Fragments inédits suivis de Das*

stille Julchen *par Helmina von Chézy* (Paris: Les Éditions Internationales, n.d.). For a study of her relationship with E.T.A. Hoffmann and Jean Paul, see Hans von Müller's work *E. T. A. Hoffmann und Jean Paul, M. Dorffer und C. Richter, Helmine von Chézy und Adelheit von Bassewitz. Ihre Beziehungen zu einander und zu gemeinsamen Bekannten im Rahmen der Zeitgeschichte,* with assistance by Eduard Berend, 1 volume published: *Die Darstellung der Vorgänge bis zu Hoffmanns Verheiratung 1802* (Köln: Gehly, 1927).

27. See Klaus Fischer's article, "Ein Weib mit Hang zum Schlendrian," *Stuttgarter Zeitung* (17 September 1988): Sonntagsbeilage, n.p. Here he adopts the stereotypical portrayal of Chézy as a "vamp," a "woman with a tendency toward sluttiness." The fact that he also calls her "eine der ersten deutschen emanzipierten Frauen" [one of the first German emancipated women] suggests his own bias against independent women in general, which colors the article.

28. See Parsons's introduction to the facsimile reprint of Helmina von Chézy, *Unvergessenes. Denkwürdigkeiten aus dem Leben* (1858), reprint with introduction by Wm. T. Parsons (Collegeville, Pa.: Pennsylvania German Studies Reprint Series #52, 1982). Cited as *Unvergessenes* in the text.

29. Susanne Kord, "'Und drinnen waltet die züchtige Hausfrau'? Caroline Pichler's Fictional Autobiographies," *Women in German Yearbook* 8 (1993): edited by Jeanette Clausen and Sara Friedrichsmeyer (Lincoln: University of Nebraska Press, 1993) 141.

30. The biographical data on Chézy is taken from: Gisela Brinker-Gabler, Karola Ludwig, and Angela Wöffen, *Lexikon deutschsprachiger Schriftstellerinnen 1800–1945* (Munich: dtv, 1986), 52–54; Hertz's book *Jewish High Society in Old Regime Berlin,* 166–71 (see note 4 above), and from Chézy's memoir *Unvergessenes.*

31. Varnhagen Collection, Boxes 65 and 147. I thank Matyáš Bečvárov for help in transcribing these letters.

32. The accusation that Chézy was "vain and worldly" is from Eva Reitz, "Helmine von Chézy," Ph.D. diss., Frankfurt a. M., 1923, 36.

33. Chézy's correspondence with George Sand is an excellent example of how Chézy envisioned her epistolary friendships to grow into published works. Georges Lubin has included ten letters of George Sand to Helmina in the 1991 volume 25 of his edition of George Sand's correspondence: *George Sand, Correspondance: Suppléments (1817–1876),* ed. Georges Lubin (Paris: Classiques Garnier, 1991); 1 June 1835] (244); [15 June 1835] (245); [25 July 1835] (246–48); 1 February [1836] (258–60); [23 May 1836] (274–75); [1 June 1836] (276–77); [10 June 1836] (278–79); 17 July 1836 (280–81); [December 1842] (399–401); [1843] (403–5). Chézy obviously was planning a project on George Sand based on their correspondence. The fact that George Sand's letters to Chézy exist in the original and in copied, edited form in the archives indicates intentions to publish, as does a note that Chézy wrote on her copy of George Sand's final letter in 1843: "Auf die Anfrage ob ich ihre Briefe drucken lassen dürfe antwortete mir George Sand . . . " [Regarding the inquiry as to whether I may publish her letters, George Sand answered me]. The original and a copy of this letter are in the Jagiellonian Library in Krakow, Box 54 in the "Autographen Sammlung." There is also a copy in the Academy Archive. The Academy Archive also holds an interesting manuscript entitled "Lettres sur l'Alsace à George Sand," written as if in preparation for publication.

34. For a biography of Dorothea Schlegel, see Carola Stern, *"Ich möchte mir Flügel wünschen:" Das Leben der Dorothea Schlegel* (Reinbek bei Hamburg: Rowohlt, 1990). For Dorothea's relationship to Helmina in Paris see pages 181–220.

35. Walter, *"Schreib oft, von Mägde Arbeit müde,"* 47–48.

36. Varnhagen Collection, Boxes 227 and 147. I am indepted to Matyáš Bečvárov for his help in transcribing the letters.

37. The first volume of Raich's 1881 edition *Dorothea v. Schlegel geb. Mendelssohn und deren Söhne Johannes und Philipp Veit*, 2 vols. (Mainz: Verlag von Franz Kirchheim, 1881) includes Dorothea's letters to Helmina [Paris 1804] (22–23); [Köln 1804] (23–25); and 19 September [1804] (25–32). Wieneke's 1914 edition *Caroline und Dorothea Schlegel in Briefen* (Weimar: Gustav Kiepenheuer, 1914) contains Dorothea's letters to Helmina from 25 August [1802] (353–55); [Paris 1803/4] (361–62); [Paris 1803/4] (362); 8 June [1804] (367–69); excerpts from the letter of 19 September [1804] (370–71); excerpt from the letter of 28 October 1804 (373–74); [Ende 1804] (375–76); excerpt from the letter from Köln [1805?] (376–77); [Ende 1809] (412–14); 15 April 1810 (414–19); [25 October 1823] (528); excerpt from the letter of 25 Feb. 1829 (535–36). Körner's 1926 collection, *Briefe von und an Friedrich und Dorothea Schlegel*, contains Helmine's letter to Dorothea 2 May 1818 (214–18) and Dorothea to Helmine 8/9 January 1835 (352–53). Körner's three-volume *Krisenjahre der Frühromantik: Briefe aus dem Schlegelkreis* (Bern: Francke Verlag, 1969) contains Dorothea's letter to Helmina from Cologne, 12 June [1804] (108–9). The *Kritische Friedrich-Schlegel Ausgabe* contains Helmine's letter to Dorothea from 2 May 1818 (29. Band, III Abteilung).

38. Raich, *Dorothea v. Schlegel*, 23–24.

39. See the letter of 28 October 1804, excerpted in Wieneke, *Caroline und Dorothea Schlegel* (273–74) and another 1804 Cologne letter in Raich (23–25). Neither Raich nor Wieneke includes Dorothea's letter from Cologne on 12 June 1804, which Körner later publishes, a letter in which Dorothea asks Helmina to send her some personal belongings they have left in Paris. (*Krisenjahre*, 108–9).

40. Raich, *Dorothea v. Schlegel*, 32.

41. Wieneke, *Caroline und Dorothea Schlegel*, 353–55.

42. Raich, *Dorothea v. Schlegel*, 23.

43. In her *Unvergessenes*, Chézy talks about the Merlin publication as being a collaborative effort between her and Dorothea Schlegel (I: 169).

44. The reference to Lavaillière is in the unpublished part of the letter from Cologne in 1804 in Raich, pp. 23–24.

45. See footnote 43 above about the Merlin story. Chézy also talks about Schlegel publishing "Geschichte des Grafen Gerhard von Revers und der schönen und tugendhaften Prinzessin Euryanthe von Savoyen, seiner Geliebten" under his name, when she also really did the translation (*Unvergessenes* I: 169).

46. Raich, *Dorothea v. Schlegel*, 23.

47. Passage edited out of the letter of 25 February 1829 in Wieneke, *Caroline und Dorothea Schlegel*, 535–36.

48. Wieneke, *Caroline und Dorothea Schlegel*, 536.

49. This letter did not appear in either Raich's or Wieneke's collection, but rather later in Josef Körner, ed., *Briefe von und an Friedrich und Dorothea Schlegel* (Berlin: Askanischer Verlag Carl Albert Kinkle), 535–36.

50. See, for example, her defense of Sophie Mereau and Karoline von Günderrode against Tieck's hostile remarks (*Unvergessenes* II: 101).

51. For an account of Amalie Struve's letters from the United States to Chézy, see my paper "Travelers' Visions/Immigrants' Realities: Amalie Struve and Amalie Schoppe in the United States", MLA Conference, Chicago, 1990. From materials in the Varnhagen Collection and in the Academy Archive, Irina Hundt and I are preparing a publication of documents connected with Chézy's relationship with Bettine von Ar-

nim, including Chézy's unpublished manuscript entitled "An die Günderrode" and the correspondence that Chézy sent to Bettine von Arnim.

52. Kord, in Appendices A and B of her *Ein Blick hinter die Kulissen: Deutschsprachige Dramatikerinnen im 18. und 19. Jahrhundert* (Stuttgart: Metzler, 1992), includes a complete list of Pichler's works and biographical material .

53. See Kord's article "Caroline Pichler's Fictional Auto/Biographies" for analysis of Pichler's friendship with other women and the influence that friendship had on her and her friends' works.

54. Varnhagen Collection, Box 142. I again thank Matyáš Bečvárov for helping to transcribe these letters.

55. Kord's essay "'Und drinnen waltet die züchtige Hausfrau'? Caroline Pichler's Fictional Auto/Biographies" questions this view.

56. Varnhagen Collection, Box 142. The letter has no date or place.

57. Varnhagen Collection, Boxes 147, 230, and 241.

58. Varnhagen, Box 230.

# Chapter 4: "Thousand Lives, Thousand Forms": Letter Writing and Publication

1. Sophie Mereau, *Amanda und Eduard*, cited in Dagmar von Gersdorff, *"Dich zu lieben kann ich nicht verlernen": Das Leben der Sophie Brentano-Mereau* (Frankfurt a.M.: Insel, 1984), 377.

2. Janet Gurkin Altman, *Epistolarity. Approaches to a Form* (Columbus: Ohio State University Press, 1982).

3. Leonore Hoffmann, Introduction to *Women's Personal Narratives: Essays in Criticism and Pedagogy*, Leonore Hoffmann and Margo Culley, ed. (New York: The Modern Language Association of America, 1985), 1.

4. James Olney, *Metaphors of Self: The Meaning of Autobiography* (Princeton: Princeton University Press, 1972).

5. See Bovenschen, *Die imaginierte Weiblichkeit*; Becker-Cantarino, "Leben als Text: Briefe im 18. Jahrhundert;" and Frederiksen, "Die Frau als Autorin zur Zeit der Romantik."

6. Lydia Schieth, *Die Entwicklung des deutschen Frauenromans im ausgehenden 18. Jahrhundert* (Frankfurt a. M.: Peter Lang, 1987).

7. Ibid., 245, n77.

8. Bovenschen, *Die imaginierte Weiblichkeit*, 211.

9. For Therese Huber, see Leuschner's essay, "Therese Huber als Briefschreiberin," in Helga Gallas and Magdalene Heuser, ed., *Untersuchungen zum Roman von Frauen um 1800*. Untersuchungen zur deutschen Literaturgeschichte 55 (Tübingen: Niemeyer, 1990), 203–12, which advocates including Huber's letters with any critical edition of her works. She would title such an edition *Briefe und Werke* to emphasize the equally significant role of letters. Dawson's essay on Sophie Albrecht focuses on the previously unknown connections that Albrecht cultivated with other women through correspondence: Ruth Dawson, "Reconstructing Women's Literary Relationships: Sophie Albrecht and Female Friendships," Goodman and Waldstein, *In the Shadow of Olympus*, 173–87.

10. Anna Louisa Karsch, *Die Karschin: Friedrich des Grossen Volksdichterin. Ein Leben in Briefen*, Elisabeth Hausmann, ed. (Frankfurt a.M.: Societäts-Verlag, 1933). Quotes from Karsch's letters come from this edition, which in the chapter will be cited by page number and otherwise as "Hausmann" with page number.

11. Karsch, Anna Louisa, *Auserlesene Gedichte* (1764), rpt. with an afterword by Alfred Anger (Stuttgart: Metzler, 1966).

12. *Gedichte, von Anna Louisa Karschin geb. Dürbach*, ed. C. L. von Klenke, 2 ed. (Berlin: F. Maurer, 1797).

13. All quotes here are from Hausmann's edition, cited as Hausmann with page numbers. Here the quote is on page 13. Recent editions of select letters include those by Gerhard Wolf, ed., *"O, mir entwischt nicht, was die Menschen fühlen:" Anna Louisa Karschin: Gedichte und Briefe; Stimmen der Zeitgenossen* (Berlin: Der Morgen, 1981); and Barbara Beuys, ed., *Herzgedanken: Das Leben der "deutschen Sappho" von ihr selbst erzählt* (Frankfurt a. M.: Societäts-Verlag, 1981). Regina Nörtemann and Ute Pott are working on a new edition of the correspondence between Karsch and Gleim (see the exhibition catalogue *Anna Louisa Karsch (1722–1791): Dichterin für Liebe, Brot und Vaterland. Ausstellung zum 200. Todestag 10. Oktober bis 16. November 1991* (Berlin: Staatsbibliothek Preußischer Kulturbesitz, 1991), 13).

14. Katherine Goodman, *Dis/Closures: Women's Autobiography in Germany Between 1790 and 1914* (New York: Peter Lang, 1986), 77.

15. Wolf, Afterword to "*O, mir entwischt nicht*," 281.

16. Scholars seem divided over how conscious Karsch was of class and gender oppression. Reinhard Nickisch, in his 1976 article on women letter writers in the Enlightenment, finds Karsch's letters lacking in an awareness of the social-economic causes of her position and of the submissive position of the woman. Thus, he deems her letters not interesting as social-historical documents, but rather as examples of how a lower-class individual could participate fully in the eighteenth-century epistolary cult, one of the largest intellectual activities of the bourgeoisie ("Die Frau als Briefschreiberin," 51). It is interesting to note that Nickisch does not include analysis of Karsch's letters in his later article on the same subject, "Briefkultur," in Brinker–Gabler's *Deutsche Literatur von Frauen*. In contrast, in the catalogue from the 1991 exhibition to commemorate two hundred years after Karsch's death, Beate Frilling and Gisela Staupe write in their foreword that from her letters we gain insight into the thoughts and reception of a female poet's existence in the middle of the eighteenth century (see footnote 13 above, page 8).

17. Wolf, "*O, mir entwischt nicht*," 299–300.

18. Cited in Hausmann, 73.

19. Wolf, "*O, mir entwischt nicht*," 294.

20. It is noteworthy that until the 1980s, the only correspondence of Mereau that was printed or reprinted systematically was that to Brentano and Schiller. Some letters to and from Mereau have been published rather haphazardly in other editions and articles, such as in Amelung's edition *Briefwechsel zwischen Clemens Brentano und Sophie Mereau. Nach den in der Königlichen Bibliothek zu Berlin befindlichen Handschriften zum ersten Mal herausgegeben*, ed. Heinz Amelung, 2 vols. (Leipzig: Insel, 1908).

21. See Weigel's treatment in her essay "Der schielende Blick;" also: Christa Bürger, "'Die mittlere Sphäre': Sophie Mereau—Schriftstellerin im Klassischen Weimar," Brinker-Gabler, ed., *Deutsche Literatur von Frauen*, vol. 1: 366–88; Helene M. Kastinger Riley, *Die weibliche Muse: Sechs Essays über künstlerisch schaffende Frauen der Goethezeit*, Studies in German Literature, Linguistics, and Culture 8 (Columbia, S.C.: Camden House, 1986), 55–88; and Uta Treder, "Sophie Mereau: Montage und Demontage einer Liebe," in Gallas and Heuser, *Untersuchungen zum Roman*, 172–83; Dagmar von Gersdorff's biography *"Dich zu lieben kann ich nicht verlernen"* and her edition of Mereau's correspondence with Clemens Brentano; Katharina von Hammerstein's *Sophie Mereau-Brentano: Freiheit—Liebe—Weiblichkeit. Tricolore sozialer und*

*individueller Selbstbestimmung um 1800* (Heidelberg: Universitätsverlag C. Winter, 1994); and Uta Fleischmann's book *Zwischen Aufbruch und Anpassung: Untersuchungen zu Werk und Leben der Sophie Mereau* (Frankfurt a. M.: Peter Lang, 1989). I thank Katharina von Hammerstein for bibliographical information on Mereau.

22. See bibliographies in Gersdorff, *"Dich zu lieben,"* and Kastinger Riley, *Die weibliche Muse.*

23. *Zeitung für Einsiedler*, ed. by L. Achim von Arnim, Nr. 19 (4. Juni 1808); and *Trost Einsamkeit*, book publication of the same (Heidelberg: Mohr & Zimmer, 1808), 149–51. I am indebted to Kastinger Riley for this information (59; 190).

24. The correspondence between Mereau and Schiller is still published in Friedrich Schiller, *Werke. Nationalausgabe* (Weimar: Böhlau, 1972), Vols. 31; 35; 36/I; 37/II; and 38/I.

25. Treder's article, "Sophie Mereau," confirms previous speculation.

26. Schiller to Goethe, 30 June 1797, in Schiller, *Werke. Nationalausgabe*, 29:93.

27. Karl August Varnhagen von Ense. *Aus dem Nachlaß Varnhagen von Enses. Tagebücher.* Ed. by Ludmilla Assing. 14 vols. (Leipzig, 1861–1870), 13: 147.

28. Gersdorff includes passages from letters by Schubart, Ahlefeld, Imhoff, Rudolpi, and Kipp in her biography of Mereau. The documentation in this biography, however, is very inconsistent, sometimes listing where documents are located, sometimes not. Nowhere does Gersdorff mention that the Varnhagen Collection is in the Jagiellonian Library in Krakow. Fleischmann and Treder have published passages from Mereau's correspondence with Kipp (see footnote 21 above).

29. Schlaffer, "Weibliche Geschichtsschreibung," 259–60.

30. Weigel, "Der schielende Blick," 95.

31. Treder, "Sophie Mereau," 172–83.

32. Bürger, *Leben Schreiben*, 387.

33. The original correspondence between Mereau and Kipp is in the Varnhagen Collection, Box 122. I am indebted to Treder and Fleischmann, whose studies contain passages from the Mereau/Kipp correspondence from which to compare my own transcriptions, when necessary. I include the date of each letter for reference in parentheses.

34. The original correspondence between Mereau and Brentano is in the Varnhagen Collection, Box 35 (under Brentano's name!). The first edition of these letters was edited by Heinz Amelung, *Briefwechsel zwischen Clemens Brentano und Sophie Mereau: Nach den in der Königlichen Bibliothek zu Berlin befindlichen Handschriften zum ersten Mal herausgegeben*, 2 vols. (Leipzig: Insel, 1908). Gersdorff reexamined the original letters for her edition, which appeared in 1981. I will cite from Gersdorff's edition, referred to as Brentano/Mereau with page number.

35. Gersdorff, *"Dich zu lieben,"* 69.

36. "Vergangenheit" appeared in *Musen-Almanach für das Jahr 1796*; "Erinnerung und Phantasie" in *Musen-Almanach für das Jahr 1796*; and "Bergphantasie" in *Damen-Calender auf das Jahr 1798.*

37. "Schwarzberg" appeared in *Die Horen* III: 9, 1795.

38. "Schwermuth" appeared in *Damen-Calender auf das Jahr 1798.*

39. The letter is undated; Fleischmann suggests Winter 1795.

40. Adelheid Hang, "Sophie Mereau in ihren Bezichungen fur Romantik," (Ph.D. diss., Frankfurt, a. M., 1934). Fleischmann, *Zwischen Aufbruch und Anpassung.*

41. There is no date on the letter. Fleischmann suspects late autumn 1796 (71).

42. Kastinger Riley, *Die weibliche Muse*, 55–88.

43. See Kastinger Riley's interpretation of two other poems that follow in the correspondence (*Die weibliche Muse*, 67–71).

44. Sophie Mereau, "Flucht nach der Hauptstadt," *Taschenbuch auf das Jahr 1806* (Frankfurt, a. M. Wilmans, 1806), 159.

45. Ibid., 184.

46. For descriptions of such conditions see Kord's study *Ein Blick hinter die Kulissen.*

47. Kord includes a nineteenth-century contract between a theater director and his actors in which one clause written specifically for actresses stipulates that the director will provide only the male costumes as needed; the women must procure their own female costumes (*Ein Blick hinter die Kulissen,* 28).

48. Sophie Mereau, ed., *Kalathiskos,* 2 vols. (1801–2); facsimile with afterword by Peter Schmidt, Heidelberg: Lamberg Schneider, 1968), 2:60.

49. In translating Bettine von Arnim's *Günderode* into English and writing essays for *The Dial,* Margaret Fuller recognized the "wild graces of style" in Günderrode's and Arnim's works; see her essay "Bettine Brentano and her Friend Günderode," *The Dial* 7 (Jan. 1842): 313–57. The correct spelling of Günderrode's name is with two r's. Bettine von Arnim spelled it incorrectly with only one in the title of her book.

50. The story of the letters is in Christa Wolf's account, "Der Schatten eine Traumes," *Der Schatten eines Traumes* (Darmstadt: Luchterhand, 1981), 37; 47.

51. See editions by Preitz and Preisendanz of the correspondence with Creuzer, Savigny, and other men: Karl Preisendanz, ed., *Die Liebe der Günderode. Friedrich Creuzers Briefe an Caroline von Günderode* (Munich: Piper, 1912); Max Preitz, "Karoline von Günderrode in ihrer Umwelt. I. Briefe von Lisette und Gottfried Nees von Esenbeck, Karoline von Günderrode, Friedrich Creuzer, Clemens Brentano und Susanne von Heyden," *Jahrbuch des Freien Deutschen Hochstifts* (1962): 208–306; Max Preitz, "Karoline von Günderrode in ihrer Umwelt. II. Karoline von Günderrodes Briefwechsel mit Friedrich Karl und Gunda von Savigny," *Jahrbuch des Freien Deutschen Hochstifts* (1964): 185–235; Max Preitz, ed., *Friedrich Schlegel und Novalis: Biographie einer Romantikerfreundschaft in ihren Briefen* (Darmstadt: Hermann Gentner Verlag, 1957); Max Preitz and Doris Hopp, "Karoline von Günderrode in ihrer Umwelt. III. Karoline von Günderrodes Studienbuch," *Jahrbuch des Freien Deutschen Hochstifts* (1975), 223–323.

52. For Günderrode, see Wolf, "Der Schatten eines Traumes;" for Mereau see Gersdorff, "Dich zu lieben."

53. Karoline von Günderrode. *Sämtliche Werke.* 3 Vols. Ed. Walter Morgenthaler with contributions from Karin Obermeier and Marianne Graf (Frankfurt/Basel: Stroemfeld/Roter Stern, 1991). (See Chapter 1, Note 65 above.)

54. Karoline von Günderrode, *"Ich sende Dir ein zärtliches Pfand": Die Briefe der Karoline von Günderrode,* Birgit Weißenborn, ed. (Frankfurt a. M.: Insel, 1992). The volume is important not only for presenting the most extensive collection of Günderrode's letters to date, but also for allowing us to see the shortfalls of previous editions. When possible, Weißenborn has examined original letters and published from those. She includes eleven previously unpublished letters. Her stress is on chronology and exchange of letters, and thus she includes relevant letters from Günderrode and her circle of relatives and acquaintances. She also documents where the letters are located. The collection is just a selection though, and unfortunately Weißenborn does not explain criteria for that selection nor for the omission of passages from letters. She has also modernized the orthography and corrected spelling, which often changes the character of the letters. For this reason, I cite from Wolf's edition *Der Schatten eines Traumes,* appearing as *Schatten* with page numbers, unless otherwise noted. Günderrode's orthography and punctuation are frequently incorrect so that I have omitted "sic" for ease of reading.

55. Margarete Lazarowicz, *Karoline von Günderrode: Portrait einer Fremden* (Frankfurt a. M.: Peter Lang, 1986).

56. Ibid., 279.

57. Robert Prutz, *Die deutsche Literatur der Gegenwart 1849–1858* (Leipzig: Voigt & Gunther, 1859), 189.

58. Weißenborn, *Briefe der Karoline von Günderrode*, 19–20; Lazarowicz, *Karoline von Günderrode*, 279.

59. Translated by Marjanne E. Goozé in Blackwell and Zantop, *Bitter Healing*, 424.

60. See Kastinger Riley's interpretation of Günderrode's story here (*Die weibliche Muse*, 101–2).

61. See Worley's article on Sophie von LaRoche's travel journals for more insights: "Sophie von LaRoche's *Reisejournale:* Reflections of a Traveling Subject," Friedrichsmeyer and Becker-Cantarino, *The Enlightenment and its Legacy*, 91–103.

62. Sara Friedrichsmeyer, "Women's Writing and the Construct of an Integrated Self," Friedrichsmeyer and Becker-Cantarino, *The Enlightenment and its Legacy*, 171–80.

63. Weigel, "Der schielende Blick," 83–137.

## Chapter 5: An Aesthetics of Letter Writing: Caroline Schlegel-Schelling and Rahel Varnhagen

1. The problem of names arises particularly in the cases of these two women. For the sake of diversity, I have opted to refer to them by many names, mostly to draw attention to the many identities they assumed. I use their first names most often, for that is the way they frequently signed their letters, and that is the name by which they were most commonly known. Although neither ever used a hyphenated form of her last name, I use that in cases to refer to their lives and works in general. I also refer to them by their last name only, using the maiden name or their married names, depending on what name they were going by at the time of the reference.

2. Isselstein published this previously unpublished quote in her essay "Rahels Schriften I. Karl August Varnhagens editorische Tätigkeit nach Dokumenten seines Archivs," Barbara Hahn and Ursula Isselstein, ed., *Rahel Levin Varnhagen: Die Wiederentdeckung einer Schriftstellerin*, Zeitschrift für Literaturwissenschaft und Linguistik Beiheft 14 (Göttingen: Vandenhoek and Ruprecht, 1987), 18 n5 (see Chapter 1, n63 above).

3. Rahel Varnhagen, *Gesammelte Werke*, ed. Konrad Feilchenfeldt, Uwe Schweikert, and Rahel E. Steiner (Munich: Matthes and Seitz, 1983), IV.2: 29. Hereafter citations from this collection will appear in parentheses as *GW* with volume and page number. As with Karoline von Günderrode's letters, Rahel's orthography and punctuation are so irregular that I have omitted "sic" for ease of reading. The same will be true for Caroline Schlegel-Schelling.

4. See Rahel's letter to Karl August on 30 October 1808 (*GW* IV.1: 89) and his letters to her on 28 October 1808 (*GW* IV.1: 84) and 24 October 1809 (*GW* IV.1: 79).

5. The translation for the major part of this quote, with some additions and modifications from me, comes from Katherine Goodman in her book *Dis/Closures*, 221–22.

6. Early studies, such as Tanneberger's *Die Frauen der Romantik und das soziale Problem* and Susman's *Frauen der Romantik*, portray her as not publishing anything. Later studies, such as Hannah Arendt's biography, saw her works as existing solely in edited versions by Karl Varnhagen and his niece Ludmilla Assing: *Rahel Varnhagen:*

*Lebensgeschichte einer deutschen Jüdin aus der Romantik*, 1959 (Munich: R. Piper & Co. Verlag, 1983). Most recent research stresses Rahel's own participation in the editing process. See in particular Ursula Isselstein's article "Rahels Schriften I," in Hahn and Isselstein, eds., Rahel Levin Varnhagen, 16–29, and Hahn's book *"Antworten Sie mir!"*

7. See Hahn's *"Antworten Sie mir!"* for a bibliography of those publications (223–24).

8. Rahel Varnhagen, *Briefe an eine Freundin: Rahel Varnhagen an Rebecca Friedländer*, Deborah Hertz, ed. (Cologne: Kiepenheuer and Witsch, 1988), 109; hereafter cited as *Briefe an eine Freundin* in parentheses with page numbers.

9. Caroline Schlegel-Schelling, *Caroline. Briefe aus der Frühromantik*, Erich Schimdt, ed., revised and enlarged by Georg Waitz, 2 vols. (Leipzig: Insel, 1913), I: 511. Citations from this volume with appear as *Caroline* with volume and page number.

10. Bovenschen, *Die imaginierte Weiblichkeit*, 216.

11. Frederiksen, "Die Frau als Autorin zur Zeit der Romantik," 99.

12. See Doris Starr Guilloton's article on Rahel Varnhagen; Gisela Dischner's book, *Caroline und der Jenaer Kreis: Ein Leben zwischen bürgerlicher Vereinzelung und romantischer Geselligkeit* (Berlin: Wagenbach, 1979); and Friedrichsmeyer's article "Caroline Schlegel-Schelling: 'A Good Woman, and No Heroine'," Goodman and Waldstein, ed., *In the Shadow of Olympus*, 115–36.

13. Dischner fits Caroline Schlegel-Schelling's life and letters into the notion of the "Geselligkeit" underlying the writings and theories of German Romantics. Dischner uses mostly male models though, especially Friedrich Schlegel, Friedrich Schleiermacher, Novalis, and Fichte, as the ones defining the ideas of community. Her very positive stance towards the men's theories prevents a more critical look at their views toward women and lacks a constructive analysis of the women who actually defined and enacted many of the community values.

14. Patricia Meyer Spacks, *Gossip* .

15. Ibid., 11.

16. Ibid., 11.

17. Ibid., 77.

18. Ibid.

19. Ibid., 18–19.

20. Eckart Kleßmann gives examples of the pejorative names Schlegel-Schelling acquired: *Caroline: Das Leben der Caroline Michaelis-Böhmer-Schlegel-Schelling 1763–1809* (Munich: Deutscher Taschenbuch Verlag, 1979), 250–58.

21. Frederiksen, "Die Frau als Autorin zur Zeit der Romantik," 99–101.

22. Rahel Varnhagen and Pauline Wiesel, *"Ein jeder machte seine Frau aus mir wie er sie liebte und verlangte": Ein Briefwechsel*, Marlis Gerhardt, ed. (Darmstadt: Luchterhand, 1987), 42. Cited hereafter as Varnhagen/Wiesel in parentheses with page numbers.

23. Friedrichsmeyer, "Caroline Schlegel-Schelling," 122–23.

24. See Heidi Thomann Tewarson's article "Jüdisches—Weibliches: Rahel Levin Varnhagens Reisen als Überschreitungen," *German Quarterly* 66.2 (Spring 1993): 145–59.

25. Cited in Katja Behrens, ed., *Frauenbriefe der Romantik* (Frankfurt a. M.: Insel, 1981), 335.

26. See expecially Brentano/Mereau, 87.

27. Elaine Showalter, *The Female Malady: Women, Madness, and English Culture, 1830–1980* (New York: Penguin, 1985).

28. Friedrichsmeyer, "Caroline Schlegel-Schelling," 126.

29. Friedrichsmeyer, "Caroline Schlegel-Schelling," 126.

30. Ibid., 124.

31. See Dale Spender's article "An Alternative to Madonna: How to deal with 'I'm not a feminist, but . . . ,'" *MS* IV.1 (July/August 1993): 44–45. I thank Diane Young for calling this article to my attention.

32. In the chapter on Rahel Varnhagen's letters with Pauline Wiesel, Hahn quotes from Rahel's last testament to Karl August, in which she asks that he return Wiesel's letters to her and tell her that Rahel remains her friend and was never angry with her (*"Antworten Sie mir,"* 101).

33. See Barbara Hahn's *Unter falschem Namen: Von der schwierigen Autorschaft der Frauen*, Gender Studies (Frankfurt a. M.: Suhrkamp, 1991), 24–32; and Hannah Arendt's *Rahel Varnhagen*, 107. For a different interpretation, see Deborah Hertz's article "Inside Assimilation: Rebecca Friedländer's Rahel Varnhagen," Joeres and Maynes, ed. *German Women in the Eighteenth and Nineteenth Centuries*, 271–88. With due respect to Hertz's rereading and her thorough research on a long-forgotten correspondence, her polarization of the issues contradicts the ambiguous messages the letters send forth.

34. Hahn observes how Rahel manifests her anger through the powerful act of naming—the two spots in which Rahel actually calls Friedländer by her name is when she talks about the new public dimension their relationship has assumed (*Unter falschem Namen*, 28–29).

35. See Hahn's article "'Nur wir sind gleich bey der Ungleichheit': Der Briefwechsel von Rahel Levin Varnhagen und Pauline Wiesel," in Hahn and Isselstein, *Rahel Levin Varnhagen*, 56–66; and the chapter "Pauline Wiesel: 'Eine hätte die Natur aus uns beiden machen sollen'" in her book *"Antworten Sie mir!"* (101–27).

36. Cited in Hahn's essay "Nur wir sind gleich bey der Ungleichheit," in Hahn and Isselstein, *Rahel Levin Varnhagen*, 65.

37. Ibid., 64.

38. Ibid., 64.

## Chapter 6: Storytelling and Poetry in Letters: Bettine von Arnim's *Goethes Briefwechsel mit einem Kinde* and *Die Günderode*

1. Gustav von Loeper, in the *Allgemeine Deutsche Biographie* (Berlin: Duncker & Humblot, 1875), 578–82, finds the "Ewig-Weibliche" (581) in Bettine von Arnim's literary and political works, stating that she displayed her feminine desires in her work with the oppressed lower classes (580). He explains his definition of "femininity" as strength of emotions and enthusiasm but weakness of logical and clear thought (581). He also views her consistent reliance on the letter form as "typically feminine." But the "feminine" entails onesidedness and a lack of historical context (581), characteristics that question the aesthetic and historical value of women's letters in general. Moritz Carriere classifies Bettine's later political works and activities, which would have placed her outside of the traditional view of women as domestic hearthkeepers, as truly "feminine," in that politics, like her poetry and music, affected her personally (259): "Bettina von Arnim," *Lebensbilder* (Leipzig: Brockhaus, 1890), 226–75. Even as late as 1960, Gustav Konrad, in his afterword to Bettine's collected works, praises Loeper's and Carriere's descriptions because both men had recognized what was "feminine" about her literary character: Bettina von

Arnim, *Werke und Briefe*, ed. Gustav Konrad, 4 vols. (Frechen: Bartmann Verlag, 1958–1963); *Briefe*, ed. Johannes Müller, vol. 5 (Frechen: Bartmann Verlag, 1961), 1: 560. For this reason, Konrad even prefers Loeper's entry in the *ADB* over the more recent entry in *NDB* by Kluckhohn. Julius Petersen and Helmuth Rogge, in their forword to the 1923 edition of Helmina von Chézy's correspondence with Adelbert von Chamisso, see Bettine von Arnim, Caroline von Wolzogen, editor of Schiller's letters, and Amöne Otto, editor of Jean Paul's letters, as belonging, in a negative way, to a tradition of women editors who followed their own interests when editing personal correspondence and thus had no sense of scrupulous editing criteria (4). To this list, Petersen and Rogge add Chézy because of the editorial license she took when she included passages from her correspondence with Chamisso in her autobiography. See: Chézy, *Bruchstücke ihres Briefwechsels* (see Chapter 3, note 26).

2. Elisabeth Lenk, "Indiscretions of the Literary Beast: Pariah Consciousness of Women Writers Since Romanticism," trans. Maureen Krause, *New German Critique* 27 (Fall 1982): 103. Georg Gottfried Gervinus, for example, views Bettine von Arnim as standing both inside what he characterizes as a not-very-distinguised tradition of women's writing while also separating herself from that tradition: *Ueber den Goetheischen Briefwechsel* (Leipzig: Friedrich Engelmann, 1836), 160.

3. See Joseph von Eichendorff "Die deutsche Salon-Poesie der Frauen," *Schriften zur Literatur*, vol. 3 of his *Werke*, 4 vols. (Munich: Winkler Verlag, 1970), 87–101. Eichendorff introduces his account of Bettine's works in his essay by condemning any kind of female creativity (90). He then explains how he, too, perceives Bettine as an anomaly because she challenged what he viewed as the "natural feminine limitations" that constrained many other women from publishing their emotions openly under their own name during their lifetime (90). He does not elevate Bettine to a position higher than that which he gives to other women, mostly because he criticizes her writing as ultimately displaying the traditional "female" characteristics, although he does not clearly define what these characteristics may be (90). See also Karl Barthel, *Deutsche Nationalliteratur der Neuzeit in einer Reihe von Vorlesungen*, 4th ed. (Braunschweig: Verlag der Hofbuchhandlung von Eduard Leibrock, 1855). For Barthel, whose widely read lectures on literary history underwent ten editions from 1850 to 1903, Arnim's unique position as a publishing woman causes her to stand out negatively among women, for in stepping into the public literary market she overstepped boundaries of feminine behavior (562).

4. See, for example, Ernst Alker, *Die deutsche Literatur im 19. Jahrhundert* (Stuttgart: Kröner, 1969). For Alker, Arnim stands out among women (63). His classification of Arnim as "outstanding," however, is undermined by his derision of her female contemporaries as idle gossipers (63). To Susmann and Nickisch, Arnim elevated herself above other women because she dared to publish her own letters in book form (Susmann, *Frauen der Romantik*, 109; Nickisch, "Die Frau als Briefschreiberin," 58). In contrast, according to Nickisch, women such as Rahel Varnhagen, Caroline Schlegel-Schelling, and Henriette Herz created no literary works with their letters and thus never posed any threat to the male-dominated literary and scholarly realm (58).

5. I refer here to the title of Kantorowicz's abridged edition of *Goethes Briefwechsel mit einem Kinde*, called *Du wunderliches Kind: Bettine und Goethe. Aus dem Briefwechsel zwischen Goethe und Bettine von Arnim* (Schwerin: Petermänken-Verlag, 1953). It is true that one must consider that Bettine labeled herself a child in her correspondence with Goethe and that she even encouraged Goethe to refer to her as "Du wunderliches Kind" [you strange child]. Very surprising, however, is the number of scholars who apply the adjective "childish" to describe other works by Arnim without trying to understand the *mythos* that Arnim was originally creating in her

letters to Goethe. See also: Ludwig Börne, "Goethes Briefwechsel mit einem Kinde. Geschrieben in Auteuil bei Paris im Sommer 1835," *Gesammelte Schriften*, 12 vols. in 4 (Vienna: Tendler & Comp., 1868) 6: 115–28; Carriere, "Bettina von Arnim;" Rudolph Gottschall, *Die deutsche Nationalliteratur in der ersten Hälfte des neunzehnten Jahrhunderts* (Breslau: Trewendt & Granier, 1855); Gutzkow, *Ausgewählte Werke*; and Heinrich Treitschke, *Deutsche Geschichte im Neunzehnten Jahrhundert*, 5 vols. (Leipzig: Verlag G. Hirzel, 1889). The portrayal these nineteenth-century literary historians give of Bettina as remaining an eternal child has persisted into more recent accounts of Bettine's life and work by Gustav Konrad, who claims that even as a mature woman she lived according to the "mute and unexplainable secrets of childhood": "Bettine von Arnim," *Deutsche Dichter der Romantik*, ed. Benno von Wiese (Munich: E. Schmidt, 1971), 310–40. See also Werner Milch, who states that Bettine experienced no development, and that from her youngest years her personality had already been formed: *Die junge Bettine 1785–1811*, Peter Küpper, ed. (Heidelberg: Lothar Stiehm Verlag, 1968), 52. For a very recent excellent examination of the child *mythos*, see Konstanze Bäumer's study on Bettine von Arnim: *"Bettine, Psyche, Mignon" Bettina von Arnim und Goethe*, Stuttgarter Arbeiten zur Germanistik 139 (Stuttgart: Akademischer Verlag, 1986).

    6. Leopold Ranke, *Das Briefwerk*, Walther Peter Fuchs, ed. (Hamburg: Hoffmann and Campe Verlag, 1949), 106.

    7. Karl Gutzkow, *Ausgewählte Werke*, Heinrich Huber Houben, ed. 12 vols. (Leipzig: Max Hesse Verlag, 1908), 12: 116.

    8. I cannot say exactly who coined this term for Bettine, but it lived on in scholarship, such as in Klara Fuhrimann's article in 1965 entitled "Kobold der Romantik: Bettina von Arnim," *Das Wort: Literarische Beilage zu 'Du-Atlantis'* 10 (1965): 795–96.

    9. Alker, for example, begins his entry on Bettine von Arnim with "the Romantic's wife and Clemens Brentano's hot-blooded sister" (*Die deutsche Literatur*, 63). Werner Milch's discussion of Goethe's relationship to Sophie von LaRoche, Maxe Brentano, and Bettine von Arnim in his essay "Goethe und die Brentanos" stresses Goethe's central position within this circle of women and does not let the women's accomplishments stand on their own: *Kleine Schriften zur Literatur-und Geistesgeschichte*, Gerhard Burkhardt, ed., Deutsche Akademie für Sprache und Dichtung 10 (Heidelberg, Darmstadt: Lambert Schneider, 1957), 145–55. Further, the number of articles that examine Bettine von Arnim's relation to Goethe outnumber articles on Bettine's other works combined. In nineteenth-century literary histories by Gottschall, Proelß, and Treitschke and in twentieth-century articles by Faber du Faur and Kelling it seems to be a great "literary" question whether Goethe really loved Bettine, or whether Bettine's love remained unrequited; see: Gottschall, *Die deutsche Nationalliteratur*; Johannes Proelss, "Rahel, Bettina und die Stieglitz," *Das junge Deutschland. Ein Buch deutscher Geistesgeschichte* (Stuttgart: Cotta, 1892), 454–534; Heinrich Treitschke, *Deutsche Geschichte im Neunzehnten Jahrhundert*, 5 vols. (Leipzig: Verlag G. Hirzel, 1889); Curt von Faber du Faur, "Goethe und Bettina von Arnim: Ein neuer Fund," *PMLA* 75 (1960): 216–30; and Hans-Wilhelm Kelling, "The Idolatry of Poetic Genius in *Goethes Briefwechsel mit einem Kinde*," *Publications of the English Goethe Society* 39 (1969): 16–30.

    10. Christine Touallion, "Frauendichtung," *Reallexikon der deutschen Literaturgeschichte*, Paul Merker and Wolfgang Stammler, ed., 1st ed. (Berlin: Walter de Gruyter & Co., 1925–26), 1: 374–76. Konrad, too, shares this opinion when he states that Bettine's personality left more of an impact than her works ("Bettine von Arnim," 311).

11. The Freies Deutsches Hochstift in Frankfurt on the Main and the Goethe-Museum in Düsseldorf commemorated the occasion with an extensive exhibit of manuscripts, letters, art works, and first editions of Arnim's works. For a catalogue of the exhibit, see *Herzhaft in die Dornen der Zeit Greifen ... Bettine von Arnim 1785–1859*, Christoph Perels, ed. (Frankfurt a. M.: Freies Deutsches Hochstift—Frankfurter Goethe Museum, 1985). The 1985 Conference of the Modern Language Association included two sessions on Arnim, comprising a total of eight papers that treated a diversity of subjects such as Bettine's later political and social works, her fairy tales, and her works in relation to other authors. The papers given during the Chicago MLA Convention were part of the session entitled "Bettina von Arnim and Her Circle" on Sunday, 29 December 1985, and the session "Bettina von Arnim in Social, Historical, and Literary Context" on Monday, 30 December.

12. I refer to Schulz's edition of the correspondence between Bettine von Arnim and the Grimm brothers: Bettine von Arnim and Jacob and Wilhelm Grimm, *Der Briefwechsel Bettine von Arnims mit den Brüdern Grimm 1838–1841*, Hartwig Schultz, ed. (Frankfurt a. M.: Insel, 1985). Heinz Härtl has published the first two volumes of this collection, which include *Goethes Briefwechsel mit einem Kinde, Die Günderode*, and *Clemens Brentanos Frühlingskranz: Bettine von Arnim, Werke* (Berlin und Weimar: Aufbau Verlag, 1986-). The Deutscher Klassiker edition, which so far has published one of the planned three-volume set, edited by Walter Schmitz and Sibylle von Steinsdorff, appeared in 1986: Bettine von Arnim, *Werke und Briefe:* Vol. I: *Clemens Brentano's Frühlingskranz. Die Günderode* (Frankfurt a. M.: Deutscher Klassiker Verlag, 1986—).

13. See the following dissertations: Konstanze Bäumer, "Goethes Briefwechsel mit einem Kinde—Ein weiblicher Bildungsroman des 19. Jahrhunderts" (Ph.D. diss., University of California, Davis, 1983); Lorely French, "Bettine von Arnim: Toward A Woman's Epistolary Aesthetics and Poetics" (Ph.D. diss., University of California, Los Angeles, 1986); Marjanne Elaine Goozé, "Bettine von Arnim, the Writer" (Ph.D. diss., University of California, Berkeley, 1984); and Edith Waldstein, "Bettina von Arnim and the Literary Salon: Women's Participation in the Cultural Life of Early Nineteenth-Century Germany" (Ph.D. diss, Washington University, 1982). The most recent publication is a collection of essays devoted solely to Bettine von Arnim, edited by Elke Frederiksen and Katherine Goodman: *Bettina Brentano-von Arnim: Gender and Politics* (Detroit: Wayne State University Press, 1995).

14. Waldstein, *Bettine von Arnim and the Politics of Romantic Conversation*.

15. Bäumer, *"Bettine, Psyche, Mignon."*

16. Goozé, "Bettine von Arnim, the Writer."

17. I refer here to Hilde Wyss, *Bettine von Arnims Stellung zwischen der Romantik und dem jungen Deutschland* (Bern and Leipzig: Paul Haupt, 1935), 48. For other, more extensive treatments of Arnim's use of the epistolary form in relation to Romantic literary theories, see the studies by Konstanze Bäumer, *"Bettine, Psyche, Mignon"* and Waldstein, *Bettine von Arnim and the Politics of Romantic Conversation.* And yet, while these studies discuss the literary theories of Friedrich Schlegel, Novalis, and other male Romantics as they relate to the epistolary form, and refer to a female aesthetic of letter writing, they provide little textual analysis of other women's letters.

18. Aside from the three dissertations on Bettine von Arnim, I refer here to articles by Bovenschen ("Über die Frage: Gibt es eine weibliche Ästhetik?"Romantik"), Frederiksen ("Die Frau als Autorin zur Zeit der Romantik"), and Goodman ("Poesis and Praxis in Rahel Varnhagen's Letters").

19. See in particular: Elke Frederiksen and Monika Shafi, "'Sich im Unbekannten suchen gehen:' Bettina von Arnims *Die Günderode* als weibliche Utopie," and Roswi-

tha Burwick, "Bettina von Arnims *Die Günderode:* Zum Selbstverständnis der Frau in der Romantik," both in *Frauensprache—Frauenliteratur? Für und Wider einer Psychoanalyse literarischer Werke,* vol. 6 of *Kontroversen, alte und neue: Akten des VII. Internationalen Germanisten-Kongresses Göttingen 1985,* 11 vols. (Tübingen: Niemeyer, 1986), 54–61; 62–67. Again, when referring to research on *Die Günderode,* the accessibility of sources favors contacts with males over those with females. In the fifth volume of Bettine von Arnim's works, for example, the volume with collected original letters, Joachim Müller reprints letters from Bettine to Clemens, Achim, Goethe, Karl von Savigny, and her sons without including important letters to Rahel, Amalie von Helvig, and her daughters. Whereas Bettine's letters to and from male correspondents have usually appeared under a separate title (correspondences with Clemens Brentano, Achim von Arnim, Rudolf Baier, Friedrich Wilhelm IV), Arnim's letters to and from other women are often tucked away in or scattered throughout biographies, such as the letters to Amalie von Helvig in Henriette von Bissing, *Das Leben der Dichterin Amalie von Helvig, geb. Freiin von Imhoff* (Berlin: Wilhelm Hertz, 1889), 392–401; and to Elizabeth von Egloffstein in Hermann von Egloffstein, ed., *Alt Weimar's Abend: Briefe und Aufzeichnungen aus dem Nachlasse der Gräfinnen Egloffstein* (Munich: Beck, 1923), 284–393; 497–504. Arnim's letters to and from women, such as Rahel Varnhagen, are also included in collections of letters exchanged with other famous people, as in Ludmilla Assing, ed., *Briefe von Stägemann, Metternich, Heine und Bettine von Arnim, nebst Briefen, Anmerkungen und Notizen von Varnhagen von Ense* (Leipzig: F. U. Brochhaus, 1865), 260–302). The paucity of studies on the women with whom Arnim had contact seems unjustified, considering that her female correspondents were also quite well known and respected in their day, including Elisabeth Goethe, the writer Karoline von Günderrode, the salonière Rahel Varnhagen, the poet and translator Amalie von Helvig, the artist Pauline Steinhäuser, and Bettine's daughters, Gisela, Armgard, and Maxe, writers and artists themselves, to name a few.

20. Gutzkow, *Ausgewählte Werke* (1839) 12: 74. Later in the essay, he refers to it as a poem (75). See also Karl Rosenkranz, "Rahel, Bettina und Charlotte Steiglitz," *Studien zur Literatur-Geschichte* (Leipzig: Koschny, 1875), 115–19.

21. Meusebach conveys the initial dilemmas over categorization in his review of *Goethes Briefwechsel* in the *Allgemeine Literaturzeitung* 115 (Halle und Leipzig, July, 1835), col. 292–93; cited by Konrad in *Bettina von Arnims Werke* 2: 732.

22. Gutzkow, *Ausgewählte Werke,* 12:75.

23. As Karl-Heinz Hahn observes in his study of Bettine's political ideas, *Goethes Briefwechsel* did not appear during a period of high admiration for Goethe: *Bettina von Arnim in ihrem Verhältnis zu Staat und Politik: mit einem Anhang ungedruckter Briefe* (Weimar: Herman Böhlaus Nachfolger, 1959), 21–22. Often, this general ebb in interest worked in favor of *Goethes Briefwechsel.* Bettine von Arnim was received quite favorably by the authors of *Junges Deutschland* mostly because her innovative form and her personality as the child in adoration of Goethe helped put Goethe into a positive light again; see: Heinrich Laube, *Moderne Charakteristiken,* vol. 49 of his *Gesammelte Werke,* ed. Heinrich Hubert Houben, 50 vols (Leipzig: Max Hesses Verlag, 1909), 297–301; and Theodor Mundt, *Geschichte der Literatur der Gegenwart,* vol. 2 of *Friedrich Schlegel's Geschichte der alten und neuern Literatur,* 2 vols (Berlin: M. Simon, 1842), 317–318. For others, such as Ludwig Börne, who was not so eager to redeem Goethe in his essay "Goethes Briefwechsel mit einem Kinde," Bettine shines through as "richly talented, god-blessed child" next to the "deaf" Goethe ("Goethes Briefwechsel mit einem Kinde," 126; see note 5 above). Also, one must be cautious about interpreting the positive views of the writers of the *Junges Deutschland* as

indicating emancipated views on women. Gutzkow, for example, believed that women had no creative talent for writing (*Ausgewählte Werke*, 12: 73). The heroine of Mundt's work *Madonna* expresses these same views (421). These writers' calls for equality in the political arena included no major steps towards educational or political equality for women. Thus, many comments about Bettine during this period are tainted with prejudicial and condescending remarks concerning her creative talents See in particular Gutzkow's account of a visit to Bettine in 1837 (*Ausgewählte Werke* 12: 113–16) and Laube's review "Bettina." Considering other men's opinions of women writers at the time, Laube's somewhat sarcastic calling of men to arms carries with it overtones of genuine surprise at women's talents, as he calls it a mockery of men that two women, Rahel and Bettina, had absorbed all the attention of readers (*Gesammelte Werke* 49: 297).

24. In *Blätter für literarische Unterhaltung* 110 (20 April 1835): 328. Cited in Konrad's afterword to *Goethes Briefwechsel* in Bettine von Arnim's *Werke* 2: 736–37.

25. See, for example, Susman's account (*Frauen der Romantik* 117), and Konrad's article "Bettina von Arnim," (note 5 above) 311. Both view Bettine's subjectivity as an obstacle to interpreting her works aesthetically.

26. For an account of Riemer's descriptions of Bettine's visits, see *Herzhaft in die Dornen der Zeit Greifen... Bettine von Arnim 1785–1859*, 45–46 (see note 11 above).

27. Friedrich Wilhelm Riemer, *Mittheilungen über Goethe. Aus mündlichen und schriftlichen, gedruckten und ungedruckten Quellen*, 2 vols. (Berlin: Duncker und Humblot, 1841), 36.

28. G. H. Lewes, *Life and Works of Goethe: with Sketches of his Age and Contemporaries, from published and unpublished sources*, 2 vols. (London: D. Nutt, 1855), 2: 362.

29. Carriere, *Lebensbilder*, 226.

30. Ibid., 227.

31. Gustav von Loeper, *Briefe Goethe's an Sophie von LaRoche und Bettina Brentano nebst dichterischen Beilagen* (Berlin: Verlag von Wilhelm Hertz, 1879).

32. Bettina von Arnim, *Bettinas Briefwechsel mit Goethe auf Grund ihres handschriftlichen Nachlasses nebst zeitgenössischen Dokumenten über ihr persönliches Verhältnis zu Goethe*, Reinhold Steig, ed. (Leipzig: Insel Verlag, 1922).

33. Bettina von Arnim, *Werke*, 5:7–129.

34. *Deutsche Rundschau*, 18 (August, 1892): 262–74. The letter from Karoline von Günderode is reprinted in Ludwig Geiger's *Karoline von Günderode und ihre Freunde* (Stuttgart, Leipzig: Deutsche Verlage-Anstalt, 1895), 125, 135. The letter from Clemens Brentano is reprinted in the 1985 Insel edition of the *Frühlingskranz*, pages 329–33.

35. For an account of the history of Bettine's manuscripts, see Gertrud Meyer-Hepner's articles "Das Bettina von Arnim-Archiv," *Sinn und Form* 6 (1954): 594–611; and "Bettina in Ost und West," *Neue Deutsche Literatur* 7,1 (1959): 152–54. Basically, Bettine's sons and then grandson who inherited the estate did not allow any entrance to the library in Wiepersdorf after Bettine's death because they did not want to cause any scandal, neither through publication of any private letters, nor through reprints of previously published works, especially *Goethes Briefwechsel*. The library remained closed until 1929 when, because of financial difficulties, it was auctioned off and then scattered all over the world. Three main archives now house Bettine's documents: The Freies Deutsches Hochstift in Frankfurt am Main, the Goethe-Schiller Forschungs- und Gedenkstätten in Weimar, and the Varnhagen Collection in the Jagiellonian library in Krakow, Poland.

36. Bettine von Arnim, *Werke*, Konrad, ed., III, 17. All citations hereafter will appear as *Werke* with volume and page numbers in parentheses.

37. Waldemar Oehlke, *Bettina von Arnims Briefromane*, Palaestra 41 (Berlin: Mayer & Müller, 1905).

38. For *Goethes Briefwechsel*, Oehlke used studies by Loeper, *Briefe Goethe's;* and by Carl Schüddekopf und Oskar Walzel. eds., "Goethe und die Romantik. Briefe mit Erläuterungen. 2. Theil," *Schriften der Goethe-Gesellschaft* 14, ed. Erich Schmidt and Bernhard Suphan (Weimar: Verlag der Goethe-Gesellschaft, 1899), 159–97. For material on the other three works, Oehlke could only refer to Steig's article from the *Deutsche Rundschau* (see footnote 34 above), as well as a letter from Bettine to Claudine von Piautaz, which Bettine had interpolated and included in *Die Günderode.*

39. See, for example, Konrad's article "Bettina von Arnim," 330. Annaliese Hopfe also classifies Bettine's works as "Briefbücher" [epistolary books] because the singular letter in the epistolary novel *(Briefroman)* has a more functional connection to the whole than it has in a *Briefbuch:* "Formen und Bereiche schöpferischen Verstehens bei Bettina von Arnim," (Ph.D. diss. Munich, 1953), 239.

40. See Goozé, "Bettine von Arnim. The Writer."

41. Meusebach viewed Goethes Briefwechsel as "ein Gedicht" (cited in Konrad, *Werke*, 2: 732). See also Gutzkow's remark about his classification (*Ausgewählte Werke*, 12: 74–75). About the passage in *Goethes Briefwechsel* concerning Günderrode, Milch also notes the amalgamation of prose and poetry (*Die junge Bettine*, 88).

42. The equation of the epistolary form to a drama was a common one in the eighteenth century. See Goethe's explanation of the reason why he chose the epistolary form for Werther in *Dichtung und Wahrheit*, in Johann Wolfgang von Goethe, *Werke: Hamburger Ausgabe*, Erich Trunz, ed., 11th rev. ed. (Munich: C. H. Beck'sche Verlagsbuchhandlung, 1978), 9: 577.

43. Konrad uses the image of fiction and truth, "Dichtung und Wahrheit," in describing Arnim's books. (*Werke* 1: 557). Also, the title of Lilienfein's study, *Bettina: Dichtung und Wahrheit ihres Leben* (Munich: R. Bruckmann, 1949), implies the connection with Goethe's autobiography.

44. See especially Gutzkow's 1837 essay "Ein Besuch bei Bettina," *Ausgewählte Werke*, 12: 114.

45. Natascha Würzbach, ed. *The Novel in Letters: Epistolary Fiction in the Early English Novel 1678–1740* (London: Routledge & Kegan Paul, 1969), XV.

46. Goodman, *Dis/Closures.*

47. Ibid., 76.

48. Artemon, in his preface to the edition of letters of Aristoteles, refers to the letter as "the half of a dialogue." The entry on the letter in the *Lexikon der Alten Welt*, contends that a letter continues the conversation between separated friends and maintains the friendship though the illusion of presence: B. Kytzler, "Brief," *Lexikon der Alten Welt*, ed. Carl Andresen, et. al. (Zurich: Artemis Verlag, 1965), col. 496–97.

49. Johann Christoph Gottsched, *Vorübungen der Beredsamkeit, zum Gebrauche der Gymnasien und grössern Schulen*, 3. ed. 1764. 201–2, cited in R. Brockmeyer, *Geschichte des deutschen Briefes* 18.

50. Altman, *Epistolarity*, 117.

51. Goozé, "Bettina von Arnim, the Writer," 227.

52. Hans von Arnim, *Bettina von Arnim* (Berlin: Haude und Spenersche Verlagsbuchhandlung, 1963), 36; Ingeborg Drewitz, *Bettine von Arnim. Romantik–Revolution–Utopie* (Düsseldorf, Cologne: Eugen Diederichs Verlag, 1969)

41–42; Goozé, "Bettine von Arnim, the Writer," 41; Gertrud Mander, *Bettina von Arnim*, Preußische Köpfe 11 (Berlin: Stapp Verlag, 1982), 43.

53. Lujo Brentano, "Der jugendliche und der gealterte Clemens Brentano über Bettine und Goethe,"*Jahrbuch des Freien Deutschen Hochstifts* (1929): 326; and Brentano/Mereau 377.

54. Ulrike Prokop, "Die Freundschaft zwischen Katharina Elisabeth Goethe and Bettina Brentano—Aspekte weiblicher Tradition," Mauser and Becker-Cantarino, *Frauenfreundschaft—Männerfreundschaft*, 241–42.

55. See Prokop's article on Cornelia Goethe in Pusch's *Schwestern berühmter Männer: Zwölf biographische Portraits* (Frankfurt a. M.: Insel Taschenbuch, 1985), 49–122; and Prokop's article "Die Einsamkeit der Imagination: Geschlechterkonflikt und literarische Produktion um 1770," Brinker-Gabler, *Deutsche Literatur von Frauen*, vol. 2, 353–59.

56. Prokop, "Die Freundschaft zwischen K. E. Goethe and B. Brentano," 252.

57. Robert Keil, ed., *Frau Rath. Briefwechsel von Katharina Elisabeth Goethe* (Leipzig: F. A. Brockhaus, 1871), 58.

58. Katharina Elisabeth Goethe, *Gesammelte Briefe*, Ludwig Geiger, ed. (Leipzig: Hesse & Becker Verlag, n.d.), 14–15. Hereafter cited as *Gesammelte Briefe* with page numbers.

59. See, for example, her letter to Klinger in May 1776, to Schönborn in 1776, and to Lavater on June 23, 1777, all in Albert Köster, *Der letzte Brief von Goethes Mutter an Bettina Brentano* (Leipzig: Insel, 1918), 40, 42, 54 respectively. Hereafter cited as Köster with page numbers.

60. Spacks, *Gossip*, 65.

61. Walter J. Ong, *The Presence of the Word: Some Prolegomena for Culture and Religious History* (Minneapolis: University of Minnesota, 1981), 70.

62. Brentano, Clemens, *Das unsterbliche Leben: Unbekannte Briefe von Clemens Brentano*, Wilhelm Schellberg and Friedrich Fuchs, ed. (Jena: Diederichs, 1939), 17.

63. Bäumer, "*Goethes Briefwechsel mit einem Kinde*—Ein weiblicher Bildungsroman des 19. Jahrhunderts," 105.

64. Clemens Brentano, *Das unsterbliche Leben*, 97.

65. Paul Beyer, "Bettinas Arbeit an Goethes Briefwechsel mit einem Kinde," *Von deutscher Sprache und Art: Beiträge zur Geschichte der neueren deutschen Sprache, zur Sprachkunst, Sprachpflege und zur Volkskunde*, Max Preitz, ed. (Frankfurt a. M.: Diesterweg, 1925), 70; Oehlke, *Bettina von Arnims Briefromane*, 48

66. In May 1807, Elisabeth Goethe writes:" . . . alle Tage die an Himmel kommen, ist sie [Bettine] bey mir das ist ihre beynahe einzige Freude—da muß ich ihr nun erzählen—von meinem Sohn—als dann Mährgen—da behaubtete sie denn; so erzähle kein Mensch" [ . . . every day that comes to heaven she [Bettine] is with me that is almost her sole joy—for then I have to tell her—about my son—as well as fairy tales—for she claims then; no person narrates as such] (*Gesammelte Briefe* 511).

67. Camillus Wendeler, *Briefwechsel des Freiherrn Karl Hartwig Gregor von Meusebach mit Jacob und Wilhelm Grimm. Nebst einleitenden Bemerkungen über den Verkehr des Sammlers mit gelehrten Freunden, Anmerkungen und einem Anhang von der Berufung der Brüder Grimm nach Berlin* (Heilbronn: Verlag von Gebr. Henninger, 1880), 400.

68. "Meine Freude war groß da ich von meiner Schwieger Tochter hörte daß du in Weimar gewesen wärest—du hast viel vergnügen dort verbreitet—nur bedauerte man daß dein Aufenthalt so kurz war" [My joy was great as I heard from my daughter-in-law that you were in Weimar—you spread a lot of pleasure there—now people only regretted that your stay there was so short] (*Gesammelte Briefe* 512).

69. The letter reads:

Liebe—Liebe Tochter!

Nenne mich ins künftige mit dem mir so theuren Nahmen Mutter—und du verdinst ihn so sehr, so gantz und gar—mein Sohn sey dein inniggeliebter Bruder—dein Freund—der dich gewiß liebt und Stoltz auf deine Freundschaft ist. Meine Schwieger Tochter hat mir geschrieben wie sehr du Ihm gefallen hast—und daß du meine Liebe Bettine bist muß du längst überzeugt seyn.

[Dear—Dear daughter!

Call me in the future with the name mother that is so dear to me—and you deserve it so much, so very much—my son shall be your cherished brother—your friend—who certainly loves you and is proud of your friendship. My daughter-in-law has written to me how much he likes you—and you must have been convinced a long time ago that you are my Dear Bettine.] (*Gesammelte Briefe* 512)

70. Beyer states about the dearth of letters between Bettine and Frau Rat that Elisabeth Goethe and Bettine were certainly people who preferred speaking to writing ("Bettinas Arbeit," 70).

71. For purposes of comparison with the quote in footnote 69, the passage in *Goethes Briefwechsel* reads:

"Liebe, liebe Tochter, mein Sohn soll Dein Freund sein, Dein Bruder, der Dich gewiß liebt, und Du sollst mich Mutter heißen in Zukunft für alle Täg, die mein spätes Alter noch zählt, es ist ja doch der einzige Name, der mein Glück umfaßt" [Dear, dear daughter, my son shall be your friend, your brother, who certainly loves you, and you should call me mother in the future for all days that my late age still counts, yes, it is the sole name that comprises my happiness] (*Werke* 2: 18).

72. Hans Hajek points out the noncompetitiveness between the two women: "Die Mystifizierung der Frau Rat durch Bettina Brentano (Ph.D. diss., Vienna, 1937), 52.

73. Carriere, "Bettina von Arnim, 252; Hans von Arnim, *Bettina von Arnim*, 82.

74. See, for example, Barthel, *Deutsche Nationalliteratur*; Proelß, "Rahel, Bettina und die Stieglitz; and Treitschke, *Deutsche Geschichte*.

75. Geiger, *Karoline von Günderrode und ihre Freunde*, 133; 136–37.

76. Theodor Mundt uses the word "Briefdichtungen" to describe the contents of *Die Günderode* (*Geschichte der Literatur der Gegenwart*, 318), praising it for its insights into religion and nature. Oehlke concludes his comparison of the original letters to the letters in the book by calling it a work of art that contains not letters or excerpts from letters, but rather epistolary thoughts, "Briefgedanken" (*Bettina von Arnims Briefromane*, 246). Konrad asserts that the authenticity of the letters in the book is immaterial. More important is the rendition of ideas in the final work ("Bettina von Arnim," 321).

77. In June 1806 she wrote to her: "Die Briefe mußt Du mir wiedergeben, denn Du kommst mir falsch vor, solange Du sie besitzest, auch leg ich einen Wert darauf, ich habe mein Herz hineingeschrieben" [You must give me the letters back, for you seem false to me as long as you possess them, I also place a value on them, I have written my heart into them] (*Werke* 5: 204).

78. See Waldstein, *Bettine von Arnim and the Politics of Romantic Conversation*, 55–57; and Wolf, "Nun ja! Das nächste Leben geht aber heute an: Ein Brief über die Bettine." Wolf is one of the first to stress the unusual and creative style of *Die Günderode*, characterizing it as an experiment of two women who tried to support each other and establish a utopia together (313).

79. Waldstein, *Bettine von Arnim and the Politics of Romantic Conversation*, 55–57.

80. Waldstein also makes this observation (Ibid., 55).

81. Some of the original letters from Karoline to Bettine and to Clemens are

included in Christa Wolf's appendix to her edition of *Die Günderode* (525–31). Bettine's original letters to Karoline are published in Bettine's *Werke* 5: 197–204. Although only a few original letters exist, it is possible to see from those that we do have the large extent to which Bettine split up letters, added passages, and chronologically rearranged the letters in the published version. Oehlke discusses the alterations in detail (*Bettina von Arnims Briefromane*, 181–246), using some original letters, factual figures, and speculation. At times he seems too hasty in his conclusions, for example, when he suspects that Bettine had used Book 13 of Goethes *Dichtung und Wahrheit* as a basis for the passages in *Die Günderode* describing Sophie von La Roche (214). Without the original letters, his argument is not convincing.

82. Most of the poems and prose pieces appeared in the early editions of Karoline's works: *Gedichte und Phantasien von Tian* (Hamburg, Frankfurt: J. C. Herrmann'schen Buchhandlung, 1804); *Poetische Fragmente von Tian* (Frankfurt a.M.: Friedrich Wilmanns, 1805); *Melete von Jon* (Heidelberg: Mohr und Zimmer, 1806). Three poems in *Die Günderode* had not appeared in any of the earlier editions: "Lethe," "An Clemens," and "Ist alles stumm und leer."

83. Oehlke, *Bettina von Arnims Briefromane*, 185.

84. Karoline von Günderrode, *Sämtliche Werke und ausgewählte Studien: Historisch-Kritische Ausgabe*, Walter Morgenthaler, ed., with assistance from Karin Obermeier and Marianne Graf, 3 vols (Stroemfeld: Roter Stern, 1990), 1: 30 (see Chapter 4, n53).

85. Ibid., 1:31.

86. Ibid., 1: 52.

87. Ibid., 1:52.

88. Bettine von Arnim and Max Prokop von Freyberg, *Der Briefwechsel zwischen Bettine Brentano und Max Prokop von Freyberg*, Sibylle Steinsdorff, ed. (Berlin and New York: de Gruyter, 1972), 11; Bettina von Arnim, *Andacht zum Menschenbild: Unbekannte Briefe von Bettine Brentano*, Wilhelm Schellberg and Friedrich Fuchs, ed. (1942; reprint Bern: Lang, 1970), 227; Goozé, "Bettine von Arnim. The Writer," 213.

# Chapter 7. Corresponding with the World: Letters and Women around the 1848 Revolution

1. This chapter contains material from my essay "Strategies of Female Persuasion: The Political Letters of Bettina von Arnim," in *Bettina Brentano-von Arnim: Gender and Politics*, edited by Elke Frederiksen and Katherine Goodman (Detroit: Wayne State University Press, 1995).

2. Fanny Lewald, "Der Cultus der Genius. Brief an Bettina von Arnim," *Blätter für literarische Unterhaltung* 171–74 (18–21 July 1849): 681.

3. Ibid., 681.

4. Ibid.

5. Ibid., 694.

6. Fanny Lewald, *Meine Lebensgeschichte*, ed. with intro. by Gisela Brinker-Gabler (Frankfurt a. M.: Fischer, 1980), 147, 160.

7. Arnim Nachlaß 332. I thank the curators of this collection for access to these manuscripts.

8. See especially the following: Shari Benstock, *The Private Self. Theory and Practice of Women's Autobiographical Writings* (Chapel Hill: North Carolina University Press, 1988); Sara Friedrichsmeyer, "'Seeds for the Sowing': The Diary of Käthe Kollwitz," *Arms and the Woman: War, Gender, and Literary Representation*, Helen Cooper,

Adrienne Auslander Munich, Susan Merrill Squier, ed. (Chapel Hill: University of North Carolina Press, 1989), 205–24; and Friedrichsmeyer, "Caroline Schlegel-Schelling;" and Goodman, *Dis/Closures.*

9. See my article "Strategies of Female Persuasion: The Political Letters of Bettina von Arnim." Arnim's political consciousness surfaces in all her published works and in private correspondence. Her letters to the King and the Berlin Magistrate contain her harshest critique of the political system and her clearest proposals of alternatives to that system, based on the individual cases she defends. Between 1838 and 1852 Arnim wrote her strongest political epistles to Crown Prince, later, King Friedrich Wilhelm IV on behalf of acquaintances who had been indicted or dismissed for their subversive actions. From 1838 to 1840 she pleaded the case of Jakob and Wilhelm Grimm, who as members of the dismissed "Göttinger Sieben" ("Göttingen Seven") had to seek new positions; in 1845 she defended Friedrich Wilhelm Schlöffel, from whom she had received lists of poor workers for her *Book of the Poor (Armenbuch),* against accusations that he was a communist; in 1846 and 1847 she wrote on behalf of Ludwig von Mieroslawski, who was sentenced to death in 1847 for his involvement in Poland's independence struggle; in 1849 she pleaded against the death sentence of the former Storkow mayor, Tschech, who had attempted to assassinate the King in 1844; in 1849 she tried to persuade the King to acquit the theologian and art historian Gottfried Kinkel, who was sentenced to life imprisonment for his participation in the 1848 Revolution. From 1846 to 1847 Arnim engaged in an involved correspondence with the Berlin Magistrate to defend her actions in publishing Achim von Arnim's and her own works privately. The Magistrate had ordered her to purchase her citizenship, which she needed to continue her own private publishing "business" that she had begun in 1846. She stated that she would not pay for the honor of citizenship, but would accept it if conferred upon her. The Magistrate was insulted by her remark and brought suit against her.

10. Paul John Eakin, *Touching the World: Reference in Autobiography* (Princeton, N.J.: Princeton University Press, 1992), 138.

11. The term "triple gaze" is a spinoff of Sigrid Weigel's term "double gaze," who in her essay "Der schielende Blick: Thesen zur Geschichte weiblicher Schreibpraxis" views the tendency of women both to accommodate and to protest norms as a necessary step toward finding a "female language of experience."

12. Ursula Püschel describes the responses of Karl Lachmann and Jakob Grimm to Bettine von Arnim's pleas on behalf of the Grimm brothers: "Weibliches und Unweibliches der Bettina von Arnim," in her *Mit allen Sinnen: Frauen in der Literatur. Essays* (Halle, Leipzig: Mitteldeutscher Verlag, 1980), 80 n3. Also, see letters by von Arnim's brother-in-law, Karl Friedrich von Savigny, and by the Berlin attorney, Otto Lewald, who worked toward having Bettine von Arnim acquitted after the Berlin Magistrate sentenced her to two years in prison. These two men, afraid that von Arnim's tendencies toward over-emotionality could have created further difficulties, insisted on writing her letter of apology to the Magistrate for her (122–23).

13. Bettine von Arnim and Friedrich Wilhelm IV, *Bettine von Arnim und Friedrich Wilhelm IV,* Ludwig Geiger, ed. (Frankfurt a. M.: Rütten und Loening, 1902), 99–101.

14. *Bettine von Arnim und Friedrich Wilhelm IV,* 100–1.

15. Iris Marion Young offers a feminist critique of the normative definitions of male-dominated Western political thought: "Impartiality and the Civic Public: Some Implications of Feminist Critiques of Moral and Political Theory," *Feminism as Critique,* Seyla Benhabib and Drucilla Cornell, ed. (Minneapolis: University of Minnesota Press, 1987), 57–76.

16. Gerhard discusses women's legal limits in nineteenth-century Germany: *Verhältnisse und Verhinderungen*, 154–89; Document 17: 396–442.

17. See Carola Lipp's articles "Bräute, Mütter, Gefährtinnen. Frauen und politische Öffentlichkeit in der Revolution 1848," *Grenzgängerinnen: Revolutionäre Frauen im 18. und 19. Jahrhundert*, Helga Grubitzsch, Hannelore Cyrus, and Elke Haarbusch, ed. (Düsseldorf: Schwann, 1985), 71–92; and "Frauen und Öffentlichkeit. Möglichkeiten und Grenzen politischer Partizipation im Vormärz und in der Revolution 1848/1849," *Schimpfende Weiber und patriotische Jungfrauen. Frauen im Vormärz und in der Revolution 1848* (Bühl-Moos: Elster Verlag, 1985), 270–301. In the latter article, Lipp points out that certain practical factors could also deter women's engagement, including impractical clothing and transportation, as well as inconvenient meeting times and places (289).

18. For particularly vivid commentary on the distance women were supposed to take from political matters, see Helmina von Chézy's *Unvergessenes*. She talks about her efforts on behalf of the wounded in Prussia after the Napoleonic wars, and not about involvement in the 1848 Revolution, but her observations are indicative of the limitations and show a woman's awareness of those limitations. At one point she remarks that one of her main problems was that she forgot that she was not a man when she became involved in politics (II, 341). At another point, she writes: "Doch so gut wie es Literaten gibt, die keiner Schriftstellerin noch Dichterin hold sind, gibt es auch Chirurgen, die weiblichen Beistand bei Kranken und Verwundeten nur ungern sehen" [Just as there are literati who like no woman writer or woman poet, there are also surgeons who look disfavorably upon women's assistance with the sick and the wounded] (II, 123).

19. Clotilde Koch-Gontard, *Clotilde Koch-Gontard an ihre Freunde: Briefe und Erinnerungen aus der Zeit der deutschen Einheitsbewegung 1843–1869*, Wolfgang Klötzer, ed. Frankfurter Lebensbilder 16 (Frankfurt a. M.: Waldemar Kramar, 1969), 57.

20. Ibid., 64.

21. Ibid., 62, 77, 78, 93.

22. Ibid., 77.

23. Ibid., 92.

24. Ibid., 309.

25. Ibid., 278–80.

26. There were other women besides the four I discuss here who were actively writing and speaking for the democratic cause around 1848. For an examination of women's published works around the 1848 Revolution and for a good bibliography of primary and secondary literature, see Lia Secci, "German Women Writers and the Revolution of 1848," *German Women in the Nineteenth Century: A Social History*, John C. Fout, ed. (New York, London: Holmes & Meier, 1984). For women's political organizations, see Eva Kuby, "Politische Frauenvereine und ihre Aktivitäten 1848 bis 1850," *Schimpfende Weiber*, Carola Lipp, ed., 248–69.

27. Gerlinde Hummel-Haasis, ed., *Schwestern zerreißt eure Ketten: Zeugnisse zur Geschichte der Frauen in der Revolution von 1848/49* (Munich: dtv, 1982), 221.

28. For Anneke's biography, see Maria Wagner, *Mathilde Franziska Anneke in Selbstzeugnissen und Dokumenten* (Frankfurt a. M.: Fischer, 1980).

29. For Aston's biography see Germaine Goetzinger, *Für die Selbstverwirklichung der Frau: Louise Aston* (Frankfurt a. M.: Fischer, 1983).

30. Emma Herwegh, *Zur Geschichte der deutschen demokratischen Legion aus Paris. Von einer Hochverräterin.* (1849) in *1848: Briefe von und an Georg Herwegh*, Marcel Herwegh, ed., 2 ed. (Munich: Albert Langen's Verlag, 1896), 127–214.

31. For interpretations and ambivalences in Lewald's fictional works and her later

turn to more conservative political attitudes, see Konstanze Bäumer, "Reisen als Moment der Erinnerung: Fanny Lewalds (1811–1889) 'Lehr- und Wanderjahr'," *Out of Line/Ausgefallen: The Paradox of Marginality in the Writings of Nineteenth-Century German Women*, Ruth Ellen B Joeres and Marianne Burkhard, ed., *Amsterdamer Beiträge zur neueren Germanistik* (Amsterdam: Rodopi, 1980), 137–57; Regula Venske, "Disciplines and Daydreaming in the Works of a Nineteenth-Century Woman Author: Fanny Lewald," in Joeres and Maynes, ed., *German Women*, 175–92; and Weigel, "Der schielende Blick."

32. Concerning personal letters, see especially Emma Herwegh's letters to Georg Herwegh. Other noteworthy personal letters include those of Clotilde Koch-Gontard to her liberal friends to describe the Parliament meetings in Frankfurt and political discussions at her salon. Carola Lipp cites the letter of Emilie Ritter as examples of political commentary from the private sphere ("Frauen und Öffentlichkeit," 285–88).

33. Mathilde Franziska Anneke, *Memoiren einer Frau aus dem badisch pfälzischen Feldzuge 1848–49* (1853, reprinted Münster: tende, 1982), 9.

34. Woolf, "Dorothy Osborne's Letters," 60.

35. Anne Hermann, "Epistolary Essays by Virginia Woolf and Christa Wolf," *New German Critique* 38 (1986): 161–80.

36. Fanny Lewald, *Erinnerungen aus dem Jahre 1848*, 2 vols. (Braunschweig: Friedrich Vieweg und Sohn, 1850), 1: vii–viii.

37. Louise Aston, *Meine Emancipation, Verweisung und Rechtfertigung* (Brüssel: C. G. Vogler, 1846), 5.

38. Herwegh, *Geschichte*, 130.

39. Ibid., 153.

40. Anneke, *Memoiren*, 10.

41. Anneke, *Memoiren*, 47–48.

42. Ibid., 48.

43. Aston, *Meine Emancipation*, 32.

44. Ibid., 32.

45. The Democrat Johannes Scherr, for example, attacked activists for defying their traditional roles, claiming that public women's groups were comprised "of ugly and hysterical spinsters" or "sloppy housewives and negligent mothers": *Von Achtundvierzig bis Einundfünfzig. Eine Komödie der Weltgeschichte* (Leipzig: , 1868), 188–89.

46. Wolf, "Nun ja! Das nächste Leben geht aber heute an," 556.

47. Lewald, *Erinnerungen*, 348–49.

48. Aston, *Meine Emancipation*, 39–40.

49. Herwegh, *Geschichte*, 129.

50. Ibid., 129.

51. Mary Catherine Bateson, *Composing A Life* (New York: Plume/Penguin, 1990), 184. I thank Esther Draznin for recommending this book to me.

52. Fuller, "Bettine Brentano and her friend Günderode," 312.

53. Ibid., 321.

54. Helene Stöcker, "Bettine von Arnim," *Neue Generation. Zeitschrift für Mutterschutz und Sexualreform* 25 (1929): 102.

55. See Bäumer's book *"Bettine, Psyche, Mignon"* for an account of contemporary reception of Bettine von Arnim's works.

56. For my line of thought here, I am indebted to Sara Friedrichsmeyer' article "'Seeds for the Sowing'": The Diary of Käthe Kollwitz," which examines the development of Kathe Kollwitz's ideas on pacifism as reflected in her diaries.

# Works Cited

## Primary Sources

Anneke, Mathilde Franziska. *Memoiren einer Frau aus dem badisch pfälzischen Feldzuge 1848–49*. 1853. Münster: tende, 1982.

Arnim, Bettina von. *Die Andacht zum Menschenbild: Unbekannte Briefe von Bettine Brentano*. Ed. Wilhelm Schellberg and Friedrich Fuchs. 1942. Reprint, Bern: Lang, 1970.

———. *Bettina von Arnims Armenbuch*. Ed. Werner Vordtriede. Frankfurt am Main: Insel, 1981.

———. "Bettina von Arnims Briefe an Julius Döring." Ed. Vordtriede. *Jahrbuch des Freien Deutschen Hochstifts* (1963): 341–488.

———. *Bettine von Arnim: Literarisches und Politisches aus ihrem Nachlass*. Ed. Karl Ernst Henrici. Auction Catologue 148. Berlin: n.p., 1929.

———. *Bettine von Arnim. Die Sehnsucht hat allemal Recht: Gedichte, Prosa, Briefe*. Ed. Gerhard Wolf. Berlin: Buchverlag der Morgen, 1984.

———. *Bettinas Briefwechsel mit Goethe auf Grund ihres handschriftlichen Nachlasses nebst zeitgenössischen Dokumenten über ihr persönliches Verhältnis zu Goethe*. Ed. Reinhold Steig. Leipzig: Insel Verlag, 1922.

———. "Briefe und Konzepte aus den Jahren 1849–1852." Ed. Gertrud Meyer-Hepner. *Sinn und Form* 5 (1953), No. 1: 38–64; No. 3/4: 27–58.

———. *Der Briefwechsel Bettine von Arnims mit den Brüdern Grimm*. Ed. Hartwig Schulz. Frankfurt a.M.: Insel, 1985.

———. *Clemens Brentanos Frühlingskranz aus Jugendbriefen ihr geflochten wie er selbst schriftlich verlangte*. Afterword by Hartwig Schultz. Frankfurt a. M.: Insel, 1985.

———. *Correspondence of Fräulein Günderode and Bettine von Arnim*. Trans. Margaret Fuller and Minna Wesselhoeft. Boston: T. O. H. P. Burnham, 1861.

———. *Dies Buch gehört dem König*. Ed. Ilse Staff. Frankfurt a. M.: Insel, 1982.

———. *Goethes Briefwechsel mit einem Kinde*. Ed. and intro. by Waldemar Oehlke. Frankfurt a. M.: Insel, 1984.

———. *Die Günderode*. Afterword by Christa Wolf. Frankfurt a. M.: Insel, 1983.

———. *II. Handschriftlicher Nachlaß der Bettine von Arnim: Dritter und Letzter Teil*. Ed. Karl Ernst Henrici. Auction Catalogue 155. Berlin: 1929.

———. *Der Magistratsprozess der Bettine von Arnim*. Ed. Meyer-Hepner. Weimar: Arion Verlag, 1960.

———. *Sämtliche Werke*. Ed. Waldemar Oehlke. 7 vols. Berlin: Propyläen-Verlag, 1920–22.

———. *Werke*. Vol. I: *Goethes Briefwechsel mit einem Kinde*. Ed. Heinz Härtl. Berlin and Weimar: Aufbau Verlag, 1986. Vol. II: *Die Günderode. Clemens Brentanos Frühlingskranz*, 1989. Three further volumes are forthcoming.

———. *Werke und Briefe*. Ed. Gustav Konrad. 4 vols. Frechen: Bartmann Verlag, 1958–63. *Briefe*. Ed. Johannes Müller. Vol. 5. Frechen: Bartmann Verlag, l961. (Cited as *Werke und Briefe*)

———. *Werke und Briefe*. Vol. I: *Clemens Brentanos Frühlingskranz. Die Günderode*. Ed. Walter Schmitz and Sibylle von Steinsdorf. Frankfurt a. M.: Deutscher Klassiker Verlag, 1986. Vol. II: *Goethes Briefwechsel mit einem Kinde*. Ed. Sibylle von Steinsdorf, 1988. Two further volumes are forthcoming.

———. "Zwei Briefe Bettinas." *Freundesgaben für Carl August Hugo Burckhardt zum siebenzigsten Geburtstag 6. Juli 1900*. Ed. Erich Schmidt. Weimar: Herman Böhlaus Nachfolger, 1900. 3–15

Arnim, Bettine von, and Achim von Arnim. *Achim und Bettina in ihren Briefen*. 2 vols. Ed. Werner Vordtriede. 1961. Frankfurt a. M.: Insel, 1981.

———. *Achim von Arnim und Bettina Brentano*. Vol. 2 of *Achim von Arnim und die ihm nahe standen*. Ed. Reinhold Steig. Stuttgart und Berlin: Cotta, 1913.

Arnim, Bettine von, and Gisela von Arnim. *Bettine und Arnim: Briefe der Freundschaft und Liebe*. Ed. Otto Betz and Veronika Straub. 2 vols. Frankfurt: Verlag Josef Knecht, 1986, 1987.

———. *Das Leben der Hochgräfin Gritta von Rattenzuhausbeiuns: Ein Märchenroman*. Ed. Shawn Jarvis. Frankfurt a.M.: Fischer, 1986.

Arnim, Bettine von, and Rudolf Baier. *Bettina von Arnim und Rudolf Baier: Unveröffentlichte Briefe und Tagebuchaufzeichnungen*. Ed. Kurt Gassen. Greifswald: L.Bamberg, 1937.

———, and Max Prokop von Freyberg. *Der Briefwechsel zwischen Bettine Brentano und Max Prokop von Freyberg*. Ed. Sibylle von Steinsdorff. Berlin and New York: de Gruyter, 1972.

———, and Jacob and Wilhelm Grimm. *Der Briefwechsel Bettine von Arnims mit den Brüdern Grimm 1838–1841*. Ed. Hartwig Schultz. Frankfurt a. M.: Insel, 1985.

———, and Hermann Fürst Pückler-Muskau. "Pückler und Bettina von Arnim." *Frauenbriefe von und an Hermann Fürsten Pückler-Muskau*. Ed. Heinrich Conrad. Munich and Leipzig: Georg Müller, 1912. 1–218

———, and Pauline Steinhäuser. "Bettina von Arnim und ihr Briefwechsel mit Pauline Steinhäuser." Ed. Karl Obser. *Neue Heidelberger Jahrbücher* 12 (1903): 85–137.

———, and Friedrich Wilhelm IV. *Bettine von Arnim und Friedrich Wilhelm IV*. Ed. Ludwig Geiger. Frankfurt am Main: Rütten und Loening, 1902.

Arnim, Ludwig Achim von. *Tröst Einsamkeit: Alte und neue Sagen und Wahrsagungen, Geschichten und Gedichte*. Heidelberg: Mohr und Zimmer, 1808.

Assing, Ludmilla, ed. *Aus dem Nachlaß Varnhagen's von Ense. Briefe von Chamisso, Gneisenau, Haugwitz, W. von Humboldt, Prinz Louis Ferdinand, Rahel, Rückert, L.Tieck u.a. Nebst Briefen, Anmerkungen und Notizen von Varnhagen von Ense*. 2 vols. Leipzig: F. A. Brockhaus, 1867.

———. *Briefe von Stägemann, Metternich, Heine und Bettine von Arnim, nebst Briefen, Anmerkungen und Notizen von Varnhagen von Ense*. Leipzig: F. A. Brockhaus, 1865.

Aston, Louise. *Meine Emancipation, Verweisung und Rechtfertigung*. Brüssel: C. G. Vogler, 1846.

Behrens, Katja, ed. *Frauenbriefe der Romantik*. Frankfurt a. M.: Insel, 1981.

*Bitter Healing: German Women Writers 1700–1830.* Ed. Jeannine Blackwell and Susanne Zantop. Lincoln: University of Nebraska Press, 1990.

Brentano, Clemens. *Briefe.* Ed. Friedrich Seebaß. 2 vols. Nürnberg: Hans Carl, 1951.

———. *Sämtliche Werke und Briefe.* Ed. Jürgen Behrens, Wolfgang Frühwald, and Detlev Lüders. Stuttgart: Verlag W. Kohlhammer, 1978.

———. *Das Unsterbliche Leben: Unbekannte Briefe von Clemens Brentano.* Ed. Wilhelm Schellberg and Friedrich Fuchs. Jena: Diederichs, 1939.

Brentano, Clemens, and Sophie Mereau. *Briefwechsel zwischen Clemens Brentano und Sophie Mereau. Nach den in der Königlichen Bibliothek zu Berlin befindlichen Handschriften zum ersten Mal herausgegeben.* Ed. Heinz Amelung. 2 vols. Leipzig: Insel, 1908.

———. *Lebe der Liebe und liebe das Leben: Der Briefwechsel von Clemens Brentano und Sophie Mereau.* Ed. Dagmar von Gersdorff. Frankfurt a. M.: Insel, 1981.

Brentano, Lujo. "Der jugendliche und der gealterte Clemens Brentano über Bettine und Goethe." *Jahrbuch des Freien Deutschen Hochstifts* (1929). 325–52.

Chamisso, Adelbert. *Correspondence d'Adalbert de Chamisso: Fragments inédits suivis de* Das stille Julchen *par Helmina von Chézy.* Ed. René Riegel. Paris: Les Éditions Internationales, n.d.

Chamisso, Adelbert v. and Helmine v. Chézy. *Bruchstücke ihres Briefwechsels.* Ed. Julius Peterson and Helmuth Rogge. Mittheilungen aus dem Literaturarchiv in Berlin, N.S. 19. Berlin: Literaturarchiv-Gesellschaft, 1923.

Chézy, Helmina von. *Briefe aus dem Briefwechsel Helmine von Chézys und Graf [Otto Henrich] Loebens 1814.* Mittheilungen aus dem Litteraturarchive in Berlin. Berlin: Litteraturarchiv-Gesellschaft, 1898. 34–86.

———. *Unvergessenes. Denkwürdigkeiten aus dem Leben.* 1858. Reprint with introduction by Wm. T. Parsons, Collegeville, Pa.: Pennsylvania German Studies Reprint Series #52, 1982.

Egloffstein, Hermann von, ed. *Alt Weimar's Abend: Briefe und Aufzeichnungen aus dem Nachlasse der Gräfinnen Egloffstein.* Munich: Beck, 1923.

Finke, Heinrich, ed. *Der Briefwechsel Friedrich und Dorothea Schlegel: 1818-1820 während Dorotheas Aufenthalt in Rom.* Munich: Josef Kösel & Friedrich Pustet, 1923.

[Friedländer, Rebecca]. *Schmerz der Liebe.* Berlin: n. p., 1810.

Goethe, Johann Wolfgang von. *Briefe an Charlotte von Stein: Kritische Gesamtausgabe.* Ed. Jonas Fränkel. 1908. Revised edition, Berlin: Akademie Verlag, 1960–62.

———. *Der Briefwechsel zwischen Schiller und Goethe.* Ed. Emil Staiger. Frankfurt a. M.: Insel, 1966.

———. *Werke: Hamburger Ausgabe.* Ed. Erich Trunz. 11th rev. edition. Munich: C. H. Beck'sche Verlagsbuchhandlung, 1978. (Cited as *HA.*)

———. *Werke.* Herausgegeben im Auftrage der Großherzogin Sophie von Sachsen. 133 vols. in 142. Weimar: Hermann Böhlau, 1891. (Cited as *WA.*)

Goethe, Katharina Elisabeth. *Gesammelte Briefe.* Ed. Ludwig Geiger. Leipzig: Hesse & Becker Verlag, n.d.

Goethe, Ottilie von. *Ottilie von Goethes Nachlaß: Briefe und Tagebücher von ihr und an sie bis 1832.* Ed. Wolfgang von Oettingen. 2 vols. Weimar: Verlag der Goethe Gesellschaft, 1913.

Gottsched, Louise Adelgunde Kulmus. *Briefe der Frau Louise Adelgunde Victorie Gottsched gebohrnen Kulmus.* 3 vols. Dresden: Joh. Wilh. Harpeter, 1771–72.

Günderrode, Karoline von. *Gesammelte Werke.* 3 vols. 1920–22. Bern: Lang, 1970.

———. *"Ich sende Dir ein Zärtliches Pfand": Die Briefe der Karoline von Günderrode.* Ed. Birgit Weißenborn. Frankfurt a. M.: Insel, 1992.

———. *Sämtliche Werke und ausgewählte Studien: Historisch-Kritische Ausgabe.* Ed. Walter Morgenthaler with assistance from Karin Obermeier and Marianne Graf. 3 vols. Stroemfeld: Roter Stern, 1990.

———. *Der Schatten eines Traumes: Gedichte, Prosa, Briefe, Zeugnisse von Zeitgenossen.* Ed. with an essay by Christa Wolf. 3rd ed. Darmstadt: Luchterhand, 1983.

Gutzkow, Karl. *Ausgewählte Werke.* Ed. Heinrich Huber Houben. 12 vols. Leipzig: Max Hesse Verlag, 1908.

Haberland, Helga and Wolfgang Pehnt. *Frauen der Goethezeit in Briefen, Dokumenten und Bildern. Von der Gottschedin bis zu Bettina von Arnim.* Stuttgart: Reclam, 1960.

Härtl, Heinz. "Briefe Friedrich Carl von Savignys an Bettina Brentano." *Wissenschaftliche Zeitschrift der Martin-Luther-Universität Halle-Wittemberg* 28 (1979):105–28.

Herwegh, Emma. *Zur Geschichte der deutschen demokratischen Legion aus Paris. Von einer Hochverräterin.* 1849. In: *1848: Briefe von und an Georg Herwegh.* Ed. Marcel Herwegh. 2nd ed. Munich: Albert Langen's Verlag, 1898. 127–214.

Herz, Henriette. *Berliner Salon. Erinnerungen und Portraits.* Ed. Ulrich Jantzki. Berlin: Ullstein, 1985.

———. *Henriette Herz in Erinnerungen, Briefen und Zeugnissen.* Ed. Rainer Schmitz. Frankfurt a. M.: Insel, 1984.

Hölderlin, Friedrich. *Hyperion.* Vol. 3 of *Sämtliche Werke.* Ed. Friedrich Beissner. Stuttgart: Kohlhammer, 1957.

Holtei, Karl von, ed. *Briefe an Ludwig Tieck.* 4 vols. Breslau: Trewendt, 1864.

Jäckel, Günter, ed *Frauen der Goethezeit in ihren Briefen.* Berlin: Verlag der Nation, 1964.

Jäckel, Günter, and Manfred Schlösser, eds. *Das Volk braucht Licht: Frauen zur Zeit des Aufbruchs 1790–1848 in ihren Briefen.* Darmstadt, Zurich: Agora, 1970. (Cited as Jäckel)

Karsch, Anna Louisa. *Auserlesene Gedichte.* 1764. Reprint with an afterword by Alfred Anger, Stuttgart: Metzler, 1966.

———. *Gedichte. Von Anna Louisa Karschin geb. Dürbach.* Ed. C. L. von Klenke. 2nd ed. Berlin: F. Maurer, 1797.

———. *Herzgedanken: Das Leben der "deutschen Sappho" von ihr selbst erzählt.* Edited with preface by Barbara Beuys. Frankfurt a. M.: Societäts-Verlag, 1981.

———. *Die Karschin: Friedrichs des Grossen Volksdichterin. Ein Leben in Briefen.* Ed. Elisabeth Hausmann. Frankfurt a. M.: Societäts-Verlag, 1933. (Cited as Hausmann)

———. *"O, mir entwischt nicht, was die Menschen fühlen:" Anna Louisa Karschin: Gedichte und Briefe; Stimmen der Zeitgenossen.* Ed. Gerhard Wolf. Berlin: Der Morgen, 1981.

Keil, Robert ed. *Frau Rath. Briefwechsel von Katharina Elisabeth Goethe.* Leipzig: F. A. Brockhaus, 1871.

Keller, Gottfried. *Gesammelte Briefe.* Ed. Carl Helbling. 4 vols. Bern: Verlag Benteli, 1951.

Klopstock, Meta. *Briefwechsel mit Klopstock, ihren Verwandten und Freunden.* Ed. with commentary by Hermann Tiemann. Vol. 1: 1751–54; 2: 1754-58; 3: Erläuterungen. With Contributions from Erich Trunz. Hamburg: Maximilian-Gesellschaft, 1956.

———. *"Es sind wunderliche Dinger, meine Briefe": Briefwechsel 1751–1758.* Bibliothek des 18. Jahrhunderts. Ed. Franziska and Hermann Tiemann. Munich: S. H. Beck, 1980.

———. *Hinterlassne Schriften.* Expanded and improved edition. In: *Klopstocks Werke,* vol. 11. Leipzig: Göschen, 1816.

Koch-Gontard, Clotilde. *Clotilde Koch-Gontard an ihre Freunde: Briefe und Erinnerungen aus der Zeit der deutschen Einheitsbewegung 1843–1869.* Frankfurter Lebensbilder 16. Ed. Wolfgang Klötzer. Frankfurt a. M.: Waldemar Kramar, 1969.

Körner, Josef, ed. *Briefe von und an Friedrich und Dorothea Schlegel.* Berlin: Askanischer Verlag Carl Albert Kinkle, 1926.

———. *Krisenjahre der Frühromantik: Briefe aus dem Schlegelkreis.* 3 vols. Bern: Francke Verlag, 1969.

Köster, Albert. *Der letzte Brief von Goethes Mutter an Bettina Brentano.* Leipzig: Insel, 1918.

La Roche, Sophie von. *Geschichte des Fräuleins von Sternheim.* Edited with an afterword by Barbara Becker-Cantarino. Stuttgart: Philipp Reclam jun., 1983.

———. *"Ich bin mehr Herz als Kopf:" Sophie von La Roche. Ein Lebensbild in Briefen.* Munich: Beck, 1983.

———. *Pomona für Teutschlands Töchter.* 24 issues.(1783–84). Reprint, edited by Jürgen Vorderstemann. 4 vols. London: Saur, 1988.

———. *Rosaliens Briefe an ihre Freundin Mariane von St.\*\*\*.* 3 vols. Altenburg: Richtersche Buchhandlung, 1779–81.

Lewald, Fanny. "Der Cultus des Genius. Brief an Bettina von Arnim." *Blätter für literarische Unterhaltung.* 171–74 (18–21 July 1849): 681–83, 685–87, 689–90, 693–94

———. *Erinnerungen aus dem Jahre 1848.* 2 vols. Braunschweig: Friedrich Vieweg und Sohn, 1850.

———. *Für und wider die Frauen: Vierzehn Briefe.* 2nd ed. Berlin: Otto Janke, 1875.

———. *Meine Lebensgeschichte.* Ed. and intro. Gisela Brinker-Gabler. Frankfurt a. M.: Fischer, 1980.

———. *Osterbriefe für die Frauen.* Berlin: Otto Janke, 1863.

Mereau, Sophie. *Amanda und Eduard. Ein Roman in Briefen.* 2 vols. Frankfurt: Wilmans, 1803.

———. *Das Blüthenalter der Empfindung* . 1794 . Reprint with an afterword and bibliography by Herman Moens, Stuttgart: Akademischer Verlag, 1982.

———. "Briefe der Ninon von Lenclos." *Erholungen.* Ed. W. G. Becker. Leipzig, 1797. 3: 189–214

———. "Bruchstücke aus den Briefen und dem Leben der Ninon de Lenclos." *Jahrbuch für Deutsche Frauen* (1805): 2,5: 111–24; 3,9: 92, 118; 3,10: 108–18; 3,12: 116–22

———. "Flucht nach der Hauptstadt." *Taschenbuch auf das Jahr 1806.* Frankfurt a. M.: Wilmans, 1806. 137–84.

———, ed. *Kalathiskos.* Berlin: Fröhlich, vols. I, II. 1801–2. Facsimile with afterword by Peter Schmidt, Heidelberg: Lamberg Schneider, 1968.

Michaelis-Böhmer-Schlegel-Schelling, Caroline. *Briefe von Caroline Michaelis-Böhmer-Schlegel-Schelling.* Ed. Sigrid Damm. Leipzig: Philipp Reclam jun., 1979.

Mundt, Theodor. *Charlotte von Stieglitz, ein Denkmal.* Berlin: Veit, 1835.

———. *Geschichte der Literatur der Gegenwart*. Vol. 2 of *Friedrich Schlegel's Geschichte der alten und neuen Literatur*. 2 vols. Berlin: M. Simon, 1842.

Naubert, Benedikte. *Heerfort und Klärchen. Etwas für empfindsame Seelen*. Afterword by Gerhard Sauder. Hildesheim: Gerstenberg, 1982.

Novalis. *Schriften: Die Werke Friedrich von Hardenbergs*. Ed. Paul Kluckhohn and Richard Samuel. 4 vols. Stuttgart: Kohlhammer, 1960-75.

Preitz, Max. "Karoline von Günderrode in ihrer Umwelt. I. Briefe von Lisette und Gottfried Nees von Esenbeck, Karoline von Günderrode, Friedrich Creuzer, Clemens Brentano und Susanne von Heyden." *Jahrbuch des Freien Deutschen Hochstifts* (1962): 208–306.

———. "Karoline von Günderrode in ihrer Umwelt. II. Karoline von Günderrodes Briefwechsel mit Friedrich Karl und Gunda von Savigny." *Jahrbuch des Freien Deutschen Hochstifts* (1964): 185–235.

———, ed. *Friedrich Schlegel und Novalis: Biographie einer Romantikerfreundschaft in ihren Briefen*. Darmstadt: Hermann Gentner Verlag, 1957.

Preitz, Max, and Doris Hopp. "Karoline von Günderrode in ihrer Umwelt. III. Karoline von Günderrodes Studienbuch." *Jahrbuch des Freien Deutschen Hochstifts* (1975): 223–323.

Raich, J. M., ed. *Dorothea v. Schlegel geb. Mendelssohn und deren Söhne Johannes und Philipp Veit. Briefwechsel im Auftrage der Familie Veit*. 2 vols. Mainz: Verlag von Franz Kirchheim, 1881.

Richter, Jean Paul. *Sämtliche Werke*. Ed. Eduard Berend. 33 vols. in 3 parts. Weimar: Hermann Böhlaus Nachfolger, 1927–64.

Runckel, Dorothee Henriette von. *Moral für Frauenzimmer nach Anleitung der Moralischen Vorlesungen des sel. Prof. Gellerts v. anderer Sittenlehrer, m. Zusätzen von Dorothee Henriette v. Runckel*. Dresden: Runckel, 1774.

Runckel, Dorothee Henriette von, ed. *Sammlung freundschaftlicher Originalbriefe, zur Bildung des Geschmacks für Frauenzimmer*. Dresden, Harpeterschen Schriften, 1777/9.

Sand, George. *Correspondance: Suppléments (1817–1876)*. Ed. Georges Lubin. Vol. XXV. Paris: Classiques Garnier, 1991.

Schiller, Friedrich. *Werke. Nationalausgabe*. Weimar: Böhlau, 1972.

Schlegel, Dorothea. *Florentin: Roman-Fragmente-Varianten*. Edited with an afterword by Lilane Weissberg. Berlin: Ullstein, 1987.

Schlegel, Dorothea Mendelssohn Veit. *Florentin. A Novel*. Translated with an intro. and essay by Edwina Lawler and Ruth Richardson. Vol. 1 of *Dorothea Mendelssohn Veit Schlegel (1764–1839): Life, Thought, and Works*. 11 vols. planned; 2 vols to date. Lewiston, N.Y.: Edwin Mellen, 1988—.

———. *Camilla. A Novella*. Ed. Ruth Richardson and Hans Eichner. Trans. Edwina Lawler. Vol. 2 of *Dorothea Mendelssohn Veit Schlegel (1764-1839): Life, Thought, and Work*, 1990.

———. *Correspondence: The Berlin and Jena Years (1764–1802)*. Translated by Edwina and Ruth Richardson. Vol. 3 of *Dorothea Mendelssohn Veit Schlegel (1764–1839): Life, Thought, and Works*. Forthcoming.

Schlegel, Dorothea and Friedrich. *Geschichte des Zauberers Merlin*. Afterword by Klaus Günzel. Cologne: Eugen Diederichs Verlag, 1984.

Schlegel, Friedrich. *Kritische Friedrich-Schlegel-Ausgabe*. Ed. Ernst Behler with the assistance of Jean-Jacques Anstett and Hans Eichner. Paderborn, Munich, Vienna: Verlag Ferdinand Schöningh; Zürich: Thomas-Verlag. 1958—. (Cited as *KFSA*.)

———. *Lessings Gedanken und Meinungen aus dessen Schriften*. Leipzig: J. C. Hinrichs, 1804.

———. *Literary Notebooks 1797–1801*. Edited with intro. and commentary by Hans Eichner. London: The Athlone Press, University of London, 1957.

———. *Werke in zwei Bänden*. Ed. Nationale Forschungs-und Gedenkstätten der Klassischen Deutschen Literatur in Weimar. 2 vols. Berlin, Weimar: Aufbau Verlag, 1980. (Cited as *Werke*).

Schlegel-Schelling, Caroline. *Caroline. Briefe aus der Frühromantik*. Ed. Erich Schmidt, revised and enlarged by Georg Waitz. 2 vols. Leipzig: Insel, 1913. (Cited as *Caroline*.)

———. *"Lieber Freund, ich komme weit her schon an diesem frühen Morgen": Caroline Schlegel-Schelling in ihren Briefen*. Ed. Sigrid Damm. Darmstadt: Luchterhand, 1980.

Varnhagen von Ense, Karl August. *Denkwürdigkeiten und vermischte Schriften*. 9 vols. 2nd ed. Leipzig: Brockhaus, 1837–59.

Varnhagen, Rahel. *Briefe an eine Freundin: Rahel Varnhagen an Rebecca Friedländer*. Ed. Deborah Hertz. Cologne: Kiepenheuer and Witsch, 1988.

———. *Gesammelte Werke*. Ed. Konrad Feilchenfeldt, Uwe Schweikert, and Rahel E. Steiner. Munich: Matthes and Seitz, 1983. (Cited as *GW*.)

———. *Jeder Wunsch wird Frivolität genannt: Briefe und Tagebücher*. Ed. Marlis Gerhardt. Darmstadt: Luchterhand, 1983.

———. *Rahel. Ein Buch des Andenkens für ihre Freunde*. Ed. Karl Varnhagen von Ense. 1834. Munich: Matthes & Seitz Verlag, 1983.

———. *Rahel Varnhagen im Umgang mit ihren Freunden (Briefe 1793–1833)*. Ed. Friedhelm Kemp. Munich: Kösel-Verlag, 1967.

Varnhagen, Rahel and Pauline Wiesel. *"Ein jeder machte seine Frau aus mir wie er sie liebte und verlangte": Ein Briefwechsel*. Ed. Marlis Gerhardt. Darmstadt: Luchterhand, 1987.

Weidemann, Luise. *Erinnerungen, nebst Lebensabrissen ihrer Geschwister und Briefen Schellings und anderer*. Ed. Julius Steinberger. Göttingen: Vereinigung Göttinger Bücherfreunde, 1929.

Wieneke, Ernst, ed. *Caroline und Dorothea Schlegel in Briefen*. Weimar: Gustav Kiepenheuer, 1914.

## Secondary Literature

Adelson, Leslie. "Racism and Feminist Aesthetics: The Provocation of Anne Duden's *Opening of the Mouth*." *Signs* 13,2 (Winter 1988): 234–52.

Alker, Ernst. *Die deutsche Literatur im 19. Jahrhundert*. Stuttgart: Kröner, 1969.

Alberti, Conrad. *Bettina von Arnim*. Leipzig: Otto Wigand, 1885.

Altman, Janet Gurkin. *Epistolarity. Approaches to a Form*. Columbus: Ohio State University Press, 1982.

Andersen, Margret, ed. *Mother Was Not a Person*. Montreal: Content Publishing Limited and Black Rose, 1972

*Anna Louisa Karsch (1722–1791): Dichterin für Liebe, Brot und Vaterland. Ausstellung zum 200. Todestag 10. Oktober bis 16. November 1991.* Berlin: Staatsbibliothek Preußischer Kulturbesitz, 1991.

Arendt, Hannah. *Rahel Varnhagen: Lebensgeschichte einer deutschen Jüdin aus der Romantik.* 1959. Munich: R. Piper & Co. Verlag, 1983.

———. *The Human Condition.* Chicago: University of Chicago Press, 1958.

Arnim, Hans von. *Bettina von Arnim.* Berlin: Haude und Spenersche Verlagsbuchhandlung, 1963.

Badinter, Elisabeth. *Mother Love: Myth and Reality: Motherhood in Modern History.* Forward by Francine du Plessix Gray. New York: Macmillan, 1980.

Bäumer, Gertrud. *Gestalt und Wandel: Frauenbildnisse.* Berlin: F. A. Herbig, 1939.

Bäumer, Konstanze. "*Goethes Briefwechsel mit einem Kinde*—Ein weiblicher Bildungsroman des 19. Jahrhunderts." Ph. D. diss., University of California, Davis, 1983.

———. *'Bettine, Psyche, Mignon' Bettina von Arnim und Goethe.* Stuttgarter Arbeiten zur Germanistik 139. Stuttgart: Akademischer Verlag, 1986.

———. "Reisen als Moment der Erinnerung: Fanny Lewalds (1811–1889) 'Lehr-und Wanderjahr'." Joeres and Burkhard. 137–57.

Barthel, Karl. *Deutsche Nationalliteratur der Neuzeit in einer Reihe von Vorlesungen.* 4th ed. Braunschweig: Verlag der Hofbuchhandlung von Eduard Leibrock, 1855.

Bateson, Mary Catherine. *Composing A Life.* New York: Plume/Penguin, 1990.

Becker-Cantarino, Bärbel. "Priesterin und Lichtbringerin. Zur Ideologie des weiblichen Charakters in der Frühromantik." Paulsen. 111–24.

———. "Schlegels *Lucinde* : Zum Frauenbild der Frühromantik." *Colloquia Germanica* 10 (1976–77): 128–39.

Becker-Cantarino, Barbara. *Der lange Weg zur Mündigkeit: Frauen und Literatur (1500–1800).* Stuttgart: J. B. Metzler, 1987.

———. "Frauen in den Glaubenskämpfen: Öffentliche Briefe, Lieder und Gelegenheitsschriften." Brinker-Gabler, *Deutsche Literatur von Frauen*, Vol. 1. 149–72.

———. "Leben als Text: Briefe im 18. Jahrhundert." *Frauen Literatur Geschichte.* 83–103.

———. "Outsiders: Women in German Literary Culture of Absolutism." *Jahrbuch für Internationale Germanistik* 16.2. (1985): 153–63.

———. "Zur Theorie der literarischen Freundschaft im 18. Jahrhundert am Beispiel der Sophie La Roche." Mauser and Becker-Cantarino. 47–74.

———, ed. *Die Frau von der Reformation zur Romantik. Die Situation der Frau vor dem Hintergrund der Literatur und Sozialgeschichte.* Bonn: Bouvier, 1980.

Bennholdt-Thomsen, Anke, and Anita Runge, eds. *Anna Louisa Karsch (1722-1791): Von schlesischer Kunst und Berliner "Natur:" Ergebnisse des Symposions zum 200. Todestag der Dichterin.* Göttingen: Wallstein Verlag, 1992.

Benstock, Shari. *The Private Self. Theory and Practice of Women's Autobiographical Writings.* Chapel Hill: North Carolina University Press, 1988.

Bergemann, Fritz. "Bettinas Leben mit Goethe". *Bettinas Leben und Briefwechsel mit Goethe.* Leipzig: Insel, 1927. 9–182.

Berghahn, Klaus. "New Historicism: Editorial Introduction." *Monatshefte* 84.2 (Summer 1992): 141–47.

Best, Otto F. *Handbuch literarischer Fachbegriffe: Definitionen und Beispiele.* Frankfurt: Fischer, 1978.

Beyer, Paul. "Bettinas Arbeit an *Goethes Briefwechsel mit einem Kinde.*" *Von deutscher Sprache und Art: Beiträge zur Geschichte der neueren deutschen Sprache, zur Sprachkunst, Sprachpflege und zur Volkskunde.* Ed. Max Preitz. Frankfurt a. M.: Diesterweg, 1925. 65–82.

Bissing, Henriette von. *Das Leben der Dichterin Amalie von Helvig, geb. Freiin von Imhoff.* Berlin: Wilhelm Hertz, 1889.

Blackall, Eric A. "The Contemporary Background to a Passage in the Lehrjahre." *Aspekte der Goethezeit.* Ed. Stanley A. Corngold, Michael Curschmann, and Theodore J. Ziolkowski. Göttingen: Vandenhoeck & Ruprecht, 1977.

———. *Goethe and the Novel.* Ithaca, London: Cornell University Press, 1976.

Blackwell, Jeannine. "Anonym, verschollen, trivial: Methodological Hindrances in Researching German Women's Literature." *Women in German Yearbook: Feminist Studies and German Culture* 1(1985). Ed. Marianne Burkhard and Edith Waldstein. Lanham: University Press of America, 1985: 39–59.

Bliven, Naomi. "Books: Old Pros." Book Review of *Bitter Healing: German Women Writers, 1700–1830.* Ed. Jeannine Blackwell and Susanne Zantop. *New Yorker,* 25 March 1991, 86–88.

Blochmann, Elisabeth. *Das "Frauenzimmer" und die "Gelehrsamkeit."* Heidelberg: Quelle & Meyer, 1966.

Börne, Ludwig. "Goethes Briefwechsel mit einem Kinde. Geschrieben in Auteuil bei Paris im Sommer 1835." *Gesammelte Schriften.* 12 vols. Vienna: Tendler & Comp., 1868. 6: 115–28.

Bovenschen, Silvia. *Die imaginierte Weiblichkeit: Exemplarische Untersuchungen zu kulturgeschichtlichen und literarischen Präsentationsformen des Weiblichen.* Frankfurt a. M.: Suhrkamp, 1980.

———. "Über die Frage: gibt es eine 'weibliche' Ästhetik." *Ästhetik und Kommunikation* 25 (1976): 60–76.

———. "Vom Tanz der Gedanken und Gefühle. Die unaufhörliche Berührung von Tiefe und Oberfläche, Alltag und Ewigkeit. Über die Freundschaft." *Frankfurter Allgemeine Zeitung,* 25 January 1986, Supplement, n. p.

Brandes, Helga. "Das Frauenzimmer-Journal: Zur Herausbildung einer journalistischen Gattung im 18. Jahrhundert." Brinker-Gabler, *Deutsche Literatur von Frauen,* vol. 1. 452–68.

*Briefe einer grossen Liebe: die private Korrespondenz aus dem Nachlass der Herzogin von Windsor.* Munich: Droemer Knaur, 1986.

*Briefe über die Liebe: von Frauen in Haft und Verbannung.* Julia Wosnessenskaja, ed. Munich: Roitmann, 1987.

*Briefwechsel mit Autoren: Rudolf Georg Binding und Thomas Mann.* Ed. Hans Wysling. Frankfurt a. M.: Fischer, 1988.

*Briefwechsel mit Autoren: Gottfried Bermann Fischer und Brigitte Bermann Fischer.* Ed. Reiner Stach with assistance from Karin Schlapp and introduction by Bernhard Zeller. Frankfurt a. M.: Fischer, 1990.

*Briefwechsel mit Autoren: Samuel Fischer und Hedwig Fischer.* Ed. Dierk Rudewald and Corinna Fiedler with introduction by Bernhard Zeller. Frankfurt a. M.: Fischer, 1989.

Brinker-Gabler, Gisela, ed. *Deutsche Literatur von Frauen.* Vol. 1: *Vom Mittelalter bis zum Ende des 18. Jahrhunderts.* Vol. 2: *19. und 20. Jahrhundert.* Munich: C. H. Beck, 1988.

Brinker-Gabler, Gisela, Karola Ludwig, and Angela Wöffen. *Lexikon deutschsprachiger Schriftstellerinnen 1800–1945.* Munich: dtv, 1986.

Brinkmann, Richard, ed. *Romantik in Deutschland.* Stuttgart: Metzler, 1978.

Brockmeyer, Rainer. "Geschichte des deutschen Briefes von Gottsched bis zum Sturm und Drang." Ph. D. diss., Münster, 1959.

Bunzel, Wolfgang. "'Phantasie ist die freie Kunst der Wahrheit.' Bettine von Arnims poetisches Verfahren in 'Goethes Briefwechsel mit einem Kinde'." *Internationales Jahrbuch der Bettina-von-Arnim-Gesellschaft* 1 (1987): 7-28.

Bürgel, Peter. "Der Privatbrief. Entwurf eines heuristischen Modells." *Deutsche Vierteljahrschrift für Literaturwissenschaft und Geistesgeschichte* 50 (1976) 281–97.

Bürger, Christa. *Leben Schreiben: Die Klassik, die Romantik und der Ort der Frauen.* Stuttgart: J. B. Metzler, 1990.

――――. "'Die mittlere Sphäre' : Sophie Mereau—Schriftstellerin im Klassischen Weimar." In Brinker-Gabler, *Deutsche Literatur von Frauen.* Vol. 1: 366-88.

Burger, Emil, ed. *Deutsche Frauenbriefe aus zwei Jahrhunderten.* Frankfurt a. M., Berlin: Moritz Diesterweg, 1908.

Burkhard, Marianne, ed. *Gestaltet und Gestaltend: Frauen in der deutschen Literatur.* Vol. 10 of *Amsterdamer Beiträge zur Germanistik.* Amsterdam: Rodopi, 1980.

Burwick, Roswitha. "Bettina von Arnims *Die Günderode:* Zum Selbstverständnis der Frau in der Romantik." *Frauensprache—Frauenliteratur.* 62–67.

Carriere, Moritz. "Bettina von Arnim." *Lebensbilder.* Leipzig: Brockhaus, 1890. 226–75.

Cott, Nancy F. *The Bonds of Womanhood.* New Haven: Yale University Press, 1977.

Critchfield, Richard. "Beyond Luise Gottsched's *Die Pietisterey im Fischbein-Rocke oder die Doctormäßige Frau." Jahrbuch für Internationale Germanistik* 17.2 (1985): 112–20.

Crumpacker, Laurie. "Letters to a Friend: Feminism and Politics in the Correspondence of Four Eighteenth-Century Women." *CEA Forum* 15.4 (1985): 7–9.

Culley, Margo. "Women's Vernacular Literature: Teaching the Mother Tongue." Hoffmann and Culley 9–17.

Dahrendorf, R. "Demokratie und Sozialstruktur in Deutschland." *Gesellschaft und Freiheit: Zur soziologischen Analyse der Gegenwart.* Munich: R. Piper, 1961.

Dawson, Ruth. "Reconstructing Women's Literary Relationships: Sophie Albrecht and Female Friendship." Goodman and Waldstein. 173–87.

de Lauretis, Teresa, ed. *Feminist Studies/Critical Studies.* Bloomington: Indiana University Press, 1986.

――――. "Feminist Studies/Critical Studies: Issues, Terms, and Contexts. de Lauretis. 1–19.

*Dichter der deutschen Romantik: Zeugnisse aus dem Besitz des Freien Deutschen Hochstifts. Ausstellung 15. Juni bis 15. September, 1976.* Ed. Detlev Lüders. Frankfurt a. M.: Freies Deutsches Hochstift, 1976.

Dischner, Gisela. *Bettina von Arnim: Eine weibliche Sozialbiographie aus dem neunzehnten Jahrhundert.* Berlin: Klaus Wagenbach, 1977.

――――. *Caroline und der Jenaer Kreis: Ein Leben zwischen bürgerlicher Vereinzelung und romantischer Geselligkeit.* Berlin: Klaus Wagenbach, 1979.

Drewitz, Ingeborg. *Bettine von Arnim: Romantik—Revolution—Utopie.* Düsseldorf/ Cologne: Eugen Diederichs Verlag, 1969.

Duden, Barbara. "Das schöne Eigentum: Zur Herausbildung des bürgerlichen Frauenbildes an der Wende vom 18. zum 19. Jahrhundert." *Kursbuch 47 (1977): 125–43.*

Dutu, Alexandru, Edgar Hösch, and Norbert Oellers. *Brief und Briefwechsel in Mittel– und Osteuropa im 18. und 19. Jahrhundert. Brief und Briefwechsel im 18. und 19. Jahrhundert als Quellen der Kulturbeziehungsforschung.* Essen: Hobbing, 1989.

Eakin, Paul John. *Touching the World: Reference in Autobiography.* Princeton, N. J.: Princeton University Press, 1992.

Ebrecht, Angelika. "Brieftheoretische Perspektiven von 1850 bis ins 20. Jahrhundert." Ebrecht, Nörtemann, Schwarz. 239–56.

Ebrecht, Angelika, Regina Nörtemann, and Herta Schwarz, eds. *Brieftheorie des 18. Jahrhunderts: Texte, Kommentare, Essays.* Stuttgart: Metzler, 1990.

Eichendorff, Joseph von. "Die Deutsche Salon-Poesie der Frauen." *Schriften zur Literatur.* Vol. 3 of his *Werke.* 4 vols. Munich: Winkler Verlag, 1970. 87–101.

———. *Geschichte der poetischen Literatur Deutschlands.* Ed. and intro. by Wilhelm Kosch. Kempten, Munich: J. Kösel, 1906.

Elbogen, Paul, ed. *Geliebter Sohn: Elternbriefe an berühmte Deutsche.* Berlin: Ernst Rowohlt Verlag, 1930.

———. *Liebste Mutter: Briefe berühmter Deutscher an ihre Mütter.* Berlin: Ernst Rowohlt Verlag, 1930.

Engelsing, Rolf. *Der Bürger als Leser: Lesergeschichte in Deutschland 1500–1800.* Stuttgart: Metzler, 1974.

Faber du Faur, Curt von. "Goethe und Bettina von Arnim: Ein neuer Fund." *PMLA* 75 (1960): 216–30.

Faderman, Lillian. *Surpassing the Love of Men: Romantic Friendship and Love Between Women from the Renaissance to the Present.* New York: Morrow, 1981.

Faludi, Susan. *Backlash: The Undeclared War Against American Women.* New York: Doubleday, 1991.

Fass, Barbara. *'La Belle Dame Sans Merçi' and the Aesthetics of Romanticism.* Detroit: Wayne State University Press, 1974.

Feilchenfeldt, Konrad. "Zwischen Textkritik und Traditionsbewusstsein: Zur Editionsgeschichte neuerer deutscher Autoren in der ersten Hälfte des 19. Jahrhunderts." *Literaturwissenschaftliches Jahrbuch im Auftrage der Görres-Gesellschaft.* N.S. 12 (1971): 205–39.

———. "'Berliner Salon' und Briefkultur um 1800." *Juden in der deutschen Literatur I.* Spec. issue of *Deutschunterricht* 36.4 (1984): 77–99.

Fetterley, Judith. *The Resisting Reader: A Feminist Approach to American Fiction.* Bloomington, London: Indiana University Press, 1978.

Fischer, Klaus. "Ein Weib mit Hang zum Schlendrian." *Stuttgarter Zeitung.* 17 September 1988: Sonntagsbeilage, n. p.

Fleischmann, Uta. *Zwischen Aufbruch und Anpassung: Untersuchungen zu Werk und Leben der Sophie Mereau.* Frankfurt a. M.: Peter Lang, 1989.

Fortmüller, Heinz-Joachim. *Clemens Brentano als Briefschreiber.* Europäische Hochschulschriften 1, 143. Frankfurt a. M.: Peter Lang, 1977.

Fout, John C, ed. *German Women in the Nineteenth Century: A Social History.* New York, London: Holmes & Meier, 1984.

Fox-Genovese, Elizabeth. "Culture and Consciousness in the Intellectual History of European Women." *Signs* 12.3 (1987): 529–47.

*Frauen Literatur Geschichte. Schreibende Frauen vom Mittelalter bis zur Gegenwart.* Ed. Hiltrud Gnüg and Renate Möhrmann. Stuttgart: Metzler, 1985.

*Frauensprache—Frauenliteratur? Für und Wider einer Psychoanalyse literarischer Werke.* Vol. 6 of *Kontroversen, alte und neue: Akten des VII. Internationalen Germanisten-Kongresses Göttingen 1985.* 11 vols. Tübingen: Niemeyer, 1986.

Frederiksen, Elke. "Die Frau als Autorin zur Zeit der Romantik: Anfänge einer weiblichen literarischen Tradition." Burkhard. 83–108.

————. "German Women Authors in the Nineteenth Century: Where Are They?" *Beyond the Eternal Feminine: Critical Essays on Women and German Literature.* Ed. Susan L. Cocalis and Kay Goodman. Stuttgart: Akademischer Verlag Hans-Dieter Heinz, 1982. 177–201.

————, and Katherine R. Goodman. *Bettine Brentano-von Arnim: Gender and Politics.* Detroit: Wayne State University Press, 1995.

————, ed. *Women Writers of Germany, Austria, and Switzerland: An Annotated Bio-Bibliographical Guide.* New York: Greenwood Press, 1989.

Frederiksen, Elke and Monika Shafi. "'Sich im Unbekannten suchen gehen:' Bettina von Arnims *Die Günderode* als weibliche Utopie." In *Frauensprache—Frauenliteratur?* 54–61.

French, Lorely. Bettine von Arnim: Toward A Women's Epistolary Aesthetics and Poetics." Ph. D. diss., University of California, Los Angeles, 1986.

————. "'. . .ich wandte mich höflich an den Mann und schrieb in seinem Beysein schnell ein Versbriefchen': Poetry in Letters of German Women in the Late-Eighteenth and Early Nineteenth Centuries. *Pacific Coast Philology* 29.1 (September 1994): 51–63.

————. "'Meine beiden Ichs': Confrontations with Language and Self in Letters by Early Nineteenth-Century Women." *Women in German Yearbook* 5 (1989): 73–89.

————. "Strategies of Female Persuasion: The Political Letters of Bettina Brentano-von Arnim." Frederiksen and Goodman. 71–94.

————. "Travelers' Visions/Immigrants' Realities: Amalie Struve and Amalie Schoppe in the United States." Paper at the Modern Languages Association Conference, Chicago, 1990.

French, Marilyn. *Beyond Power: On Women, Men, and Morals.* New York: Ballantine, 1985.

Friedrichsmeyer, Sara. *The Androgyne in Early German Romanticism: Friedrich Schlegel, Novalis and the Metaphysics of Love* (Bern, New York: Peter Lang, 1983).

————. "Caroline Schlegel-Schelling: A Good Woman, and No Heroine." Goodman and Waldstein. 115–36.

————. "Paula Modersohn-Becker and the Fictions of Artistic Self-Representation." *German Studies Review* XIV, 3 (October 1991): 490–510.

————. "Romanticism and the Dream of Androgynous Perfection." *Deutsche Romantik and English Romanticism.* Ed. Thomas G. Gish and Sandra G. Frieden. Houston German Studies 5. Munich: Wilhelm Fink, 1984.

————. "'Seeds for the Sowing': The Diary of Käthe Kollwitz." *Arms and the Woman: War, Gender, and Literary Representation.* Ed. Helen Cooper, Adrienne Auslander Munich, Susan Merrill Squier. Chapel Hill: University of North Carolina Press, 1989. 205–24.

————. "Women's Writing and the Construct of an Integrated Self." In Friedrichsmeyer and Becker-Cantarino. 171–80.

Friedrichsmeyer, Sara, and Barbara Becker-Cantarino, eds. *The Enlightenment and its Legacy. Studies in German Literature in Honor of Helga Slessarev.* Bonn: Bouvier, 1991.

Friedrichsmeyer, Sara, and Jeanette Clausen. "What's Missing in New Historicism or the 'Poetics' of Feminist Literary Criticism." *Women in German Yearbook* 9 (1993). Ed. Jeanette Clausen and Sara Friedricksmeyer. Lanham: University of Nebraska Press, 1993, 253–58.

Frühwald, Wolfgang. "Clemens Brentano." *Deutsche Dichter der Romantik.* Ed. Benno von Wiese. Berlin: Erich Schmidt, 1971.

———, ed. *Probleme der Brief-Edition: Kolloquium der Deutschen Forschungsgemeinschaft, Schloß Tutzing am Starnberger See, 8.-11. September 1975.* Boppard: Boldt, 1977.

Fuhrimann, Klara. "Kobold der Romantik: Bettina von Arnim." *Das Wort: Literarische Beilage zu 'Du—Atlantis'* 10 (1965): 795–96.

Fuller, Margaret. "Bettine Brentano and her Friend Günderode." *The Dial* 7 (Jan. 1842): 313–57.

Fuss, Diana. *Essentially Speaking: Feminism, Nature and Difference.* New York: Routledge, 1989.

Gallas, Helga and Magdalene Heuser, eds. *Untersuchungen zum Roman von Frauen um 1800.* Untersuchungen zur deutschen Literaturgeschichte 55. Tübingen: Niemeyer, 1990.

Geertz, Clifford. *The Interpretation of Cultures.* New York: Basic Books, 1973.

Geiger, Ludwig. *Karoline von Günderode und ihre Freunde.* Stuttgart, Leipzig, Berlin, Vienna: Deutsche Verlage-Anstalt, 1895.

Gellert, Christian Fürchtegott. *Briefe an Fräulein Erdmuth von Schönfeld, nachmals Gräfin Bunau von Dahlen aus den Jahren 1758–1768.* Leipzig: Hirschfeld, 1861.

———. *Briefe, nebst einigen damit verwandten Briefen seiner Freunde.* Ed. Johann Adolf Schlegel and Gottlieb Leberecht Heyer. Leipzig: Weidmanns Erben und Reich, 1774.

———. *Briefwechsel Christian Fürchtegott Gellert's mit Demoiselle Lucius. Nebst einem Anhange . . . Sämmtlich aus den bisher meist noch ungedruckten originalen.* Ed. Friedrich Adolf Ebert. Leipzig: F. A. Brockhaus, 1823.

———. *Werke.* Ed. Gottfried Honnefelder. 2 vols. Frankfurt a. M.: Insel, 1979.

Gerhard, Ute. *Verhältnisse und Verhinderungen: Frauenarbeit, Familie und Rechte der Frauen im 19. Jahrhundert: Mit Dokumenten.* Frankfurt a. M.: Suhrkamp, 1978.

Gersdorff, Dagmar von. *"Dich zu lieben kann ich nicht verlernen": Das Leben der Sophie Brentano-Mereau.* Frankfurt a. M.: Insel,1984.

Gervinus, G[eorg] G[ottfried]. *Ueber den Goetheischen Briefwechsel.* Leipzig: Friedrich Engelmann, 1836.

Gilbert, Sandra M., and Susan Gubar. *The Madwoman in the Attic: The Woman Writer and the Nineteenth-Century Literary Imagination.* New Haven, London: Yale University Press, 1979.

Glaser, Horst Albert, ed. *Deutsche Literatur. Eine Sozialgeschichte zwischen Revolution und Restauration: Klassik, Romantik 1786–1815.* Vol. 5. Reinbeck bei Hamburg: Rowohlt, 1980.

Goetzinger, Germaine. *Für die Selbstverwirklichung der Frau: Louise Aston.* Frankfurt a. M.: Fischer, 1983.

Goldsmith, Elizabeth, ed. *Writing the Female Voice: Essays on Epistolary Literature.* Boston: Northeastern University Press, 1989.

Goodman, Katherine. *Dis/Closures: Women's Autobiography in Germany Between 1790 and 1914.* New York: Peter Lang, 1986.

———. "The Impact of Rahel Varnhagen on Women in the Nineteenth Century." Burkhard. 125–53.

———. "Poesis and Praxis in Rahel Varnhagen's Letters." *New German Critique* 27 (1982): 123–39.

———. "The Sign Speaks: Charlotte von Stein's Matinees." Goodman and Waldstein. 71–93.

Goodman, Katherine R., and Edith Waldstein, eds. *In the Shadow of Olympus: German Women Writers Around 1800.* Albany: State University of New York Press, 1992.

Goozé Marjanne Elaine. "Bettine von Arnim, the Writer." Ph. D. diss., University of California, Berkeley, 1984.

———. "The Seduction of Don Juan: Karoline von Günderrode's Romantic Reading of a Classic Story." In Friedrichsmeyer and Becker-Cantarino. 117–29.

Gotsmann, Elsie, ed. *Deutsche Briefe der Liebe und Freundschaft.* Berlin: Kiepenheuer, 1937.

Gottschall, Rudolph. *Die deutsche Nationalliteratur in der ersten Hälfte des neunzehnten Jahrhunderts.* Breslau: Trewendt & Granier, 1855.

Grenzmann, Wilhelm. "Brief." *Reallexikon der deutschen Literaturgeschichte.* Ed. Paul Merker and Wolfgang Stammler. 2nd ed., revised and enlarged by Werner Kohlschmidt and Wolfgang Mohr. Berlin: Walter de Gruyter & Co., 1958. 1: 186–93.

Guilloton, Doris Starr. "Rahel Varnhagen und die Frauenfrage in der deutschen Romantik: Eine Untersuchung ihrer Briefe und Tagebuchnotizen." *Monatshefte für deutschen Unterricht* 69 (1977): 391–403.

Gundelfinger, Friedrich, ed. *Romantiker-Briefe.* Jena: Eugen Diederichs, 1907.

Gundolf, Friedrich. *Romantiker.* Berlin-Wilmersdorf: H. Keller, 1930.

Gustedt, Jenny von. "Rahel Varnhagen, Bettina von Arnim und Charlotte Stieglitz." *Aus Goethes Freundeskreise.* Ed. Lily von Kretschmann. Braunschweig: Westermann, 1892. 35–55.

Habermas, Jürgen. *Strukturwandel der Öffentlichkeit: Untersuchungen zu einer Kategorie der bürgerlichen Gesellschaft.* Darmstadt: Luchterhand, 1982.

Hahn, Barbara. *"Antworten Sie mir!": Rahel Levin Varnhagens Briefwechsel.* Stroemfeld: Roter Stern, 1990.

———. "Rahel Levin Varnhagen und Bettine von Arnim: Briefe, Bücher, Biographien." *Frauen Literatur Politik,* Ed. Annegret Pelz, et. al. Literatur im historischen Prozeß, Neue Folge 21/22. Argument-Sonderband 172/173. Berlin: Argument-Verlag, 1988.

———. *Unter falschem Namen. Von der schwierigen Autorschaft der Frauen.* Gender Studies. Frankfurt a. M.: Suhrkamp, 1991.

———. "'Weiber verstehen alles à la lettre:' Briefkultur im beginnenden 19. Jahrhundert." Brinker-Gabler, *Deutsche Literatur von Frauen,* vol. 2. 13–27.

———, ed."*Im Schlaf bin ich wacher": Die Träume der Rahel Levin Varnhagen.* Frankfurt a. M.: Luchterhand, 1990.

Hahn, Barbara and Ursula Isselstein eds. *Rahel Levin Varnhagen: Die Wiederentdeck-*

*ung einer Schriftstellerin.* Zeitschrift für Literaturwissenschaft und Linguistik Beiheft 14. Göttingen: Vandenhoek and Ruprecht, 1987.

Hahn, Karl-Heinz. *Bettina von Arnim in ihrem Verhältnis zu Staat und Politik: mit einem Anhang ungedruckter Briefe.* Weimar: Herman Böhlaus Nachfolger, 1959.

Hajek, Hans. "Die Mystifizierung der Frau Rat durch Bettina Brentano." Ph. D. diss., Vienna, 1937.

Hammerstein, Katharina von. *Sophie Mereau-Brentano: Freiheit—Liebe—Weiblichkeit: Tricolore sozialer und individueller Selbstbestimmung um 1800.* Heidelberg: Universitätsverlag C. Winter, 1994.

Hang, Adelheid. "Sophie Mereau in ihren Beziehungen zur Romantik." Ph. D. diss., Frankfurt, 1934.

Hartwig, Helmut. "Zwischen Briefsteller und Briefpostkarte. Briefverkehr und Strukturwandel bürgerlicher Öffentlichkeit." *Gebrauchsliteratur. Methodische Überlegungen und Beispielanalysen.* Ed. Ludwig Fischer and Knut Hickethier. Stuttgart: Metzler, 1976. 114–26.

Hausen, Karin. "Die Polarisierung der Geschlechtscharaktere—Eine Spiegelung der Dissoziation von Erwerbs-und Familienleben." *Sozialgeschichte der Familie in der Neuzeit Europas.* Ed. Werner Conze. Stuttgart: Klett, 1976.

Haustein, Jens, ed. *Briefe an den Vater: Zeugnisse aus 3 Jahrhunderten.* Frankfurt a. M.: Insel, 1987.

Havelock, Eric A. *Preface to Plato.* Cambridge: Belknap Press of Harvard University Press, 1963.

Heilbrun, Carolyn G. *Writing A Woman's Life.* New York: W. H. Norton & Co., 1988.

Heiligenstaedt, Fritz, ed. *Deutsche Briefe von Gellert bis zur Romantik. Für den Schulgebrauch.* Schöninghs Ausgaben deutscher Klassiker. Erg. Bd. 11. Paderbon: Schöningh, 1914.

Heinrichs, Norbert and Horst Weeland, eds. *Briefe deutscher Philosophen (1750-1850): Microfiche-Edition.* Munich: K. G. Saur, 1990.

Henrichs, Norbert, ed. *Briefe deutscher Philosphen (1750–1850).* Munich: Saur, 1990.

Hermann, Anne. "Epistolary Essays by Virginia Woolf and Christa Wolf. *New German Critique* 38 (1986): 161–80.

Herminghouse, Patricia. "Die Wiederentdeckung der Romantik: Zur Funktion der Dichterfiguren in der neueren DDR-Literatur." *DDR-Roman und Literaturgesellschaft.* Ed. Jos Hoogeven and Gerd Labroisse. *Amsterdamer Beiträge zur neueren Germanistik* 11 and 12. Amsterdam: Rodopi, 1981, 217–48.

———. "Women and the Literary Enterprise in Ninetennth-Century Germany." Joeres and Maynes. 78–93.

Hertz, Deborah. "Inside Assimilation: Rebecca Friedländer's Rahel Varnhagen." Joeres and Maynes. 271–88.

———. *Jewish High Society in Old Regime Berlin.* New Haven: Yale University Press, 1988.

—. "The Literary Salon in Berlin, 1790–1806: The Social History of an Intellectual Institution." Ph. D. diss., University of Minnesota, 1979.

———. "Salonières and Literary Women." *New German Critique* 14 (Spring 1978): 97–108.

———. "The Varnhagen Collection is in Krakow." *American Archivist* 44 (1981): 223–28.

*Herzhaft in die Dornen der Zeit greifen* . . . : *Bettine von Arnim 1785–1859. Ausstellung 1985.* Ed. Christoph Perels. Frankfurt a. M.: Freies Deutsches Hochstift—Frankfurter Goethe Museum, 1985.

Heuser, Magdalene. "'Das beständige Angedencken vertritt die Stelle der Gegenwart.' Frauen und Freundschaften in Briefen der Frühaufklärung und Empfindsamkeit." Mauser and Becker-Cantarino. 141–65.

———. "Das Musenchor mit neuer Ehre zieren. Schriftstellerinnen zur Zeit der Frühaufklärung." Brinker-Gabler. Vol. 1: 293–313.

Hillard, Gustav. "Vom Wandel und Verfall des Briefes." *Merkur* 23 (1969): 342-51.

Hoffmann, Leonore and Margo Culley, eds. *Women's Personal Narratives: Essays in Criticism and Pedagogy.* New York: The Modern Language Association of America, 1985.

Hohendahl, Peter U. "Interdisciplinary German Studies: Tentative Conclusions." *German Quarterly* 62.2 (Spring 1989): 227–34.

Honnefelder, Gottfried. *Der Brief im Roman. Untersuchungen zur erzähltechnischen Verwendung des Briefes im deutschen Roman.* Bonn: Bouvier, 1975.

Hopfe, Annaliese. "Formen und Bereiche schöpferischen Verstehens bei Bettina von Arnim." Ph. D. diss., Munich, 1953.

Hummel-Haasis, Gerlinde, ed. *Schwestern zerreißt eure Ketten: Zeugnisse zur Geschichte der Frauen in der Revolution von 1848/49.* Munich: dtv, 1982.

"International Bookshelf." Book Review of *Bitter Healing: German Women Writers, 1700–1830.* Ed. Blackwell and Zantop. *MS* Nov./Dec. 1990: 57.

Isselstein, Ursula. "Rahels Schriften I. Karl August Varnhagens editorische Tätigkeit nach Dokumenten seines Archivs." Hahn und Isselstein. 16–29.

Jacobus, Mary. *Reading Woman: Essays in Feminist Criticism.* New York: Columbia University Press, 1986.

Jappe, Georg. "Vom Briefwechsel zum Schriftwechsel." *Merkur* 23 (1969): 351-62.

Joeres, Ruth-Ellen B. "That girl is an entirely different character! Yes, but is she a feminist?': Observations on Sophie von la Roche's *Geschichte des Fräuleins von Sternheim.*" Joeres and Maynes. 137–56.

———. "Self-Conscious Histories: Biographies of German Women in the Nineteenth Century." Fout. 172–96.

Joeres, Ruth Ellen B., and Marianne Burkhard, ed. *Out of Line/Ausgefallen: The Paradox of Marginality in the Writings of Nineteenth-Century German Women.* Vol. 28 of *Amsterdamer Beiträge zur neueren Germanistik.* Amsterdam: Rodopi, 1980.

Joeres, Ruth-Ellen B. and Mary Jo Maynes, eds. *German Women in the Eighteenth and Nineteenth Centuries: A Social and Literary History.* Bloomington: Indiana University Press, 1986.

Johnson, Barbara. *The Critical Difference: Essays in the Contemporary Rhetoric of Reading.* Baltimore: Johns Hopkins University Press, 1980.

Jonas, Ludwig and Wilhelm Dilthey, eds. *Aus Schleiermacher's Leben In Briefen.* 4 vols. Berlin: Georg Reimer, 1860–63.

Jones, Ann Rosalind. "Writing the Body: Toward and Understanding of *l'Écriture féminine.*" Showalter *The New Feminist Criticism: Essays on Women, Literature, and Theory.* 361–77.

Kaes, Anton. "New Historicism and the Study of German Literature." *German Quarterly* 62, no. 2 (Spring 1989): 210–19.

Kantorowicz, Alfred, ed. *Du wunderliches Kind: Bettine und Goethe. Aus dem Briefwechsel zwischen Goethe und Bettine von Arnim.* Schwerin: Petermänken-Verlag, 1953.

Kelling, Hans-Wilhelm. "The Idolatry of Poetic Genius in *Goethes Briefwechsel mit einem Kinde.*" *Publications of the English Goethe Society* 39 (1969): 16–30.

Kelly, Joan. "The Social Relations of the Sexes: Methodological Implications of Women's History and Theory." *The Essays of Joan Kelly.* Chicago: University of Chicago Press, 1984.

Kermode, Frank. "The High Cost of New History": Book Review of *Forms of Nationhood: The Elizabethan Writing of England* by Richard Helgerson, University of Chicago Press. *The New York Review of Books* 39.12 (25 June 1992): 43–45.

Kern, Bärbel and Horst Kern. *Madame Doctorin Schlözer: Ein Frauenleben in den Widersprüchen der Aufklärung.* Munich: C. H. Beck, 1990.

Kessler, Wolfgang. "Brief und Briefwechsel im 18. und 19. Jahrhundert als Quelle der historischen Kulturbeziehungsforschung." Dutu, Hösch, and Oellers. 341–48.

Kiesel, Helmuth and Paul Münch. *Gesellschaft und Literatur im 18. Jahrhundert: Voraussetzungen und Entstehung des literarischen Markts in Deutschland.* Munich: Verlag C. H. Beck, 1977.

Kirchner, Friedrich. *Die deutsche Nationalliteratur des neunzehnten Jahrhunderts.* Heidelberg: G. Weiss, 1894.

Kirsch, Sarah. "Wiepersdorf." *Rückenwind: Gedichte.* Ebenhausen bei Munich: Langewiesche-Brandt, 1978.

Kissel, Susan S. "Writer Anxiety versus the Need for Community in the Botts Family Letters." Hoffmann and Culley. 48–56.

Kleßmann, Eckart. *Caroline: Das Leben der Caroline Michaelis-Böhmer-Schlegel-Schelling 1763–1809.* Munich: Deutscher Taschenbuch Verlag, 1979.

Kletke, Hermann, ed. *Auserwählte Briefe deutscher Männer und Frauen.* Berlin: Hasselberg, 1860.

Kluckhohn, Paul. "Bettina von Arnim." *Neue Deutsche Biographie.* 1: 370–71.

Kolodny, Annette. "Some Notes on Defining a 'Feminist Literary Criticism'." *Critical Inquiry* 2 (1975): 75–92.

Konrad, Gustav. "Bettina von Arnim." *Deutsche Dichter der Romantik.* Ed. Benno von Wiese. Munich: E. Schmidt, 1971. 310–40.

Kord, Susanne. *Ein Blick hinter die Kulissen. Deutschsprachige Dramatikerinnen im 18. und 19. Jahrhundert.* Stuttgart: Metzler, 1992.

———. "'Und drinnen waltet die züchtige Hausfrau'? Caroline Pichler's Fictional Auto/Biographies." *Women in German Yearbook* 8 (1993). Ed. Jeanette Clausen and Sara Friedrichsmeyer. Lincoln: University of Nebraska Press, 1993: 141–58.

Kuby, Eva. "Politische Frauenvereine und ihre Aktivitäten 1848 bis 1850." *Schimpfende Weiber und patriotrische Jungfrauen. Frauen im Vormärz und in der Revolution 1848.* Carola Lipp, ed. Bühl-Moos: Elster Verlag, 1985. 248–69.

Kytzler, B. "Brief." *Lexikon der Alten Welt.* Ed. Carl Andresen, et. al. Zurich: Artemis Verlag, 1965. 496–501.

Laube, Heinrich. *Moderne Charakteristiken.* Vol. 49 of his *Gesammelte Werke.* Ed. Heinrich Hubert Houben. 50 vols. Leipzig: Max Hesses Verlag, 1909.

Lazarowicz, Margarete. *Karoline von Günderrode: Portrait einer Fremden.* Frankfurt a. M.: Peter Lang, 1986.

Lenk, Elisabeth. "Die Sich selbst verdoppelnde Frau." *Ästhetik und Kommunikation* 25 (1976): 84–87.

———. "Indiscretions of the Literary Beast: Pariah Consciousness of Women Writers Since Romanticism." Trans. Maureen Krause. *New German Critique* 27 (Fall 1982): 101–14.

Lennox, Sara. "Christa Wolf and the Women Romantics." *Studies in GDR Culture and Society* 2. Washington D.C.: University Press of America, 1982.

———. "Feminism and New Historicism." *Monatshefte* 84.2 (Summer 1992): 159-70.

———. "Feminist Scholarship and *Germanistik*." *German Quarterly* 62.2 (Spring 1989): 158–70.

———. "Some Proposals for Feminist Literary Criticism." *Women in German Yearbook* 7 (1991). Ed. Jeanette Clausen and Sara Friedrichsmeyer. Lincoln: University of Nebraska Press, 1991. 91–97.

Lerche Otto. "Einleitung" *Frauenbriefe aus Zeiten deutscher Not*. Cologne: Schmidt, 1929.

Leuschner, Brigitte. "Therese Huber als Briefschreiberin." Gallas and Heuser. 203–12.

Lewes, G. H. *Life and Works of Goethe: with Sketches of his Age and Contemporaries, from published and unpublished sources*. 2 vols. London: D. Nutt, 1855.

Lewis, Nigel. *Paperchase: Mozart, Beethoven, Bach ... The Search for Their Lost Music*. London: Hamish Hamilton, 1981.

Lilienfein, Heinrich. *Bettina: Dichtung und Wahrheit ihres Leben*. Munich: R. Bruckmann, 1949.

Lipp, Carola. "Bräute, Mütter, Gefährtinnen. Frauen und politische Öffentlichkeit in der Revolution 1848." *Grenzgängerinnen: Revolutionäre Frauen im 18. und 19. Jahrhundert*. Ed. Helga Grubitzsch, Hannelore Cyrus, and Elke Haarbusch. Düsseldorf: Schwann, 1985. 71–92.

———. "Frauen und Öffentlichkeit. Möglichkeiten und Grenzen politischer Partizipation im Vormärz und in der Revolution 1848/1849." *Schimpfende Weiber und patriotische Jungfrauen. Frauen im Vormärz und in der Revolution 1848*. Bühl-Moos: Elster Verlag, 1985. 270–301.

Loeper, Gustav von. "Bettina." *Allgemeine Deutsche Biographie*. Vol. 2. Berlin: Duncker & Humblot, 1875. 578–82.

———, ed. *Briefe Goethe's an Sophie von LaRoche und Bettina Brentano nebst dichterischen Beilagen*. Berlin: Verlag von Wilhelm Hertz, 1879.

Lützeler, Paul Michael, ed. *Romane und Erzählungen der deutschen Romantik: Neue Interpretationen*. Stuttgart: Reclam, 1981.

———. *Romane und Erzählungen zwischen Romantik und Realismus: Neue Interpretationen*. Stuttgart: Reclam, 1983.

Mallachow, Lore. *Bettina*. Berlin: Das Neue Berlin, 1952.

Mallon, Otto. "Bibliographische Bemerkungen zu Bettina von Arnims Sämtlichen Werken." *Zeitschrift für deutsche Philologie*. Sonderdruck (1931), 446-65.

Mander, Gertrud. *Bettina von Arnim*. Preußische Köpfe 11. Berlin: Stapp Verlag, 1982.

Marks, Elaine and Isabelle de Courtivron, eds. and introds. *New French Feminisms: An Anthology*. New York: Shocken Books, 1981.

Martens, Wolfgang. *Die Botschaft der Tugend: Die Aufklärung im Spiegel der deutschen Moralischen Wochenschriften*. Stuttgart: J. B. Metzler, 1968.

Mattenklott, Gert. *Jüdische Intelligenz in deutschen Briefen 1619–1988*. Frankfurt: Frankfurter Bund für Volksbildung, 1988.

Mattenklott, Gert, Hannelore and Heinz Schlaffer. *Deutsche Briefe 1750–1950*. Frankfurt a. M.: S. Fischer, 1988.

Maurer, Michael. "Das Gute und das Schöne." *Euphorion* 79 (1985), Vol. 2, 111-38.

Mauser, Wolfram and Barbara Becker-Cantarino. *Frauenfreundschaft-Männerfreundschaft: Literarische Diskurse im 18.Jahrhundert*. Tübingen: Max Niemeyer, 1991.

Mellor, Anne K. "On Romanticism and Feminism". In her *Romanticism and Feminism*. Bloomington: Indiana University Press, 1988. 3–9.

Menninghaus, Winfried. "Afterword." *Friedrich Schlegel: Theorie der Weiblichkeit*. Frankfurt a. M.: Insel, 1983.

Meyer, Eva. "Briefe oder die Autobiographie der Schrift." *Manuskripte* 94 (1986): 18–22.

Meyer-Hepner, Gertrud. "Bettina in Ost und West." *Neue Deutsche Literatur* 7,1 (1959): 152–54.

———. "Das Bettina von Arnim-Archiv." *Sinn und Form* 6 (1954): 594–611.

Milch, Werner. "Goethe und die Brentanos." *Kleine Schriften zur Literatur-und Geistesgeschichte*. Ed. Gerhard Burkhardt. Deutsche Akademie für Sprache und Dichtung 10. Heidelberg, Darmstadt: Lambert Schneider, 1957. 145–55.

———. *Die junge Bettine 1785–1811*. Ed. Peter Küpper. Heidelberg: Lothar Stiehm Verlag, 1968.

Miller, Nancy K. "Changing the Subject: Authorship, Writing, and the Reader." de Lauretis, *Feminist Studies/Critical Studies*. 102–20.

Modleski, Tania. "Feminism and the Power of Interpretation: Some Critical Readings." de Lauretis, *Feminist Studies/Critical Studies*. 121–38.

Mohr, Heinrich. "'Freundschaftliche Briefe'—Literatur oder Privatsache? Der Streit um Wilhelm Gleims Nachlaß." *Jahrbuch des Freien Deutschen Hochstifts* (1973): 14–75.

Moi, Toril. *Sexual/Textual Politics: Feminist Literary Theory*. London: Methuen, 1985.

Montrose, Louis A. "Professing the Renaissance: The Poetics and Politics of Culture." Vesser. *The New Historicism*. 15–36.

Müller, Hans von. *E. T. A. Hoffmann und Jean Paul, M. Dorffer und C. Richter, Helmine von Chézy und Adelheit von Bassewitz. Ihre Beziehungen zu einander und zu gemeinsamen Bekannten im Rahmen der Zeitgeschichte*. With assistance by Eduard Berend. 1 volume published: *Die Darstellung der Vorgänge bis zu Hoffmanns Verheiratung 1802*. Cologne: Gehly, 1927.

Müller, Wolfgang. G. "Der Brief." In: *Prosakunst ohne Erzählen: Die Gattungen der nicht-fiktionalen Kunstprosa*. Klaus Wiesenburger, ed. Konzepte der Sprach-und Literaturwissenschaft 34. Tübingen: Niemeyer, 1985, 67–87.

Muller, John P., and William J. Richardson, eds. *The Purloined Poe: Lacan, Derrida, and Psychoanalytic Reading*. Baltimore: Johns Hopkins University Press, 1988.

Neidhardt, Friedhelm. *Die Familie in Deutschland: Gesellschaftliche Stellung, Struktur und Funktionen*. Beiträge zur Sozialkunde 5. Opladen: Leske, 1966.

Nestor, Pauline. *Female Friendships and Communities: Charlotte Brontë, George Eliot, Elizabeth Gaskell*. Oxford: Clarendon Press, 1985.

Newton, Judith Lowder. "History as Usual? Feminism and the New Historicism." Veeser 152–67.

Nickisch, Reinhard M. G. "Briefkultur: Entwicklung und sozialgeschichtliche Bedeutung des Frauenbriefs im 18. Jahrhundert." Brinker-Gabler 1: 389-409.

————. "Die Frau als Briefschreiberin im Zeitalter der deutschen Aufklärung." *Wolfenbütteler Studien zur Aufklärung* 3 (1976): 29–65.

————. *Die Stilprinzipien in den deutschen Briefstellern des 17. und 18. Jahrhunderts.* Palaestra 254. Göttingen: Vandenhoeck & Ruprecht, 1969.

Nörtemann, Regina. "Brieftheoretische Konzepte im 18. Jahrhundert und ihre Genese." Ebrecht, Nörtemann, and Schwarz. 211–24.

Oehlke, Waldemar. *Bettina von Arnims Briefromane,* Palaestra 41. Berlin: Mayer & Müller, 1905.

Oellers, Norbert. "Der Brief als Mittel privater und öffentlicher Kommunikation in Deutschland im 18. Jahrhundert." Dutu, Hösch, and Oellers, 9–36.

Olney, James. *Metaphors of Self: The Meaning of Autobiography.* Princeton: Princeton University Press, 1972.

Ong, Walter J. *Orality and Literacy. The Technologizing of the Word.* New York and London: Methuen, 1982.

————. *The Presence of the Word: Some Prolegomena for Culture and Religious History.* Minneapolis: University of Minnesota, 1981.

Ortner, Sherry B. "Is Female to Male as Nature Is to Culture?" *Women, Culture, and Society.* Ed. Michelle Zimbalist Rosaldo and Louise Lamphere. Stanford: Stanford University Press, l974. 67–89.

Paulsen, Wolfgang, ed. *Die Frau als Heldin und Autorin: Neue kritische Ansätze zur deutschen Literatur.* Bern, Munich: Francke Verlag, 1979.

Pechter, Edward. "The New Historicism and Its Discontents: Politicizing Renaissance Drama." *PLMA* 102.2 (1987): 292–303.

Peck, Jeffrey. "There's No Place Like Home? Remapping the Topography of German Studies." *German Quarterly* 62.2 (Spring 1989): 178–87.

Perry, Ruth. *Women, Letters, and the Novel.* New York: AMS Press, Inc, 1980.

Peter, Klaus, ed. *Romantikforschung seit 1945.* Königstein/Ts.: Verlagsgruppe Athenäum-Hain-Scriptor Hanstein, 1980.

Pichler, Karoline. *Denkwürdigkeiten aus meinem Leben.* Edited with foreword and notes by Emil Karl Blümml. 2 vols. Münich: Georg Muller, 1914.

Pockels, Carl Friedrich. "Freundschaft der Weiber untereinander." In volume 2 of his *Versuch einer Charakteristik des weiblichen Geschlechts. Ein Sittengemählde des Menschen, des Zeitalters und des geselligen Lebens.* 4 vols. Hannover: Ritschersche Buchhandlung, 1798. 2: 168–232.

Poovey, Mary. *The Proper Lady and the Woman Writer: Ideology as Style in the Works of Mary Wollstonecraft, Mary Shelley, and Jane Austen.* Chicago, London: University of Chicago Press, 1984.

Proelss, Johannes. "Rahel, Bettina und die Stieglitz." *Das junge Deutschland. Ein Buch deutscher Geistesgeschichte.* Stuttgart: Cotta, 1892. 454–534.

Prokop, Ulrike. "Die Einsamkeit der Imagination: Geschlechterkonflikt und literarische Produktion um 1770." Brinker-Gabler 1. 325–65.

————. "Die Freundschaft zwischen Katharina Elisabeth Goethe und Bettina Brentano—Aspekte weiblicher Tradition." Mauser and Becker-Cantarino. 237–73.

Prutz, Robert. *Die deutsche Literatur der Gegenwart 1849–1858.* Leipzig: Voigt & Gunther, 1859.

Püschel, Ursula. "Bettina von Arnims politische Schriften." Diss. Berlin (Humboldt Universität), 1965.

————. "Weibliches und Unweibliches der Bettina von Arnim." *Mit allen Sinnen: Frauen in der Literatur. Essays.* Halle-Leipzig: Mitteldeutscher Verlag, 1980. 51–86.

Pusch, Luise F., ed. *Schwestern berühmter Männer: Zwölf biographische Portraits.* Frankfurt a. M.: Insel Taschenbuch, 1985.

Ranke, Leopold. *Das Briefwerk.* Ed. Walther Peter Fuchs. Hamburg: Hoffmann and Campe Verlag, 1949.

Rasch, Wolfdietrich. *Freundschaftskult und Freundschaftsdichtung im deutschen Schrifttum des 18. Jahrhunderts: Vom Ausgang des Barock bis zu Klopstock.* Halle/ Saale: Max Niemeyer, 1936.

Reitz, Eva. "Helmina von Chézy." Ph. D. diss., Frankfurt a. M., 1923.

Richel, Veronica C. *Luise Gottsched: A Reconsideration.* Bern: Peter Lang, 1973.

————. "Luise Gottsched's *Der Lockenraub* and Alexander Pope's *The Rape of the Lock.* A Comparative Analysis." *Neuphilologicale Mitteilungen* 76 (1975): 473–87.

Richter, Bruno. *Der Brief und seine Stellung in der Erziehung und im Unterricht seit Gellert..* Diss. Leipzig, 1900. Meissen: Richard Haubold, 1900.

Riemer, Friedrich Wilhelm. *Mittheilungen über Goethe. Aus mündlichen und schriftlichen, gedruckten und ungedruckten Quellen.* 2 vols. Berlin: Duncker und Humblot, 1841.

Riley, Helene M. Kastinger. *Die weibliche Muse: Sechs Essays über künstlerisch schaffende Frauen der Goethezeit.* Studies in German Literature, Linguistics, and Culture 8. Columbia, S.C.: Camden House, 1986.

Rosenblatt, Louise M. *The Reader, the Text, the Poem: the Transactional Theory of the Literary Work* . Carbondale: Southern Illinois University Press, 1978.

Rosenkranz, Karl. "Rahel, Bettina und Charlotte Stieglitz." *Studien zur Literatur-Geschichte.* Leipzig: Koschny, 1875. 102–23.

Runge, Anita and Lieselotte Steinbrügge, eds. *Die Frau im Dialog. Studien zur Geschichte und Theorie des Briefs.* Weinheim, Basel: Beltz, 1990.

Rupp, Leila J. "'Imagine My Surprise': Women's Relationships in Historical Perspective." *Frontiers* 5.3 (1980): 61–70.

Sanders, Ruth. "'Ein kleiner Umweg:' Das literarische Schaffen der Luise Gottsched." In Becker-Cantarino, ed. *Die Frau von der Reformation zur Romantik.* 170–94.

Scherr, Johannes. *Von Achtundvierzig bis Einundfünfzig. Eine Komödie der Weltgeschichte.* Leipzig: O. Wigand, 1868.

Schieth, Lydia. *Die Entwicklung des deutschen Frauenromans im ausgehenden 18. Jahrhundert.* Frankfurt a. M.: Peter Lang, 1987.

Schlaffer, Hannelore. "Weibliche Geschichtsschreibung—ein Dilemma." *Merkur* 445 (März 1986): 256–60.

Schlawe, Fritz. *Die Briefsammlungen des 19. Jahrhunderts. 1815–1915. Bibliographie der Briefausgaben und Geszwitregister der Briefschreiben und Briefempfänger.* 2 vols. Stuttgart: Metzler, 1969.

Schmidt-Fischer, Hildegard, ed. *"und immer weiter Schlägt das Herz." Briefe deutscher Frauen ausgew.* Berlin: Deutsche Buch-Gemeinschaft, 1938. n. p.

Schultz, H.J. *Frauen. Porträts aus zwei Jahrhunderten.* Stuttgart, 1981.

Schröder, Hannelore. "Das 'Recht' der Väter." *Feminismus: Inspektion der Herrenkultur: Ein Handbuch.* Ed. Luise F. Pusch. Frankfurt a. M.: Suhrkamp, 1983. 477–506.

Schüddekopf, Carl, and Oskar Walzel, eds. "Goethe und die Romantik. Briefe mit

Erläuterungen. 2. Theil." *Schriften der Goethe-Gesellschaft* 14. Ed. Erich Schmidt and Bernhard Suphan. Weimar: Verlag der Goethe-Gesellschaft, 1899. 159–97.

Schuller, Marianne. *Im Unterschied: Lesen/Korrespondieren/Adressieren.* Frankfurt a. M.: Verlag Neue Kritik, 1990.

Schultz, Hartwig. "Nachwort." *Clemens Brentanos Frühlingskranz* by Bettine von Arnim. Frankfurt a. M.: Insel Taschenbuch, 1985.

Secci, Lia. "German Women Writers and the Revolution of 1848." Fout. 151–71.

Segebrecht, Wulf. "Nachwort." *Clemens Brentanos Frühlingskranz aus Jugendbriefen ihm geflochten wie er selbst verlangt* by Bettine von Arnim. Munich: Winkler Verlag, l967.

Sennett, Richard. *The Fall of Public Man.* New York: Knopf, 1977.

Seyhan, Azade. "Prospects for Feminist Literary Theory in German Studies: A Response to Sara Lennox's Paper." *German Quarterly* 62.2 (Spring 1989): 171–77.

Showalter, Elaine. *The Female Malady: Women, Madness, and English Culture, 1830–1980.* New York: Penguin, 1985.

———. "Feminist Criticism in the Wilderness." In her *The New Feminist Criticism.* 243–70.

———, ed. *The New Feminist Criticism: Essays on Women, Literature and Theory.* New York: Pantheon Books, 1985.

Smith-Rosenberg, Carroll. "The Female World of Love and Ritual: Relations between Women in Nineteenth-Century America." *Signs* 1.1 (1975): 1–29.

Spacks, Patricia Meyer. *Gossip.* Chicago: University of Chicago Press, 1985.

Spender, Dale. "An Alternative to Madonna: How to deal with 'I'm not a feminist, but . . . .'" *MS* IV.1 (July/August 1993): 44–45.

Steinhausen, Georg. *Geschichte des deutschen Briefes: Zur Kulturgeschichte des deutschen Volkes.* 1889. Dublin, Zurich: Weidmann, 1968.

Stephan, Inge, and Sigrid Weigel. *Die verborgene Frau: Sechs Beiträge zu einer feministischen Literaturwissenschaft.* Argument Sonderband 96. Berlin: Argument Verlag, 1983.

Stern, Carola. *"Ich möchte mir Flügel wünschen:" Das Leben der Dorothea Schlegel.* Reinbek bei Hamburg: Rowohlt, 1990.

Stern, Guy. "Wieland als Herausgeber der *Sternheim.*" *Christoph Martin Wieland: Nordamerikanische Forschungsbeiträge zur 250. Wiederkehr seines Geburtstages 1983.* Ed. Hansjörg Schelle. Tübingen: Max Niemeyer, 1984. 195–208.

Stern, Ludwig. *Die Varnhagen von Ensesche Sammlung in der Königlichen Bibliothek zu Berlin.* Berlin: Behrend & Co., 1911.

Stöcker, Helene. "Bettina von Arnim." *Neue Generation. Zeitschrift für Mutterschutz und Sexualreform* 25 (1929): 99–105.

Susman, Margarethe. *Frauen der Romantik.* 1929. Reprint Cologne: Metzler, 1960.

———. *Deutung einer grossen Liebe: Goethe und Charlotte von Stein.* Zurich: Artemis Verlag, 1951.

Tanneberger, Irmgard. *Die Frauen der Romantik und das soziale Problem.* Oldenburg: Schulzesche Hofbuchdruckerei und Verlagsbuchhandlung, 1928.

Teraoka, Arlene Akiko. "Is Culture to us What Text is to Anthropology? A Response to Jeffrey M. Peck's Paper." *German Quarterly* 62.2 (Spring 1989): 188–91.

Tewarson, Heidi Thomann. "Jüdisches—Weibliches: Rahel Levin Varnhagens Reisen als Überschreitungen." *German Quarterly* 66.2 (Spring 1993): 145–59.

Todd, Janet. *Women's Friendship in Literature.* New York: Columbia University Press, 1980.

Touallion, Christine. *Der deutsche Frauenroman des 18. Jahrhunderts.* 1919. Bern: Peter Lang 1979.

———. "Frauendichtung." *Reallexikon der deutschen Literaturgeschichte.* Ed. Paul Merker and Wolfgang Stammler. 1st ed. Berlin: Walter de Gruyter & Co., 1925–26. 1: 374–76.

Treder, Uta. "Sophie Mereau: Montage und Demontage einer Liebe." Gallas and Heuser 172–83.

Treitschke, Heinrich. *Deutsche Geschichte im Neunzehnten Jahrhundert.* 5 vols. Leipzig: Verlag G. Hirzel, 1889.

Veeser, H. Aram, ed. *The New Historicism.* New York: Routledge, 1989.

Venske, Regula. "Disciplines and Daydreaming in the Works of a Nineteenth-Century Woman Author: Fanny Lewald." In Joeres and Maynes. 175–92.

Vosskamp, Wilhelm. "Dialogische Vergegenwärtigung beim Schreiben und Lesen: Zur Poetik des Briefromans im 18.Jahrhunderts." *Deutsche Vierteljahrsschrift* 45 (1971): 80–116.

Wagner, Maria. *Mathilde Franziska Anneke in Selbstzeugnissen und Dokumenten.* Frankfurt a. M.: Fischer, 1980.

Waldstein, Edith. *Bettine von Arnim and the Politics of Romantic Conversation.* Studies in German Literature, Linguistics, and Culture 33. Columbia, S.C.: Camden House, 1988.

———. "Bettina von Arnim and the Literary Salon: Women's Participation in the Cultural Life of Early Nineteenth-Century Germany." Ph. D. diss., Washington University, 1982.

Walter, Eva. *"Schreib oft, von Mägde Arbeit müde:" Lebenszusammenhänge deutscher Schriftstellerinnen um 1800—Schritte zur bürgerlichen Weiblichkeit.* Düsseldorf: Schwann, 1985.

Warhol, Robyn R. and Diane Price Herndl. *Feminisms: An Anthology of Literary Theory and Criticism.* New Brunswick, N.J.: Rutgers University Press, 1991.

Wasserzieher, Ernst. "Einleitung." *Briefe deutscher Frauen.* Berlin, Bonn: Ferd. Dümmlers Verlagsbuchhandlung, 1925. v–viii.

Weigel, Sigrid. "Der schielende Blick: Thesen zur Geschichte weiblicher Schreibpraxis." Stephan and Weigel. 83–137.

Weissberg, Liliane. "Turns of Emancipation: On Rahel Varnhagen's Letters." Goodman and Waldstein. 53–70.

Wellek, Albert. "Zur Phänomenologie des Briefes." *Witz, Lyrik, Sprache: Beiträge zur Literatur-und Sprachtheorie mit einem Anhang über den Fortschritt der Wissenschaft.* Bern, Munich: Francke, 1970. 43–67.

Wendeler, Camillus. *Briefwechsel des Freiherrn Karl Hartwig Gregor von Meusebach mit Jacob und Wilhelm Grimm. Nebst einleitenden Bemerkungen über den Verkehr des Sammlers mit gelehrten Freunden, Anmerkungen und einem Anhang von der Berufung der Brüder Grimm nach Berlin.* Heilbronn: Verlag von Gebr. Henninger, 1880.

Westermann, Charlotte, ed. *Briefe der Liebe aus drei Jahrhunderten deutscher Vergangenheit.* Ebenhausen. Munich: Wilhelm Langwiesche-Brandt, 1913.

Widmann, Hans, Ed. *Der deutsche Buchhandel in Urkunden und Quellen.* 2 vols. Hamburg: Dr. Ernst Hauswedel & Co., 1965.

Wieland, Christoph Martin. *C. M. Wieland's Briefe an Sophie von La Roche, nebst einem Schreiben von Gellert und Lavater.* Ed. Franz Horn. Berlin: E. H. G. Christiani, 1820.

———. *Gesammelte Schriften.* Ed. Deutsche Kommission der Königlich Preußischen Akademie der Wissenschaften. 33 vols. in 2 parts. Berlin: Weidmannische Buchhandlung, 1909–75.

Wilpert, Gero von. *Sachwörterbuch der Literatur.* 5th ed. Stuttgart: Alfred Kröner, 1969.

Winkle, Sally. *Woman as Bourgeois Ideal. A Study of Sophie von La Roche's "Geschichte des Fräuleins von Sternheim" and Goethe's "Werther."* New York: Peter Lang, 1988.

Wittmann, Reinhard, ed. *"Die Post will fort, ich muß schließen . . ." Briefe aus dem 18. Jahrhundert.* Munich: C. H. Beck, 1985.

Wolf, Christa. "Nun ja! Das nächste Leben geht aber heute an. Ein Brief über Bettine." *Die Günderode* by Bettine von Arnim. Frankfurt a. M.: Insel, 1983. 545–84.

———. *Kein Ort. Nirgends.* Darmstadt: Luchterhand, 1979.

———. "Kultur ist, was gelebt wird." *Alternative.* 143/44 (April/June 1982): 118–27.

———. *Nachdenken über Christa T.* Darmstadt: Luchterhand, 1971.

———. "Der Schatten eines Traumes: Karoline von Günderrode—ein Entwurf." *Der Schatten eines Traumes.* Darmstadt: Luchterhand, 1981. 5–52.

Woolf, Virginia. "Dorothy Osborne's Letters." *Collected Essays.* Vol 3. London: The Hogarth Press, 1966–67. 59–65.

———. *A Room of One's Own.* New York, London: Harcourt Brace Jovanovich, 1929.

Worley, Linda Kraus. "Sophie von LaRoche's Reisejournale: Reflections of a Traveling Subject." Friedrichsmeyer and Becker-Cantarino. 91–103.

Würzbach, Natascha, ed. *The Novel in Letters: Epistolary Fiction in the Early English Novel 1678–1740.* London: Routledge & Kegan Paul, 1969.

Wyss, Hilde. *Bettine von Arnims Stellung zwischen der Romantik und dem jungen Deutschland.* Bern and Leipzig: Paul Haupt, 1935.

Young, Iris Marion. "Impartiality and the Civic Public: Some Implications of Feminist Critiques of Moral and Political Theory." *Feminism as Critique.* Ed. Seyla Benhabib and Drucilla Cornell. Minneapolis: University of Minnesota Press, 1987. 57–76.

Zeitler, Julius, ed. *Deutsche Liebesbriefe.* Leipzig: Julius Zeitler, 1907.

# Index

Aesthetics, 63; 159–61; and Bettine von Arnim's letters, 208, 235, 237; and Karoline von Günderrode's letters, 145; and history, 242; of letter writing, 71–72, 115, 127, 131, 162–202, 236; and Sophie Mereau's letters, 143; and politics, 239; "pre-aesthetic forms," 72, 115; and reading, 44–45, 262 n. 62; and Caroline Schlegel-Schelling's letters, 189; as theme in letters, 225. *See also* Art

Ahlefeld, Charlotte von, 96, 106, 130

Albrecht, Sophie, 114

Allgemeines Landrecht der Preußischen Staaten, 64

Altman, Janet Gurkin, 112

Ambiguity: and ambivalence 125, 170, 246–48; in Sophie Mereau's letters 138, 142–43; in Rahel Varnhagen's letters, 198; in views of women's letters, 64, 65–67, 165; in women's letters, 58, 74, 77, 182; in women's lives, 251–52

Amelung, Heinz, 131

Anneke, Mathilda Franziska, 23, 25, 239; biography of, 242–43; husband Fritz Anneke, 243; letters, 244–51

Apologies: in women's letters, 95, 137, 179, 216, 226, 249

Archives, 45–46; Academy Archive of the Berlin-Brandenburger Academy of Sciences, 96; Bettine von Arnim's manuscripts in Wiepersdorf, 285 n. 35; Goethe-Schiller Archive in Weimar, 239; Leske family archive, 144. *See also* Varnhagen Collection

Arendt, Hannah, 191, 194, 195

Arnim, Achim von, 31, 64, 115, 143, 204, 215

Arnim, Bettine von, 13, 22–23, 25, 31–32, 41, 44, 54, 75, 78, 106, 143, 144, 155, 238–39, 240; *Goethes Briefwechsel mit einem Kinde*, 203–22; *Die Günderode*, 222–37; reception of, 203–14

Art: letters as, 39–42, 50, 206, 208, 210, 212, 222; masculine and feminine, 66, 69, 71; 129; and reality, 209. *See also* Aesthetics

Assing, Ludmilla, 29, 109

Aston, Louise, 23, 25, 239; biography 243; letters, 244–51

Autobiographical writings, 159, 207, 248

Autobiography: epistolary, 212; and fiction, 252; and form, 239; letter as, 40; and war, 240; of women, 34, 99, 108, 124, 126, 165, 210, 245, 259 n. 24

Badinter, Elisabeth, 55–56

Barkhaus, Karoline von, 144, 151, 155

Bateson, Mary Catherine, 251

Bäumer, Konstanze, 217

Becker-Cantarino, Barbara, 46, 49–50, 66, 75, 76, 79

Beethoven, Ludwig van, 41

Biography, 43, 75; of Bettine von Arnim, 215; and autobiography, 252; of Helmina von Chézy, 99; form of, 222; and letters, 21, 112–13, 115; of Elisabeth Goethe, 216; of Johann Wolfgang von Goethe, 208; of Karoline von Günderrode, 144, 147; of Anna L. Karsch, 115–16, 118; of Meta Klopstock, 89; of Sophie Mereau, 46, 128, 130–31, 144; women's interest in, 172–73, 93

Blackwell, Jeannine, 13, 35

Böhmer, Johann Franz Wilhelm, 169, 185

Bovenschen, Silvia, 55–56, 75, 114–15

Brachmann, Luise, 106

Brentano, Bettine. *See* Bettine von Arnim

Brentano, Clemens, 22, 68–70, 131, 204; and Bettine von Arnim, 208, 215, 217, 224, 226; and Karoline von Günderrode, 143, 144–49, 151–53, 155, 156,

157; and Sophie Mereau, 127–28, 136–42

Brentano, Franz, 217

Brentano, Gunda, 70, 78, 143, 158

Brentano, Maximiliane, 61

Brinckmann, Carl Gustav von, 181, 171, 179

Brinkmann, Richard, 43

Brion, Friederike, 33

Buff, Charlotte, 33

Carriere, Moritz, 208

Chamisso, Adelbert von, 96

Chézy, Helmina von, 20–21, 25, 44, 141, 165, 239; and Anton von Chézy, 102; correspondence with friends, 96–111, 113–14, 229; and Karl Freiherr von Hastfer, 100

Children: child image in Bettine von Arnim, 203, 207, 210, 281–82 n. 5; and Louise Gottsched, 87; and Meta Klopstock, 92; and Sophie Mereau, 127; and Caroline Schlegel-Schelling, 180, 185; women's role with, 55–56, 59–60, 77, 108

Christlich-Deutsche Tischgesellschaft, 64

Classicism: German, 143, 144

Creuzer, Friedrich, 33, 143, 144, 149, 151, 222; and Sophie Creuzer, 144

Death: of Helmina von Chézy, 97; of Elisabeth Goethe, 215; of Louise Gottsched, 32; of Karoline von Günderrode, 143–44; of Anna Karsch, 125; of Meta Klopstock, 89; 94–95; 183; of Sophie Mereau, 144; as metaphor in letters, 83, 143–44, 179, 183, 225, 227; of Dorothea Schlegel, 105; of Rahel Varnhagen, 34, 165

Derrida, Jacques, 14

Dialogue: epistolary, 30; in letters, 171, 212, 219, 224, 225, 226, 228, 229–34, 286 n. 48

Divorce: of Helmina von Chézy, 99, 100, 105; of Anna Karsch, 181; of Sophie Mereau, 127; of Caroline Schlegel-Schelling, 179, 186; of Pauline Wiesel, 175; of women, 180. See also Marriage

Drama: of Karoline von Günderrode, 229–34; and letters, 39, 210, 228;

women's interest in, 92. See also Theater

Drewitz, Ingeborg, 252

Editing: letters of Helmina von Chézy, 97–98; letters of Meta Klopstock, 89–90; and nationalism, 258 n. 10; process of, 19, 29–36, 45–47

Editions of letters: of Louise Gottsched, 79–80; of Karoline von Günderrode, 45, 143–44, 158, 263 n. 65; of Emma Herwegh, 244; of Sophie Mereau, 144; of Rahel Varnhagen, 45–46; of women, 13, 20, 29–36, 45–46

Editors: Bettine von Arnim as, 22, 205, 207, 218–22; men as, 29–30, 70–72, 189, 201, 236; Dorothee Runckel, 79–80, 87–89; Caroline Schlegel-Schelling as, 170; women as, 179

Education, 51, 55, 58, 64–65, 79, 159; Louise Gottsched's views on, 79, 81–82, 86; Fanny Lewald's views on, 244; men's and women's, 49, 60–61, 216–17; of Sophie Mereau, 127; of Caroline Schlegel-Schelling, 169; of Rahel Varnhagen, 170; women's in the eighteenth century, 51–53, 57–58

Eichendorff, Joseph von, 73

Ehrmann, Marianne, 64

Engelsing, Rolf, 51

Enlightenment, 37, 79, 143, 159

Epistolary: feminist interpretations of form, 14; form, 37, 245–46; novel, 50, 51, 135, 210; tradition for women, 20, 22, 23, 38–47, 252–53

Essay: by Helmine von Chézy, 101; form and letters, 23, 246, 251; by Sophie Mereau, 127; by Caroline Schlegel-Schelling, 72; and women, 50, 216

Fantasy: in Karoline von Günderrode's letters, 150, 151, 227; in Sophie Mereau's letters: 133–35, 138, 139, 140, 145

Femininity: and Bettine von Arnim, 217, 235–36, 237, 280–81 n. 1 and 3; devaluation of, 205; the feminine and feminist criticism, 13–14; and Karoline von Günderrode, 146, 148, 151–52, 160; and illness, 182–83; in letters, 35, 38–39, 40–41, 203; and masculinity, views on, 73, 240; and Sophie Mereau,

129; norms of, 54–55, 56–58; and politics, 23, 240–41, 249–50; and Caroline Schlegel-Schelling, 190. *See also* Gender

Feminism: and Bettine von Arnim, 204; and Helmina von Chézy, 99; and Sophie Mereau, 130; and politics, 191–92; and the women's movement, 166, 191

Feminist literary criticism: Anglo-American, 14–15, 255 n. 9; French, 14–15, 255 n. 9; and deconstruction, 14; and new historicism, 16–18; and letter editions, 35–36, 46–47

Fichte, Johann, 73, 235

Finke, Heinrich, 30–31

Flachsland, Caroline, 32, 61

Forster, Therese. *See* Therese Huber

Fouqué, Jean de la Motte, 109, 162

Fox-Genovese, Elizabeth, 23, 60

Freedom: in Louise Aston's life, 243, 245; in Elisabeth Goethe's letters, 221; in Karoline von Günderrode's poetry, 227; in Sophie Mereau's letters, 133, 141, 181; in Caroline Schlegel-Schelling's letters, 185; in Rahel Varnhagen's letters, 184, 195; of women and men, 252

French: Helmina von Chézy's translations from, 101; Chézy's views on, 99–100; feminists, 14–15; Gellert's views on, 52; in Louise Gottsched's letters, 51–52, 79, 86; in Meta Klopstock's letters, 92; troops in Germany, 187, 193; in Rahel Varnhagen's letters, 52

French, Marilyn, 22

Friedländer, Rebecca, 162–63, 170, 172, 174; correspondence with Rahel Varnhagen, 192–202

Friedrich II ("the Great"), 126

Friedrich Wilhelm II, 125

Friedrich Wilhelm III, 100–101, 240

Friedrichsmeyer, Sara, 16, 66–67, 159, 172, 185, 188, 191

Friendship: Bettine von Arnim and Elisabeth Goethe, 214–22; Bettine von Arnim and Karoline von Günderrode, 222–37; and Helmine von Chézy, 96–111; difference between men's and women's, 91–92; in the eighteenth century, 53–54; Louise Gottsched and Dorothee Runckel, 79–89; Karoline von Günderrode with Savigny and Gunda

Brentano, 146; and Meta Klopstock, 89–96; and letters, 113, 211, 239; men's, 33; Sophie Mereau and Charlotte von Ahlefeld, 130; Caroline Schlegel-Schelling and Huber, 190; Rahel Varnhagen and Rebecca Friedländer, 192–202; Rahel Varnhagen and Pauline Wiesel, 175, 184, 200; women's, 20, 25, 169, 201

Frohberg, Regina. *See* Friedländer, Rebecca

Frühwald, Wolfgang, 41, 42

Fuller, Margaret, 252

Fuss, Diana, 15

Gagern, Heinrich von, 242

Geertz, Clifford, 16, 21

Gellert, Christian Fürchtegott, 48, 50, 51, 52–54, 55–59, 67, 70, 183

Gender: constraints, 155; and freedom, 252; and friendship, 75–77; and genre, 24, 58, 98, 203, 228, 242; in Karoline von Günderrode's letters, 147, 148, 150; as historical determinant, 17, 24–25, 47, 73, 98; ideology, 18, 55, 153, 160, 203, 245; and illness, 183; and letter writing, 20, 24–25, 40–41; in Sophie Mereau's letters, 137, 141; norms, 20, 24, 52, 78, 81, 161, 178, 246; relationships, 16; roles, 14, 31, 74, 84, 91, 123–24, 235; in Caroline Schlegel-Schelling's letters, 189; stereotypes, 126, 186; transcendence of, 250–51. *See also* Femininity; Women

Genlis, Madame de, 100–101, 106, 108, 111

Gentz, Friedrich, 38

Gersdorff, Dagmar von, 46, 130, 131

Giseke, Dietrich and Eleonore, 90, 95

Gleim, Johann Wilhelm Ludwig, 51, 62, 115, 117–25

Goethe, Cornelia, 33, 52, 61

Goethe, Elisabeth, 32, 61, 78, 113, 205, 213–22, 236, 287 n. 66 and 68, 288 n. 69 and 71

Goethe, Johann Wolfgang von, 19, 22, 32–35, 51, 54, 56, 115, 123, 125, 127, 129, 160, 167, 187, 204, 206, 210, 215, 222

Goodman, Katherine, 117, 211, 212

Gossip, 166, 167–68, 173, 179, 180, 182, 215, 241

Gotter, F. W., 190
Gotter, Julie, 187, 201
Gotter, Luise, 54, 78, 169, 180–81, 186, 187, 201
Gotter, Pauline, 186
Göttinger Hain, 53
Gottsched, Johann Christoph, 32, 51–52, 55, 212, 229; correspondence with Louise Gottsched, 81–82, 86–88
Gottsched, Louise, 25, 32–33, 36, 42, 48, 51–52, 54, 95–96, 97, 111, 113–14, 123, 125, 135, 136, 165, 182; correspondence, 78–89
Grumbach, Argula von, 50
Günderrode, Karoline von, 21, 22, 25, 33, 46, 54, 75, 78, 114–15, 127, 142, 173, 175, 179, 182, 183, 204, 205, 208, 212–13, 218, correspondence, 143–61; in Bettine von Arnim's *Die Günderode*, 222–37, 246
Gundolf, Friedrich, 30
Gutzkow, Karl, 73

Habermas, Jürgen, 51
Hahn, Barbara, 30, 33, 35, 37, 45–46, 195, 199
Hausen, Karin, 61
Hausmann, Elizabeth, 115
Health: in Louise Gottsched's letters, 85; in Dorothea Schlegel's letters, 104–5; in Caroline Schlegel-Schelling's letters, 179–80; as theme in women's letters, 182–84; in Rahel Varnhagen's letters, 183–84, 192
Heilbrun, Carolyn, 75
Heine, Heinrich, 248
Helvig, Amalie von, 96, 106, 109
Hermann, Anne, 15, 246
Hertz, Deborah, 193, 194, 195
Herwegh, Emma, 23, 239, 243–44; correspondence, 244–51; and Georg Herwegh, 244, 248
Herz, Henriette, 46
Heyden, Susanne von, 33, 143, 144
History: exclusion of women from, 246; and letters, 14, 29–37, 48–74, 88, 163, 167, 168, 174, 193, 205, 239; and literature, 205, 209, 210, 222; Rahel Varnhagen's views on, 164–65, 201; in women's letters, 224. *See also* New Historicism
Hoffmann, E. T. A., 99

Hohenhausen, Elisa von, 96, 109
Hölderlin, Friedrich, 67
Honnefelder, Gottfried, 40
Huber, L. F.: Caroline Schlegel-Schelling's letters to, 188–90
Huber, Therese, 144, 169, 180
Humboldt, Alexander von, 193
Humboldt, Karoline von, 32, 54, 63, 193
Humboldt, Wilhlm von, 56, 63, 67, 193

Ingarden, Roman, 40

Jacobi, Friedrich Heinrich, 62, 125, 224
Jean Paul (Richter), 35, 99
Jews: and antisemitism, 193–94; Bettine von Arnim on, 204; and German letters, 46; Rebecca Friedländer as, 193; Emma Herwegh as, 243; Rahel Varnhagen as, 169–70, 194
Joeres, Ruth-Ellen B., 15, 17
Johnson, Barbara, 14

Karsch, Anna Louisa, 13, 21, 25, 36, 42, 100, 102, 142, 144, 145, 165, 175, 181, 212, 213, 215, 246; correspondence, 113–27; marriage to Hirsedorn, 116, 123
Keller, Gottfried, 29
Kelly, Joan, 17–18
Kipp, Johann Heinrich, 127, 130; Sophie Mereau's correspondence with, 131–36, 138, 140, 165
Kirsch, Sarah, 252
Klenke, Caroline von, 100, 101, 106, 115
Klettenberg, Susanne von, 61, 215
Klopstock, Friedrich Gottlieb, 54, 112, 120, 142, 149, 215; correspondence with Meta Klopstock, 89–92
Klopstock, Meta, 13, 25, 33, 42, 48, 54, 61, 125, 229; correspondence, 89–96, 97, 111–12, 142, 149, 165, 183
Koch-Gontard, Clotilde, 241–42
Kolodny, Annette, 36
Kord, Susanne, 100
Krickeberg, Friederike, 38

Lacan, Jacques, 14
Lacretelle, Pierre-Louis, 103
Language, 24, 45, 49–50, 51–53, 235; in feminist theories, 14; Gottsched's reforms of, 80; as theme in letters, 81, 90

LaRoche, Sophie von, 13, 46, 52, 54, 59, 64, 224; and Chancellor Michael von LaRoche, 236–37; and *Pomona*, 64
Latin, 49, 54, 92
Lavaillière, Louise Françoise de, 103, 111
Lazarowicz, Margarete, 144, 153
Legal rights of women, 64–65, 191, 242
Lenclos, Ninon, 141–42
Lengefeld, Charlotte von, 32
Lenk, Elisabeth, 203
Lennox, Sara, 17, 24
Lessing, Gotthold Ephraim, 120
Letters: form of, 159–61; and Latin, 49–50, 52; men's in comparison with women's, 42; "naturalness" of, 52–53, 67, 71, 126, 235; and the novel, 113–14; praise of women's, 265 n. 29; theories on, 13–14, 254 n. 7, 260 n. 37. *See also* Epistolary, Editing, Editions of Letters, Editors, Letter-writing manuals; Publication of letters
Letter-writing manuals, 18, 50, 53, 55, 59, 264 n. 21
Lewald, Fanny, 23, 25, 34, 36, 44; *Erinnerungen aus dem Jahr* 1848, 48, 244–51; *Meine Lebensgeschichte*, 34
Liebeskind, Meta, 173, 188
Love, 25, 29; Mathilde F. Anneke's views on, 247; in Bettine von Arnim's letters, 218, 220, 238; in Helmina von Chézy's letters, 99; and Karoline von Günderrode, 147, 151; in Anna Karsch's letters, 125; in Meta Klopstock's letters, 54, 61, 90–91, 93, 95; in Friedrich Schlegel's *Lucinde*, 66–67; in Sophie Mereau's letters, 68–70, 136, 140; in men's and women's letters, 49, 53, 54; "motherly," 55–56, 265 n. 32; between Rahel Varnhagen and Rebecca Friedländer, 198
Luther, Martin, 50
Lützeler, Paul Michael, 43

Maltitz, Alexander, 107
Marriage: of Louise Aston, 243; of Helmina von Chézy, 100; Louise Gottsched's advice on, Karoline von Günderrode's views on, 82; 146–47; of Anna Karsch, 123; Meta Klopstock's view on, 89, 92–93; in letters, 25, 31, 77; of Fanny Lewald, 244; of Sophie Mereau, 127, 131–32, 135, 136; in Romanticism, 182,

243; of Caroline Schlegel-Schelling, 169; of Amalie Schoppe, 110; of Rahel Varnhagen, 170; in women's letters, 54, 96. *See also* Divorce, Love
Marwitz, Alexander von, 172
Marxism, 16
Mendelssohn, Moses, 102, 122–23
Mereau, Sophie, 13, 21, 25, 33, 36, 46, 68–69, 114–15, 122, 149, 151, 165, 175, 179, 180, 181, 215, 246; correspondence, 127–45; and Henriette Schubart, (sister), 130
Merlin, story of, 103–4
Metaphors: in Bettine von Arnim's letters, 220; in Louise Gottsched's letters, 83; in Anna Karsch's letters; 124; in letters, 17; in Sophie Mereau's letters, 131, 132–33, 138, 139, 141, 142; of selves, 74, 160. *See also* Death, Fantasy, Freedom, Language
Meysenbug, Malwida von, 36
Michaelis, Caroline. *See* Schlegel-Schelling, Caroline
Mittermaier, Karl, 241, 242
Moi, Toril, 17
Moller, Meta. *See* Meta Klopstock
Montrose, Louis, 19
Mundt, Theodor, 205–6, 208

Napoleon, 167, 170, 186–87, 189–90
Napoleonic Code, 64
Nathusius, Phillip, 207, 223
Nature: in Helmina von Chézy's works, 99; and creativity of women, 48, 190, 217; equation of women with, 61–65, 67–68; feminine, 20, 23, 55–57, 59; in Karoline von Günderrode's works, 234; Rahel Varnhagen's views on, 164, 178, 201
Nees, Lisette von, 143, 144, 157
New Historicism, 16–25, 46, 159–61, 256 n. 17, 257 n. 38
Newton, Judith, 16–17, 18
Nickisch, R. M. G., 52, 58
Novalis, 67, 73, 166

Oehlike, Waldemar, 209
Oellers, Norbert, 42, 44
Olney, James, 112
Ong, Walter, 49–50
Outsiders, 78, 177, 219

Phenomenology, 40

Philosophers, 36, 44, 80; Bettine von Arnim's views on, 234–36; Louise Gottsched as, 80

Philosophical empiricism, 54–55

Pichler, Caroline, 96, 100, 106–8

Pockels, Carl Friedrich, on women's friendship, 76–77

Poetry: Bettine von Arnim and, 210, 224–37; and Louise Aston, 248; and Helmina von Chézy 106–7; and Anna Karsch, 124–25, 160; and Karoline von Günderrode, 127, 150, 151–52, 160; 224–37; letters as, 206, 213; and Sophie Mereau, 127, 130, 134, 137–38, 139

Political engagement, 25; and Bettine von Arnim, 204, 238–39, 290 nn. 9 and 12; and Helmina von Chézy, 99, 291 n. 18; exclusion of women from, 60, 64–65; and feminism, 191–92; and Madame de Genlis, 100; and letters, 18–19, 20, 23, 168, 170–71, 202, 238–53; men's reaction to, 240; and Caroline Pichler, 107; and Caroline Schlegel-Schelling, 169, 181, 184–92; of women in 1848 Revolution, 238–53

Poststructuralism, 14, 16

Preußisches Vereinsgesetz, 49, 64

Prince Louis Ferdinand of Prussia, 170, 175

Private sphere, 59–60, 209; and the letter, 18, 20, 39–40, 56–65; and politics, 191–92, 240

Prokop, Ulrike, 61, 215

Prutz, Robert, 151

Publication of letters: and Bettine von Arnim, 205, 214–15, 236–37, 288–89 n. 81; controversies over, 62–63; criteria for, 29–37; and Louise Gottsched, 87–89; and Karoline von Günderrode, 156; and Anna Karsch, 125–26; and Meta Klopstock, 94–95; and Clotilde Koch-Gontard, 242; and Caroline Schlegel-Schelling, 70–73, 192, 202; and Rahel Varnhagen, 162–66, 192, 194–96, 202. See also Editing, Editions of letters; Editors

Pückler, Muskau, Hermann Ludwig Heinrich von, 29, 206

Raich, J. M., 102

Reading: "aesthetic" and "efferent," 44–

45, 262 n. 62; and Bettine von Arnim, 222–23, 224; and feminism, 14, 17; and Louise Gottsched, 81, 82, 84; and Karoline von Günderrode, 144, 153, 155, 157; and new historicism, 19–20; process of in letters, 20, 50–51, 58, 64, 175, 212–13

Recke, Elisa von, 36, 106

1848 Revolution, 49, 23; women in: 238–53

Richardson, Samuel, 51, 91

Riemer, Friedrich Wilhelm, 207

Riley, Helene M. Kastinger, 137

Ritter, Johann Wilhelm, 68

Role-playing: in Karoline von Günderrode's letters, 149–50; in Meta Klopstock's letters, 149; in Sophie Mereau's letters, 140, 141, 149

Romanticism, 30, 39, 42–43, 45; and Bettine von Arnim, 204; early, 169; and Karoline von Günderrode, 143, 144; views on women, 65–73

Rosenblatt, Louise, 44

Rousseau, Jean-Jacques, 55–56, 66–67

Runckel, Dorothee, 32–33, 36, 48, 54, 113, 229; as editor of Louise Gottsched's correspondence, 79–89, 95, 97, 123; on women's friendship, 76

Salons, 20, 50–51, 65, 74, 75, 102, 267 n. 62; of Clothilde Koch Gontard, 241–42; of Rahel Varnhagen, 170, 175, 177, 193

Sand, George, 96, 98, 101, 243; 272 n. 33

Sappho, 121

Savigny, Karl von, 143, 144, 151, 154–55, 156–57, 158

Schelling, Friedrich Wilhelm Joseph, 36, 166, 173, 182, 187, 235

Schieth, Lydia, 113–15

Schiller, Charlotte von Lengefeld, 54

Schiller, Friedrich, 32–33, 36, 56, 66–67, 120, 127–29, 160, 185

Schlaffer, Hannelore, 23, 130

Schlawe, Fritz, 43–44

Schlegel, August Wilhelm, 36, 72–73, 166, 169, 173–74, 179–80, 182, 188

Schlegel, Dorothea Mendelssohn Veit, 13, 41, 44, 30–31, 33, 63, 73, 96, 99, 100, 108, 169; correspondence with Helmina von Chézy 101–5; on divorce, 180, 181

Schlegel, Friedrich, 30–31, 33, 63, 65–67,

160, 185, 192; *Athenäum Fragments*, 66; and Helmina von Chézy, 99, 101–3; and Karoline von Günderrode, 143; *Lucinde*, 66–67; and Caroline Schlegel-Schelling, 70–73, 166, 182

Schlegel-Schelling, Caroline, 13, 21–22, 25, 36, 41, 52, 54, 70–73, 78, 113, 141, 203, 240; correspondence of, 162–202, 212

Schmidt, Elisabeth Moller, 33, 94, 95

Schönfeld, Fräulein Erdmuth von, 33, 51, 54

Schoppe, Amalie, 96, 109–11

Self: in Bettine von Arnim's letters, 205, 207; in autobiographies, 211, 213, 239; in Karoline von Günderrode's letters, 145, 154, 158–61, 183, 212; image of in letters, 21, 45; in Sophie Mereau's letters, 131, 142; in political letters, 248; in Caroline Schlegel-Schelling's letters, 171, 180; in Rahel Varnhagen's letters, 171, 172, 174, 175–76, 212

Sennett, Richard, 61

Sentimentalism and sentimentality, 37, 40, 42, 53, 56, 59, 76, 77, 260n. 36

Showalter, Elaine, 13, 17, 182–83

Spacks, Patricia, 216

Spontaneity in letters, 56, 212, 221, 235

Staël, Madame Germaine de, 69, 99,101

Stahr, Adolf, 239

Steig, Reinhold, 208

Stein, Charlotte von, 32–33, 141

Steinhausen, Georg, *Die Geschichte des deutschen Briefes*, 37–39, 49

Stieglitz, Charlotte, 205

Stöcker, Helene, 252

Stolberg, Auguste, 54

Storm and Stress, 37

Storytelling, 163, 167–68, 186, 205, 214–15, 216; in Bettine von Arnim's *Goethes Briefwechsel mit einem Kinde*, 218–22; 236

Structuralism, 40

Struve, Amalie, 96, 106, 108

Subjectivity, 16–17, 59, 61–62, 204, 207, 260n. 31; in Karoline von Günderrode's letters, 144–45; and interpretation of letters, 21–22, 43, 167, 174, 190–91, 210

Sulzer, J. G., 115–16, 118–19, 122

Susmann, Margarethe, 34, 42–43

Tanneberger, Irmgard, 42–43

Tarnow, Fanny, 96, 106, 109–11

Theater, interest in, 102, 173, 216. *See also* Drama

Tian or Jon. See Günderrode, Karoline von

Tieck, Ludwig, 38

Tiemann, Hermann, 89

Touallion, Christine, 204

Translations: by Helmine von Chézy, 101, 102, 103, 111; by Emma Herwegh, 244; by Louise Gottsched, 79, 82; by Sophie Mereau, 127, 160; by Caroline Pichler, 106; by Caroline Schlegel-Schelling, 170; by Rahel Varnhagen, 194

Travel: and Bettine von Arnim, 219; and Helmina von Chézy, 106; and Louise Gottsched, 84; in letters, 30, 51, 79, 206; and Fanny Lewald, 244, 245; as male domain, 60; and Caroline Schlegel-Schelling, 180; and Rahel Varnhagen and Pauline Wiesel, 177

Trotta, Margarethe von, 252

Truth, as theme in letters, 165, 167, 172, 174, 176–77, 184, 198, 201, 235

Unger, Helene, 34

Unger, J. F., 34

Urquijo, Don Raphael d', 162, 193

Varnhagen Collection, 20, 45, 96, 102; Helmine von Chézy's correspondence in, 96–111; Sophie Mereau's correspondence in, 131–36; Rahel Varnhagen's correspondence with Rebecca Friedländer in, 193

Varnhagen von Ense, Karl, 34, 46, 108, 109, 162–63, 165, 170, 192, 205–6, 208, 212

Varnhagen von Ense, Rahel, 13, 21–22, 25, 30, 34, 35, 41, 44, 45, 46, 52, 63, 65, 74, 78, 203, 212, 213, 240; correspondence of, 162–202

Veit, David, 174

Vortriede, Werner, 31

Voß, Johann Heinrich, 62

Vulpius, Christiane (von Goethe), 187, 218

Walter, Eva, 55

War: Napoleonic War, 109; Caroline

Schlegel-Schelling's portrayal of, 186, 188; women in war, 106, 240; women's views on, 167, 247

Wasserzieher, Ernst, 31

Weber, Karl Maria von, 99

Weigel, Siegfried, 15

Weißenborn, Birgit, 153

Wellek, Albert, 40–41

Wieland, Christoph Martin, 52, 54, 59, 64, 120, 189

Wieneke, Ernst, 102, 103

Wiesel, Pauline, 78, 162, 170, 172, 174; Rahel Varnhagen's correspondence with, 175–79, 184, 192, 198, 199; and Friedrich Ferdinand Wiesel, husband, 175

Winkle, Sally, 55

Wolf, Christa, 143, 155, 246, 252

Wolf, Gerhard, 118, 120

Women's emancipation: Louise Aston's views on, 248, 250; and Sophie Mereau, 129; Caroline Pichler's views on, 107–8

Woolf, Virginia, 50, 65, 75, 246, 248–49

Writing: discussions about in letters, 93–94, 179; process of, 210–11. *See also* Editing, Editions, Editors; Publication of letters

Young, Iris Marion, 191

Zäunemann, Sidonia Hedwig, 79

Zell, Katharina, 50

Ziegler, Christiane Mariane von, 79